Audiophile Record Collector's Handbook

By

Phil Rees, BSc BA PhD

Cumbria
England

Cranmore Publications

Reading
England

Copyright © 1999-2012 by Phil Rees

All rights reserved. This book, or parts thereof, may not
be reproduced in any form without permission.

A catalogue record for this book is available from the British Library

First Edition December 1991

Second Edition May 1992

Third Edition December 1992

Fourth Edition July 1993

Fifth Edition May 1995
(re-printed May 1996)

Sixth Edition November 1999

Seventh Edition October 2003
(re-printed January 2006, January 2012)

ISBN: 978-1-907962-60-8

Please note that there is now a companion to this book, giving complete listings of many English mono LPs. Specifically, ALP, BLP, CLP, DLP, 33CX, 33C, COLH, RLS, XLP, LXT, LX, LW, BR, etc. It is available from the same source as this book and is called:

Mono Record Collector's Handbook

Table of Contents

Prefaces and Acknowledgements 2

RCA Living Stereo 5

RCA Living Stereo 'SB' English Pressings 19

RCA Victrola 24

Mercury Living Presence 27

Mercury: English EMI Pressings 39

Decca 45

Decca SET box sets 47

SXL2000 series 57

SXL6000 series 65

Decca London (1958-64) 83

Decca Argo (ZNF, ZRG) 89

Decca L'Oiseau-Lyree 98

Decca Reissue Labels 101

Brunswick Stereo SXA 116

Telefunken Stereo SMA 118

EMI 119

Early EMIs (1958-1964) 122

SAX: EMI Columbia (1958-1964) 129

Later EMIs (from about 1964) 136

EMI Box sets 160

Other EMI labels 169

SAN (HMV Angel) Series 174
Lyrita 186
Readers Digest 189
Useful Names and Addresses 190
Bibliography 190

About the Author

I have a BSc degree in mathematics from Manchester University and worked as a designer in the computer industry until retiring in 1993.

I have been a record collector and/or dealer for many years. I first became aware of the great sound quality of some of the early Deccas and RCA "shaded dogs" during the mid 80s. I then formed a collection including practically every worthwhile RCA shaded dog, Mercury, Decca SXL, EMI ASD, SAX, Lyrita, etc. This collection was acquired by a process of swapping records with many internationally based fellow collectors.

Around 1989 I started selling records in my spare time, and in 1993 this became a full time activity. The business was joined by my wife, Jan, in 1994 and has since supplied many thousands of audiophile records to collectors all over the world, being generally regarded as the premier international source of quality English vinyl.

To keep my brain active I have been studying philosophy part time and was recently awarded a PhD from Reading University.

Prefaces and Acknowledgements

Preface to this edition

New lists have been added – Telefunken SMA; these are all believed to be complete listings.

Preface to the first edition

This guide is aimed mainly at collectors of fine sounding analogue stereo LP records. It concentrates largely on orchestral repertoire - that is what such collectors listen to in the main. I have started from the assumption that the analogue stereo recordings from the period late 50s to mid 70s are far more satisfying than any other recordings ever made. The great majority of good recordings from that period are to be found on the RCA, Mercury, Decca, EMI, and Lyrita labels.

The information in this guide represents the labour of many years, not just by the author, but by many others too. Back in the mid 80s, when I owned just 5 Mercurys, I wanted to know what else was available on Mercury. So I started compiling a list from the information on the Mercury paper record sleeves. I noticed that every issue of the USA based "The Absolute Sound" magazine (TAS) reviewed various records, so I started adding this review information to the growing catalogue. Then I discovered that a group of collectors in New York (Robert Hunt, David Nemzer, Louis Cardona, etc) had already compiled Mercury and RCA listings. So their information (which at that time was far from complete) was painstakingly typed into the computer. Thus the catalogues started to grow. Later I received copies of the sale catalogues when Bob Corsetti sold his unique 100% RCA & Mercury collection.

The Decca work began with a visit to Decca's London offices and permission to photocopy some old catalogue information. At the same time, Carol Keasler (a collector from Illinois, USA) was working along the same lines for the 'London' catalogue. It was natural that we compared results and cross referenced between Decca and London.

Then I met Mike Langhorne who collected English pressing Mercurys and early EMIs (ASD and SAX). He had some very complete listings that formed the beginnings of the English Mercurys and EMI lists herein.

The most important acknowledgement has to be to TAS in general, to Sid Marks's reviews therein, and to its publisher, Harry Pearson. In the midst of the growth of CD that magazine was a beacon for early vinyl recordings, and a constant inspiration. When 'Gramophone' published one more CD eulogy it was great to find the real truth in TAS - that the original vinyl was much better.

The "TAS Index" is now available. It may be said that this renders obsolescent the TAS references included in many of the listings herein. Perhaps this is so, perhaps not. In any event, I commend the TAS index to all readers of this book.

There is still plenty left to do, the main omission now being Philips, American Columbia (CBS), DGG. Generally, these labels are not in the front rank along with those described in this book. Nevertheless, there are many fine recordings to be found amongst them, and I hope that we shall gradually discover them.

As the 1990s unfold LP production has come to a halt. It is fairly safe to say that no more worthwhile classical recordings will ever again be released on vinyl. Consequently, all the great analogue records are now **history**. Getting to know that history can be a most rewarding pastime and I commend it to all.

Phil Rees,   Wokingham, 1991

Preface to the second edition

Errors have been corrected and some records have been added to the EMI ASD and SXL6000 series listings.

Some entries in the SXL2000 series were marked "?", indicating that **almost certainly** no such record ever existed. These have been removed since they proved misleading.

Mercurys having a Philips SAL reissue have been appropriately cross-referenced.

Preface to the third edition

Errors have been corrected and more records have been added to the EMI ASD, EMI SAN, and SXL6000 series listings.

Details of the most important records on the Decca reissue labels (Ace of Diamonds, Eclipse, and "World of" have been added. These reissues have been cross-referenced back to their originals (sometimes Decca SXLs and sometimes RCA LSCs)

Preface to the fourth edition

A section on Decca Argo has been added, further miscellaneous additions to the ASDnnnn and SXL6000s have been made, and errors have been corrected.

Preface to the fifth edition

Further miscellaneous additions have been made, and errors have been corrected.

Preface to the sixth edition

This edition sees an additional 30-40 pages. Nearly all the lists have been extensively updated. In particular, the ASDnnnn, SLS, SDD, etc lists have been greatly expanded, and are now very close to complete. The Argo list has been greatly extended. New lists have been added: SWL (Decca), SOL (Oiseau-Lyre), SXLP (EMI reissue), SCX (EMI).

This will probably be the last edition of the book to include photos. Peter Fulop's superb labelography gives all the photos of labels anyone could wish for and the reader is recommended to obtain a copy (refer to bibliography at end of this book).

I would like to thank Tony Kind for his considerable help in extending these lists, and for his constant interest and encouragement.

Preface to the seventh edition

The Decca section has had the new HEAD list added.

The ASDnnnn, SLS, SET, SXL, SDD/GOS, ZRG, SOL, SAN, and SXLP lists have been extensively updated and I now regard them as complete. For the ASD and SLS lists I have now noted digital issues. For the SAN and SXLP lists, as well as making them complete, they have been extensively cross referenced to their original recordings.

The TWO list has been extended to include all classical material.

New lists have been added – Brunswick SXA, Decca HEAD, Decca Dnnn and nBB sets; these are all believed to be complete listings.

As predicted in the previous edition, I have dropped the label photos. The reader is commended to Peter Fulop's labelography.

* * * * *

RCA Living Stereo

The lists: The lists "RCA Living Stereo Series" and "RCA Soria Series" are based upon the author's own collection of RCA Living Stereo records, as well as earlier lists produced by James Mitchell, Robert Hunt & David Nemzer, and Bob Corsetti respectively.

They are believed to be complete for LSC/LDS Living stereos up to around LSC2800, and very complete from there up to LSC3000.

The "RCA Living Stereo 'SB' English Pressings" list is not claimed to be 100% complete, but is a very full list, close to complete, at least for the SB2000 series.

Where a record has been discussed in The Absolute Sound (TAS) the volume numbers are shown by Tv followed by 1 to 3 + marks, indicating the degree of praise, for example T60++. This is of course a very crude assessment, and no substitute for reading the reviews. The page number is sometimes also shown, e.g. Tv/p+++.

If the record has **ever** been on the TAS "Editors Choice" list this is shown by "TASEC". "TASEC*" indicates it received a special commendation on the Editor's Choice list. Sometimes the volume number in which the record first appeared on the list is also shown - e.g. TASEC44 indicates that it was first listed in volume 44.

If the TAS review was by Sid Marks it is indicated by "SM".

Note that LSC signifies regular LSC Living Stereo, and that LDS signifies RCA's 'Soria' series.

Where appropriate, the rating given in James Mitchell's excellent paper is also shown, e.g. JM10+. JM10++* indicates that Mitchell placed the record in his "best of all the RCAs" paper.

Where VICS pressing alternatives exist, these are shown in brackets. Note that the VICS numbers are those assigned to the English Decca pressed VICS. Up to around VICS1200 these are the same as the US VICS. Thereafter they are sometimes different.

Many of the LSC series that were recorded in England by Decca were later reissued by Decca on the Eclipse (ECS) and "World Of" (SPA) labels. Where such pressing alternatives exist, these are shown in brackets.

Dynagroove: Around LSC2650 RCA began to use a cutting process known as "Dynagroove". In simple terms, this process amounted to using a computer controlled cutter head which continuously varied the gap between the grooves depending on the level of the sound. The process is now felt to have had a bad effect on the sound quality. Nevertheless, there are some Dynagroove records with very fine sound. Where the record is known to have been made with the "Dynagroove" process this is shown by the letters "DG".

A note about LSC 2068: This was originally issued without the Liszt Concerto and with the Rachmaninov concerto spread over both sides. Later issues compressed the Rachmaninov onto one side and the quality was sharply reduced as a result.

Labels and Pressings

RCA and Decca: During the period from the start of the stereo era to around 1961, RCA and Decca had a co-operation agreement. Under this agreement Decca made a number of recordings in Europe for RCA. The engineer on most of these recordings (like LSC2225 "Witches Brew", and LSC2313 "Venice") was Kenneth Wilkinson, and they are generally among the finest in the RCA catalogue. Indeed, in terms of recorded sound quality, they are amongst the finest recordings ever made. In addition, RCA used Decca's pressing facilities for the English issues of all their LSC series. The Decca pressing facilities were amongst the finest in the world at that time, and the Decca pressings are of very high quality. This is particularly true for those recordings made in England by Decca themselves.

US pressings: The earliest label on the American pressings is the famous "Shaded Dog". The background colour is brick red. This label was used from 1958 up to around 1964. The second label is usually referred to as "White Dog", and the colour is a brighter red.

The engraving on the vinyl shows the stamper number 1S, 2S, etc, 1S being the earliest. In addition, if you look closely you will also see a single letter R, H, or I. This letter indicates which pressing plant produced the record - Rockaway, Hollywood, or Indianapolis.

English pressings: There are two different types of English pressings. Those with numbers like SBxxxx (or SFxxxx for more 'popular' repertoire) were pressed in England for RCA by Decca at the same time as the corresponding LSC.

Those with numbers like LSBxxxx were pressed in England by RCA, generally slightly later than the corresponding LSC, and after the agreement between RCA and Decca had lapsed. The LSBs correspond generally to the later Dynagroove LSCs and are generally preferable to the LSC since the computer controlled cutter head used by the Dynagroove process was not used by RCA's English subsidiary.

You will not find the "Nipper dog" anywhere on SBs. This is because EMI owned the copyright to the Nipper logo in England. The early SBs have numbers like SB2nnn. The label is dark red with silver lettering. The emblem LIVING STEREO is found in the upper part of the label, with an RCA logo in the form of a 2 cms silver circle. These are standard Decca pressings of the period and the stamper numbers use the same encoding as for the Decca SXL series. Most of these early SBs were deleted long before the second SB label was introduced, so there are fewer problems with 1st labels, 2nd labels, etc.

The second SB label is a more orange shade of red. The LIVING STEREO legend is no longer used, and the 'RCA' legend is now a slightly smaller black circle with white lettering. Generally these labels are found on the slightly later SB6nnn series, these corresponding (very approximately) to RCAs from around LSC2650 onwards.

Victrola pressings: The early Victrola pressings are of very high quality, showing little degradation compared to the original issue. The American Victrola pressings have stamper information in the same form as the original LSCs. English pressings were all pressed by Decca and issued at exactly the same time as the USA pressings. As with the originals, the Decca pressings of those records that were recorded by Decca in England are among the finest of all.

For both USA and English pressings the earliest label is a dark maroon ('plum') colour and the second label is pink.

Abbreviations:

AdSC	Accademia di St Cecilia
BPO	Boston Pops Orchestra
BSO	Boston Symphony Orchestra
CSO	Chicago Symphony Orchestra
Festival Quartet	Goldberg/Primrose/Graudan/Babin
LPSO	London Proms Symphony Orchestra
MMF	Maggio Musicale Fiorentino
NSOL	New Symphony Orchestra of London
OdLOC	Orchestra de L'Opera Comique
PCO	Paris Conservatoire Orchestra
RCAVO	RCA Victor Orchestra
ROHCG	Royal Opera House Covent Garden Orchestra
ROHO	Rome Opera House Orchestra
RomeOp	Rome Opera Orchestra
RSC	Roger Shaw Chorale
SdZ	Solisti di Zagreb
SOA	Symphony of the Air
SOoN	Symphony Orchestra of Naples
VSOp	Vienna State Opera
VV	Vienna Volksoper
ZIM	Zimbler Sinfonietta

* * * * *

RCA Soria Series

The Soria series was a small set of the RCA Living Stereo series that were provided with the most lavish packaging. Most of them have very high quality books by 'Skira' and heavy duty boxes. Musically, and in terms of the sound quality, they are of the same standard as the standard LSCs.

Cat. No.	Work	Artist	Orchestra	Notes
LDS 2346	Strauss,J: Vienna of Johann Strauss	Karajan	VPO	(SB2091) JM10
LDS 2347	Mozart: Symphony 40/Haydn Symphony 104	Karajan	VPO	(SB2092) JM10-
LDS 2348	Beethoven: Symphony 7	Karajan	VPO	(SB2087)
LDS 2351	Brahms: Symphony 1	Karajan	VPO	(SB2086)
LDS 2384	Strauss,R: Don Quixote	Reiner	CSO	(SB2099) JM10+
LDS 2385	Poulenc-Cocteau: La Voix Humane	Pretre	OdLOC Duvall	
LDS 2447	Handel: Messiah (extracts)	Beecham	RPO	JM10+
LDS 2513	Brahms: Double Concerto	Wallenstein Heifetz Piatigorsky		(SB2140) SM81
LDS 2554	Chopin: Sonata in B flat min/Sonata 3	Rubinstein		JM10+
LDS 2560	Bream: English Lute Music	Bream		(SB2150) SM81++
LDS 2625	Milhaud: Creation du Monde/Suite Provencale	Munch	BSO	(SB6511) JM9
LDS 2656	Bream: Evening of Elizabethan Music	Bream Consort		TAS44/163 SM59/123++
LDS 6065	Royal Ballet Gala Performance	Ansermet	ROHCG	(VICS1066)
LDS 6075	Spoken: "J.B." Play by Archibald Macleish			
LDS 6077	Berlioz: Requiem	Munch	BSO	(SB2096/7) TAS36/126
LDS 6091	Verdi: Requiem	Reiner	VPO	(SER4526/7) JM10 SM90
LDS 6098	Berlioz: Romeo and Juliet (complete)	Munch	BSO	TAS36/126,39/139 JM10
LDS 6152	Strauss,R: Ariadne Auf Naxos	Leinsdorf	VPO	
LDS 6155	Verdi: Otello	Serafin	RomeOp	
LDS 6159	Heifetz/Piatigorsky Concerts	Festival Quartet		JM10+
LDS 6164	Bizet: Carmen	Karajan	VPO	TASEC98
LDS 6407	Vienna Philharmonic Festival	Karajan	VPO	(LDS2535-8)
LDS 6409	Handel: Messiah (complete)	Beecham	RPO Vickers	(SER4501) JM10++*
LDS 6706	Wagner: Die Walkure	Leinsdorf	LSO Vickers	JM10+
LDS 7022	Puccini: Tosca	Karajan	VPO Price/DiStefano	JM9 TASEC98x

RCA Living Stereo Series

LSC 1806	Strauss,R: Also S2prach Zarathustra	Reiner	CSO		(VICS1265) TAS44/128 JM10+
LSC 1817	Offenbach: Gaite Parisienne	Fiedler	BPO		(VICS1012) TAS34,32 JM10++
LSC 1893	Ravel: Daphnis&Chloe	Munch	BSO		(VICS1271) TAS36/162 JM10+
LSC 1901	Tchaikovsky: Symphony 6	Monteux	BSO		(SB2024 VICS1009) JM10+
LSC 1903	Brahms: Violin Concerto	Reiner	CSO	Heifetz	TAS32/98 JM10++ SM77/138++
LSC 1934	Bartok: Conc for Orchestra	Reiner	CSO		(VICS1110/2005) JM10+ TASEC34
LSC 1984	Ravel Bolero/Valse/Rhaps Esp/Debussy: Faun Prelude	Munch	BSO		(SB2019 VICS1041) JM10++*
LSC 1990	Offenbach: Offenbach in America	Fiedler	BPO		JM10++
LSC 1991	Beethoven: Symphony 7/Fidelio Ov	Reiner	CSO		(SB2010) JM10+
LSC 1992	Beethoven: Violin Concerto	Munch	BSO	Heifetz	(SB2047) TAS36/160 JM10+
LSC 1994	Jungle Drums(Malaguena/Fire Dance/etc)	Gould			SM64/127
LSC 2028	Strauss,J: Waltzes by the Strauss Family	Fiedler	BPO		JM10
LSC 2052	Tchaikovsky: Nutcracker Suite (extracts)	Fiedler	BPO		(SF5004) JM10+
LSC 2068	Rachmaninov: Piano Concerto 2	Reiner	CSO	Rubinstein	(SB2139) TAS40/136 JM10++*
LSC 2068	Rachmaninov: Piano Concerto 2/Liszt Concerto 1	Reiner	CSO	Rubinstein	(SB2139) TAS40/136 SM100

Note that LSC2068 comes in two forms – in later issues of the record RCA squeezed more music on at the expense of sound quality. In the earlier issue the Rachmaninov is spread over two sides with benefits to sound quality.

LSC 2077	Strauss,R: Death&Transfiguration/Till Eulenspiegel	Reiner	VPO		(SB2036 VICS1004 ECS674) JM10 SM100+
LSC 2080	Brass and Percussion	Gould			JM10 SM57/138
LSC 2084	Rossini-Respighi: La Boutique Fantasque/Ibert	Fiedler	BPO		(VICS1053) TAS36/123 JM10++
LSC 2085	Stravinsky: Rite of Spring	Monteux	PCO		(SB2005 ECS750) JM10+ SM69/144-
LSC 2097	Brahms: Symphony 1	Munch	BSO		JM10
LSC 2100	HiFi Fiedler (William Tell/Marche Slave/etc)	Fiedler	BPO		JM10++* SM57/136+
LSC 2104	Blues in the Night	Gould			JM9 SM61/125++
LSC 2105	Tchaikovsky: Srnd for Strings/Elgar Intr & Allegro	Munch	BSO		TAS36/122 JM10+ SM77-
LSC 2109	Walton: Cello Conc/Bloch: Schelomo	Munch	BSO	Piatigorsky	(SB6676 LSB4101) TAS36/123 JM10
LSC 2111	Debussy: La Mer/Ibert: Ports of Call	Munch	BSO		(VICS1041=TAS36/161) JM10+ TAS78/146++
LSC 2112	Strauss,J: Vienna(Emporor/Blue Danube/etc)	Reiner	CSO		JM10+
LSC 2113	Stravinsky: Petrouchka/Firebird Suite	Monteux	PCO	Katchen	(SB2037 SPA152) never issued in USA
LSC 2120	Beethoven: Piano Concerto 1	Krips	SOA	Rubinstein	(SB2046) JM10
LSC 2121	Beethoven: Piano Concerto 2	Krips	SOA	Rubinstein	JM10
LSC 2122	Beethoven: Piano Concerto 3	Krips	SOA	Rubinstein	
LSC 2123	Beethoven: Piano Concerto 4	Krips	SOA	Rubinstein	JM9+
LSC 2124	Beethoven: Piano Concerto 5	Krips	SOA	Rubinstein	(SB2015)
LSC 2125	Grieg: Peer Gynt/Lyric Suite	Fiedler	BPO	Farrell	TAS36/128 JM10+
LSC 2129	Tchaikovsky: Violin Concerto	Reiner	CSO	Heifetz	(SB2002) TAS36/162 JM10
LSC 2130	Strauss,J: Fledermaus/Gypsy Baron (excerpts)	Fiedler	BPO		JM10++
LSC 2131	Franck: Symphony in D Min	Munch	BSO		(SB2009 VICS1034)
LSC 2134	Overture! (Suppe/Herold/Auber/Adam)	Agoult	NSOL		JM10++*
LSC 2135	Prokofiev: Cinderella	Rignold	PCO		(VICS1138 ECS597) LSC not issued in USA
LSC 2139	Xmas Hymns and Carols Vol 1	Shaw	RSC		JM9
LSC 2147	Schubert: Trout Quintet	Festival Quartet			
LSC 2150	Prokofiev: Lt Kije/Stravinsky: Song of Nightingale	Reiner	CSO		(VICS1290) TASEC44
LSC 2177	Tchaikovsky: Sleeping Beauty excerpts	Monteux	LSO		(SB2013 VICS1011 ECS575) JM9+/10+
LSC 2183	The Reiner Sound (Rachmaninov Isle of Dead/Ravel)	Reiner	CSO		(SB2042) TASEC*42 TAS21/165 JM10++
LSC 2185	Rachmaninov: Sym 3/Rimsky-K: Russian Easter Ov	Boult	LPO		(SB2035 ECS573) Issued England, but not USA
LSC 2195	Copland: Billy the Kid/Rodeo	Gould			JM10++ SM90
LSC 2199	A Mighty Fortress	Shaw	RSC		
LSC 2201	Mussorgsky: Pictures at an Exhibition	Reiner	CSO		(SB2001) JM10++* TAS27/108 SM98++
LSC 2202	Pops Caviar (Russian Easter/Prince Igor/etc)	Fiedler	BPO		JM10+
LSC 2207	Schumann: Carnaval/Fantasy	Ania Dorfman (piano)			JM10
LSC 2208	Rimsky Korsakov: Scheherazade	Monteux	LSO		(SB2003 VICS1013 SPA89)
LSC 2209	Brahms: Symphony 3	Reiner	CSO		(SB2007 VICS1117) JM10

Catalog	Title	Conductor/Artist	Orchestra	Notes
LSC 2213	Boston Tea Party	Fiedler	BPO	JM10 SM61/126++
LSC 2214	Dvorak: New World Symphony	Reiner	CSO	(SB2031) JM10+ TAS78/140--
LSC 2216	Tchaikovsky: Symphony 6	Reiner	CSO	(VICS1163) JM10+
LSC 2217	Batons and Bows	Gould		JM9 SM59/123+
LSC 2219	Brahms: Piano Concerto 2	Reiner	CSO Gilels	(SB2032 VICS1026) JM10+ TAS78/146--
LSC 2221	Mendelssohn: Symphonies 4/5	Munch	BSO	TAS36/162 JM10 SM58/137
LSC 2222	Ravel: Alborado/Valses/Debussy Iberia	Reiner	CSO	(SB2044 VICS1199+ VICS1025) JM10+
LSC 2223	Mendelssohn: Midsmr Nts Drm/Schubert: Rosamunde	VPO	Monteux	(SB2014) Never issued USA
LSC 2224	Wheres the Melody	Gould		JM10
LSC 2225	Witches Brew	Gibson	NSOL	(SB2020 SPA175) JM10++* TASEC65
LSC 2226	Rodgers, Richard: Victory at Sea Vol 2	Bennett	RCAVO	SM57/137+
LSC 2227	Tchaikovsky: Swan Lake	Morel	ROHCG	(SB2012 VICS1002) Never issued USA
LSC 2228	Berlioz: Harold in Italy	Munch	BSO Primrose	(SB2016) JM10+ TAS36/126 SM100-
LSC 2229	Marches in HiFi	Fiedler	BPO	JM10+ SM60/133+
LSC 2230	Spain (Iberia/Three Cornered Hat/etc)	Reiner	CSO	(VICS1294) TASEC44 JM10+
LSC 2231	On Stage with Robert Shaw	Shaw	RSC	JM8
LSC 2232	Moon Wind and Stars	Gould		JM9
LSC 2233	Beethoven: Symphony 3	Munch	BSO	JM10 SM60/135++
LSC 2234	Saint-Saens: Conc 2/Franck Symph Varns	Wallenstein	SOA Rubinstein	(SB2023) JM10+ TAS73/144+ TASEC
LSC 2235	Music to have fun with	Fiedler	BPO	(SF5041)
LSC 2237	Rachmaninov: Piano Concerto 3.	Munch	BSO Janis	(VICS1032: JM10)
LSC 2238	Its Classic but its Good	Bennett	RCAVO	
LSC 2239	Tchaikovsky: Symphony 5	Monteux	BSO	TAS36/124 JM10+ SM61/128++
LSC 2240	Sousa: Stars & Stripes/Gotshalk-Kay Cakewalk	Fiedler	BPO	JM10++
LSC 2241	1812 Ov/Tragic Ov/Liszt Mephisto/Fingals Cave	Reiner	CSO	(SB2059 VICS1025) JM10+
LSC 2247	Deep River and other Spirituals	Shaw	RSC	SM64/125++
LSC 2249	Ponchielli: La Gioconda (extracts)	Previtalli		JM10
LSC 2251	Hovanness: Mysterious Mountain/Stravinsky	Reiner	CSO	(VICS1295) JM10+ SM59/123++
LSC 2252	Tchaikovsky: Piano Concerto 1	Kondrashin	Van Cliburn	(SB2006) JM10 SM65/184+
LSC 2253	Gluck: Orfeo & Euridice (abridged)	Monteux	RomeOp	JM10
LSC 2254	Victoria: Requiem Mass	Mount Angel Choir		JM10+
LSC 2255	Wagner: Brunnhilde's Immolation/Liebestod	Munch	BSO Farrell	TAS36/163 JM10
LSC 2256	Schumann: Piano Concerto	Krips RCAVO Rubinstein		(SB2033) SM60/135
LSC 2257	Bliss: Pomp & Circ/Welcome to the Queen/etc	Bliss	LSO	(SB2026 SDD255)
LSC 2261	Shostakovich: Symphony 5	Mitchell	NatSO	JM10+ SM60/134+
LSC 2265	Chopin: Rubinstein Story(Conc 2)	Wallenstein	SOA Rubinstein	JM10+
LSC 2267	Offenbach: Gaite Parisienne/Khachtrn Gayne Suite	Fiedler	BPO	(SF5036) JM9+
LSC 2268	Encores (Riverside Church organ)	Virgil Fox		JM10+
LSC 2270	Pops Stoppers	Fiedler	BPO	JM10+
LSC 2271	Ravel: Piano Concerto/D'Indy	Munch	BSO Henriot-Schweitzer	(SB2053 VICS1060/1071) JM10+
LSC 2272	Prokofiev: Symphony 5	Martinon	PCO	(SB2034 VICS1169 ECS593) JM9 SM98-
LSC 2273	Bach,J.S: Cantata 4/Motet 3	Shaw	RSC	JM10
LSC 2274	Brahms: Piano Concerto 1	Munch	BSO Graffman	(SB2040 VICS1109 SB2040) JM10+
LSC 2275	Brahms: A Brahms/Schumann Recital	Forrester		(SB2116)
LSC 2276	Brailowsky Encores	Brailowsky (piano)		
LSC 2279	Program of Song	Leontyne Price (Soprano)		JM8
LSC 2280	The Art of Song	Valletti		JM10
LSC 2281	Brahms: Violin Concerto	Monteux	LSO Szeryng	(SB2049 VICS1028) JM10+ SM65/176+
LSC 2282	Debussy: Images for Orchestra	Munch	BSO	TAS36/122 JM10+ SM90+
LSC 2285	Walton: Facade/Lecocq: Mamzelle Angot	Fistoulari	ROHCG	(SB2039 VICS1168 ECS586) JM10+
LSC 2287	Mozart: Piano Conc 25/Don Giovanni Ov	Reiner	CSO Tchaikovsky	(VICS1167) JM10+ SM60/133-
LSC 2288	Prokofiev: Symphony 7/Overture Russe	Martinon	PCO	(SB2061 ECS619) SM59/123+
LSC 2292	The French Touch (Dukas/Ravel/etc)	Munch	BSO	(SB2041 VICS1060) JM10+ SM64/127+++
LSC 2293	Stravinsky: Suite Italienne/Debussy Sonata	Piatigorsky (Cello)		
LSC 2294	Rodgers: Slaughter on 10th Ave/etc	Fiedler	BPO	TAS36/129 JM10++
LSC 2295	Foster: Stephen Foster Song Book	Shaw	RSC	JM9 SM67/144++

Catalog	Work	Performer / Orchestra	Notes
LSC 2296	Brahms: Piano Concerto 2	Krips RCAVO Rubinstein	(SB2069) JM10+ SM59/123
LSC 2297	Brahms: Symphony 4	Munch BSO	(SB2060) JM10+
LSC 2298	Borodin: Symphony 2/Rims Kors: Capr Esp	Martinon PCO	(SB2105 SPA281) JM10++ SM58/136++
LSC 2299	Lehar: Waltzes(Merry Widow/Gypsy Love/etc)	Sharples LSO	(VICS1106) JM10+
LSC 2301	Adam: Giselle (extracts)	Wolff PCO	(SB2018 ECS677) SM61/127
LSC 2302	Sullivan: Gilbert & Sullivan Overtures.	Alan Ward & Orchestra	JM10++
LSC 2303	Milanov Operatic Arias	Basile RCAVO Milanov (Sop)	
LSC 2304	Chopin: Ballades/Andante Spinato/Grand Polonaise	Graffman	(VICS1077) JM10++
LSC 2307	Destination Stereo	Various incl Reiner	JM10++*
LSC 2308	Doubling in Brass (Dixie/Yankee Doodle/etc)	Gould	JM10+
LSC 2309	Saint-Saens: Samson & Delilah (opera abridged)	Cleva Metop Stevens	JM10+
LSC 2312	Bach,J.S: Cantatas	Shaw RSC	
LSC 2313	Venice - Verdi/Rossini/Offenbach	Solti ROHCG	(SB2058 SPA347) JM10+ SM77/140+++
LSC 2314	Mendelssohn: Vln Conc/Prokofiev Vln Conc	Munch BSO Heifetz	(SB2066) JM10 SM65/182++ TASEC65
LSC 2316	Beethoven: Symphony 6	Monteux VPO	(SB2065 VICS1006 SPA113)
LSC 2317	Living Strings	Gould	
LSC 2318	Rossini: Overtures(Tell/Barber/etc)	Reiner CSO	(SB2075) TAS27/123 JM10+ SM83/234+
LSC 2320	Song of India (Thunder & Lightning Polka/etc)	Fiedler BPO	JM10+ SM58/138++
LSC 2322	Shostakovich: Symphony 1/Age of Gold	Martinon LSO	(SB2051 ECS580) JM10++ SM64/125++
LSC 2323	Rimsky Korsakov: Capr Esp/Tchaik: Capr It	Kondrashin RCAVO Shumsky	(SB2064) JM10++ SM83/242+
LSC 2325	Music for Frustrated Conductors	Fiedler BPO	JM9/10 SM64/124
LSC 2326	Fauré: "Claire de Lune" (Massenet, Fauré, Debussy, etc)	Agoult LPSO	(SF5054 ECS805 SPA111)
LSC 2327	Bizet: L'Arlesienne Suites 1&2/Chabrier Espana	Morel ROHCG	(SB2057 VICS1057 SPA173/SPA220) JM10++
LSC 2328	Tchaikovsky: Nutcracker Suite (extracts)	Reiner CSO	(SB2107 VICS1460) TASEC44 JM10+
LSC 2329	Pops Xmas Party	Fiedler BPO	JM10+
LSC 2330	Brahms: Quartet 3/Piano Quartet	Festival Quartet	
LSC 2331	"Mario!"	Lanza	
LSC 2332	Hello World! Little Society Orchestra	Scherman narr E Roosevelt	
LSC 2334	Lanza,Mario: Lanza - Xmas Carols	Lanza	
LSC 2335	Rodgers, Richard: Victory at Sea Vol 1.	Bennett RCAVO	JM9 SM57/137+
LSC 2336	Finlandia (Sibelius/Grieg)	Mackerras NSOL	(SB2063 VICS1069 SPA91) SM73++
LSC 2338	Lanza,Mario:For the First Time	Lanza	JM10
LSC 2339	Romberg: Student Prince	Lanza	
LSC 2340	Gershwin: Porgy&Bess/Sym Picture of Gershwins	Bennett RCAVO	JM10 SM100++
LSC 2341	Saint-Saens: Symphony 3	Munch BSO	(SB2089) TAS36/162 44/179 JM10++/8
LSC 2342	Sibelius: Symphony 2	Monteux LSO	(SB2070 ECS789) JM10+ SM98++
LSC 2343	Beethoven: Symphony 5/Coriolan Ov	Reiner CSO	(VICS1161) JM10- SM61/125-
LSC 2344	Schubert: Symphony 9	Munch BSO	(SB2085) TAS36/129
LSC 2345	Tchaikovsky: 1812 Ov/Ravel Bolero	Gould	(SB2083) JM9/10+
LSC 2350	Yuletide Songfest for the Entire Family	Engle	
LSC 2352	Blackwood: Symphony 1/Haieff Symphony 2	Munch BSO	JM10+ SM77/136++
LSC 2353	Vivaldi: 4 Bassoon Concertos	ZIM Sherman Walt	(members of BSO) SM61/128++
LSC 2354	Mozart: Fantasia in Cmin/Sonatas K457/K330	Andre Tchaikowsky	JM10+
LSC 2355	Rachmaninov: Piano Concerto 3	Kondrashin SOA Van Cliburn	(SB2048) JM10+
LSC 2360	Chopin: Preludes	Andre Tchaikowsky	
LSC 2362	Berlioz: Symphonie Fantastique	Monteux VPO	(SB2090 VICS1031) JM10+ SM77-
LSC 2363	Tchaikovsky: Violin Concerto	Munch BSO Szeryng	(SB2080 VICS1037) TAS 36/162 SM58/136
LSC 2364	Mahler: Symphony 4	Reiner CSO Della Casa	(SB2081) JM10++ SM100
LSC 2365	Boccherini: Cello Conc/Vivaldi	Janigro SdZ	JM10+ SM61/126
LSC 2366	Beethoven: Sonata 7/Appassionata	Horowitz (piano)	JM10
LSC 2367	Gershwin: American in Paris/Rhapsody in Blue	Fiedler BPO Wild	TAS35/107,42/83 TASEC*44 JM10++
LSC 2368	Chopin: Scherzos	Rubinstein JM10++	TAS78/136+
LSC 2369	Tchaikovsky: Symphony 4	Monteux BSO	(SB2093) TASEC44 TAS32,36,42 JM10+
LSC 2370	Chopin: Ballades	Rubinstein	JM10++ SM58/137
LSC 2371	Mahler: Kindertotenlieder	Munch BSO Forrester	JM10
LSC 2373	Presenting Jamie Laredo	Jaime Laredo	(SB2074)

Catalog	Title	Artist/Orchestra	Notes
LSC 2374	Bartok: Music for Strings, Percussion and Celeste	Reiner CSO	TAS40/138 JM10++
LSC 2376	Stravinsky: Petrouchka	Monteux BSO	TAS36/127- JM10+
LSC 2377	Beethoven: Sonatas-Spring/Kreutzer	Rubinstein Szeryng	(SB2084) JM10+
LSC 2378	Schubert: Death & The Maiden	Juilliard String Quartet	(SB2079) TASEC42 JM10+ SM61/129++
LSC 2379	Roberta Peters Recital	Peters	JM10
LSC 2380	Music from million $ movies	Fiedler BPO	JM8 SM59/123++
LSC 2390	Christmas Songs	Verreau Grassi	(Only issued Canada)
LSC 2391	Opera: Opera for People who Hate Opera	Various	
LSC 2393	Opera: Caruso Favourites	Lanza	JM8
LSC 2394	Haydn: Symphonies 94/101	Monteux VPO	(SB2111 ECS574) JM10+ SM58/136++
LSC 2395	Prokofiev: Alexander Nevsky	Reiner CSO	(SB6530) JM10++ TAS9 SM67/139++
LSC 2396	Beethoven: Piano Concerto 3	Hendl CSO Graffman	(VICS1059) JM10++*
LSC 2398	Kabalevsky: The Comedians	Kondrashin RCAVO	(VICS1007) TASEC44 JM10++
LSC 2399	Mendelssohniana (extracts)	Binge NSOL	(SF5087) JM10+ Recorded England
LSC 2400	Ballet Music From the Opera	Fistoulari ROHCG	(SB2094) JM10++*
LSC 2401	Copland: App Spring/Tender Land suite	Copland BSO	(SB2104) TAS36/127- JM10 SM58/136+
LSC 2402	A Chorus Of Love	Shaw RSC	
LSC 2403	What Wondrous Love (American hymns)	Shaw RSC	
LSC 2405	Sibelius: Symphony 5	Gibson LSO	(SB2068 VICS1016 SPA122) SM65/184++
LSC 2406	Kalman: Countess Maritza (hlts)	VV	(SF5105) JM10+
LSC 2407	Strauss,J: Waltz Dream (hlts)	VV	JM10+
LSC 2411	Town Hall Recital	Valletti	
LSC 2412	Schumann: Dichterliebe	Valletti	JM10+
LSC 2413	Ravel: String Quartet	Juilliard String Quartet	TAS78/136++
LSC 2414	Brahms: Sonata 3/Bach Partita 3	Laredo/Sokoloff	
LSC 2415	Debussy: Preludes Book 1	Casadessus (piano)	
LSC 2416	Operatic Choruses	Shaw RSC	
LSC 2417	176 Keys: Music for 2 Pianos	Vronsky/Babin	JM10+
LSC 2418	Elgar: Enigma variations	Monteux LSO	(SB2108 VICS1107 SPA121)
LSC 2419	Dvorak: Slavonic Dances	Martinon LSO	(SB2115) SM81-
LSC 2420	Brahms: Trio in E flat/Beethoven Sonata	Szeryng Begley	SM98+
LSC 2421	Szeryng in Recital	Szeryng	(SB2109)
LSC 2423	Festival: Marche Slave etc	Reiner CSO	(VICS1068) JM10+ TASEC 65
LSC 2424	Vivaldi: Four Seasons	Societa Correlli	(SB2100)
LSC 2427	The Fabulous Josephine Baker	Jo Bouillon Baker	
LSC 2429	Grieg: Piano Concerto/Liszt	Wallenstein Rubinstein	(SB2112) JM10+
LSC 2430	Rachmaninov: Rhapsody on a Theme of Paganini, Falla : Nights in the Gardens of Spain	Jorda SFSO Rubinstein Reiner CSO Rubinstein	(SB2144) TAS30/139 TASEC44 JM10++*
LSC 2433	Grofe: Grand Canyon/Beethoven Wellingtons Victory	Gould	(SF5071) JM9+
LSC 2435	Sibelius: Violin Concerto	Hendl CSO Heifetz	(SB2101) JM10 TAS30/140 TASEC65
LSC 2436	Respighi: Pines/Fountains of Rome	Reiner CSO	(SB2103) TAS29/120 TAS49/64 TASEC65
LSC 2437	Bizet: Carmen for Orchestra	Gould	
LSC 2438	Berlioz: Overtures	Munch BSO	(SB2125) JM10+ SM69/150++
LSC 2439	All Time Favourites	Fiedler BPO	JM10+
LSC 2440	Romberg: The Desert Song	Lanza	
LSC 2441	Wagner: Reiner conducts Wagner	Reiner CSO	JM10+ SM77+
LSC 2442	Liszt: Music of Liszt	Fiedler BPO	JM10++ SM69/150++
LSC 2443	Liszt: The Virtuoso Liszt	Graffman	JM10++
LSC 2445	Armed Forces Suite	Bennett RCAVO	JM9+ SM59/123+
LSC 2446	Rimsky Korsakov: Scheherazade	Reiner CSO	TAS27/108 49/148 TASEC* 44 JM10++
LSC 2448	Bream: Art of Julian Bream	Bream	JM10++ SM73/190++
LSC 2449	Bizet: Carmen suite/Gounod: Faust	Gibson ROHCG	(VICS1108 SPA173/SPA220) JM10++*
LSC 2450	Schumann: Carnaval/Meyerbeer Les Patineurs	Rignold ROHCG	
LSC 2454	A Mario Lanza Program	Lanza	
LSC 2455	Schumann: Piano Concerto	Reiner CSO Van Cliburn	JM10++ SM69/146+
LSC 2456	Lalo: Symphonie Espagnole	Hendl CSO Szeryng	(SB2120 VICS1065 SB2120) JM10++ SM86++
LSC 2458	Operatic arias	Verreau (tenor)	(Only issued Canada)

Cat. No.	Title	Conductor/Artist	Orchestra/Soloist	Notes
LSC 2459	Brahms: Sonata 3/Interlude in E/Romance in F		Rubinstein	SM61/126+
LSC 2460	Bach,J.S: St 2 for Flute&strings etc	Janigro	SdZ	JM10+
LSC 2461	Mozart: Piano Concerto no 24/etc	Krips	Rubinstein	(SB2117) JM10+
LSC 2462	Debussy: La Mer/Strauss Don Juan.	Reiner	CSO	(SB2128) JM10+ SM100
LSC 2465	Prokofiev: Piano Concerto 2	Leibowitz	PCO Frager	TASEC44 TAS29/119 JM10++
LSC 2466	Brahms: Piano Concerto 2	Leinsdorf	CSO Richter	(SB2106) JM10+ SM64/126
LSC 2468	Chopin: Concerto 1/Mendelssohn Capriccio Brillant	Munch	BSO Graffman	(VICS1030)
LSC 2470	More classical music for people who hate classical music	Fiedler	BPO	(SF5109) JM10+
LSC 2471	Rhapsodies:Liszt Hung/Enescu Roumanian 1	Stokowski	RCAVO	(SB2130) JM10+ SM65/180++ TASEC73
LSC 2472	Bruch: Violin Conc 1/Mozart	Mitchell	NatSO Laredo	(VICS1129) JM10+
LSC 2473	Brahms: Piano Qt in Gmin	Festival Quartet		(SB2136)
LSC 2474	Schumann: Symphony 1/Manfred Ov	Munch	BSO	(SB2126) JM10 SM65/180+
LSC 2481	Schumann: Quartet 3/Carter Quartet 2	Juilliard String Quartet		
LSC 2485	Delibes: Sylvia & Coppelia	Rignold	PCO	(SB2152 VICS1130 SB2152)
LSC 2486	Loesser: Music of Frank Loesser	Fiedler	BPO	JM10 SM83/239+
LSC 2487	Bream: Giuliani/Arnold Guitar Concertos	Melos Ensemble Bream		JM10++ TASEC73
LSC 2488	Fauré: Sonata 1/Debussy Sonata 3	Senofsky Graffman		
LSC 2489	Dvorak: Symphony 2 (7)	Monteux	LSO	(SB2155 VICS1310 ECS779)
LSC 2490	Dvorak: Cello Concerto	Munch	BSO Piatigorsky	(VICS2002) JM10+
LSC 2491	Beethoven: Symphonies 1/8	Monteux	BSO	(SB2127 ECS638) JM10+
LSC 2493	Schubert: Sonata in D	Gilels (piano)		JM10 SM81-
LSC 2495	Heart of the Concerto	Reiner etc	Rubinstein	JM10++
LSC 2496	Heart of the Symphony	Reiner etc		JM10+
LSC 2497	Prokofiev: Ugly Duckling/Cinderella	Galina Vishnevskaya		(SB2141)
LSC 2498	Jan Peerce Sings Hebrew Melodies	J Peerce		
LSC 2500	Strauss,J: Waltzes	Reiner	CSO	TASEC44 JM10++
LSC 2502	Serenade		Verreau	Believed only Canadian pressing exists
LSC 2504	Arias from Faust,Boheme, Carmen, etc	Anna Moffo (soprano)		(SB2156) JM10+
LSC 2505	Berlioz: Romeo and Juliet	Munch	BSO	Believed never issued in USA
LSC 2506	Arias from Aida, Butterfly, Traviata	Fabritis	Price	
LSC 2507	Prokofiev: Piano Concerto 3/MacDowell Pno Conc 2	Hendl	CSO Van Cliburn	(SB2113) JM10++* SM100++
LSC 2509	Friml: The Vagabond King	Lanza		
LSC 2514	Franck: Symphony in D Min	Monteux	CSO	(SB6631) TAS29/122 JM10+ SM90+-
LSC 2515	Herbert: The Immortal Victor Herbert	Shaw	RSC	SM83/240++
LSC 2516	Schubert: Symphonies 5/8	Reiner	CSO	(SB2134) JM10 SL6/82+ SM86
LSC 2517	Brahms: Piano Quartet in A	Festival Quartet		SM69/148
LSC 2520	Mendelssohn: Symphony 3	Munch	BSO	(SB2129) TAS44/178 JM9 SM98
LSC 2522	Schubert: Symphony 2/Beethoven Prometheus Music	Munch BSO		(SB6508) JM10
LSC 2523	Rodgers, Richard: Victory at Sea Vol 3	Bennett	RCAVO	SM57/137
LSC 2524	Dvorak: Quartet in C/Wolf Ital Serenade	Juilliard Quartet/Begley		JM9
LSC 2531	Berg: Lyric Suite/Webern 5 Pieces	Juilliard String Quartet		JM10
LSC 2532	Gould: Fall River Legend/etc	Gould		TAS39/139+
LSC 2535	Mozart: Symphony 40/Haydn Symphony 104	Karajan	VPO	JM10- See LDS 2347
LSC 2536	Beethoven: Symphony 7	Karajan	VPO	See LDS 2348
LSC 2537	Brahms: Symphony 1	Karajan	VPO	(SB2086) See LDS 2351
LSC 2538	Strauss,J: Vienna of Johann Strauss	Karajan	VPO	JM10 See LDS 2346
LSC 2539	Puccini: Turandot (hlts)	Nilsson Bjorling		
LSC 2540	Favourite Songs	Valletti		
LSC 2541	Rachmaninov: Pno Conc 1/Liszt Todtentanz	Reiner	CSO Janis	(VICS1205) JM10+
LSC 2542	Moonlight Sonata (various)	Gould		
LSC 2544	Beethoven: Piano Concerto 1/Sonata 22	Munch	BSO Richter	(VICS1478) TAS23, 36/125 50/180 JM10
LSC 2545	Beethoven: Piano Snts Appassionata/Op 26	Richter		(SB2119 VICS1427) TAS23,50/180 JM10+
LSC 2546	Liebestraum	Fiedler	BPO	JM10+
LSC 2547	Light Classics	Fiedler	BPO	(SF5122) JM10+
LSC 2548	Viennese Night	Fiedler	BPO	
LSC 2549	Family Fun With Familiar Music	Fiedler	BPO	JM10+

Catalog	Title	Artist/Orchestra	Notes
LSC 2550	Beethoven: Trio Op 8/Kodaly Duo	Piatigorsky Primrose Heifetz	SM83/240++
LSC 2551	Sea Shanties	Shaw RSC	JM9
LSC 2552	Beyond the Blue Horizon	Gould	JM10
LSC 2553	Shostakovich: Cello Sonata/Schubert Arpeggione	Shafran Pecherskaya	JM10++
LSC 2555	Wagner: The Sound of Stokowski and Wagner	Stokowski SOA	(SB2148) JM10++ SM81+++
LSC 2556	Hearts in 3/4 Time	Fiedler BPO	JM10+
LSC 2557	Bach: Organ Music	Carl Weinrich	
LSC 2558	Foss: Studies in Improvisation	Lukas Foss Improvisation Chamber Ensemble	
LSC 2559	Kern/Porter: Favourites	Gould	
LSC 2561	Verdi: La Traviata (hlts)	Previtalli ROHO	JM10
LSC 2562	Beethoven: Emperor Concerto	Reiner CSO Van Cliburn	JM10+ SM83/242+
LSC 2563	Beethoven, Bach, Schubert Trios	Piatigorsky Primrose Heifetz	
LSC 2565	Tchaikovsky Romeo&Juliet/Strauss:Till Eulenspiegel	Munch BSO	JM10++* SM59/123++
LSC 2566	Grieg: Concerto in A min	Wallenstein Rubinstein	JM10+ TASEC65
LSC 2567	Poulenc: Conc for Organ/Stravinsky Jeu de Cartes	Munch BSO	(SB2147) JM10 SM90++
LSC 2568	Ravel: Daphnis&Chloe	Munch BSO	(SB2137) JM10+ SM67/146++
LSC 2569	Sousa: Sousa Forever	Gould	
LSC 2570	Incomparable Bjorling	Bjorling	
LSC 2573	Kreutzer variations	Smith Heifetz	Never issued in USA
LSC 2575	Chopin: Concerto 1	Skrowacsewski NSOL Rubinstein	(SB2145) JM10+ SM90+
LSC 2576	Chopin: My Favourite Chopin	Van Cliburn	(SB2143) JM10
LSC 2577	Beethoven: Kreutzer Sonata/Bach,J.S Double Conc	Sargent Heifetz Friedman	(SB2146) JM10+ SM86+
LSC 2578	Birgit Nilsson	Nilsson	JM10+
LSC 2579	Piano Favourites Played by the Orchestra	Gould	
LSC 2580	I'm Going to Sing	Shaw RSC	
LSC 2581	Brahms: Piano Concerto 2	Reiner CSO Van Cliburn	(SB6545) JM10+
LSC 2586	Gershwin: Concerto in F/Cuban Ov	Fiedler BPO Wild	TAS42/83 TAS35/107 36/130 JM10+
LSC 2591	Hellelujah & other choruses	Shaw RSC	
LSC 2592	He's Got the Whole World in His Hands	Marion Anderson	(SB2153)
LSC 2593	Inspiration Music	Stokowski NSOL Luboff Choir	JM10++*
LSC 2595	Pops Round-Up (Yellow Rose of Texas, etc)	Fiedler BPO	JM9 TAS78/148++
LSC 2596	Saint-Saens: Carnival of the Animals/Britten YPGO	Fiedler BPO	
LSC 2598	23 Glee Club Favourites	Shaw RSC	SM58/140+++
LSC 2599	Our Man in Boston	Fiedler BPO	JM10
LSC 2600	Swing Low Sweet Chariot	Price	
LSC 2601	Rachmaninov: Piano Concerto 2	Reiner CSO Van Cliburn	(SB6502) JM10++ SM86+
LSC 2603	Bruch: Scottish Fantasy/etc	Sargent NSOL Heifetz	(SB6503) JM10
LSC 2604	Opera without Singing	Fiedler BPO	
LSC 2605	Highlights from Rubinstein at Carnegie Hall	Rubinstein	(SB6504)
LSC 2606	Bream: Popular Classics from Spain	Bream	
LSC 2608	Berlioz: Symphonie Fantastique	Munch BSO	TAS36/161 JM10++
LSC 2609	Strauss,R: Also Sprach Zarathustra	Reiner CSO	(SB6518) TAS44/128 JM10
LSC 2610	Paganini: Conc 1/Saint-Saens Intr&Rondo	Hendl CSO Friedman	JM10+
LSC 2611	Chopin/Rachmaninov/Ravel/Prokofiev	Richter	JM10+
LSC 2612	Handel: Music for Royal Fireworks	Stokowski RCAVO	JM10+ TAS39/139
LSC 2613	Christmas Carols	Anderson	
LSC 2614	Beethoven: Symphony 6	Reiner CSO	(SB6510) DG JM10 1st numbered DG
LSC 2615	Massenet: Great Scenes from Werther	Leibowitz ROHO Valletti	
LSC 2616	Verdi: Aida (extracts)	Solti RomeOp	JM10+
LSC 2617	Verdi: Il Trovatore (extracts)	Basile RomeOp	JM10+
LSC 2619	Brahms: Sonatas 2/3	Rubinstein Szeryng	(SB6520) JM10+ SM64/126++
LSC 2620	Beethoven: Sonata 8/Brahms Sonata 1	Rubinstein Szeryng	(SB6513) JM10+ SM90++
LSC 2621	Prokofiev: Love of 3 Oranges/Chopin	Fiedler BPO	JM10+
LSC 2626	Beethoven: Quartet Op 131	Juilliard String Quartet	
LSC 2629	Dvorak: Symphony 4(8)	Munch BSO	(SB6509) JM10
LSC 2632	Beethoven: Quartets Fmin Op 95/Fmaj Op 135	Juilliard String Quartet	(SB6534)

Catalog	Title	Artist/Conductor	Orchestra/Soloist	Notes
LSC 2633	Love Walked In	Gould		
LSC 2634	Mozart: Piano Concerto no 21/23	Wallenstein	Rubinstein	(SB6532) JM10+ SM65/178++
LSC 2635	Mozart: Piano Concerto no 20/Haydn	Wallenstein	Rubinstein	JM10+
LSC 2636	Mozart: Piano Concerto no 17/Schubert	Wallenstein	Rubinstein	JM10+ SM73++
LSC 2637	State Fair: Music of Richard Rodgers	Gould		
LSC 2638	Leroy Anderson: Fiddle Faddle...	Fiedler	BPO	JM9 TAS33/136 SM73/191++
LSC 2640	Romantic Italian Songs	Franchi		
LSC 2641	Strauss,R: Ein Heldenleben	Leinsdorf	BSO	(SB6565) DG JM9+
LSC 2642	Mahler: Symphony 1	Leinsdorf	BSO	DG JM9
LSC 2643	Bartok: Conc for Orchestra	Leinsdorf	BSO	JM10+
LSC 2644	Beethoven: Symphony 3	Leinsdorf	BSO	DG JM9
LSC 2645	Concert	Verreau (tenor)		Issued Canada only
LSC 2646	Violin Recital	Lillian Garner		Only Canadian pressing exists
LSC 2647	Chausson: Sym in Bflat/Franck: Le Chasseur Maudit	Munch	BSO	(SB6528) JM10+
LSC 2648	Rachmaninov: Suite for 2 Pianos	Vronsky Babin		JM10
LSC 2649	Bach: Organ Music Vol 2	Weinrich		
LSC 2652	Bruch: Violin Concerto 1/Mozart	Sargent	NSOL Heifetz	(SB6527) Ken Wilkinson
LSC 2653	Music for Strings	Janigro	SdZ	
LSC 2654	Beethoven: Sonatas-Moonlight/Pathetique/Les Adieux	Rubinstein		JM10+
LSC 2655	Puccini: La Boheme (hlts)	Leinsdorf	ROHO	JM10
LSC 2657	Our Man from Italy	Franchi		
LSC 2658	Recital	Bruyères (baritone)		Issued Canada only
VCS 2659	The Power of the Orchestra	Leibowitz	RPO	JM10++ Gerhardt, Wilkinson
LSC 2661	Jalousie & other Latin Favs	Fiedler	BPO	DG JM10+
LSC 2662	America the Beautiful	Shaw	RSC	DG
LSC 2664	Ravel: Bolero/Pavane	Munch	BSO	DG JM9
LSC 2666	Sibelius: Music of Finlandia	Gould		DG JM9
LSC 2667	Ravel: Concerto in G	Leinsdorf	BSO Hollander	DG JM10
LSC 2668	Debussy: Afternoon of a Faun	Munch	BSO	DG JM9
LSC 2669	Schumann: 'Rubinstein' (Carnival/Fantasie)	Rubinstein		DG JM9
LSC 2670	Stardust (Claire de Lune, Deep Purple, etc)	Fiedler	BPO	DG JM8
LSC 2671	Szymanowski: Romance for Violin & Piano	Fieldman		
LSC 2673	Mendelssohn: Midsummer Night's Dream	Leinsdorf	BSO	DG JM9
LSC 2674	Broadway I Love You	Franchi		DG
LSC 2675	The Dream Duets	Franchi Moffo		
LSC 2676	Robert Shaw Chorale on Tour	Shaw	RSC	
LSC 2677	Concert in the Park	Fiedler	BPO	DG
LSC 2678	Rachmaninov: Rhapsody on Paganini	Fiedler	BPO Pennario	DG JM10
LSC 2679	Gershwin: Porgy and Bess	Price		DG
LSC 2680	Beethoven: Piano Concerto 4	Reiner	CSO Van Cliburn	DG TAS36/160 JM9+
LSC 2683	Tchaikovsky: Symphony 6	Munch	BSO	DG JM10
LSC 2686	Gould: Spirituals for Orchestra	Gould		DG
LSC 2688	Tchaikovsky: Swan Lake excerpts	Fiedler	BPO	DG JM9+
LSC 2689	Chausson Poeme/Sarasate/Ravel/S-Saens	Sargent	LSO Friedman	DG Rec England, Gerhardt, Perry
LSC 2690	Liszt: Concertos 1&2	Leibowitz	LSO Pennario	(SB6568) DG JM10 Wilkinson
LSC 2692	Wagner: Die Walkure excerpts	Leinsdorf	LSO	
LSC 2693	Vocal Recital	Colette Boky		Issued Canada only
LSC 2694	Mozart: Symphony 41/Eine Kleine Nachtmusik	Leinsdorf	BSO	DG JM10
LSC 2695	Berlioz: Nuits d'Ete/Falla El Amor Brujo	Reiner	CSO Price	(SB6566) DG
LSC 2701	Schumann: Symphony 4	Leinsdorf	BSO	DG JM10
LSC 2702	Milhaud: Frenchman in NY/Gershwin: Am in Paris	Fiedler	BPO	DG JM10
LSC 2703	Prokofiev: Sym & Con for Cello & Orchestra	Leinsdorf	BSO	DG
LSC 2704	Music to have fun by	Mitchell	NSOL	
LSC 2705	Masters of the Guitar	Presti Lagoya		
LSC 2707	Prokofiev: Symphony 5	Leinsdorf	BSO	(SB6576)
LSC 2709	Verdi: La Gioconda/Force of Destiny	Previtalli		

Catalog	Title	Performers	Notes
LSC 2711	Brahms: Symphony 1	Leinsdorf BSO	DG JM9
LSC 2713	For the young in heart	Mitchell NSOL	
LSC 2715	Brahms: Trio 2/Beethoven Trio in G	Senofsky Trepel Graffman	
LSC 2717	Ramos-Diaz: Masters of the Guitar Vol 2	Pomponio Zarate	
LSC 2718	Music for voice & guitar	Britten Pears	Recorded England
LSC 2719	V Williams: Greensleeves/Tallis/Eng Folk Songs Suite	Gould	DG
LSC 2724	Brahms: Piano Concerto 1	Leinsdorf BSO Van Cliburn	DG JM9
LSC 2725	Rimsky-Korsakov: Le Coq D'Or	Leinsdorf BSO	DG JM10+
LSC 2726	Chopin: Waltzes	Rubinstein	DG JM10+
LSC 2730	Rodrigo: Concierto Aranjuez/Vivaldi/Britten	Melos CO Bream	(SB6635) DG
LSC 2734	Glazunov: Vln Conc/Mozart	Hendl CSO Heifetz	JM10+ SM57/139++
LSC 2735	Fauré: Piano Quartet	Festival Quartet	
LSC 2737	Schubert: Quintet in C maj	Piatigorsky Heifetz	On LDS6159
LSC 2738	Mendelssohn: Octet/Mozart G Min Quintet	Piatigorsky Heifetz	On LDS6159
LSC 2739	Franck: Quintet/Brahms: Sextet.	Piatigorsky Heifetz	On LDS6159
LSC 2740	Walton: Violin conc/Castelnuova-Tedesca Concerto	Heifetz	(LSB4102)
LSC 2741	Italian Arias	Vickers	
LSC 2742	Haydn: Symphonies 95/101	Reiner CSO	(SB6584) DG Last Reiner LSC
LSC 2743	Vivaldi: Concertos 5,6,7,8	Societa Corelli Redditi	
LSC 2744	Favourite Dances & marches	Fiedler BPO	
LSC 2745	Music America Loves Best	Fiedler BPO	DG
LSC 2746	Enesco/Liszt/Gershwin/Chabrier	Fiedler BPO	JM10+
LSC 2747	Slaughter on 10th Ave and Other Show Hits	Fiedler BPO	JM10+
LSC 2748	Lanza,Mario: The Best of Mario Lanza	Lanza	Electronic stereo
LSC 2749	Strauss,R: Songs	Lisa Della Casa	
LSC 2751	A French Program	Rubinstein	DG
LSC 2757	World's Greatest Marches	Fiedler/Leinsdorf BPO/BSO	DG JM10
LSC 2759	Britten: A Ceremony of Carols/Rejoice in the Lamb	Shaw RSC	
LSC 2760	"Songs of Faith and Inspiration"	Shaw RSC	
LSC 2762	Menoti: Amahl and the Night Visitors	NBC Opera Company Grossman	(SB6634 LSB4075) DG TASEC65
LSC 2765	Beethoven: Quartet Op 132	Juilliard String Quartet	
LSC 2766	Music to Tell a Story By	Mitchell NSOL	
LSC 2767	Rosza: Violin Concerto/Benjamin Romatic Fantasy	Hendl Dallas Heifetz	(SB6605)
LSC 2768	More Jungle Drums	Gould	
LSC 2770	Beethoven/Haydn/Rosza	Piatigorsky Heifetz	DG
LSC 2772	Masters of the Guitar: Haydn/Schubert	Pomponio Zarate	Not DG
LSC 2779	Schumann: Sonata in Gmin	Turini	
LSC 2782	More Music from Million $ Movies	Fiedler BPO	DG
LSC 2783	Prokofiev: Peter & the Wolf/Classical Symphony	Sargent LSO	
LSC 2785	Menoti: Death of the Bishop of Brindisi/Schonberg	Leinsdorf BSO	
LSC 2786	Chants of the Church	Mount Angel Choir	JM10+
LSC 2789	Grofe Grand Canyon St/Bernstein Candide Ov	Fiedler BPO	DG
LSC 2800	Great Music for Relaxation	Gould/Agoult/etc	
LSC 2801	Khachaturian: Piano Concerto/Bloch	Previn RPO Hollander	DG
LSC 2806	Ravel: Daphnis&Chloe St 2/Roussel Bacchus&Ariadne	Martinon CSO	DG (SB6627)
LSC 2807	V Williams: Serenade to Music	Van Cliburn	(Van Cliburn conducts)
LSC 2810	The Best of Arthur Fiedler & the Boston Pops	Fiedler BPO	
LSC 2813	Music to have fun by (Reiner/Kije etc)	Various incl Reiner	DG
LSC 2815	Alkan: Piano Music of Alkan	Lewenthal	
LSC 2816	Respighi: Feste Romane/Strauss: Don Juan	Mehta LAPO	
LSC 2819	Bream: Julian Bream in Concert	Bream Peter Pears	Rec England
LSC 2822	Stravinsky: Symphony of Psalms/Poulenc: Gloria	Shaw RSC	DG
LSC 2827	An Evening at the "Pops" (Live)	Fiedler BPO	DG
LSC 2832	Beethoven: Quartets 1/3	Barchett Quartet	DG
LSC 2834	Prokofiev: Symphony 6	Leinsdorf BSO	(SB6662)
LSC 2839	Wagner: Die Meistersinger (highlights, live)	Munich National Theatre	

Catalog	Title	Performers	Notes
LSC 2841	Puccini: Tosca (highlights)	Karajan VPO	
LSC 2845	Wagner: Flyign Dutchman (highlights)	Dorati ROHO	
LSC 2850	Gould: Spirituals/Copland: Dance Symphony	Gould CSO	DG
LSC 2852	Bartok: Concerto 2/Stravinsky Violin Concerto	Leinsdorf BSO Silverstein	
LSC 2856	Gershwin: Heifetz Plays Music of Gershwin & France	Heifetz	DG
LSC 2857	The Duke at Tanglewood (live)	Fiedler BPO Ellington	
LSC 2867	Heifetz-Piatigorsky Concerts	Piatigorsky Heifetz	DG
LSC 2878	The Baroque Guitar	Bream	DG
LSC 2879	Stravinsky: Agon/Schuller: 7 Studies on Paul Klee	Leinsdorf BSO	DG (SB6677)
LSC 2887	Dvorak: Strinq Quartet op 105/Smetana Qt	Guarneri Quartet	DG
LSC 2893	Ives: Symphony 1/The Unanswered Question	Gould	DG
LSC 2896	Bach: Lute Suites 1/2	Bream	DG (SB6684)
LSC 2899	Rachmaninov: Symphony 2	Previn LSO	DG Wilkinson JM10
LSC 2909	Howard Ferguson:/Karen Khachaturian Sonatas	Heifetz Steuber	DG
LSC 2914	Varese: Arcana/Martin	Martinon CSO	(SB6710) TAS4/234
LSC 2920	Nielsen Symphony 4/Clarinet Concerto	Gould CSO Goodman	
LSC 2923	Strauss,R: Alpine Symphony	Kempe RPO	(SB6696) DG JM9 Wilkinson
LSC2924	Lute Music from the Royal Courts of Europe	Bream	(SB6698)
LSC 2927	Walton: Symphony 1	Previn LSO	DG
LSC 2934	Prokofiev: Symphony 3, Scythian Suite	Leinsdorf BSO	(SB6705)
LSC 2941	Ives: Piano Sonata 1	William Masselos	(SB6709)
LSC 2957	Mozart Violin Concertos K219/Turina	Piatigorsky Heifetz	DG
LSC 2964	Bream: Bream's Favourite Modern Guitar Music	Bream	
LSC 2971	Brahms: Piano Quintet op 34	Guarneri Qt Rubinstein	DG (SB6737)
LSC 2974	Viola recital: Hindemith,Stravinsky,Reger	Trampler	(SB6789)
LSC 2985	Dvorak: Piano Quintet in A/Francaix	Piatigorsky Heifetz	
LSC 2987	Bream: Dances of Dowland	Bream (lute)	DG
LSC 2990	Rachmaninov: Symphony 3	Previn LSO	(SB6729 LSB4090)
LSC 2994	Prokofiev: Music from Romeo and Juliet	Leinsdorf BSO	
LSC 3009	Brahms: Piano Quartet/Bocherini/Toch	Piatigorsky Heifetz	DG
LSC 3019	Prokofiev: Piano Concertos 3, 4	Leinsdorf BSO Browning	
LSC 3048	Mozart Quintet in C/Mendelssohn Trio 2 in Cmin	Piatigorsky Heifetz	DG
LSC 3061	Prokofiev: Symphony 2, Lt Kije Suite	Leinsdorf BSO	
LSC 6052	Puccini: Tosca	Leinsdorf RomeOp Milanov	
LSC 6059	Mascagni: Cavalleria Rusticana	Tebaldi Bjorling	(SB2021/2) JM8
LSC 6066	Beethoven: Symphonies 8/9	Munch BSO	(VICS1114) JM8
LSC 6068	Beethoven/Brahms Schumann Pno Qnts	Festival Quartet	
LSC 6076	Verdi: Macbeth	Leinsdorf	(SER4505-7)
LSC 6079	Mozart: Marriage of Figaro	Leinsdorf Tozzi/Peters	
LSC 6082	'Everything But The Beer' (concert)	Fiedler BPO	JM10++* SM86++
LSC 6087	Mahler: Das Lied Von Der Erde/Haydn Symphony 88	Reiner CSO	(VICS1390) JM10+ TAS30 SM81/118+
LSC 6094	Albeniz: Iberia/Rhapsody Espagnole	Morel PCO	(SB2131/2) SM58/138++
LSC 6095	Puccini: La Boheme	Leinsdorf RCAVO Tucker/Moffo JM10	
LSC 6096	Beethoven: Symphonies 1/9	Reiner CSO	(SB6500/1) WD JM10
LSC 6097	Summer Festival (Ov Russlan&Ludmilla/Reiner)	Various	(SB6542)
LSC 6135	Puccini: Madame Butterfly	RomeOp Leinsdorf Moffo	JM10+
LSC 6139	Ponchielli: La Gioconda	Previtalli AdSC	(SB2027/30)
LSC 6140	Bach: 6 Brandenburg Concertos	Munch BSO	
LSC 6141	Donizetti: Lucia Di Lammermoor	Leinsdorf RomeOp	
LSC 6143	Rossini: Barber of Seville (cplt)	Leinsdorf MetOp	
LSC 6149	Puccini: Turandot	Rome Op Leinsdorf Nilsson Tebaldi Bjorling	(SER4520-2) JM10+
LSC 6150	Verdi: Il Trovatore	Basile RomeOp	
LSC 6154	Verdi: La Traviata	Previtalli RomeOp	
LSC 6156	Wagner: Flying Dutchman	Dorati ROHO	(SER4535/7)
LSC 6157	Bach: B Minor Mass	Shaw RSC	
LSC 6158	Verdi: Aida	Solti RomeOp	(SER4538-40)

LSC 6160	Puccini: Madama Butterfly			
LSC 6163	Verdi: Falstaff	Solti		(SER5509-11)
LSC 6167	BSO Chamber Players	Various		(SB6692)
LSC6176	Donizetti: Lucrezia Borgia	RCA Italian Opera Perlea		(SER5553-5)
LSC 6179	Verdi: Un Ballo in Maschera	Leinsdorf		
LSC 6198	Verdi: Aida	Leinsdorf	LSO Bumbry	(SER5609-11)
LSC 6406	Verdi: The Force of Destiny	Previtalli	AdSC	
LSC 6408	Mozart: Marriage of Figaro	VPO	Leinsdorf	(SER4508-11)
LSC 6410	Mozart: Don Giovanni	VPO	Leinsdorf Nilssson	(SER4528-31)
LSC 6411	Brahms: 4 Symphonies	Munch	BSO	
LSC 6702	Beethoven: The 5 Piano Concertos	Various	Rubinstein	
LSC 6708	Wagner: Die Meistersinger	?		
LSC 6709	Schubert: The Symphonies of F. Schubert	Vaughan	SOoN	
LSC 6710	Wagner: Lohengrin	Leinsdorf	BSO	DG
LSC 6803	Tchaikovsky: Omnibus (2129/2177/2216/2239/2565)	Various		JM10/10
LSC 6805	Haydn: Symphonies 82-92	Vaughan	SOoN	
LSC 6902	8 Great Symphonies	Various		(LSC1901, 2239, 2097, 2297, 2131, 2221, 2233)
LSC 7027	Verdi: Rigoletto	Solti RCAVO Moffo/Merrill		JM10
LSC 7029	Strauss,J: Die Fledermaus	Stevens/Konya		JM10+
LSC 7030	Mozart: Requiem/Requiem for Death of JFK	Leinsdorf	BSO	JM9
LSC 7031	Mahler: Symphony 5	BSO	Leinsdorf	(SER5518-9)
LSC 7040	Verdi: Requiem	BSO	Leinsdorf	(SER5537-8)
LSC 7046	Mahler: Symphony 3	BSO	Leinsdorf	(SB6765-6)
LSC 9300	Stereo for the Joy of It	Various		(LSC2233, 1901, 2214, 2100, 1903, 2195, 2234, 2201, 1984, 2150)
SPS 3313	Sounds in Space. (2150/2085/1991/2131/etc)	Various		(SF 5015)
SPS 3350	New Golden Age of Sound ('Breck' sampler)	Various		

* * * * *

RCA Living Stereo 'SB' English Pressings

SB2001	Mussorgsky: Pictures at an Exhibition	Reiner	CSO	(LSC 2201)
SB2002	Tchaikovsky: Violin Concerto	Reiner	CSO Heifetz	(LSC 2129)
SB2003	Rimsky Korsakov: Scheherazade	Monteux	LSO	(LSC 2208)
SB2005	Stravinsky: Rite of Spring	Monteux	PCO	(LSC 2085)
SB2006	Tchaikovsky: Piano Concerto 1	Kondrashin	Van Cliburn	(LSC 2252)
SB2007	Brahms: Symphony 3, Tragic Overture	Reiner	CSO	(LSC 2209)
SB2008	Beethoven: Piano Concerto 3	SOA	Krips Rubinstein	(LSC 2122)
SB2009	Franck: Symphony in D Min	Munch	BSO	(LSC 2131)
SB2010	Beethoven: Symphony 7/Fidelio Ov	Reiner	CSO	(LSC 1991)
SB2011	'South Pacific'	Original 1958 Soundtrack recording		
SB2012	Tchaikovsky: Swan Lake	Morel	ROHCG	(LSC 2227)
SB2013	Tchaikovsky: Sleeping Beauty excerpts	Monteux	LSO	(LSC 2177)
SB2014	Mendelssohn: Midsmr Nts Drm/Schubert: Rosamunde	Monteux	VPO	(LSC 2223)
SB2015	Beethoven: Piano Concerto 5	Krips	SOA Rubinstein	(LSC 2124)
SB2016	Berlioz: Harold in Italy	Munch	BSO Primrose	(LSC 2228)
SB2017	Beethoven: Piano Concerto 4	Krips	SOA Rubinstein	(LSC 2123)
SB2018	Adam: Giselle (extracts)	Wolff	PCO	(LSC 2301)
SB2019	Ravel Bolero/Valse/Rhaps Esp/Debussy: Faun Prelude	Monteux	BSO	(LSC 1984)
SB2020	Witches Brew (Mussorgsky, Arnold, St-Saens, Liszt, etc)	Gibson	NSOL	(LSC 2225)
SB2021-2	Mascagni: Cavalleria Rusticana	Florence May Orch Erede Tebaldi Bjorling		(LSC 6059)
SB2023	Saint-Saens: Conc 2/Franck Symph Varns	Wallenstein	SOA Rubinstein	(LSC 2234)
SB2024	Tchaikovsky: Symphony 6	Monteux	BSO	(LSC 1901)
SB2025	Beethoven: Symphony 3	BSO	Munch	(LSC 2233)
SB2026	Elgar: Pomp & Circ 1-5, Bliss: Things to Come, etc	Bliss	LSO	(LSC 2257)
SB2027-30	Ponchielli: La Gioconda	Previtalli	AdSC Milanov di Stefano	(LSC 6139)
SB2031	Dvorak: New World Symphony	Reiner	CSO	(LSC 2214)
SB2032	Brahms: Piano Concerto 2	Reiner	CSO Gilels	(LSC 2219)
SB2033	Schumann: Piano Concerto	Krips	RCAVO Rubinstein	(LSC 2256)
SB2034	Prokofiev: Symphony 5	Martinon	PCO	(LSC 2272)
SB2035	Rachmaninov: Sym 3/Rimsky-K: Russian Easter Ov	Boult	LPO	(LSC 2185)
SB2036	Strauss,R: Death&Transfiguration/Till Eulenspiegel	Reiner	VPO	(LSC 2077)
SB2037	Stravinsky: Petrouchka/Firebird Suite	Monteux	PCO Katchen	(LSC 2113 SPA152)
SB2039	Walton: Facade/Lecocq: Mamzelle Angot	Fistoulari	ROHCG	(LSC 2285)
SB2040	Brahms: Piano Concerto 1	Munch	BSO Graffman	(LSC 2274)
SB2041	The French Touch (Dukas/Ravel/etc)	Munch	BSO	(LSC2292 VICS1060)
SB2042	The Reiner Sound (Rachmaninov Isle of Dead/Ravel)	Reiner	CSO	(LSC 2183)
SB2043	Rachmaninov: Piano Concerto 2 (earliest issue)	Reiner	CSO Rubinstein	(LSC 2068)
SB2043	Rachmaninov: Piano Concerto 2/Liszt: Piano Concerto 1	Reiner	CSO Rubinstein	(LSC 2068)

Note that SB2043 comes in two forms corresponding to the two forms of the American issued LSC2068.
In the earlier issue the Rachmaninov is spread over two sides with benefits to sound quality.

SB2044	Ravel: Alborado/Valses/Debussy Iberia	Reiner	CSO	(LSC 2222)
SB2045	Tchaikovsky: Symphony 5	BSO	Monteux	(LSC 2239)
SB2046	Beethoven: Piano Concerto 1	Krips	SOA Rubinstein	(LSC 2120)
SB2047	Beethoven: Violin Concerto	Munch	BSO Heifetz	(LSC 1992)
SB2048	Rachmaninov: Piano Concerto 3	Kondrashin	SOA Van Cliburn	(LSC 2355)
SB2049	Brahms: Violin Concerto	Monteux	LSO Szeryng	(LSC 2281)
SB2050	"Music for Frustrated Conductors" (supplied with baton!)	Various	Fiedler/Gould/Bennett/etc	(LSC2325)
SB2051	Shostakovich: Symphony 1/Age of Gold	Martinon	LSO	(LSC 2322)
SB2052	St-Saens: Samson et Dalilah (hlts)	Cleva	MetOp del Monaco Stevens	(LSC2309)
SB2053	Ravel: Piano Concerto, D'Indy: Symphony on a French Mt Air	Munch	BSO Henriot-Schweitzer	(LSC 2271)
SB2057	Bizet: L'Arlesienne Suites 1&2/Chabrier Espana	Morel	ROHCG	(LSC 2327)
SB2058	Venice (Verdi, Rossini, Offenbach, Ponchielli)	Solti	ROHCG	(LSC 2313)
SB2059	1812 Ov/Tragic Ov/Liszt Mephisto/Fingals Cave	Reiner	CSO	(LSC 2241)
SB2060	Brahms: Symphony 4	Munch	BSO	(LSC 2297)

SB2061	Prokofiev: Symphony 7/Overture Russe	Martinon PCO	(LSC 2288)
SB2063	Finlandia (Sibelius/Grieg)	Mackerras NSOL	(LSC 2336)
SB2064	Rimsky Korsakov: Capr Esp/Tchaik: Capr It	Kondrashin RCAVO Shumsky	(LSC 2323)
SB2065	Beethoven: Symphony 6	Monteux VPO	(LSC 2316)
SB2066	Mendelssohn: Violin Conc/Prokofiev Violin Conc 2	Munch BSO Heifetz	(LSC 2314)
SB2067	Chopin: Piao Concerto 2 ("The Rubinstein Story")	SOA Wallenstein Rubinstein	(LSC 2265)
SB2068	Sibelius: Symphony 5, Karelia Suite	Gibson LSO	(LSC 2405)
SB2069	Brahms: Piano Concerto 2	Krips RCAVO Rubinstein	(LSC 2296)
SB2070	Sibelius: Symphony 2	Monteux LSO	(LSC 2342)
SB2074	Presenting Jaime Laredo (Vivaldi, Falla, Wieniawski, Bach))	Jaime Laredo Sokolov (piano)	(LSC 2373)
SB2075	Rossini: Overtures(Tell/Barber/etc)	Reiner CSO	(LSC 2318)
SB2079	Schubert: String Quartets 12, 14 (Death & The Maiden)	Juilliard String Quartet	(LSC 2378)
SB2080	Tchaikovsky: Violin Concerto	Munch BSO Szeryng	(LSC 2363)
SB2081	Mahler: Symphony 4	Reiner CSO Della Casa	(LSC 2364)
SB2082	Chopin: Ballades	Rubinstein	(LSC 2370)
SB2083	Tchaikovsky: 1812 Ov/Ravel Bolero	Gould	(LSC 2345)
SB2084	Beethoven: Sonatas-Spring/Kreutzer	Rubinstein Szeryng	(LSC 2377)
SB2085	Schubert: Symphony 9	Munch BSO	(LSC 2344)
SB2086	Brahms: Symphony 1	Karajan VPO	(LSC 2537 LDS2351)
SB2087	Beethoven: Symphony 7	Karajan VPO	(LDS 2348)
SB2089	Saint-Saens: Symphony 3	Munch BSO	(LSC 2341)
SB2090	Berlioz: Symphonie Fantastique	Monteux VPO	(LSC 2362)
SB2091	Strauss,J: Vienna of Johann Strauss	Karajan VPO	(LDS 2346)
SB2092	Mozart: Symphony 40/Haydn Symphony 104	Karajan VPO	(LDS 2347)
SB2093	Tchaikovsky: Symphony 4	Monteux BSO	(LSC 2369)
SB2094	Ballet Music From the Opera	Fistoulari PCO	(LSC 2400)
SB2095	Chopin: Scherzos 1-4	Rubinstein	(LSC 2368)
SB2096-7	Berlioz: Requiem	Munch BSO Simoneau	(LDS 6077)
SB2098	Romberg: "The Desert Song"	Lanza Raskin	(LSC 2440)
SB2099	Strauss,R: Don Quixote	Reiner CSO Janigro (cello)	(LDS 2384)
SB2100	Vivaldi: Four Seasons	Societa Correlli Vittorio Emanuele (violin)	(LSC 2424)
SB2101	Sibelius: Violin Concerto	Hendl CSO Heifetz	(LSC 2435)
SB2102	Beethoven: Piano Sonatas 7, 23 (Appassionata)	Horowtiz	(LSC2366)
SB2103	Respighi: Pines/Fountains of Rome	Reiner CSO	(LSC 2436)
SB2104	Copland: App Spring/Tender Land suite	Copland BSO	(LSC 2401)
SB2105	Borodin: Symphony 2/Rimsky-Korsakov: Capriccio Espagnol	Martinon LSO	(LSC 2298)
SB2106	Brahms: Piano Concerto 2	Leinsdorf CSO Richter	(LSC 2466)
SB2107	Tchaikovsky: Nutcracker Suite (extracts)	Reiner CSO	(LSC 2328)
SB2108	Elgar: Enigma Variations, Brahms : St Anthony Variations	Monteux LSO	(LSC 2418)
SB2109	Szeryng Recital (Tartini, Gluck, Kreisler, Schumann)	Szeryng Charles Reiner (piano)	(LSC 2421)
SB2110	Brahms: Symphony 2	VPO Monteux	(VICS1055 ECS596)
SB2111	Haydn: Symphonies 94/101	Monteux VPO	(LSC 2394)
SB2112	Grieg: Piano Concerto/Liszt: Piano Concerto 1	Wallenstein RCAVO Rubinstein	(LSC 2429)
SB2113	Prokofiev: Piano Concerto 3/MacDowell Pno Conc 2	Hendl CSO Van Cliburn	(LSC 2507)
SB2114	Dvorak: Cello Concerto	BSO Munch Piatigorsky	(LSC 2490)
SB2115	Dvorak: Slavonic Dances op 46/1-8, op 72/7	Martinon LSO	(LSC 2419)
SB2116	Brahms: A Brahms/Schumann Recital	Forrester John Newmark (piano)	(LSC 2275)
SB2117	Mozart: Piano Concerto no 24/etc	Krips Rubinstein	(LSC 2461)
SB2118	Liszt: The Virtuoso Liszt	Graffman	(LSC 2443)
SB2119	Beethoven: Piano Sonatas 12 (Funeral March), 23 (Appassionata)	Richter	(LSC 2545)
SB2120	Lalo: Symphonie Espagnole	Hendl CSO Szeryng	(LSC 2456)
SB2121	Mussorgsky : Pictures at an Exhibition	Toscanini NBCSO	(ALP1218)
SB2122	Respighi : Fountains of Rome, Pines of Rome	Toscanini NBCSO (Elec reprocessed stereo)	(RB16108)
SB2123	Dvorak: Symphony 9	Toscanini NBCSO	(RB16116)
SB2124	Mario Lanza Recital	Lanza	
SB2125	Berlioz: Overtures	Munch BSO	(LSC 2438)

SB2126	Schumann: Symphony 1/Manfred Ov	Munch	BSO	(LSC 2474)
SB2127	Beethoven: Symphonies 1/8	Monteux	VPO	(LSC 2491)
SB2128	Debussy: La Mer/Strauss Don Juan.	Reiner	CSO	(LSC 2462)
SB2129	Mendelssohn: Symphony 3	Munch	BSO	(LSC 2520)
SB2130	Rhapsodies:Liszt Hung/Enescu Roumanian 1	Stokowski	RCAVO	(LSC 2471)
SB2131-2	Albeniz: Iberia/Ravel: Rhapsody Espagnole	Morel	PCO	(LSC 6094)
SB2133	Beethoven: Emperor Concerto	CSO	Reiner Van Cliburn	(LSC 2562)
SB2134	Schubert: Symphonies 5/8	Reiner	CSO	(LSC 2516)
SB2136	Brahms: Piano Qt in Gmin	Festival Quartet		(LSC 2473)
SB2137	Ravel: Daphnis&Chloe	Munch	BSO	(LSC 2568)
SB2138	Puccini: Turandot (hlts)	Leinsdorf	Rome Op Nilsson Bjorling	(LSC 2539 SER4520-2)
SB2139	"Heart of the Concerto" (Beethoven,Chopin,Grieg,Liszt,etc)	Reiner	Rubinstein	(LSC 2495)
SB2140	Brahms: Double Concerto	Wallenstein	Heifetz/Piatigorsky	(LDS 2513)
SB2141	Song Recital (Prokofiev, Rachmaninov, Shostakovich, etc)	Vishnevskaya	Dedyukhin (piano)	(LSC 2497)
SB2143	Chopin: My Favourite Chopin	Van Cliburn		(LSC 2576)
SB2144	Rachmaninov: Rhapsody on a Theme of Paganini,	Jorda	San Francisco SO Rubinstein	
	Falla : Nights in the Gardens of Spain	Reiner	CSO Rubinstein	(LSC 2430)
SB2145	Chopin: Concerto 1	Skrowacsewski	NSOL Rubinstein	(LSC 2575)
SB2146	Beethoven: Kreutzer Sonata/Bach,J.S Double Conc	Sargent	NSOL Heifetz Friedman	(LSC 2577)
SB2147	Poulenc: Conc for Organ/Stravinsky Jeu de Cartes	Munch	BSO	(LSC 2567)
SB2148	Wagner: The Sound of Stokowski and Wagner	Stokowski	SOA	(LSC 2555)
SB2149	Beethoven: Piano Concerto 1, Piano Sonata Op54	BSO	Munch Richter	(LSC 2544)
SB2150	Bream: English Lute Music		Bream	(LDS 2560)
SB2151	Chopin: Piano Sonata in B flat min, Piano Sonata 3		Rubinstein	(LDS 2554)
SB2152	Delibes: Sylvia & Coppelia	Rignold	PCO	(LSC 2485)
SB2153	He's Got the Whole World in His Hands	Marion Anderson Franz Rupp (piano)		(LSC 2592)
SB2155	Dvorak: Symphony 7	Monteux	LSO	(LSC 2489)
SB2156	Arias from Faust, Boheme, Carmen, etc	Serafin	Rome Op Anna Moffo (soprano)	(LSC 2504)
SB6500-1	Beethoven: Symphonies 1/9	Reiner	CSO	(LSC 6096)
SB6502	Rachmaninov: Piano Concerto 2	Reiner	CSO Van Cliburn	(LSC 2601)
SB6503	Bruch: Scottish Fantasy/etc Sargent	NSOL Heifetz		(LSC 2603)
SB6504	Highlights from Rubinstein at Carnegie Hall		Rubinstein	(LSC 2605)
SB6508	Schubert: Symphony 2/Beethoven Prometheus Music	Munch	BSO	(LSC 2522)
SB6509	Dvorak: Symphony 4(8)	Munch	BSO	(LSC 2629)
SB6510	Beethoven: Symphony 6	Reiner	CSO	(LSC 2614)
SB6511	Milhaud: Creation du Monde/Suite Provencale	Monteux	BSO	(LDS 2625)
SB6512	Massenet: Great Scenes from Werther	ROHCG	Leibowitz Valletti	(LSC 2615)
SB6513	Beethoven: Sonata 8/Brahms Sonata 1	Rubinstein	Szeryng	(LSC 2620)
SB6514	Paganini:Violin Concerto, St-Saens: Intro&Rondo Capriccioso	CSO	Hendl Friedman	(LSC 2610)
SB6518	Strauss,R: Also Sprach Zarathustra	Reiner	CSO	(LSC 2609)
SB6520	Brahms: Sonatas 2/3	Rubinstein	Szeryng	(LSC 2619)
SB6526	Mahler: Symphony 1	BSO	Leinsdorf	
SB6527	Bruch: Violin Concerto 1/Mozart	Sargent	NSOL Heifetz	(LSC 2652)
SB6528	Chausson: Sym in Bflat/Franck: Le Chasseur Maudit	Munch	BSO	(LSC 2647)
SB6530	Prokofiev: Alexander Nevsky	Reiner	CSO	(LSC 2395)
SB6532	Mozart: Piano Concerto no 21/23	Wallenstein	Rubinstein	(LSC 2634)
SB6534	Beethoven: Quartets Fmin Op 95/Fmaj Op 135	Juilliard String Quartet		(LSC 2632)
SB6540	Debussy: Afternoon of a Faun, Nuages, Fetes, Printemps	BSO	Munch	(LSC 2668)
SB6542	Summer Festival (Ov Russlan&Ludmilla/Reiner)	Various		(LSC 6097)
SB6545	Brahms: Piano Concerto 2	Reiner	CSO Van Cliburn	(LSC 2581)
SB6550	Tchaikovsky: Symphony 6	BSO	Munch	(LSC 2683)
SB6553	Sibelius: Finlandia, Tuonela, Valse Triste, Pohjola's Daughter, etc		Morton Gould	(LSC 2666)
SB6556	Ravel: Bolero, La Valse, Pavane	BSO	Munch	(LSC 2664)
SB6561	"Concert in the Park"(Wedding Dance,Victor Herbert Favs,etc)	BPO	Feidler	(LSC 2677)
SB6564	Rachmaninov: Rhapsody on a theme of Paganini,	BPO	Fiedler Pennario	(LSC2678)
	Franck: Symphonic Variations			
SB6565	Strauss,R: Ein Heldenleben	Leinsdorf	BSO	(LSC 2641) DG

Catalog	Work	Orchestra/Ensemble	Conductor/Artist	(Original)
SB6566	Berlioz: Nuits d'Ete/Falla El Amor Brujo	Reiner	CSO Price	(LSC 2695)
SB6568	Liszt: Concertos 1&2	Leibowitz	LSO Pennario	(LSC 2690)
SB6570	Mozart:Piano Concerto K466,Haydn: Andante & Vns in Fmin	Wallenstein	Rubinstein	
SB6584	Haydn: Symphonies 95/101	Reiner	CSO	(LSC 2742)
SB6597	Prokofiev: Violin Concerto 1, Piano Concerto 5	BSO	Leinsdorf Friedman	(LSC 2732)
SB6605	Rosza: Violin Concerto/Benjamin Romatic Fantasy	Hendl Dallas	Heifetz	(LSC 2767)
SB6611	Recital: Chopin, Rachmaninov, Prokofiev, Ravel		Richter	(LSC 2611)
SB6618	Rachmaninov: Piano Concertos 1, 4	RPO	Previn Pennario	(LSC 2788)
SB6627	Ravel: Daphnis&Chloe St 2/Roussel Bacchus&Ariadne	Martinon	CSO	(LSC 2806)
SB6631	Franck: Symphony in D Min	Monteux	CSO	(LSC 2514)
SB6634	Menoti: Amahl and the Night Visitors	NBC Opera Company	Grossman	(LSC 2762)
SB6635	Rodrigo: Concierto Aranjuez/Vivaldi/Britten	Melos CO	Bream	(LSC 2730)
SB6644	Gershwin: Porgy and Bess selections, etc		Heifitz	(LSC 2856)
SB6647	"Presenting Montserrat Caballe" (Opera extracts)			(LSC 2862)
SB6651	Shostakovich: Symphony 5	LSO	Previn	(LSC 2866)
SB6662	Prokofiev: Symphony 6	BSO	Leinsdorf	(LSC 2834)
SB6668	Schubert: Piano Sonatas D784, D850		Gilels	(LSC 2493)
SB6670	Tchaikovsky: Symphony 2, Liadov: 8 Russian Folk Songs	LSO	Previn	
SB6676	Walton: Cello Conc/Bloch: Schelomo	Munch	BSO Piatigorsky	(LSC 2109)
SB6678	Shostakovich: Piano Sonata 2, Liszt: Piano Sonata in Bmin		Gilels	
SB6685	Rachmaninov: Symphony 2	LSO	Previn	(LSC 2899)
SB6686	"Songs of Granados"		Caballe	(LSC 2910)
SB6691	Walton: Symphony 1	LSO	Previn	(LSC 2927)
SB6694	BSO Chamber Players	Various		(LSC 6167)
SB6696	Strauss,R: Alpine Symphony	Kempe	RPO	(LSC 2923)
SB6699	Zarzuela Arias		Caballe	(LSC 2894)
SB6705	Prokofiev: Symphony 3, Scythian Suite	BSO	Leinsdorf	
SB6709	Ives: Piano Sonata 1		William Masselos	(LSC 2941)
SB6714	Nielsen: Symphony 1	LSO	Previn	(LSC 2961)
SB6720	Nielsen: Symphony 4, Helios Ov	CSO	Martinon	
SB6729	Rachmaninov: Symphony 3	Previn	LSO	(LSC 2990)
SB6734	Brahms: Sonatas 1 & 2 for Viola and Piano	Horszowski	Trampler	(LSC 2933)
SB6736	V Williams: Sinfonia Antartica	LSO	Previn	
SB6737	Brahms: Piano Quintet op 34	Guarneri Qt	Rubinstein	(LSC2971)
SB6752	Bartok: Miraculous Mandarin, Hindemith: Nobilissima Visione		CSO	Martinon
SB6754	Brahms: Serenade in D op 11,	Philadelphia Chamber Orch	Brusilow	
SB6761-2	Messiaen: Turangalila, Takemitsu	Toronto SO	Ozawa	(LSC 7051)
SB6765-6	Mahler: Symphony 3	BSO	Leinsdorf	(LSC 7046)
SB6787	Beethoven: Piano Concertos 3, 4	BSO	Leinsdorf Rubinstein	
SB6806	Bax: Symphony 3, The Happy Forest	LSO	Downes	
SB6842	V-Williams: Symphony 9, 3 Portraits from the England of Elizabeth	LSO	Previn	
SER4501	Handel: Messiah (complete)	Beecham	RPO Vickers	(LDS 6409)
SER4505-7	Verdi: Macbeth		Leinsdorf	(LSC 6076-8)
SER4508-11	Mozart: Marriage of Figaro	VPO	Leinsdorf	(LSC 6408)
SER4520-2	Puccini: Turandot	Rome Op	Leinsdorf	(LSC 6149-51)
SER4523-5	Strauss,R: Ariadne Auf Naxos	VPO	Leinsdorf	(LDS 6152)
SER4526-7	Verdi: Requiem	Reiner	VPO	(LDS 6091)
SER4528-31	Mozart: Don Giovanni	VPO	Leinsdorf Nilssson (LSC 6410)	
SER4535-7	Wagner: Flying Dutchman	Dorati	ROHO	(LSC 6156)
SER4538-40	Verdi: Aida	Solti	RomeOp	(LSC 6158)
SER5500-1	Puccini: La Boheme	Rome Opera	Leinsdorf	(LSC 6095)
SER5504-6	Puccini: Madame Butterfly	Rome	Leinsdorf	(LSC 6135)
SER5507-8	Puccini: Tosca	VPO	Karajan	
SER5509-1	Verdi: Falstaff		Solti	(LSC 6163)
SER5512-3	Portrait of Manon	RCA Orch	Leibowitz Moffo Di Stefano	(LSC7028)

SER5518-9	Mahler: Symphony 5	BSO	Leinsdorf	(LSC 7031)
SER5524-6	Bellini: Norma	LSO	Bonynge Sutherland Horne Schippers	
SER5527-30	Verdi: The Force of Destiny			
SER5537-8	Verdi: Requiem	BSO	Leinsdorf	(LSC 7040)
SER5534-6	Verdi: Luisa Miller	RCA Orch	Cleva Moffo Bergonzi	
SER5544-8	Wagner: Lohengrin	BSO	Leinsdorf	(LSC 6710-5)
SER5553-5	Donizetti: Lucrezia Borgia	RCA Italian Opera	Perlea	(LSC6176)
SER5559-0	Puccini: La Rondine	RCA Iralian Opera	Molinari-Pradelli Moffo	(LSC7048)
SER5561-3	Handel: Julius Caesar	NY City Opera	Rudel Treigle Sills Forrester	(LSC6182)
SER5569-71	Handel: Hercules	Vienna Radio Orch	Priestman Stich-Randall	(LSC6181)
SER5572-4	Verdi: Ernani	RCA Italian Opera	Schippers Price Bergonzi	(LSC6183)
SER5600-2	Bizet: Carmen	VPO	Karajan	
SER5609-1	Verdi: Aida	Leinsdorf	LSO Bumbry	(LSC 6198)
SER5620	Tippett: The Vision of St Augustine	LSO	Tippett	
SER5649	V Williams: The 9 Symphonies	LSO	Previn	
SER5664	Classic Film Scores: The Sea Hawk	NPO	Gerhardt	
SER5701-3	Beethoven: Violin Sonatas op 47, op 24, op 30/3, Brahms: Violin Sonatas op 78, op 100, op 108	Szeryng	Rubinstein	
SER5729-31	Beethoven: Complete String Trios	Heifetz	Primrose Piatigorsky	
SF5004	Tchaikovsky: Nutcracker Suite (extracts)	Fiedler	BPO	(LSC 2052)
SF5023	Bob & Ray Throw a Stereo Spectacular			(LSP 1773)
SF5035	Lehar: Waltzes	LSO	Sharples	(LSC 2299)
SF5036	Offenbach: Gaite Parisienne/Khachtrn Gayne Suite	Fiedler	BPO	(LSC 2267)
SF5041	"Music to Have Fun With"	Fiedler	BPO	(LSC 2235)
SF5054	"Claire de Lune" (Massenet, Tchaikovsky, Fauré, Debussy, etc)	Agoult	LPSO	(LSC 2326)
SF5063	"The Music of Sigmund Romberg"	George Melachrino & His Orchestra		
SF5067	"Twilight in Vienna" (Lehar, Stolz, Kalman, etc)	Vienna State Orch Stolz		
SF5068	"Marching around the World"	Band of the Coldstream Guards		
SF5071	Beethoven: Wellington's Victory, Grofe: Grand Canyon Suite	Morton Gould Morton Gould Orch		(LSC 2433)
SF5087	Mendelssohniana (extracts)	Binge	NSOL	(LSC 2399)
SF5092	Victory at Sea vol 1	RCAVO	Bennett	(LSC 2335)
SF5095	"A Scottish Anthology"	Wishart Campbell with Orch		
SF5096	Oscar Strauss: A Waltz Dream (hlts)	Bauer-Theussl Vienna Volksoper		
SF5105	Kalman: Countess Maritza (hlts)	VV	Paulik	(LSC 2406)
SF5109	"More Classical Music for People who Hate Classical Music"	BPO	Fiedler	(LSC 2470)
SF5122	Light Classics (Falla, Chabrier, Wagner, Rimsky-Korsakov, etc)	Fiedler	BPO	(LSC 2547)
SF5131	"Overtures on Parade"	Band of the Coldstream Guards		

RCA Victrola

The numbers used for Victrola in USA and England are the same up to about VICS1200. However, after that number they are different. The numbers used herein are the English pressing numbers.

The list is very complete for original Victrola VICS orchestral records.

Victrolas that are straight reissues of previous Living Stereos are not listed. If a Victrola contains at least one piece never before released then it is listed. If there are also non-original pieces on the disc, then the LSC number on which they were originally issued is also shown.

Number	Title			
VICS1002	Tchaikovsky: Swan Lake	Morel	PCO	(LSC2277 not iss USA)
VICS1004	Strauss,R Till Eulenspiegel, Death & Transfiguration	VPO	Reiner	
VICS1006	Beethoven: Symphony 6	VPO	Monteux	
VICS1007	Kabalevsky: The Comedians	Kondrashin	RCAVO	(LSC2398)
VICS1011	Tchaikovsky: The Sleeping Beauty	LSO	Monteux	(LSC2177)
VICS1013	Rimsky Korsakov: Scheherazade	LSO	Monteux	(LSC2208)
VICS1016	Sibelius: Symphony 5	Gibson	LSO	(LSC2405)
VICS1017	Stravinsky: Rite of Spring	Monteux	PCO	(LSC2085)
VICS1023	Mendelssohn: Midsmr Nts Dream/Schubert Rosamund	Monteux	VPO	JM10++
VICS1024	Rachmaninov: Piano Conc 2/Weber/Mendelssohn	Jorda	SFO Brailowsky	
VICS1025	Tchaikovsky: 1812, Liszt: Mephisto, Debussy: Iberia	CSO	Reiner	
VICS1026	Brahms: Piano Concerto 2	CSO	Reiner Gilels	(LSC2219)
VICS1027	Stravinsky: Firebird/Debussy: Nocturnes	Monteux	PCO/BSO	
VICS1028	Brahms: Violin Concerto	Monteux	LSO Szeryng	(LSC2281)
VICS1030	Chopin: Piano Concerto 1, Mendelssohn: Capriccio Brillant	BSO	Munch Graffman	(LSC2468)
VICS1031	Berlioz: Symphonie Fantastique	VPO	Monteux	(LSC2362)
VICS1032	Rachmaninov: Piano Concerto 3	BSO	Munch Janis	(LSC2237)
VICS1033	Mendelssohn: Violin Concerto/Bruch Violin Concerto	Munch BSO Laredo		JM10
VICS1034	Franck: Symphony in D min	BSO	Munch	(LSC2131)
VICS1035	Beethoven: Symphony 5/Schubert Symphony 8	Munch	BSO	JM10
VICS1036	Beethoven: Symphony 3	Monteux	VPO	JM10
VICS1037	Tchaikovsky: Violin Concerto,	BSO	Munch Szeryng	(LSC2363, SB2080)
	Tartini: Devil's Trill	Szeryng	Reiner (piano)	(LSC2421, SB2109)
VICS1039	Tchaikovsky: Piano Concerto 1	Reiner	CSO Gilels	JM10
VICS1040	Matton: Mouvement Sym/Mercures: Lignes & Pointes	Montreal SO		
VICS1041	Ravel: Rapsodie Espagnol, Mother Goose, Debussy: La Mer	BSO	Munch	(LSC1984)
VICS1042	Strauss,R: Ein Heldenleben	Reiner	CSO	JM10++
VICS1044	Berlioz: Overtures Vol 3	Munch	BSO	
VICS1048	Mahler: Symphony 4	CSO	Reiner	(LSC2364)
VICS1053	Rossini-Respighi: Boutique Fantasque, Ibert Divertissement	BPO	Fiedler	(LSC2084)
VICS1054	Dvorak: Slavonic Dances	LSO	Martinon	(LSC2419)
VICS1055	Brahms Symphony 2	Monteux	VPO	(SB2110 ECS596) No US LSC number assigned
VICS1057	Bizet: L'Arlesienne Suites 1&2, Chabrier Espana	Morel	ROHCG	(SB2057 LSC2327) JM10++
VICS1058	Chausson: Poeme/Saint-Saens Intr&Rondo	Munch	BSO Oistrakh	
VICS1059	Beethoven: Piano Concerto 3	CSO	Hendl Graffman	(LSC2396)
VICS1060	Ravel: Mother Goose, d'Indy: Symphony on French Mt Air	BSO	Munch	(LSC2271)
VICS1061	Beethoven: Symphony 7	LSO	Monteux	(not issued LSC)
VICS1062	Brahms: Symphony 1	BSO	Munch	
VICS1064	Lalo: Rhapsodie Espagnol	CSO	Hendl Szeryng	(LSC2456)
VICS1065	Wagner: Tannhauser/Walkure/Gotterdamerung ovs	Munch BSO		
VICS1066	'Ballet Favourites'	ROHCG	Ansermet	(LDS6065)

Cat. No.	Work	Performer(s)	Orchestra/Details	Notes
VICS1067	Grieg: Piano Concerto/Peer Gynt	Gruner-Hege	Oslo Philh with Baekkelund	
VICS1068	Festival of Russian Music (Marche Slave, Bare Mt, Igor, etc)	CSO	Reiner	(LSC2423)
VICS1069	Finlandia: Sibelius: Pelleas & Melisande, Finlandia	LPSO	Mackerras	(LSC2336)
VICS1071	Ravel: Piano Concerto, Prokofiev Concerto 2	BSO	Munch Henriot-Schweitzer	(LSC2271)
VICS1077	Chopin: Ballades, Andante Spinato, Grand Polonaise		Graffman	(LSC2304)
VICS1079	Rossini: Overtures	Reiner	CSO	(LSC2318)
VICS1100	Tchaikovsky: Symphony 4	Munch	BSO	
VICS1101	Rachmaninov: Concerto 1 Strauss Burleske.	Reiner	CSO	JM10+
VICS1102	Beethoven Symphony 4	Monteux	LSO	JM10 (ECS671)
VICS1104	Strauss,R: Symphonia Domestica	Reiner	CSO	JM10
VICS1105	Prokofiev: Piano Concerto 3/Classical Symphony	Jorda	SFO Graffman	
VICS1107	Elgar: Enigma variations/Brahms: Haydn Vns	Monteux	LSO	(LSC2418 & orig]
VICS1108	Bizet: Carmen suite, Gounod: Faust	Gibson	ROHCG	(LSC2449)
VICS1110	Bartok: Concerto for Orchestra	CSO	Reiner	(LSC1934)
VICS1138	Prokofiev: Cinderella	Rignold	ROHCG	(LSC 2135: not issued in USA, ECS597)
VICS1139	Rachmaninov: Symphony 2	Boult	LPO	
VICS1148	Nielsen: Symphony 4/Helios Overture	Martinon	CSO	
VICS1153	Khachaturian: Vln Conc/Saint-Saens Havanaise	Monteux	BSO Kogan	SM77+
VICS1160	Bartok: Music for Strings Percussion & Celesta, Hungn Sketches	CSO	Reiner	(LSC2374)
VICS1162	Debussy: Images (complete)	BSO	Munch	(LSC2282)
VICS1170	Beethoven: Symphony 2 Ovs Fidelio King Stephen	Monteux	LSO	
VICS1171	Italian Opera Preludes & Intermezzi	Basile		
VICS1174	Popular Classics		Gould	
VICS1197	Tchaikovsky Romeo & Juliet/Francesca da Rimini	Munch	BSO	(LSC2565+original) JM10+
VICS1199	Ravel Pavan Alb Strauss Bourgeois Gent.	Reiner	CSO	(LSC2222 & original) JM10++
VICS1265	Strauss,R: Zarathustra, Don Juan	Reiner	CSO	(LSC2462 & LSC2609) JM10++
VICS1322	Rodrigo: Concerto de Aranjuez/etc	Hafler De Falla Orch Maza		JM10+
VICS1328	Dance Music of the Renaissance	Various		
VICS1366	Mozart: Symphony 41/Haydn 88	Reiner	CSO	
VICS1392	Strauss,R: Don Juan/Salome (last scene)	Reiner	CSO Borkhe	
VICS1412	Prokofiev: Romeo and Juliet excerpts	Munch	BSO	
VICS1424	Weinberger: Schwanda Dvorak Strauss Smetana	Reiner	CSO	TASEC 44 JM10+
VICS2009	Strauss,R: Scenes from Elektra	Reiner	CSO Borkhe	TAS 35/177+
VICS6006	Berlioz L'Enfance du Christ	Munch	BSO	
VICS6007	Sullivan: Pirates of Penzance	Alan Ward & Orchestra		JM10++
VICS6015	Penderecki: Passion according to St Luke	Cologne Ch & Orch		
VICS6016	Vivaldi: Juditha Triumphans (complete opera)			
VICS6018	Couperin Complete Organ works	Chapuis		
VICS6023	Bach: The Brandenburg Concertos	Collegium Aureum		

Mercury Living Presence

The list: This list is based upon the author's own collection of Mercury Living Presence records, as well as earlier lists produced by Robert Hunt, David Nemzer, and Bob Corsetti. The list is believed to be complete, but corrections are always welcomed. Where English EMI pressing alternatives exist these are shown in brackets (English EMI pressings have numbers AMS16xxx). Where the disc has been discussed in The Absolute Sound (TAS) the volume & page is shown along with 1 to 3 + marks. These indicate the degree of praise, for example TAS60/123++ (this is of course a very crude assessment, and no substitute for reading the reviews). TAS 'Editors Choice' discs are also shown by "TASEC".

In the later Mercury period two 'economy' series were issued called "Great Music" and "Curtain-Up" respectively. These are indicated.

The definitive source for information on the sound quality of Mercurys is Sid Marks's historic series in TAS. At the end of that series he gave an overall ranking for about 50 of the best Mercurys. Discs included in this ranking are marked Nnn, nn showing the ordering Sid Marks gave.

Mercury labels and pressings: Without doubt, of all the 'audiophile' record labels, the situation with the USA pressed Mercurys is the most complex. To get a full appreciation of all the nuances of Mercury labels and pressings you need to collect them for many years. However, here is a summary of the position:

The earliest American pressings have dark maroon labels, and the later pressings have progressively lighter labels. Very late pressings have a very pale maroon label and these were mainly pressed by Philips. There is also an even later Philips pressing with an orange label.

Up to around SR90265 the earliest Mercury pressings were produced for Mercury by RCA. Consequently they have stamper engravings that are clearly machine made and have the recognisable RCA type face (as found on shaded dog stampers). The stampers of these are FR1, FR2, etc, FR1 being the earliest pressing.

Slightly later pressings were made at Mercury's own pressing facility at Richmond, Indiana. These have stamper engravings that appear scratched by hand. The stampers of these are RFR1, RFR2, etc, RFR1 being the earliest. Of course, for Mercurys after SR90265, these are the 1st pressings.

There are also pressings of the form CTFR1, CTFR2, etc, and also CBFR1, CBFR2, etc. These were specially pressed for the "Columbia Record Club". This was an LP record mail order company founded in 1958. They are more or less contemporary with the later pressings in the RFR series. I have had reports that this record club requested Mercury to cut the masters for their issues at a lower level in order not to cause problems for the record playing equipment of its members.

Philips pressings: The later Philips pressings have stamper engravings that are clearly machine made, of the form M1, M2, etc. Sometimes you will find a Mercury with an 'M' pressing on one side and a RFR on the other side - this just means that Philips used an old RFR stamper for that second side. After about SR90500 there are only Philips pressings.

There are also promotional ("promo") Mercurys with white, green, or yellow labels - these pressings are very desirable - they are usually the very first pressings. Around the SR90400 region there are also gold labels.

Pressing variations: How does the sound quality vary between these various pressings? Well, there are many different opinions on this, and I do not want to get into a big argument with other "experts". I will just give a few guidelines:

FR pressings are of similar quality to RCA shaded dogs - i.e. very reliable. RFRn pressings are generally fine, but can sometimes be noisy and gritty and the higher the RFR number (e.g. RFR8) the higher the chances this will be so. However, this is certainly not an absolute rule.

CTFR and CBFR pressings invariably have quite noisy vinyl. The late Philips M pressings are, in my opinion, very good, and are bargains. This is because, being 'late' pressings they are often cheap. Generally, they have very quiet vinyl surfaces. OK, if the FR pressing has sound quality 10 out of 10, these may be 8 out of 10 - still superb.

Vendor pressings: Then there is the difficult question of 'Vendor' pressings. This is the most misunderstood and confused subject in this whole area! Here is my understanding of the position: Some Mercurys have "Vendor" marked on the label. It is a mistake to automatically assume that these are not good. Some Mercurys were only ever issued as vendor pressings. A lot of Vendor pressings were also quite late pressings. It is the fact that they are late pressings that make them noisy, not the fact that they are vendors. If you get an early pressing vendor it sounds fine. I once had 2 RFR1 copies of the same Mercury and one was a vendor pressing - they both sounded identical.

Someone once told me that all Vendor pressings were in the range SR90300 - 90370. I might agree that **most** are in this range, but I certainly know of exceptions - I have had vendor copies down to SR90206, and I know of them up to SR90442.

English pressings: There are two groups of English pressed Mercurys: A very large group pressed by EMI, and a very small group that was pressed by Philips a little later. The first group were pressed by EMI at the same time as the US originals. They are described in detail in a later section. I will just say here that one of the great things about English EMI Mercury pressings is that there are none of these pressing variations - all have dark maroon labels and very thick vinyl pressings.

The second group were pressed by Philips in the mid 60s. Philips Mercurys have a similar audio relationship to the American SR as do the EMI pressings. An example is SAL3569 Miraculous Mandarin (from SR90416) which again has the same jacket design as the SR, and also a dark maroon label. There are only about 7 or 8 'Mercurys' in this SAL series, and I have tried to indicate them in the listing.

French pressings: A number of the Mercurys were pressed in France in the "Magie du Son" series. I cannot present much information about them (such as pressing and label details, etc) because I do not have much. What I can say is that I have had about 10 different records in this series and they are all absolutely superb. For example, in my opinion the French pressing of SR90153 'The Birds' is superior to any other I have heard, including a USA 1st pressing. There is much variation in label colour - I have seen 3 different - bright blue, bright red, and green.

Mercury Record Jackets: There is considerable variation in the quality of the record jackets on USA pressed Mercurys. As the years went by and the company became more and more short of money, the quality went steadily downhill.

The earliest jackets are superb. The colour photograph on the front is in a very high gloss, and there is a colour panel on the back that continues the photo on the front. Amongst collectors, when this panel is present the record is called a "Colour Back" (or CB for short). As time went on the panel on the back remained but it became black and white. At the same time the artwork quality on the front dropped - the high gloss was replaced by a more matt appearance. It is difficult to explain but the later jackets just look "cheap" when compared to the sumptuous earliest jackets.

The inner sleeves on the early pressings are again of high quality and are informative because they give a lot of detail about others in the series, even including colour photos in some cases.

The English pressed records show no such variation in jacket quality. They are all of very high quality. The jackets are very similar to their USA counterparts. The artwork is identical, and the text on the back is also the same. However, the colour panel on the back is not found on these records.

Box Sets: The Mercury numbering system clearly indicates box sets. The numbering for a box set is, e.g. SR2-9006 which indicates a 2 record box.

'Curtain Up'/'Great Music': These are two series within the later Mercury time frame. They clearly indicate the way in which Mercury had lost its way. They consist of mainly reissue material, and many carry the legend "One hour of music" - and you can imagine the compression this causes. If you're looking for the music alone then buy them, but if you expect great Mercury sound you **may** be disappointed.

Disclaimer: The subject of Mercury labels, pressings, vendor pressings, etc, is among the most complex in the field of classical records. I have tried to give some guidance to help you through this minefield. However, there will always be someone ready to produce a counter example for each point I have made. Nevertheless, these are reasonable guidelines based on my personal experience over many years with many hundreds of Mercurys.

Abbreviations:

DSO	Detroit Symphony Orchestra
ERO	Eastman Rochester Orchestra
ERPO	Eastman Rochester Pops Orchestra
ERSO	Eastman Rochester Symphony Orchestra
EWE	Eastman Wind Ensemble
LSO	London Symphony Orchestra
MIN	Minneapolis Symphony Orchestra
MPO	Moscow Philharmonic Orchestra

Catalog	Title	Conductor	Orchestra	Notes
LPS-9000	Beethoven: Wellington's Victory/Leonora/Prometheus	Dorati	LSO	(AMS16091) TAS35/108+
LPS2-901	Civil War Vol I (Fort Sumter to Gettysburg)	Fennell	EWE	TAS32/148+
LPS2-902	Civil War Vol II (Gettysburg to Appomattox)	Fennell	EWE	
SR3-9000	Cherubini: Medea (complete)	La Scala	Serafin/Callas	Recorded at La Scala
SR2-9005	Delibes: Coppelia	Dorati	MIN	(AMS16018/9) TAS38/143,36/166
SR2-9006	Delibes: Sylvia (complete ballet)	Fistoulari	LSO	(AMS16032/3) TAS38/143++ 40/16
SR2-9007	Dvorak: Slavonic Dances	Dorati	MIN	(AMS16046/7)
SR2-9008	Donizetti: Lucia di Lammermoor (complete)	La Scala	Sanzogno/Scotto	
SR2-9009	Rossini: La Cambiale di Matrimonio	VdR	Fasano/Scotto	
SR2-9010	Paisiello: The Barber of Seville (complete)	VdR		(SR90243/4) with libretto
SR2-9011	Adam: Giselle (complete)	Fistoulari	LSO	(AMS16087/8) TAS34/180++ RFR1/2
SR3-9012	Verdi: Rigoletto (complete)	MMF	Scotto Bastiani	
SR2-9013	Tchaikovsky: Nutcracker Suite	Dorati	LSO	(AMS16143/4) TAS44/142++ TAS52/211++
SR6-9014	Tchaikovsky: Nutcracker/Swan Lake/Sleeping Beauty	Dorati	LSO	Electronic stereo
SR2-9015	Tchaikovsky: Symphonies 1/2/3	Dorati	LSO	(SR90398/9) RFR2/3/4 TAS51/174
SR3-9016	Bach: Cello suites (complete)	Starker		TAS32/143
SR3-9017	4 Great Violin Concertos	Issersdedt	LSO Szeryng	Beethoven, Sibelius, Tchaikovsky, Prokofiev
SR3-9018	Tchaikovsky: Four suites for Orchestra.	Dorati	Philh	(SR90454-6) TAS40/136++
SR2-9019	Tchaikovsky: Suites 3/4, Nutcracker excerpts	Dorati	LSO	
SR2-9120	World of Flamenco	Romeros		(SR90464/5) TAS52/213+
SR6-9121	Tchaikovsky: 6 Symphonies	Dorati	LSO	TAS51/174++
SR4-9122	Portugal's Golden Age	Gulbenkian CO	Gerlin Jonas	
SR2-9123	A Panorama of Experimental Music	Pierre Henry		
SR3-9124	Handel: Concerti Grossi Op 6	Leppard	ECO	
SR2-9125	Bach: 7 Sonatas for Flute/Harpsichord	Puyana Larrieu		
SR2-9126	Tchaikovsky: Greatest Hits	various		
SR2-9127	Heart of the Ballet	various		
SR2-9128	Heart of the Symphony	various		
SR2-9129	Heart of the Concerto	various		
SR2-9130	Heart of the Opera	various		
SR2-9131	Heart of the March	various		
SR2-9132	Music for Musing	various		
SR2-9133	The Spoleto Festival	various		
SR2-9134	Music for The Morning	various		
SR90001	Bizet: Carmen suite/L'Arlesienne 1&2	Paray	DSO	(AMS16053) TAS42/133+
SR90002	Gershwin: Rhapsody in Blue/Conc in F	Hanson	ERSO List	(AMS16026) TAS35/107+
SR90003	Bartok: Violin concerto	Dorati	MIN Menuhin	TAS33/134++
SR90005	Ravel: Bolero/Mother Goose/Chabrier	Paray	DSO	(AMS16120 has Chabrier) TAS43/148 SM64/130
SR90006	Prokofiev: 3 Oranges Suite/Scythian Suite	Dorati	LSO	N23 (AMS16009) TAS40/139++ TAS73+++ (TASEC)
SR90007	Albeniz Iberia 1-5/Falla Dances from La Vida Breve	Dorati	MIN	(AMS16002) TAS33/135+
SR90008	Strauss,J: Fruhlingsstimmenc Champagne Polka/etc	Dorati	MIN	(AMS16001)
SR90009	Leroy Anderson: Music of Leroy Anderson Vol 1	Fennell	ERPO	(AMS16044) TAS33/136
SR90010	Debussy La Mer/Iberia	Paray	DSO	(AMS16094) TAS42/134 TAS73/141++ TASEC73
SR90011	Beethoven: Symphony 3	Dorati	MIN	TAS45/156-
SR90012	Saint-Saens: Symphony 3	Paray	DSO Dupre	(AMS16004) TAS44++ 36+ TASEC65
SR90013-5	Cherubini: Medea (complete)	La Scala	Serafin Callas	see SR3-9000
SR90016	Offenbach Gaite Parisienne/Strauss Graduation Ball	Dorati	MIN	(AMS16005) TAS34/177+
SR90017	Chausson: Symphony in B flat	Paray	DSO	TAS37/96+-
SR90018	Chadwick: Symphonic Sketches Suite for Orchestra	Hanson	ERSO	TAS37/96
SR90019	Rachmaninov: Symphony 2	Paray	DSO	(AMS16003) TAS37/96
SR90043	Leroy Anderson: Music of Leroy Anderson Vol 2	Fennell	ERPO	(AMS16037) TAS33/136+ TASEC
SR90049	Grofe: Grand Canyon/Mississipi Suite	Hanson	ERSO	(AMS16011) TAS34/177+
SR90053	Music for Quiet Listening	Hanson	ERSO	TAS34/180+

SR90054	Tchaikovsky: Overture 1812/Capriccio Italien	Dorati	MIN	(AMS16010) TAS34/179-
SR90060	Shostakovich: Symphony 5	Skrowaczewski	MIN	(AMS16128) TAS51/176++ 53/116++
SR90098	Bartok: Second suite for Orchestra	Dorati	MIN	TAS39/127++ FR1
SR90099	Strauss,R: Der Rosenkavalier St/Till Eulenspiegel	Dorati	MIN	(AMS16014) TAS37/94
SR90102	Schumann: Symphony 2	Paray	DSO	TAS35/110-
SR90103	Sessions: The Black Maskers/McPhee Tabuh Tabuhan	Hanson	ERO	(AMS16093) TASEC44 TAS39+++ 53++
SR90105	Marching Along	Fennell	EWE	(AMS16020) TAS35/107+-
SR90107	Wagner: Orch excerpts	Paray	DSO	(AMS16049) TAS50/196
SR90109	Boardwalk Pipes	Robert Elmore (Theatre Organ)		
SR90111	Spirit of '76 (Fifes and Drums)	Fennell	EWE	TAS33/134
SR90112	Ruffles and Flourishes: (Trumpets & Drums)	Fennell	EWE	TAS47/142++-
SR90115	Vaughan Williams: Symphony 8/Butterworth/Bax	Barbirolli	HO	1st recording TAS41++ 54+++
SR90121	Mozart: Eine Kleine Nachtmusik/Symphony 36	Dorati	LSO	TAS34/176
SR90122	Borodin: Polvn Dances/Rimsky:Le Coq d'Or Suite	Dorati	LSO	(AMS16008) TAS37/95
SR90123	Mendelssohn: Symphony 3/Ov Fingals Cave.	Dorati	LSO	TAS44/178
SR90124	Strauss,J: Viennese night at the Proms.	Barbirolli	HO	TAS40/136+
SR90125	Elgar: Enigma Varns/Purcell: Suite for Strings	Barbirolli	HO	TAS38/143
SR90126	Liszt: Piano Conc 1/Grieg Piano Conc.	Weldon	HO Farrell	TAS33/137-
SR90127	Bach on the Biggest	Robert Elmore		TAS47/142+-
SR90128	Paray Mass for 500 Anniv of Death of Joanne of Arc	Paray	DSO	TAS36/166+-
SR90129	Mozart: Symphony 35/Haydn: Symphony 96	Paray	DSO	(AMS16052) TAS33/134-
SR90132	Kodaly: Hary Janos Suite	Dorati	MIN	N7 (AMS16025) TASEC44 TAS53+++
SR90133	Schumann: Symphony 3	Paray	DSO	(AMS16035) TAS35/110-
SR90134	Fiesta in Hi-Fi	Hanson	ERO	(AMS16016) TASEC44 TAS33++ 53++
SR90136	Carpenter: Adventures in a Perambulator, Phillips: McGuffey's Reader Hanson ERO			N34 (AMS16015) TAS39/125+
SR90137	Khachaturian: Gayne/Flight of the Bumblebee	Weldon	HO	
SR90139	Rossini: Ovs: Gazza Ladra/Barber of Seville/etc	Dorati	MIN	(AMS16090) TAS37/93
SR90143	Hindemith:Sym for Band/Stravinsky/Schoenberg	Fennell	EWE	(AMS16106)
SR90144	Hi-Fi a la Espanola	Fennell	ERO	N14 (AMS16089) TAS52+++ 53+++
SR90147	Kennan: Three Pieces/Rogers/Bergsma	Hanson	ERO	N30 (AMS16104) 46/150++
SR90149	Ives: Symphony 3/3 Places In New England	Hanson	ERO	N41 (AMS16083) TAS42/134++
SR90150	Hanson: Song of Democracy/Elegy	Hanson	ERO	TAS47/142+ TASEC65
SR90153	Respighi: Brazilian Impressions/The Birds	Dorati	LSO	N1 (AMS16036) TAS34++ 54+++ TASEC
SR90154	Brahms: 6 Hungarian Dances/Haydn Variations	Dorati	LSO	(AMS16006)
SR90155	Haydn: Symphonies 100/101	Dorati	LSO	TAS44/176++
SR90156	Verdi: Overtures	Dorati	LSO	(AMS16058) TAS42/132+
SR90158	Handel-Harty: Water Music/Royal Fireworks Music	Dorati	LSO	N11 (AMS16031) TAS36/167++
SR90159	Dvorak: Symphony 7	Barbirolli	HO	Never issued, came out as mono MG50159
SR90160	Suppe: Overtures	Barbirolli	HO	TAS42/122
SR90161	Encore Please Sir John	Barbirolli	HO	TAS50/196++ 54/159+++
SR90162	Dvorak: Symphony 8	Barbirolli	HO	Never issued, came out as mono MG50162
SR90163	Herbert: Cello Concerto 2/Peter: Sinfonia in G	Hanson	ERO	TAS46/157+-
SR90164	Grieg: Peer Gynt Suite 1/Symphonic Dances	Barbirolli	HO	TAS38/141-
SR90165	Hanson: Symphony 1 ("Nordic")	Hanson	ERO	TAS31/96+
SR90166	Gershwin: Cuban Overture/McBride	Hanson	ERO	
SR90168	Dupre: Franck: Trois Chorales/Pieces Heroique	Dupre		(AMS16030) TAS45++ 53++ TASEC65
SR90169	Dupre: Widor Allegro from Symphony 6/etc	Dupre		N9 (AMS16097) TAS27++ 53++ TASEC44
SR90170	March Time	Fennell	EWE	(AMS16012) TAS31/96+
SR90171	Brahms: Symphony 2	Dorati	MIN	TAS45/154-
SR90172	Copland: Rodeo/El Salon Mexico,etc	Dorati	MIN	N16 (AMS16021) TAS42+++ 53+++
SR90173	Winds in Hi-Fi:Grainger/Milhaud/Strauss/etc.	Fennell	EWE	(AMS16023) TAS36/165++ 53/120++ TASEC65
SR90174	Mendelssohn: Sym 5/Music from Midsmr Nts Dream	Paray	DSO	(AMS16022) TAS49/144-
SR90175	Hanson: Composer and His Orch Vol 1	Hanson	ERO	N25 (AMS16007) TAS21+++ 44/174+++ 53/118++ TASEC*
SR90176	Mozart: Serenade 10 for winds	Fennell	EWE	N31 TAS49/144-
SR90177	Schmitt: La Tragedie de Salome/etc	Paray	DSO	TASEC44 TAS43/152++
SR90178	Strauss,J: Strauss Family Album	Dorati	MIN	(AMS16024) TAS36/167-

Catalog	Title	Conductor	Orchestra	Notes
SR90179	Kodaly: Dances of Galanta/Bartok	Dorati	PHun	(AMS16027) TAS35/106-
SR90183	Bartok: Dance Suite/Deux Portraits	Dorati	PHun	N 8 (AMS16068) TAS36/168++ 54/159+++
SR90184	Mozart: Symphonies 39/41	Issersdedt	LSO	(AMS16050) TAS34/179-
SR90185-6	Delibes: Coppelia	Dorati	MIN	see SR2-9005
SR90187-8	Delibes: Sylvia (complete ballet)	Fistoulari	LSO	see SR2-9006
SR90189	The Magic of the Bells	Lefevre		
SR90190	Wienerwalzer Paprika - Viennese Waltzes	Dorati	PHun	(AMS16063)
SR90191	French Overtures (Berlioz, Lalo, Bizet)	Paray	DSO	(AMS16013) TAS39/124 TAS73/141+
SR90192	Hanson: Symphony 2/Lament for Beowulf	Hanson	ERO	TAS35/108++ TASEC65
SR90193-4	Dvorak: Slavonic Dances	Dorati	MIN	see SR2-9007
SR90195	Rimsky Korsakov: Scheherazade	Dorati	MIN	(AMS16057) TAS45/153-
SR90196	Schubert: Symphonies 4/6.	Schmitt-Issersledt LSO Susskind		(AMS16029) TAS38/142
SR90197	British Band Classics Vol II	Fennell	EWE	N10 (AMS16043) TASEC44 TAS45/154++ 53/118+++
SR90198	Schumann: Symphony 1/Manfred Ov	Paray	DSO	(AMS16017) TAS35/110-
SR90199	Respighi: Ancient Dances & Airs for Lute.	Dorati	PHun	N29 (AMS16028) TAS37, 46/150++ 54/159+++ TASEC44
SR90200	Tchaikovsky: Serenade for Strings/Arensky	Dorati	PHun	(AMS16040) TAS42/136++ SM77/135+
SR90201	Tchaikovsky: Marche Slave/Francesca Da Rimini/etc	Dorati	MIN	(AMS16059) TAS45/156+-
SR90202	Strauss,R: Tod und Verklarung/Don Juan	Dorati	MIN	(AMS16072) TAS45/152++-
SR90203	Bouquet de Paray (Rossini/Liszt/Weber/etc)	Paray	DSO	(AMS16042) TAS34/176
SR90204	Sibelius: Symphony 2	Paray	DSO	(AMS16061) TASEC44 TAS41/123 53++
SR90205	Beethoven: Symphonies 1/2	Paray	DSO	(AMS16039)
SR90206	Piston: Incredible Flutist/Moore	Hanson	ERO	(AMS16129) TAS31/96++ 32+ 53++
SR90207	Hands Across the Sea	Fennell	EWE	(AMS16048) TAS31/97+
SR90208	Haydn: Symphonies 94/103	Dorati	PHun	(AMS16085) TAS44/176 40/167+
SR90209	Khachaturian: Music from ballet Gayne/etc	Dorati	LSO	(AMS16116) TAS33/137++
SR90210	Brahms: Horn Trio/Violin sonata 2	Szigeti Horszowski Barrow		(AMS16076) TAS35/105++-
SR90211	Vive La Marche	Paray	DSO	(AMS16077) TAS34/176+
SR90212	Chabrier: Espana/Suite Pastorale etc	Paray	DSO	(AMS16107) TAS47/142++ 53/116++
SR90213	Ravel Tomb de Couperin/Valses/Debussy:Petite Suite	Paray	DSO	N24 (AMS16066) 46/150++ 53+++
SR90214	Smetana: Moldau/Mussorgsky: Bare Mt/Sibelius/Liszt	Dorati	LSO	(AMS16105) TAS33/134+
SR90215	Offenbach: Overtures by Offenbach & Auber	Paray	DSO	(AMS16045) TAS37/93+
SR90216	Stravinsky: Petrouchka	Dorati	MIN	(AMS16056) TAS31/97+
SR90217	Moussorgsky: Pictures at an Exhibition	Dorati	MIN	N19 (AMS16051) TAS51/177++ 53++
SR90218	Schubert: Symphony 8/Rosamunde music	Skrowaczewski	MIN	(AMS16108) TAS50/195-
SR90219	Grainger: Country Gardens and Other Favourites	Fennell	ERPO	N12 (AMS16060) TAS41+++ 53+++
SR90220	Gould: West Point Symphony/Bennett Symphonic Songs	Fennell	EWE	N22 (AMS16100) TAS44/175++ 53++
SR90221	Diverse Winds: Hartley/Grainger/etc	Fennell	EWE	(AMS16078) TAS33/135+ 53/120++
SR90222	Popovers	Fennell	ERPO	(AMS16041) TAS35/105
SR90223	Bloch: Concerto Grosso nos 1/2	Hanson	ERO	(AMS16098) TASEC44 TAS31++ 49+
SR90224	Barber: Medea/Capricorn Concerto	Hanson	ERO	N32 (AMS16096) TAS35/106+
SR90225	Brahms: Violin Concerto	Menges	LSO Szigeti	(AMS16034) TAS49/144-
SR90226	Stravinsky: Firebird	Dorati	LSO	N17 (AMS16038) TASEC44,35++,44+
SR90227	Dupre: Marcel Dupre at St Supplice V1	Dupre		(AMS16054) TAS39/125+ (Bach)
SR90228	Dupre: Marcel Dupre at St Supplice V3	Dupre		(AMS16064) (Music by Franck)
SR90229	Dupre: Marcel Dupre at St Supplice V2	Dupre		(AMS16062) (Dupre) TAS32/141
SR90230	Dupre: Marcel Dupre at St Supplice V4	Dupre		(AMS16069) (Music by Bach)
SR90231	Dupre: Marcel Dupre at St Supplice V5	Dupre		(AMS16074) (Music by Messiaen)
SR90232	Wagner:Dutchman/Rienzi/Meistersinger/etc (hlts)	Paray	DSO	(AMS16095)
SR90233	Cherubini: Medea (highlights)	La Scala	Serafin/Callas	
SR90234	Wagner: Lohengrin/Tannhauser/Tristan (hlts)	Dorati	LSO	(AMS16067) TAS34/178
SR90235	Liszt: Hungarian Rhaps/Enesco Roum Rhaps 1&2	Dorati	LSO	N13 (AMS16101) TAS50/195++
SR90236	Dvorak: Symphony 4(8)/Ov Carnaval	Dorati	LSO	N27 (AMS16075) TAS34/180+
SR90238-9	Adam: Giselle (complete)	Fistoulari	LSO	see SR2-9011
SR90240	Pergolesi: La Serva Padrona (opera)	VdR	Scotto	TAS40/138
SR90241-2	Rossini: La Cambiale di Matrimonio	VdR	Fasano/Scotto	see SR2-9009

Catalog	Title	Conductor	Orchestra/Soloist	Notes
SR90243-4	Paisiello: The Barber of Seville (comp)	VdR		SR2-9010
SR90245	Gabrieli: Music for Brasses	Fennell	EWE	(AMS16119) TAS31/97+
SR90246	Copland: Appalachian Spring/Billy the Kid	Dorati	LSO	N36 (AMS16122) TAS38/140++-
SR90247	French Overtures (Herold, Auber, Adam, Thomas)	Paray	DSO	(AMS16121) TAS39/124++-
SR90248	Dorati Symph,Nocturne&Capriccio for Oboe&String Qt	Dorati	MIN	TAS31/97++ 53/116++
SR90250-1	Donizetti: Lucia di Lammermoor (cplt)	La Scala	Sanzogno Scotto	see SR2-9008
SR90253	Stravinsky: Rite of Spring	Dorati	MIN	(AMS16065) TAS33/137++ 35 SM69+
SR90254	Berlioz: Symphonie Fantastique	Paray	DSO	(AMS16055) TAS50/199+- SM77/136+
SR90255	Tchaikovsky: Symphony 5	Dorati	LSO	N37 (AMS16125) TAS31/97+
SR90256	Ballet for Band: Sullivan/Ross-Respighi/etc	Fennell	EWE	(AMS16070) TAS51/178++ 53++ TASEC
SR90257	Still: Sahdji Ballet/Ginastera/Guarnieri	Hanson	ERO	N33 TAS33/136++
SR90258	Prokofiev: Symphony 5	Dorati	MIN	(AMS16073) TAS37/92++ SM98++
SR90259	Picchi: Balli d'Arpicordo/Frescobaldi	Puyana		(AMS16142)
SR90260	Rachmaninov: Piano Concerto 2	Dorati	MIN Janis	(AMS16071) TAS40/135,32/142
SR90261	Donizetti: Lucia di Lammermoor (hlts)	La Scala	Sanzogno/Scotto	
SR90262	Dvorak: Symphony 5 (New World)	Paray	DSO	(AMS16079) TAS34/177 53/116++ 78/140++
SR90263	Gould: Fall River Legend/Spirituals	Hanson	ERO	(AMS16080) TAS44/177++ 53/120++
SR90264	Sousa: Sound off	Fennell	EWE	(AMS16081) TAS40/135+ 53/120++
SR90265	Borodin Polvn Dances/Rimsky:Russian Easter Fest Ov	Dorati	LSO	(AMS16102) Last RCPA TAS51/178
SR90266	Tchaikovsky: Piano Concerto 1	Menges	LSO Janis	(AMS16086) TAS50/194+
SR90267	Hanson: Composer and His Orch Vol 2 'Mosaics'	Hanson	ERO	TAS31/98+
SR90268	Brahms: Symphony 1	Dorati	LSO	(AMS16082) TAS45/154-
SR90269	Suppe: Ov Poet & Peasant etc	Paray	DSO	(AMS16084) TAS41/122+
SR90271	Marches for Orchestra	Fennell	ERPO	(AMS16092) TAS34/180
SR90272	Schubert: Symphony 7 (9 in C maj)	Skrowaczewski	MIN	(AMS16124) TAS50/196+
SR90273-5	Verdi: Rigoletto (cplt)	MMF	Scotto Bastiani	see SR3-9012
SR90276	Wagner: Wagner for Band	Fennell	EWE	(AMS16103) TASEC44 TAS52++ 53++
SR90277	Loeffler:2 Rhapsodies/McCauley/Barlow	Hanson	ERO	N 4 TAS49/144++ 53/118+++
SR90278	Berg: Suites from Wozzeck and Lulu	Dorati	LSO	(AMS16117) TAS34/180++,58+++ TASEC73
SR90279	Tchaikovsky: Symphony 4	Dorati	LSO	(AMS16118) TAS49/147+
SR90280	Mozart: Symphony 40/Haydn: Farewell Symphony	Dorati	LSO	TAS50/200+
SR90281	Ravel: Daphnis&Chloe/Debussy: 3 Nocturnes for Orch	Paray	DSO	N26 (AMS16120) TASEC TAS41++ 53+++
SR90282	Fetler: Contrasts for Orchestra	Dorati	MIN	N20 (AMS16099) TAS31/98 53/116++
SR90283	Rachmaninov: Piano Concerto 3	Dorati	MIN Janis	N18 (AMS16109) TASEC TAS40+,46++
SR90284	Sousa: Sousa on Review	Fennell	EWE	(AMS16110) TAS43/150+
SR90285	Franck: Symphony in D Min	Paray	DSO	(AMS16115) TAS47/142+
SR90286	Bloch: Schelomo/Herbert: Cello Conc 2	Hanson	ERO Miquelle	(AMS16123)
SR90287	Wagner: excts: Meist/Tann/Parsifal/Lohengrin	Dorati	LSO	(AMS16126) TAS51/176
SR90288	Bloch: Sinfonia Breve/Peterson	Dorati	MIN	N21 (AMS16127) TAS37/94+ 53++
SR90289	Viennese Waltz Favourites	Various		TAS31/98 Curtain-Up
SR90290	Gershwin: Gershwin Favs(Am in P/Cub Ov)	Hanson	ERO	(AMS16135) Curtain-Up
SR90291	Sousa: John Philip Sousa Favourites	Fennell	EWE	Curtain-Up
SR90292	Orchestral March Favourites	Various		Curtain-Up
SR90293	Symphonic Dance Favourites	Various		Curtain-Up
SR90294	Frederick Fennell Favourites	Fennell		Curtain-Up
SR90295	Royal Family of the Spanish Guitar	Romeros		(AMS16131)
SR90296	Guitar Music from Courts of Spain.	Romero (Celedonio)		
SR90297	Flamenco! (Ten improvisations)	Romero (Pepe)		
SR90298	Respighi: Pines/Fountains of Rome	Dorati	MIN	TAS50/203-
SR90299	Musical Diplomats USA	Hanson	EPhil	TAS50/200+
SR90300	Prokofiev: Pno Concerto 3/Rachmaninov Concerto 1	Kondrashin	MPh Janis	(AMS16130) TASEC44 TAS34++ 54+++
SR90301	Brahms: Piano Concerto 2	Skrowaczewski	LSO Bacchaur	(AMS16137) TAS49/144+-
SR90303	Dvorak: Cello Concerto/Bruch Kol Nidrei	Dorati	LSO Starker	N28 (AMS16133) TASEC TAS33++ 44++
SR90304	Harpsichord Recital - various	Puyana		(AMS16132) TAS39/127++ 53/120++
SR90305	Encore Byron Janis	Janis		(AMS16136) TAS43/147++ 54+++
SR90306-7	Tchaikovsky: Nutcracker Suite	Dorati	LSO	see SR2-9013

Mercury Living Presence

Catalog	Title	Artist/Orchestra	Notes
SR90308	Brahms: Violin Concerto	Dorati LSO Szeryng	(AMS16134) TAS31/98+- 33/141-
SR90309	Shostakovich: String Quartets 4/8	Borodin Quartet	
SR90310	Balalaika Favourites	Osipov State Russian Folk Orch	N6 (AMS16139) TASEC45+++ 54+++
SR90311	Bartok: Bluebeard's Castle (complete)	Dorati LSO Szonyi Szekely	(AMS16140) TAS49/144+
SR90312	Tchaikovsky: Symphony 6	Dorati LSO	N38 TAS42/124++
SR90313	Ravel: Rhaps Esp/Pavane/La Valse/etc/Ibert Escales	Paray DSO	N5 TAS39/126+++ 53/116+++
SR90314	Screamers! : Circus Marches	Fennell EWE	TAS47/142+
SR90315	Prokofiev: Romeo and Juliet Suites 1/2.	Scrowaczewski MIN	TAS34/178+-. Reissued Philips SAL3463
SR90316	Vienna 1908-1914: Webern/Berg/Schoenberg	Dorati LSO	N3 TAS47/149+++ TAS54/159+++ TAS58/134+++ 59/122+++ TASEC73. Reissued Philips SAL
SR90317	Beethoven: Symphony 5/Egmont/Consecration of House	Dorati LSO	
SR90318	Ballet Highlights from French Opera	Paray DSO	(AMS16138) TAS49/144++ 53/118++
SR90319	Prokofiev: Violin Sonatas 1/2	Szigeti Balsam	
SR90320	Mendelssohn: Cello Sonata/Chopin: Cello Sonata	Starker Sebok	TAS33/135++
SR90321	Beethoven: Piano Concerto 5	Skrowaczewski LSO	N39 TAS47/146+-
SR90322	Concertos & duets for 2 Harpsds		
SR90323	Favourite Concert Overtures	Various	Curtain-Up
SR90324	Favourite Opera Overtures	Various	Curtain-Up
SR90325	March Favourites	Various	Curtain-Up
SR90326	American Dance Favourites	Various	Curtain-Up
SR90327	Opera Ballet Favourites	Various	Curtain-Up
SR90328	Ballet Favs (Coppelia/Sylvia)	Various	Curtain-up (AMS16112=Sylvia extracts)
SR90329	Liszt: Piano Concertos 1/2	Kondrashin MPh Janis	
SR90330	Schumann: Symphonies 1/3	Paray DSO	Great Music
SR90331	Saint-Saens Symphony 3/Chausson Sym in B Flat	Paray DSO	Great Music
SR90332	Rimsky Korsakov: Scheherazade/Russian Easter Ov	Dorati MIN	Great Music
SR90333	Wagner Meistersinger/Tristan/Parsifal/Gott	Paray MIN	Great Music
SR90334	Strauss,R Till/Juan/Death & Trans/Dance of 7 Veils	Dorati MIN	Great Music
SR90335	Dvorak: Slavonic Dances Op 46/72	Dorati MIN	Great Music
SR90336	Brahms: Acad Fest/Tragic/Haydn Varns/Hungrn Dances	Dorati LSO	Great Music
SR90337	Musical Almanac Fennell	Hanson EWE	Curtain-Up
SR90338	Music & Plunk, Tinkle, Ting-a-Ling	Various	Curtain-Up
SR90339	Gala Favourites	Various	Curtain-Up
SR90340	Fennell and the "Pops"	Fennell ERPO	Curtain-Up
SR90342	Mussorgsky: Pictures/Bare Mt/Prokofiev	Dorati MIN	Great Music
SR90343	Prokofiev: Symphony 5/Scythian Suite	Dorati MIN	Great Music
SR90344	Tchaikovsky: Sernd for Strings/Rimsky:Le Coq d'Or	Dorati	Great Music
SR90345	Rachmaninov: Sym 2/Tchaikovsky:Fran da Rimini	Paray	Great Music
SR90346	Borodin: Prince Igor (excerpts)/Arensky	Dorati	Great Music
SR90347	Schumann: Cello Conc/Lalo: Cello conc	Skrowaczewski LSO Starker	TAS38/145++ 35mm. Reissued Philips SAL3482
SR90348	Szeryng plays Kreisler	Szeryng Charles Reiner	TAS39/124 TAS52/210+
SR90349	Gina Bachauer: Queen of the keyboard	Gina Bachauer	TAS37/94
SR90350-5	Tchaikovsky: Nutcracker/Swan Lake/Sleeping Beauty	Dorati LSO	see SR6-9014
SR90356	Mendelssohn: Symphony 4/Schubert 5	Skrowaczewski MIN	TAS34/181
SR90357	Hanson: Composer and Orch Vol 3 'For the 1st Time'	Hanson ERO	
SR90358	Beethoven: Violin Concerto	Dorati LSO Szigeti	
SR90359	Heroic Overtures.	Paray DSO	Curtain-Up
SR90360	Bravoes in Brass (Picadore,Col Bogey...)	Fennell EWE	Curtain-Up
SR90361	Holidays Around the World	Various	Curtain-Up
SR90366	Hovaness: Symphony 4/Giannini: Symphony 4	Roller EWE	N 2 TAS35/108++ 53/118+++
SR90367	Treasures for the Violin	Szeryng Charles Reiner	TAS52/210+
SR90368	Chopin: Piano concerto 1,Nocturne op27/1,3 Etudes op25	Dorati LSO Bachauer	TAS40/139
SR90369	Bach: Ov in French Manner/Toccata in F sharp min	Puyana	
SR90370	Bach: Cello suites 2/5	Starker	TAS40/138+++ 32/143 53/120++
SR90371	Liszt: Hungarian Rhapsodies 1,4,5,6	Dorati LSO	N15 TAS38/143++ 54/159+++
SR90372	Debussy: La Mer/Iberia/Petite Suite	Paray DSO	Great Music

Catalog	Title	Conductor/Orch	Notes
SR90373	Ravel: Bolero/Valse/Pavane/etc	Paray DSO	Great Music
SR90374	Bizet: Carmen/L'Arlesienne/Chabrier/etc.	Paray DSO	Great Music
SR90375	Berlioz: Fantastic Symph/Ovs	Paray DSO	Great Music
SR90376	Franck: Symphony/Le Roi d'Ys	Paray DSO	Great Music
SR90377	Overtures & Excerpts from French Operas.	Paray DSO	Great Music
SR90378	Bartok: Conc for Orchestra	Dorati LSO	TAS35/105+++
SR90379	Schuman,W: New England Tryptich/Griffes/Mennin	Hanson ERO	TASEC11 TAS46/154++
SR90380	4 Concertos for 2 Guitars	Presti Lagoya	
SR90381	Beethoven: Piano Concerto 4/Sonata op 14/1.	Dorati LSO Bachauer	TAS47/142-
SR90382	Songs of New nations	Leonard De Paur Chorus	
SR90383	Schumann: Piano Conc in A min/solos	Skrowaczewski MIN Janis	TAS52/210+
SR90385	Concs for Trumpets	Faerber Holy	
SR90386	Rossini: Overtures	Lamoureux Orch/Benzi	TAS36/169--
SR90387	Stravinsky: Song of the Nightingale/4 Etudes.	Dorati LSO	TAS52/212++
SR90388	Folksong Suites&Other British Band Classics	Fennell EWE	Elec stereo (B Band Classics V 1)
SR90390	Broadway Marches	Fennell Symphonic Winds	TAS46/156++
SR90391	Ravel: Gaspard de la Nuit/Debussy Pour le Pno.	Bachauer Gielgud	
SR90392	Brahms: Sonatas 1&2 for Cello&Piano	Starker Sebok	TAS51/177++
SR90393	Khachaturian: Violin Concerto	Dorati LSO Szeryng	TAS38/142++-
SR90394	Gershwin: Porgy & Bess Latin Suite	Hanson ERO	Reprocessed stereo
SR90395	Tchaikovsky: Waltzes	Dorati MIN	
SR90396	Haydn: Concs for Trumpet/Horn/Oboe	Sevenstern Sotijn Wouden	
SR90397	Music in Shakespeare's England	Krainis Consort	
SR90398-9	Tchaikovsky: Symphonies 1/2/3	Dorati LSO	see SR2-9015
SR90400	Leroy Anderson: Music of Leroy Anderson Vol 3	Fennell ERPO	TAS33/136
SR90401	Vivaldi Concertos for Harpsd,Piccolo,etc	Ensemble cond by Duhamel	
SR90402	Couperin: Les Nations/Rameau	Stuttgart Baroque Ens Couraud	
SR90403	Baroque Concertos	Paumgartner VSO Van Tricht	Great Music
SR90404	Rampal: Baroque Dances&Diversions	Andre Lagorce Rampal Birbaum	
SR90405	Mendelssohn: Varns Concertantes/Chopin/Bartok	Starker Sebok	TAS42/134++
SR90406	Mendelssohn: Vln Concerto/Schumann Vln Concerto	Dorati LSO Szeryng	TAS35/108-
SR90407	Mozart: 4 Horn Concertos	VSO Paumgartner Penzel	
SR90408	Baroque Flute Concerto	Orch Antiqua Musica Roussel Rampal	
SR90409	Tchaikovsky: Rococo Varns/S-Saens:Cello Conc	Dorati LSO Starker	N35 TAS43/151++. Reissued Philips SAL
SR90410	3 Concertos for Clav & Orch.	Moscow Chamber Orch Barshai	
SR90411	Baroque Masterpieces	Puyana	
SR90412	Mozart: Serenades for Winds & Strings K525/K361	Dorati/Fennell	
SR90413	Mozart: Piano Concs 20/23	VSO Paumgartner Haskill	
SR90414	Haydn: Syms 55/85, Pno Conc in D	Lamoureux Orch Benzi Haebler	
SR90415	Beethoven: Symphony 6/Haydn Symphony 100	Dorati LSO	
SR90416	Bartok: Miraculous Mandarin/Div for Strings	Dorati BBCSO	TAS32/142+ 51/174++ Reissued Philips SAL3569
SR90417	Baroque Concertos for 4 guitars.	Romeros	
SR90418	Danse Calinda!	Leonard De Paur Chorus	
SR90419	Prokofiev: Violin Concerto/Stravinsky	Menges LSO Szigeti Bogas	
SR90420	Barber: Music of Samuel Barber	Hanson ERO	Electronic stereo
SR90421	Copland: Symphony 3/Harris: Symphony 3	Hanson ERO	Electronic stereo
SR90422	Macdowell: Suite 2 (Indian)/Griffes	Hanson ERO	Electronic stereo
SR90423	Piston/Sessions/Hanson/Hovhaness	Hanson ERO	Great Music
SR90425	Vivaldi: Concs for Strings&Oboes	Moscow Chamber Orch/Barshai	
SR90426	Bartok: Wooden Prince	Dorati LSO	TAS38/141+-. Reissued Philips SAL3670
SR90427	Spanish Music for 2 Guitars	Presti Lagoya	
SR90428	Mozart: Piano Concertos 15/16	Davis LSO Haebler	TAS38/142-
SR90429	Thomson, Virgil: Symphony on a Hymn Tune/Hanson	Hanson ERO	TAS34/181++
SR90430	Hanson Piano Conc/La Montaine Birds of Paradise	Hanson ERO La Montaine	TAS38/144++
SR90431	Offenbach: Gaite Parisienne/Gershwin Am in Paris	Dorati MIN	
SR90432	Chopin: Piano concerto 2/Fantasy in Fmin op 49	Dorati LSO Bachauer	

Catalog	Title	Artist	Orchestra/Notes	Reference
SR90434	Evening of Flamenco Music	Romeros		(AMS16141) TAS33/136+
SR90435	Paris 1917-38: Satie/Milhaud/Auric/Francaux	Dorati	LSO	TAS33/134+++. Reissued Philips SAL
SR90436	Haydn: Symphonies 59/81	Dorati	FCO	TAS38/141++
SR90437	Brahms: 16 Hungarian Dances	Dorati	LSO	
SR90438	Mozart: Mozarteana (Marches,Dances,etc)	Dorati	FCO	
SR90439	Coates: Music by Eric Coates	Fennell	LPO	
SR90440	Carousel Waltz and other favourites	Fennell	EWE	
SR90442	Sonatas by Debussy, Ives, Honegger,etc	Szigeti	Bogas	
SR90443	Conc for Recorder&strings	Marriner London Strings Kroner	Lond Strings=ASMF	
SR90444	Champagne & Roses & Bonbons	Dorati	MIN	
SR90445-7	Bach: Cello suites (complete)	Starker		see SR3-9016
SR90448	Rachmaninov: P C 2/Tchaikovsky Piano Concerto 1	Dorati	MIN	reissues
SR90449	Hanson: Symphony 3/MacDowell: Suite 1	Hanson	ERO	Only recording of McDowell TAS37/95+
SR90450	Neilsen: Fynsk Forar;12 songs	Woldike	Danish Radio SO & Chorus	
SR90451-3	4 Great Violin Concertos	Issersdedt	LSO Szeryng	See SR3-9017
SR90454-6	Tchaikovsky: Four suites for Orchestra.	Dorati	Philh	see SR3-9018
SR90457	Baroque Music for 2 Guitars	Presti	Lagoya	
SR90458	18th Century French Flute Concertos	AMCO Roussel Rampal		
SR90459	Soler: Music for the Harpsd	Puyana		
SR90460	Italian Cello Sonatas	Starker		
SR90461	Lumbye: Concert in the Tivoli Gardens	Royal Danish O/Hammelboe		
SR90462-3	Tchaikovsky: Highlights	?		
SR90464-5	World of Flamenco	Romeros		
SR90466	Bach: V Concs Em,Dm,Am	Collegium Musicum Winterthur Szeryng (as soloist+conductor)		
SR90467	Brahms: Alt Rpsdy/Kodaly Psalmus Hung.	Markevitch Russian St SO		
SR90468-73	Tchaikovsky: 6 Symphonies	Dorati	LSO	see SR6-9121
SR90474-7	Portugal's Golden Age	Gulbenkian CO Gerlin Jonas		see SR4-9122
SR90480	Bach: Three Sonatas for Cello/Piano	Starker	Sebok	TAS36/167++
SR90481	Classical Ragas of India No artists listed	Recorded in India by Deben Bhattachuya		
SR90482	A Panorama of Experimental Music Vol 2.	Pierre Henry		
SR90483-5	Handel: Concerti Grossi Op 6	ECO	Leppard	see SR3-9124
SR90487	Vivaldi: Romeros Play Vivaldi(Guitar Concs)	Romeros Alessandro		
SR90488	Rodrigo: Concierto Andaluz/Aranjuez	San Antonio SO Alessandro		N40 TASEC44 TAS51/179++
SR90489-90	Bach: 7 Sonatas for Flute/Harpsichord	Larrieu	Puyana	see SR2-9125
SR90491-2	Tchaikovsky: Greatest Hits	various		see SR2-9126
SR90493-4	Heart of the Ballet		see SR2-9127	
SR90495-6	Heart of the Symphony		see SR2-9128	
SR90497-8	Heart of the Concerto		see SR2-9129	
SR90499	Dorati Symph,Nocturne&Capriccio for Oboe&String Qt	Dorati	MIN	TAS31/97+- see SR90248
SR90500	Scriabin: Nocturnes/Etudes/Preludes	Hilde Somer		
SR90502	Brahms: Symphony 3/Haydn Variations	Dorati	LSO	TAS45/154-
SR90503	Brahms: Symphony 4/Acad Fest Ov	Dorati	LSO	TAS45/154-
SR90506-7	Heart of the Opera		see SR2-9130	
SR90508-9	Music for Musing		see SR2-9132	
SR90510	Fennell Spectaculars	Fennell	EWE	
SR90511	Schumann: Symphony 4/Mozart Symph 40	Dorati	LSO	Believed to be reissue
SR90513-4	The Spoleto Festival			see SR2-9133
SR90515	Bartok: Music for Strings, Percussion & Celeste.	Dorati	LSO	
SR90516	Dvorak: Symphony 7	Dorati	LSO	TAS33/136+
SR90517	Corigliano: Pno Conc/Strauss R	San Antonio SO Alessandro Somer		
SR90518	"A Flamenco Wedding"	Romeros	Maria Victora (vocals)	
SR90519	Bach: Transcriptions by Liszt and Busoni	Crochet		
SR90520	Shura Cherkassky Recital (piano)	Shura Cherkassky		
SR90521	Menotti: Old Lady and the Thief (opera)	Trieste Teatro Verdi		
SR90522	?			
SR90523	Beethoven: Symphony 7	Dorati	LSO	

SR90524	Hanson: Merry Mount (complete)	Hanson	ERO	
SR90525	Scriabin: Sonatas 7/9	Hilde Somer		
SR90526	Encore Dorati	Dorati	MIN	
SR90527	Tchaikovsky: Violin Concerto	Dorati	LSO Szeryng	
SR90528	Tchaikovsky: The Saint Petersburg Sugar Plum	Dorati	LSO	(Nutcracker Suite Op 71a)
SR90529-30	Music for The Morning		see SR2-9134	
SR90531	Bartok: Miraculous Mandarin/Prokofiev Scythian Suite	Dorati	BBCSO/LSO	
SR90532	Love, What the World Needs Now	Various artists		
SR90533	Bartok: Suite 2/Dance Suite	Dorati	MIN	Reissues
SR93016	Delibes: Sylvia (excerpts)	Fistoulari	LSO	(AMS16112) (SR90328=some of this)

* * * * *

Mercury: English EMI Pressings

The list: This list is based upon the author's own collection of Mercury Living Presence records, as well as an earlier list produced by Mike Langhorne. Its main purpose is to enable you to discover if there is an AMS for any given SR. Consequently it is sorted in SR number order.

EMI Pressings: Many of the Mercury series were also pressed and issued in England by EMI in the period 1958-1963 under a licence issued by Mercury to EMI. They were issued at more or less the same time as were the US pressings.

The contract with EMI made stipulations on cutting equipment, and Mercury's Fine and Cozart were personally involved in inspecting and approving EMI's pressing arrangements. All of these EMI discs have the same design of the jacket front. The cover notes are the same as on the US discs, and they look very similar, even down to a similar dark maroon label. The stereo discs have numbers like AMS16xxx, and also carry the SR number on the front cover (there is also a mono series of MMA11xxx discs, not catalogued here). The programmes on these discs are nearly always identical with their SR counterparts.

They are of the very highest pressing quality, and throughout the 5 year period in which these discs were pressed there is little variation in quality, all being of thick, quiet vinyl. EMI achieved very good pressing consistency. There are no 'Vendor', nor 'promo' labels, though there are discs with 'for broadcast only' stickers on the label. There are also 2-disc test pressings, though these are very rare.

Sound Quality: How does the sound quality of these discs compare to the SRs? There is controversy over this question, but I'll stick my neck out! For those unfamiliar with Mercury pressing details, the simple answer is that the AMS is sometimes smoother in the treble than the SR. Still having much of the famed Mercury dynamics, the AMS is usually cut at about 1-2 dB lower level with a consequent reduction in dynamic power (This level reduction may also account for the less fierce treble).

Many English pressings have sound quality close to the US original. Unfortunately, some do not. I believe the explanation is that when Mercury made available a recording to EMI, in some cases they sent the tape and in other cases they sent a master pressing. In the former case EMI were able to alter the sound and they did so for the worst. However, in the latter case they couldn't do anything to change the sound quality with the result that these sound great. At this point in time I am still not clear how to distinguish these two groups.

AMS pressing quality is very consistent and you know exactly what you are going to get. Experienced Mercury collectors will know that with the SR pressings it all depends on exactly what pressing you get.

For those prepared to think about pressing variations among SRs, the answer is more complex: If the SR is one of the earlier Mercurys (pre about SR90265), then the early FR1,2,3 pressings (which were made in RCA pressing facilities) will usually have greater impact and dynamics. After these FR pressings the SRs become less reliable.

For later Mercurys where RFR1 is the first pressing, in my experience only the early RFR pressings are better. With all CBFR and CTFR pressings the AMS is nearly always preferable. In other words, unless it is a genuinely early SR pressing, the greater pressing consistency of the AMSs make them a safer bet than the SR.

General: Only a selection of the US stereo Mercurys were issued in this series - 143 in total. They come from Mercury's early and middle periods, the majority being before SR90300. During Mercury's final period, EMI dropped out and European pressing was gradually taken over by Philips. There are a small number of mid 60s Philips Mercurys which are extremely good, and have a similar audio relationship to the American SR as do the EMI pressings. An example is SAL3569 Miraculous Mandarin (from SR90416) which again has the same jacket design as the SR, and also a dark maroon label. There are only about 7 or 8 'Mercurys' in this SAL series. However, slightly later Philips reissue series also include a number of "Mercurys". In particular the best of the Mercury Paray recordings are on the Philips SGL series, and several of the Starker recordings are on the Philips "Festivo" label - these are both early-mid 60s labels. I know of no listing of these Philips Mercury reissues.

Nearly all AMS Mercurys have the identical programme to the SR originals. One exception is AMS16120. This has the whole of SR90281, plus the Chabrier Bouree Fantasque from SR90005. The only other example is AMS16112 Delibes: Sylvia extracts. The jacket of this bears the unusual SR number SR93016. This is again because there is no 100% SR equivalent, so they made up a 'fictitious' SR number. The closest equivalent, SR90328, contains extracts from both the Coppelia and Sylvia records.

Work	Orchestra/Conductor	Cat. 1	Cat. 2
Beethoven: Wellington's Victory/Prometheus/etc	LSO Dorati	16091	LPS9000
Delibes: Coppelia	MIN Dorati	16018/9	2-9005
Delibes: Sylvia (complete ballet)	LSO Fistoulari	16032/3	2-9006
Dvorak: Slavonic Dances	MIN Dorati	16046/7	2-9007
Adam: Giselle (complete)	LSO Fistoulari	16087/8	2-9011
Tchaikovsky: Nutcracker Suite	LSO Dorati	16143	2-9013
Bizet: Carmen suite/L'Arlesienne 1&2	DSO Paray	16053	90001
Gershwin: Rhapsody in Blue/Conc in F	ERSO Hanson List	16026	90002
Prokofiev: Love for 3 Oranges Suite/Scythian St	LSO Dorati	16009	90006
Albeniz: Iberia 1-5/Falla	MIN Dorati	16002	90007
Strauss,J: Champagne Polka/etc	MIN Dorati	16001	90008
Leroy Anderson: Music of Leroy Anderson Vol 1	ERPO Fennell	16044	90009
Debussy: La Mer/Iberia/Petite Suite	DSO Paray	16094	90010
Saint-Saens: Symphony 3	DSO Paray Dupre	16004	90012
Offenbach: Gaite Parisienne/Strauss	MIN Dorati	16005	90016
Rachmaninov: Symphony 2	DSO Paray	16003	90019
Leroy Anderson: Music of Leroy Anderson Vol 2	ERPO Fennell	16037	90043
Grofe: Grand Canyon/Mississipi Suite	ERSO Hanson	16011	90049
Tchaikovsky: Overture 1812/Capriccio Italien	MIN Dorati	16010	90054
Shostakovich: Symphony 5	MIN Skrowaczewski	16128	90060
Strauss,R: Der Rosenkavalier St/Till Eulenspiegel	MIN Dorati	16014	90099
Sessions: Black Maskers/McPhee: Tabuh Tabuhan	ERO Hanson	16093	90103
Marching Along	EWE Fennell	16020	90105
Wagner: Orch excerpts	DSO Paray	16049	90107
Borodin: Polvn Dances/Rimsky:Le Coq d'Or St	LSO Dorati	16008	90122
Mozart: Symphony 35/Haydn: Symphony 96	DSO Paray	16052	90129
Kodaly: Hary Janos Suite	MIN Dorati	16025	90132
Schumann: Symphony 3	DSO Paray	16035	90133
Fiesta in Hi-Fi	ERO Hanson	16016	90134
Carpenter: Adventures in a Perambulator/etc	ERO Hanson	16015	90136
Rossini: Ovs: Gazza Ladra/Barber of Seville/etc	MIN Dorati	16090	90139
Hindemith:Sym for Band/Stravinsky/Schoenberg	EWE Fennell	16106	90143
Hi-Fi a la Espanola	ERO Hanson	16089	90144
Kennan: Three Pieces/Rogers/Bergsma	ERO Hanson	16104	90147
Ives: Symphony 3/3 Places In New England	ERO Hanson	16083	90149
Respighi: Brazilian Impressions/The Birds	LSO Dorati	16036	90153
Brahms: 16 Hungarian Dances/Haydn Variations	LSO Dorati	16006	90154
Verdi: Overtures	LSO Dorati	16058	90156
Handel: Water Music/Royal Fireworks	LSO Dorati	16031	90158
Dupre: Franck: Trois Chorales/Pieces Heroique	Dupre	16030	90168
Dupre: Widor Allegro from Symphony 6/etc	Dupre	16097	90169
March Time	EWE Fennell	16012	90170
Copland: Rodeo/El Salon Mexico/etc	MIN Dorati	16021	90172
Winds in Hi-Fi:Grainger/Milhaud/Strauss/etc	EWE Fennell	16023	90173
Mendelssohn: Sym 5/Midsmr Nights Dream	DSO Paray	16022	90174
Hanson: Composer and His Orch Vol 1	ERO Hanson	16007	90175
Strauss,J: Strauss Family Album	MIN Dorati	16024	90178

Title	Performer	Cat 1	Cat 2
Kodaly: Dances of Galanta/Bartok	PHun Dorati	16027	90179
Bartok: Dance Suite/Deux Portraits	PHun Dorati	16068	90183
Mozart: Symphonies 39/41	LSO Schmidt-Issersdedt	16050	90184
Wienerwalzer Paprika - Viennese Waltzes	PHun Dorati	16063	90190
French Ovs (Ambroise/Auber/Herold)	DSO Paray	16013	90191
Rimsky Korsakov: Scheherazade	MIN Dorati	16057	90195
Schubert: Symphonies 4/6	LSO Schmidt-Isserstedt Susskind	16029	90196
British Band Classics Vol II	EWE Fennell	16043	90197
Schumann: Symphony 1/Manfred Ov	DSO Paray	16017	90198
Respighi: Ancient Dances & Airs for Lute	PHun Dorati	16028	90199
Tchaikovsky: Serenade for Strings/Arensky	PHun Dorati	16040	90200
Tchaikovsky: Marche Slave/Francesca Da Rimini/etc	MIN Dorati	16059	90201
Strauss,R: Tod und Verklarung/Don Juan	MIN Dorati	16072	90202
Bouquet de Paray (Rossini/Liszt/Weber/etc)	DSO Paray	16042	90203
Sibelius: Symphony 2	DSO Paray	16061	90204
Beethoven: Symphonies 1/2	DSO Paray	16039	90205
Piston: The Incredible Flutist/Moore	ERO Hanson	16129	90206
Hands Across the Sea	EWE Fennell	16048	90207
Haydn: Symphonies 94/103	PHun Dorati	16085	90208
Khachaturian: Music from ballet Gayne/etc	LSO Dorati	16116	90209
Brahms: Horn Trio/Violin sonata 2	Szigeti Horszowski Barrow	16076	90210
Vive La Marche	DSO Paray	16077	90211
Chabrier: Espana/Suite Pastorale etc	DSO Paray	16107	90212
Ravel: Le Tomb de Couperin/Valses/Debussy	DSO Paray	16066	90213
Smetana: Moldau/Mussorgsky/Sibelius/Liszt	LSO Dorati	16105	90214
Offenbach: Overtures by Offenbach & Auber	DSO Paray	16045	90215
Stravinsky: Petrouchka	MIN Dorati	16056	90216
Moussorgsky: Pictures at an Exhibition	MIN Dorati	16051	90217
Schubert: Symphony 8/Rosamunde music	MIN Skrowaczewski	16108	90218
Grainger: Country Gardens and Other Favourites	ERPO Fennell	16060	90219
Gould: West Point Symphony/Bennett	EWE Fennell	16100	90220
Diverse Winds: Hartley/Grainger/etc	EWE Fennell	16078	90221
Popovers	ERPO Fennell	16041	90222
Bloch: Conc Grosso nos 1/2	ERO Hanson	16098	90223
Barber: Medea/Capricorn Concerto	ERO Hanson	16096	90224
Brahms: Violin Concerto	LSO Menges Szigeti	16034	90225
Stravinsky: Firebird	LSO Dorati	16038	90226
Dupre: Marcel Dupre at St Supplice V1 (Bach: Preludes & Fugues)		16054	90227
Dupre: Marcel Dupre at St Supplice V3 (Organ Music by Franck)		16064	90228
Dupre: Marcel Dupre at St Supplice V2 (Dupre)		16062	90229
Dupre: Marcel Dupre at St Supplice V4 (Bach:Chorales/Fantasias)		16069	90230
Dupre: Marcel Dupre at St Supplice V5 (Dupre & Messiaen)		16074	90231
Wagner: Dutchman/Rienzi/Magic Fire/Meist (hlts)	DSO Paray	16095	90232
Wagner: Lohengrin/Tannhauser/Tristan (hlts)	LSO Dorati	16067	90234
Liszt: Hungn Rhaps 2&3/Enesco Roum Rhaps 1&2	LSO Dorati	16101	90235
Dvorak: Symphony 4(8)/Ov Carnaval	LSO Dorati	16075	90236
Gabrieli: Music for Brasses	EWE Fennell	16119	90245

Title	Performers	Cat1	Cat2
Copland: Appalachian Spring/Billy the Kid	LSO Dorati	16122	90246
French Ovs: Herold/Auber/Adam	DSO Paray	16121	90247
Stravinsky: Rite of Spring	MIN Dorati	16065	90253
Berlioz: Symphonie Fantastique	DSO Paray	16055	90254
Tchaikovsky: Symphony 5	LSO Dorati	16125	90255
Ballet for Band: Sullivan/Ross-Respighi/etc	EWE Fennell	16070	90256
Prokofiev: Symphony 5	MIN Dorati	16073	90258
Picchi: Balli d'Arpicordo/Frescobaldi	Puyana	16142	90259
Rachmaninov: Piano Concerto 2	MIN Dorati Janis	16071	90260
Dvorak: Symphony 5 (New World)	DSO Paray	16079	90262
Gould: Fall River Legend/Spirituals	ERO Hanson	16080	90263
Sousa: Marches	EWE Fennell	16081	90264
Borodin: Polvn Dances/Rimsky:Russian Easter Ov	LSO Dorati	16102	90265
Tchaikovsky: Piano Concerto 1	LSO Menges Janis	16086	90266
Brahms: Symphony 1	LSO Dorati	16082	90268
Suppe: Ov Poet & Peasant etc	DSO Paray	16084	90269
Marches for Orchestra	ERPO Fennell	16092	90271
Schubert: Symphony 7 (9 in C maj)	MIN Skrowaczewski	16124	90272
Wagner: Wagner for Band	EWE Fennell	16103	90276
Berg: Suites from Wozzeck and Lulu	LSO Dorati	16117	90278
Tchaikovsky: Symphony 4	LSO Dorati	16118	90279
Debussy: 3 Nocturnes/Ravel/Chabrier	DSO Paray	16120	90281
Fetler: Contrasts for Orchestra	MIN Dorati	16099	90282
Rachmaninov: Piano Concerto 3	MIN Dorati Janis	16109	90283
Sousa: Sousa on Review	EWE Fennell	16110	90284
Franck: Symphony in D Min	DSO Paray	16115	90285
Bloch: Schelomo/Herbert: Cello Conc 2	ERO Hanson Miquelle	16123	90286
Wagner: excts: Meist/Tann/Parsifal/Lohengrin	LSO Dorati	16126	90287
Bloch: Sinfonia Breve/Peterson	MIN Dorati	16127	90288
Gershwin: Gershwin Favs(Am in P/Cub Ov)	ERO Hanson/MIN Dorati	16135	90290
Royal Family of the Sp Guitar	The Romeros	16131	90295
Prokofiev: Pno Conc 3/Rach Conc 1	MPO Kondrashin Janis	16130	90300
Brahms: Piano Concerto 2	LSO Skrowaczewski Bacchaur	16137	90301
Dvorak: Cello Conc/Bruch Kol Nidrei	LSO Dorati Starker	16133	90303
Harpsichord Recital - various	Rafael Puyana	16132	90304
Encore Byron Janis	Byron Janis	16136	90305
Brahms: Violin Concerto	LSO Dorati Szeryng	16134	90308
Balalaika Favourites	Osipov State Russian Folk Orch	16139	90310
Bartok: Bluebeard's Castle (complete)	LSO Dorati Szonyi Szekely	16140	90311
Ballet: Hlts from French Opera	DSO Paray	16138	90318
Delibes: Sylvia (excerpts)	LSO Fistoulari	16112	90328
An Evening of Flamenco Music	The Romeros	16141	90434

Decca

The lists:

The lists for SET, Dnnn sets, SXL2000, SXL6000, SWL, HEAD are all now believed to be complete.

This London CS list is believed to be complete for the early blue-back issues (from the period 1958-1964).

CS numbers in () are the American London CS numbers where appropriate.

Where the record has been discussed in The Absolute Sound (TAS) the volume number is shown by Tv (sometimes the page number is also shown by Tv/p). TAS 'Editors Choice' discs are also shown ('TASEC').

Where the record was mentioned in Robert Moon's booklet "Full Frequency Stereophonic Sound", this is shown by RMnn, where nn is the rating (maximum of 20) Moon gave the record.

London: The word "Decca" could not be used in USA because the name was already in use there. So Decca records were marketed there under the name London. The Londons were pressed in England at exactly the same pressing plant as the Deccas and at exactly the same time. There are different opinions as to whether or not there are differences between Deccas and Londons. Some say they are identical. Others say that the London US pressings were cut at a slightly higher level, giving more treble emphasis. Sorry folks, I'm not entering this controversy!

Some of the very earliest London pressings are called "pancake" pressings. These do not have the "groove guard" at the edge of the record, and they also have a label that appears to be slightly larger than it ought to be - the lead out groove at the centre of the record runs into the label. I have only ever seen these pressings on London, and never on SXLs. I don't know why this should be so - one of the little mysteries of the record business!

Dutch pressings: In the late 70s Decca abandoned their famous New Malden pressing plant and started pressing in Holland. Records of this vintage are thin and floppy and a shadow of their former quality. I avoid them.

Non existent entries: Note that entries with just * for the title indicate that no such record is believed to exist. However, in the Decca catalogues there is a blank entry reserved for them. What this probably means is that a number was allocated by Decca for a record, but it was never actually issued. What it may also mean is that the record was issued only in some other country, such as France, Australia, South Africa. Where a record is definitely known to have been issued, but only in one specific country, it is listed here, but with a note to that effect. Of course, such records will have non-standard labels. An example is SXL2061: Some believe that there is a foreign issue of this and that it is Debussy: La Mer/Faun Prelude/Ravel: Rapsodie Espagnol with OSR and Ansermet. I offer this as rumour only.

Abbreviations: As well as the usual abbreviations, the following are used:

AAM	Academy of Ancient Music
AdSC	Accademia di Santa Cecilia
Ccgbw	Amsterdam Concertgebouw Orchestra
Clvlnd	Cleveland Orchestra
CSO	Chicago Symphony Orchestra
IPO	Israel Philharmonic Orchestra
KCC	Choir of Kings College Cambridge
LAPO	Los Angeles Philharmonic Orchestra
LPO	London Philharmonic Orchestra
LSO	London Symphony Orchestra
LWS	London Wind Soloists
NOS	National Orchestra of Spain
NSOL	New Symphony Orchestra of London
OdP	Orchestre de Paris
OSR	Orchestre de la Suisse Romande
PCO	Paris Conservatoire Orchestra
POO	Orchestra of the Paris Opera
PJBE	Philip Jones Brass Ensemble
ROHCG	Orchestra of the Royal Opera House Covent Garden
StCO	Stuttgart Chamber Orchestra
StPh	Stuttgart Philharmonic Orchestra
VME	Vienna Mozart Ensemble
VPO	Vienna Philharmonic Orchestra
VSOp	Vienna State Opera
VV	Vienna Volksoper

Decca SET box sets

Decca started using the SET numbering scheme for sets around 1959/60. Decca used the SET number not just for box sets, but for anything which had an accompanying leaflet. For example, SET311 (Bluebeard's Castle) is a single record, but it has an accompanying leaflet. Box sets prior to the start of the SET series used the SXL numbering and the labels were then black. A good example of this confusing situation is the Solti Das Rheingold box set. The earliest form of this is SXL2101, but this later became SET382.

Label: SET labels are the same as SXL labels except that the colour is purple instead of black.

Number	Work	Orch	Artists	Notes
RING1-22	Wagner: The Ring (complete)	VPO	Solti Cooke	In wooden presentation case
SET 201-3	Strauss,J: Fledermaus Gala Performance	VPO	Karajan	
SET204-8	Wagner: Tristan & Isolde	VPO	Solti Nilsson	
SET209-11	Verdi: Otello	VPO	Karajan	
SET212-4	Donizetti: Lucia di Lammermoor	AdSC	Pritchard	
SET215-7	Verdi: Un Ballo in Maschera	AdSC	Solti	
SET218-20	Handel: Messiah	LSO	Boult Sutherland Bumbry	
SET221-3	Cilea: Adriana Lecouvreur	AdSC	Capuana	
SET224-6	Verdi: Rigoletto	AdSC	Santagno	
SET227	Solti conducts Wagner	VPO	Solti	
SET228-9	Strauss,R: Salome	VPO	Solti Nilsson	TAS 30/125+
SET230	"Dali in Venice" Homage to Salvatore Dali. (Dali interview, Scarlatti: The Spanish Lady & Roman Cavalier, etc)	Complesso Strumentale Confalonieri	Confalonieri Cossotto Alvary	
SET231	Brahms: Symphony 3, Tragic Ov	VPO	Karajan	
SET232-4	Handel: Alcina	LSO	Bonynge Sutherland Berganza	
SET236-8	Puccini: Il Triticco	MMF	Gardelli	
SET239-41	Bellini: La Sonnambula	AdSC	Bonynge	
SET242-6	Wagner: Siegfried	VPO	Solti	
SET247-8	"Command performance"	LSO	Bonynge Sutherland	
SET249-51	Verdi: La Traviata		Pritchard Sutherland Bergonzi Merrill	
SET252-3	Britten: War Requiem	LSO	Britten	
SET254-5	Art of the Ballerina	LSO	Bonynge	
SET256-8	Bizet: Carmen	OSR	Schippers Resnik Del Monaco Sutherland	
SET259-61	Bellini: I Puritani		Bonynge Sutherland	
SET262-4	Rossini: Italian in Algiers	Varviso	Berganza	
SET265-7	Rossini: La Cenerentola	Simionato	Bruscantini	
SET268-9	The Age of Bel Canto	LSO	Bonynge Sutherland Horne	
SET270-1	Schubert: Winterreise/Dichterliebe	Britten	Pears	
SET272-3	Beethoven: Fidelio	VPO	Maazel Nilsson McCracken Krause	
SET274-6	Britten: Albert Herring	LSO	Britten	
SET277-9	Debussy: Pelleas et Melisande	OSR	Ansermet	
SET280-1	Donizetti: Don Pasquale	Vienna Op Orch	Kertesz	
SET282-4	Verdi: Macbeth	AdSC	Schippers	
SET285-7	Rossini: Barber of Seville	Varviso	Berganza	
SET288-91	Bach,J.S: St Matthew Passion	StCO	Munchinger	
SET292-7	Wagner: Gotterdammerung	VPO	Solti	TAS 44/144+ TASEC65
SET298-300	Verdi: Nabucco	VSOp	Gardelli	
SET301	Britten: Curlew River		Britten	
SET302	Mozart: Requiem	VPO	Kertesz	(SPA476)
SET303-4	Bach: The Art of Fugue	StCO	Munchinger	
SET305-8	Verdi: Don Carlo	ROHCG	Solti	

Catalog	Title	Orchestra	Conductor/Artists	Notes
SET309-10	"Souvenir of a Golden Era"	OSR	Lewis Horne	
SET311	Bartok: Bluebeards Castle	Kertesz Ludwig Berry		TAS 49/146+
SET312-6	Wagner: Die Walkure	VPO	Solti	
SET317-9	Rossini: Semiramide	LSO	Bonynge Sutherland	
SET320-2	Bellini: Beatrice di Tenda	LSO	Bonynge Pavarotti Sutherland	
SET323-4	Bruckner: Symphony 7, Wagner Siegfried Idyll	VPO	Solti	
SET325-6	Mahler: Symphony 2	CSO	Solti Harper Watts	TAS 11/384
SET327-30	Gounod: Faust	LSO	Bonynge Sutherland	
SET331	Mahler: Das Lied von der Erde	Bernstein VPO King Dieskau		
SET332	Mozart: Symphony 36/Piano Concerto 15	VPO	Bernstein	
SET333-4	Brahms: German Requiem	OSR	Ansermet	(DPA583/4)
SET335-6	Bruckner: Symphony 8	VPO	Solti	
SET337	Donizetti: Don Pasquale (hlts)	VSO	Kertesz Sciutti	
SET338-40	Britten: A Midsummer Night's Dream	LSO	Britten	
SET341-2	Puccini: Tosca	AdSC	Maazel Nilsson Corelli Fischer-Dieskau	
SET343-4	Mascagni: Cavalleria Rusticana	Rome	Varviso	
SET345	Rossini: La Cenerentola (hlts)	MMF	de Fabritiis Simionato Bruscantini	
SET346-8	Bach,J.S: Christmas Oratorio	StCO	Munchinger	
SET349-50	Love Live Forever	Philh	Bonynge Sutherland	
SET351	Graun: Montezuma (hlts)	LPO	Bonynge Sutherland	
SET352	Bononcini: Griselda	LPO	Bonynge	
SET353	Verdi: Don Carlos (hlts)	ROHCG	Solti	(from SET305-8)
SET354-5	Strauss,R: Elektra	VPO	Solti	
SET356	Britten: The Burning Fiery Furnace	English Opera Britten Pears		
SET357-9	Mozart: Clemenza di Tito	Vienna SO Kertesz		
SET360-1	Mahler: Symphony 9	LSO	Solti	
SET362-3	Haydn: The Creation	VPO	Munchinger	
SET364-6	Ponchielli: La Gioconda	Rome	Gardelli	
SET367	Verdi: Nabucco (hlts)	VSOp	Gardelli	
SET368-9	Bellini: Norma	AdSC	Varviso Del Monaco	
SET370-1	Liszt: Faust Symphony	OSR	Ansermet	
SET372-3	Donizetti: La Fille Du Regiment	ROHCG	Bonynge Pavarotti Sutherland	
SET374-5	Verdi: Requiem	VPO	Solti Pavarotti Sutherland Talvela Horne	
SET376-8	Cherubini: Medea	AdSC	Gardelli Lorengar Jones	
SET379-81	Britten: Billy Budd	LSO	Britten	
SET382-4	Wagner: Das Rheingold	VPO	Solti	
SET385-6	Mahler: Symphony 3	LSO	Solti	
SET387-9	Delibes: Lakme	Bonynge Sutherland		
SET390	Wagner: Die Walkure (excerpts)	VPO	Solti	
SET391	Rossini: Semiramide (hlts)	LSO	Bonynge Sutherland	
SET392-3	"Royal Opera House Covent Garden Anniversary Album"			
SET394-6	Catalani: La Wally	Monte Carlo Cleva Tebaldi Del Monaco		
SET397	Britten: A Midsummer Night's Dream	LSO	Britten	
SET398	Bach,J.S: Easter Oratorio	StCO	Munchinger	
SET399-400	Kodaly: Hari Janos (complete)	LSO	Kertesz	
SET401-2	Verdi: La Traviata	VPO	Maazel Lorengar Malagu Fischer-Dieskau	
SET403-4	Leoncavallo: I Pagliacci	AdSC	Gardelli	
SET406-8	"An Introduction to the Ring by Deryck Cooke"	VPO	Solti	
SET409	Verdi: Macbeth (hlts)	AdSC	Schippers	
SET410-11	Bach: Brandenburg Concertos	ECO	Britten	
SET412-5	Mozart: Don Giovanni	ECO	Bonynge	
SET416-7	Dvorak: Requiem	LSO	Kertesz	
SET418-21	Strauss,R Der Rosenkavalier	VPO	Solti Crespin Dermota	
SET422	Zandonai: Francesca da Rimini	Monte Carlo Rescigno Del Monaco		
SET423	Bach,JS: Christmas Oratorio (hlts)	StCO	Munchinger	

SET424-6	Bellini: Norma	LSO	Bonynge
SET427-9	Verdi: Aida	Rome Opera	Solti
SET430	Bellini: Beatrice di Tenda (hlts)	LSO	Bonynge Sutherland
SET431	Gounod: Faust (hlts)	LSO	Bonynge Sutherland
SET432	Mozart: La Clemenza di Tito (hlts)	Vienna SO	Kertesz
SET433-4	Adam: Giselle	Monte Carlo	Bonynge
SET435-6	Giordano: Fedora	Monte Carlo	Gardelli
SET438	Britten: The Prodigal Son	English Opera	Britten Pears
SET439-40	"A Tebaldi Festival"	NPO	Bonynge Tebaldi
SET443-4	Gluck: Orfeo ed Euridice	ROHCG	Solti
SET445	Britten: The Golden Vanity (Children's Crusade)	Britten	
SET446-9	Donizetti: Anna Bolena	Vienna Opera	Varviso
SET450	Ponchielli: La Gioconda (hlts)	AdSC	Gardelli Tebaldi
SET451	Puccini: Tosca (hlts)	AdSC	Maazel Nilsson
SET452	Britten: Billy Budd (hlts)	LSO	Britten Pears
SET453	Britten: Albert Herring (hlts)	ECO	Britten Pears
SET454-5	"Romantic French Arias"	OSR	Bonynge Sutherland
SET456	Duets from Bellini: Norma, Rossini: Semiramide	LSO	Bonynge Sutherland Horne
SET457	Strauss,R: Salome (hlts)	VPO	Solti
SET458	Bellini: Norma (hlts)	AdSC	Varviso
SET459	Strauss: Elektra (hlts)	VPO	Solti Nilsson
SET460-3	Meyerbeer: Les Huguenots	NPO	Bonynge Sutherland
SET464	Verdi: 4 Sacred Pieces	LAPO	Mehta
SET465-7	Handel: Messiah	ECO	Bonynge Sutherland Krause
SET468	Stravinsky: The Firebird (+ rehearsal)	OSR	Ansermet
SET469-70	Mahler: Symphony 6/etc	CSO	Solti
SET471-2	Mahler: Symphony 5	CSO	Solti
SET473-4	Delibes: Coppelia	OSR	Bonynge
SET475	Debussy: Pelleas & Melisande (hlts)	OSR	Ansermet
SET476	Cherubini: Medea (hlts)	AdSC	Gardelli Lorengar Jones
SET477-8	Bach,J.S: Mass in Bmin	StCO	Munchinger
SET479-81	Mozart: Magic Flute	VPO	Solti
SET482	Wagner: Das Rheingold (excerpts)	VPO	Solti
SET483	Verdi: La Traviata (hlts)	Berlin	Maazel
SET484-6	Verdi: Un Ballo in Maschera	AdSC	Bartoletti Tebaldi Pavarotti
SET487	Strauss,R: Der Rosenkavalier (hlts)	VPO	Solti
SET488	Delibes: Lakme (hlts)		Bonynge Sutherland
SET489	Catalani: La Wally (hlts)	Monte Carlo	Cleva Del Monaco
SET490	Leoncavallo: Pagliacci, Mascagni: Cavalleria Rusticana (hlts)	AdSC	Gardelli etc
SET491	Donizetti: La Fille du Regiment (hlts)	ROHCG	Bonynge Sutherland Pavarotti
SET492-3	Britten: The Rape of Lucretia	ECO	Britten
SET494	Giordano: Fedora (hlts)	Monte Carlo	Gardelli Del Monaco
SET495	Gluck: Orfeo ed Euridice (hlts)	ROHCG	Solti
SET496	Mozart: Don Giovanni (hlts)	ECO	Bonynge Sutherland Lorengar
SET497-8	"Vienna, Women, and Song" (Gypsy Baron, Merry Widow, etc)	VV	
SET499-500	Purcell: The Fairy Queen	ECO	Britten Vyvyan
SET501-2	Britten: Owen Wingrave	ECO	Britten
SET503-5	Donizetti: L'Elisir d'Amore	ECO	Bonynge Pavarotti Sutherland
SET506-9	Wagner: Tannhauser	VPO	Solti Kollo Dernesch
SET510-2	Verdi: Macbeth	LPO	Gardelli Pavarotti etc
SET513	Meyerbeer: Les Huguenots (hlts)	Philh	Bonynge Sutherland
SET514-7	Mussorgsky: Boris Godunov	VPO	Karajan
SET518-9	Mahler: Symphony 7	CSO	Solti
SET520-1	"Regine Crespin: Prima Donna in Paris"	VV	Crespin
SET522	Donizetti: Anna Bolena (hlts)	VSOp	Varviso Suliotis Horne

Catalog	Work	Orchestra	Conductor/Artists	TAS
SET523-4	"Homage to Pavlova"	LSO	Bonynge	
SET525-6	Elgar: The Dream of Gerontius	LSO	Britten	
SET527	Mozart: Magic Flute (hlts)	VPO	Solti	
SET528-30	Donizetti: Lucia di Lammermoor	ROHCG	Bonynge Sutherland Pavarotti	
SET531-3	Bach, J.S: St John Passion	ECO	Britten	
SET534-5	Mahler: Symphony 8	CSO	Solti	TAS44/169
SET536	Britten: Owen Wingrave (hlts)	ECO	Britten	
SET537	Britten: The Rape of Lucretia (hlts)	ECO	Britten Pears	
SET538	Verdi: Un Ballo in Maschera (hlts)	AdSC	Bartoletti Tebaldi	
SET539	Verdi: Macbeth (hlts)	LPO	Gardelli Pavarotti	
SET540-1	Strauss, J: Die Fledermaus	VPO	Bohm	
SET542-4	Verdi: Rigoletto	LSO	Bonynge Sutherland Pavarotti	
SET545-7	Offenbach: Tales of Hoffmann	OSR	Bonynge Sutherland Domingo	
SET548-9	"Mozart Opera Festival"	Vienna Haydn Orch	Kertesz Popp Fassbaender Krause	
SET550-4	Wagner: Parsifal	VPO	Solti	
SET555	Mahler: Das Lied von der Erde	CSO	Solti Kollo Minton	
SET556	Wagner: Tannhauser (hlts)	VPO	Solti Dernesch Ludwig	
SET557	Mussorgsky: Boris Godunov (hlts)	VPO	Karajan Ghiaurov	
SET558	Boito: Mefistofele (hlts)	AdSC	Serafin Tebaldi di Stefano	
SET559	Donizetti: Lucia di Lammermoor (hlts)	ROHCG	Bonynge Sutherland	
SET560	Purcell: The Fairy Queen (hlts)	ECO	Britten	
SET561-3	Puccini: Turandot	LPO	Mehta Pav Suth	TASEC 11, TASEC 44
SET564	Donizetti: L'Elisir d'Amore (hlts)	ECO	Bonynge Sutherland Pavarotti	
SET565-6	Puccini: La Boheme	BPO	Karajan	TASEC 2
SET567-8	Schumann: Scenes from Goethe's Faust	ECO	Britten	
SET569	Offenbach: Les Contes D'Hoffmann (hlts)	OSR	Bonynge Sutherland	
SET570-1	Berlioz: Romeo & Juliet	VPO	Maazel	
SET572	Massenet: Therese	Philh	Bonynge	
SET573	Puccini: Turandot (hlts)	LPO	Mehta Sutherland Pavarotti	
SET574	Wagner: Parsifal (hlts)	VPO	Solti	
SET575-8	Mozart: Cosi fan Tutte	LPO	Solti	
SET579	Puccini: La Boheme (hlts)	BPO	Karajan Pavarotti	
SET580	Verdi: Rigoletto (hlts)	LSO	Bonynge Sutherland Pavarotti	
SET581-3	Britten: Death in Venice	ECO	Bedford	
SET584-6	Puccini: Madame Butterfly	VPO	Karajan	
SET587-9	Bellini: I Puritani	LSO	Bonynge Pavarotti Sutherland	
SET590-2	Bach: St John Passion	StCO	Munchinger	
SET593-4	Monteverdi Vespers of 1610	Monteverdi Orch & Choir	Gardiner Munrow	
SET595	Mozart: Cosi fan Tutte (hlts)	LPO	Solti	
SET596-8	Tchaikovsky: Eugene Onegin	ROHCG	Solti	
SET599	Tchaikovsky: Eugene Onegin (hlts)	ROHCG	Solti	
SET600	Strauss, J: Die Fledermaus (hlts)	VPO	Bohm Windgassen Janowitz	
SET601	Strauss, R: Ein Heldenleben	VPO	Solti	
SET602	Verdi: 4 Sacred Pieces	CSO	Solti	
SET605	Puccini: Madama Butterfly (hlts)	VPO	Karajan Pavarotti	
SET606-8	Verdi: Luisa Miller	NPO	Maag	
SET609-11	Gershwin: Porgy and Bess	Clvlnd	Maazel	
SET612-4	Massenet: Esclarmonde	NPO	Bonynge Sutherland	
SET615	Purcell: Dido and Aeneas	Aldeburgh	Bedford	
SET616	Stravinsky: Oedipus Rex	LPO	Solti	
SET617	Wolf-Ferrari: Il Segretto di Susanna	ROHCG	Gardelli	
SET618	Walton: Belshazzar's Feast	LPO	Solti	
SET619	Bellini: I Puritani (hlts)	LSO	Bonynge Sutherland Pavarotti	
SET621	Bizet: Carmen (hlts)	LPO	Solti Domingo Te Kanawa	
SET622	Bizet: Carmen/Borodin: Prince Igor/Tchaikovsky	LSO	Solti	

SET623	Verdi: Luisa Miller (hlts)	NPO	Maag Pavarotti etc	
SET624	Donizetti: Maria Stuarda (hlts)	Teatro Comunale Bologna	Bonynge Pavarotti	
SET625	Wagner: Die Meistersinger (hlts)	VPO	Solti Kollo Bailey	
SET626	Wagner: Flying Dutchman (hlts)	CSO	Solti	
SET627	Puccini: Suor Angelica	NPO	Bonynge Sutherland Ludwig	
SET628	Holst: The Planets	LPO	Solti	
SET629	Lehar (arr Bonynge): The Merry Widow (hlts)	NPO	Bonynge Sutherland	
SET630	Bartok: Duke Bluebeard's Castle	LPO	Solti	
SET631	Verdi: Il Trovatore (hlts)	NPO	Bonynge Sutherland Pavarotti	
SET632	Verdi: Otello (hlts)	VPO	Solti	(from D102D 3)
SET633	Humperdinck: Hansel and Gretel (hlts)	VPO	Solti Popp Fassbaender	

Later Decca Group Sets (including Argo & Oiseau Lyre)

The following SXLAnnnn-SXLMnnnn box sets are, in effect, part of the SXL6000 series and entries corresponding to them are listed therein.

Label: The labels are identical to the late SXL6000 labels.

SXLA6452	Beethoven: The Piano Sonatas (complete)		Backhaus	10 discs
SXLB6470	Beethoven: The 9 Symphonies	VPO	Schmidt-Isserstedt	6 discs
SXLC6476	Tchaikovsky: Symphonies 1-6	VPO	Maazel	5 discs
SXLD6515	Dvorak: The 9 Symphonies	LSO	Kertesz	7 discs
SXLE6558	Sibelius: The 7 Symphonies	VPO	Maazel	4 discs
SXLF6565	Rachmaninov: Piano Concertos 1-4, Rhapsody on theme of Paganini	LSO	Previn Ashkenazy	3 discs
SXLG6594	Beethoven: The 5 Piano Concertos	CSO	Solti Ashkenazy	4 discs
SXLH6610	Brahms: Symphonies 1-4/Vns on Theme by Haydn	VPO	Kertesz	4 discs
SXLJ6644	Schubert: The Symphonies	VPO	Kertesz	5 discs
SXLK6660	Schoenberg: Complete Orch Works	LSO	Atherton	5 discs
SXLM6665	Kodaly: Complete Orch works	PHun	Dorati	3 discs

Decca BB Sets

The BB series of Decca, Argo, and Oiseau Lyre sets were issued between 1971 and 1976 and most were available at a lower price ('BB' probably means 'Bargain Box').

Label: BB labels are the same as later SXL6000 labels but are in various colours – black, red, pale blue.

1BB101-3	Britten: Church Parables (Curlew River, Prodigal Son, Furnace)	English Opera Group	Britten	
2BB104-6	Verdi: Falstaff	RCA Italiana	Solti	
3BB107-8	Debussy: Preludes (complete)		Rodolphe Kars (pno)	
2BB109-11	Wagner: Flying Dutchman	ROHCG	Dorati London Rysanek	
2BB112-4	Strauss,R: Ariadne auf Naxos	VPO	Leinsdorf	
4BB115-8	Strauss,R: Der Rosenkavalier	VPO	Kleiber	[mono]
5BB119-20	25 Years at the Aldeburgh Festival	various	Britten	
6BB121-2	Beethoven: Symphony 9	CSO	Solti	
5BB123-4	Puccini: Tosca	VPO	Karajan DiStefano	
7BB125-9	Wagner: Die Walkure	LSO	Leinsdorf Nilsson	
5BB130-1	Bach: Brandenburg Concertos	StCO	Munchinger	
8BB132-5	Liszt: Complete Piano Works for Piano vol 1		France Clidat	
10BB168-70	Tchaikovsky: Swan Lake (complete)	Netherlands Radio Philh	Fistoulari Ricci	
6BB171-2	Bruckner: Symphony 4	VPO	Bohm	
7BB173-7	Mahler: Symphonies 1, 2, 3	CSO	Solti	

7BB178-82	Mahler: Symphonies 5, 6, 7	CSO	Solti	
7BB183-7	Mahler: Symphonies 4, 8, 9	CSO/ Ccgbw /LSO	Solti	
11BB188-196	Beethoven: Complete Symphonies + Ovs	CSO	Solti	
6BB197-8	Recital by Ferrier/Walter (Schubert,Schumann,Brahms)	Ferrier	Walter (pno)	[mono]
12BB203-6	Musicke of Sundrie Kindes (Renaissance Music)	Consort of Musicke Rooley		[Oiseau Lyre]
13BB207-12	Mozart: Violin Sonatas 17-28, 32-34	Goldberg Lupu		
14BB213-17	Bach,JS: Brandenburg Concertos 1-6, etc	StCO	Munchinger Malcolm (hpsd)	
15BB218-20	Prokofiev: Piano Concerto 1-5, etc	LSO	Previn Ashkenazy	
5BB221-2	Rachmaninov: 24 Preludes		Ashkenazy (pno)	
16BB223-32	"Your Hundred Best Tunes"	various		
6BB236-7	Beethoven:Symphony 3, Berlioz, Sibelius, Wagner	LPO	De Sabata	[mono]
1BBA1001-4	Handel:Coronation&Chandos Anthems,St Cecilia's Day Ode	KCC	Willcocks	[Argo]
2BBA1005-7	Messiaen: Catalogue d'Oiseau		Sherlaw Johnson (pno)	[Argo]
3BBA1008-10	Wolf: Morike Lieder		Luxon	[Argo]
4BBA1011-2	Couperin: Masses		Weir (organ)	[Argo]
5BBA1013-5	Organ Recital		Preston	[Argo]

Decca Dnnn Sets

The Dnnn series of sets were issued from 1976 and the final digit indicates the number of discs in the set.

Label: Dnnn labels are the same as later purple coloured SET labels.

D2D 3	Donizetti: Maria Stuarda	Bologna	Bonynge Sutherland Pavarotti	
D3D 4	Handel: Organ Concertos op 4/1-6, op 7/1-6 & 13-16	ASMF	Marriner Malcolm	[Argo]
D4D 3	Puccini: Madama Butterfly	AdSC	Serafin Tebaldi	[SXL2054-6]
D5D 2	Puccini: La Boheme	AdSC	Serafin Tebaldi Bergonzi	[SXL2170-1]
D6D 7	Dvorak: The 9 Symphonies	LSO	Kertesz	[SXLD6515]
D7D 4	Sibelius: The 7 Symphonies	VPO	Maazel	[SXLE6558]
D8D 6	Tchaikovsky: The 6 Symphonies, Manfred	VPO	Maazel	[SXLC6476]
D9D 3	Rachmaninov: The 3 Symphonies, The Rock	OSR	Weller	
D10D 4	Mozart: Don Giovanni	VPO	Leinsdorf Nilsson Price	[SER4528-31]
D11D 3	Bizet: Carmen	LPO	Solti Domingo	
D12D 5	Wagner: Lohengrin	Bayreuth 1953 Keilberth		[LXT2880-4]
D13D 5	Wagner: The Mastersingers of Nurnberg	VPO	Solti	
D18D 3	Handel: Messiah	ASMF	Marriner	[Argo]
D24D 3	Wagner: The Flying Dutchman	CSO	Solti Bailey Martin	
D26D 4	A Festival of English Music (Butterworth,Britten,Elgar,etc)	ASMF	Marriner	[Argo]
D29D 4	Byrd: My Ladye Nevells Booke		Hogwood (kbd)	[Oiseau Lyre]
D34D 2	Leoni: L'Oracolo	NPO	Bonynge Sutherland	
D37D 3	Tchaikovsky: Swan Lake	NPO	Bonynge	
D38D 3	Rossini: Barber of Seville	MMF	Erede Simionato Bastianini	[LXT5283-5]
D39D 4	Brahms: 4 Symphonies, Tragic Ov, Haydn Vns, Acad Fest Ov	Clvlnd	Maazel	[SXL6783, original]
D40D 3	Festival of Early Music	EMCL	Munrow	[Argo]
D41D 5	Wagner: Tristan & Isolde	VPO	Solti	[SET204-8]
D42D 3	Bach,JS: St Matthew Passion	Jacques Orch	Jacques	[from 78s]
D47D 3	Verdi: Aida	AdSC	Erede Tebaldi del Monaco	[LXT2735-7, electronic stereo]
D48D 3	Berg: Lulu	VPO	Dohnanyi	
D50D 2	Haydn: The Creation	RPO	Dorati etc	
D51D 2	Janacek: Kata Kabanova	VPO	Mackerras Söderström Dvorsky	
D55D 3	Verdi: Otello	VPO	Karajan Tebaldi del Monaco	[SET209-11]
D56D 4	Mozart: Cosi fan Tutte	LPO	Solti	[SET575-8]
D62D 4	Piano Concertos (Tchaikovsky,Rachmaninov,Beethoven,etc)	Various Orch&conductors	Ashkenazy	[SXLs]
D63D 3	Ponchielli: La Gioconda	AdSC	Previtali Milanov di Stefano	[SB2027-30]

D65D 3	"The Voice of the Century" (Puccini, Rossini, Gounod, etc)		Sutherland	[SXLs, SETs]
D68D 3	Puccini: Madama Butterfly	Barcelona SO	Gatto	
D69D 3	"A Baroque Festival" (Concertos by Vivaldi, Bach, Corelli, etc)	ASMF	Marriner	[Argo]
D77D 5	Beethoven: Symphonies 5,6,9, Piano Concerto 5, etc	various		[various]
D78D 3	Tchaikovsky: Sleeping Beauty	NPO	Bonynge	
D82D 3	Verdi: Il Trovatore	NPO	Bonynge Sutherland Pavarotti	
D83D 3	Leoncavallo: I Pagliacci	NPO	Patané Pavarotti	
	Mascagni: Cavalleria Rusticana	NPO	Gavazzeni Pavarotti	
D86D 3	Nicolai: Merry Wives of Windsor	BavSO	Kubelik	
D87D 2	Beethoven: Missa Solemnis	CSO	Solti Popp Minton	
D88D 3	Haydn: The Seasons	RPO	Dorati Cotrubas Sotin	
D92D 5	Beethoven: Violin Sonatas (complete)	Perlman	Ashkenazy	[SXL originals]
D93D 3	Donizetti: Lucrezia Borgia	NPO	Bonynge	
D94D 2	"Leopold Stokowski 1882-1977"	various	Stokowski	[PFS originals]
D95D 6	Tchaikovsky: Symphonies 1-6	LAPO	Mehta	
D96D 3	Donizetti: La Favorita	Teatro Comunale Bologna	Bonynge	
D97D 3	Wagner: Flying Dutchman	Bayreuth 1955	Keilberth	[LXT5150-2]
D99D 3	Vivaldi: Violin Concertos op 9/1-12 'La Cetra'	ASMF	Brown	[Argo]
D100D 19	Wagner: Der Ring des Nibelungen	VPO	Solti	[RING1-22]
D101D 10	Vivaldi: 4 Seasons,L'Estro Armonico,Stravaganza,La Cetra,etc	ASMF	Marriner	[Argo]
D102D 3	Verdi: Otello	VPO	Solti	
D103D 3	Strauss,R: Ariadne Auf Naxos	LPO	Solti Price Kollo	
D104D 3	Handel: Messiah	LSO	Boult Bumbry Sutherland	[SET218-20]
D105D 5	Schubert: The Symphonies (complete)	VPO	Kertesz	[SXL originals]
D108D 2	Smetana: Ma Vlast	IPO	Weller	
D112D 3	Choral Festival	St Johns Cambridge	Guest	[Argo]
D117D 2	Mahler: Symphony 3	LAPO	Mehta Forrester	
D120D 3	Bach,JS: Organ Works vol 1		Hurford	[Argo]
D121D 10	Mozart: Complete Dances and Marches	VPO	Boskowsky	[SXL originals]
D125D 3	Serate Musicali	Sutherland	Bonynge (pno)	
D129D 2	Operatic Recital	various	Pavarotti	[SXL,SET originals]
D130D 3	Paer: Leonora	BavRSO	Maag	
D131D 2	Humperdinck: Hansel and Gretel	VPO	Solti Popp Fassbender/etc	
D132D 4	Mozart: Marriage of Figaro	VPO	Karajan	
D133D 2	Mendelssohn: Walpurgis Nacht, Symphony 2	VPO	Dohnanyi	
D134D 2	Puccini: Tosca	NPO	Rescigno Freni Pavarotti	
D135D 2	Brahms: German Requiem, Haydn Variations	CSO	Solti Te Kanawa	
D137D 2	Berlioz: Requiem Mass	Clvlnd	Maazel	
D138D 3	Bach,JS: Organ Works vol 2		Hurford	[Argo]
D139D 4	Bach,JS: St Matthew Passion	Thames CO	Willcocks	
D144D 2	Janacek: The Makropoulos Affair	VPO	Mackerras	
D147D 2	New Year's Day Concert in Vienna, 1979	VPO	Boskovsky	
D148D 4	"Festival of Kings" (Allegri,Gibbons,Byrd,Tallis,Bach,etc)	KCC	Willcocks/Ledger	[Argo]
D150D 3	Bach,JS: Organ Works vol 3		Hurford	[Argo]
D151D 4	Brahms: Symphonies 1-4	CSO	Solti	[SXL6890, originals]
D155D 4	Beethoven: String Quartets 12-16, Grosse Fuge	Aeolian Quartet		[Argo]
D156D 3	Massenet: Don Quichotte	OSR	Kord Ghiaurov	
D162D 4	Mozart: Don Giovanni	LPO	Solti	
D165D 3	Franck: Organ Works		Steed	
D167D 3	Mozart: The Complete Symphonies vol 1	AAM	Hogwood/Schröder	[Oiseau Lyre]
D168D 3	Mozart: The Symphonies vol 2 (9,14-17, etc)	AAM	Hogwood/Schröder	[Oiseau Lyre]
D169D 3	Mozart: The Salzburg Symphonies vol 1 (18-24, 26,27)	AAM	Hogwood/Schröder	[Oiseau Lyre]
D170D 3	Mozart: Salzburg Symphonies vol 2 (25,28-30,etc)	AAM	Hogwood Schröder	[Oiseau Lyre]
D171D 4	Mozart: The Symphonies vol 5 (32-36, etc)	AAM	Hogwood/Schröder	[Oiseau Lyre]
D172D 4	Mozart: Symphonies vol 6 (31,35,38-41)	AAM	Hogwood/Schröder	[Oiseau Lyre,digital]
D173D 3	Mozart: Symphonies vol 7 (6, 7, 8, 37, etc)	AAM	Hogwood/Schröder	[Oiseau Lyre, digital]

D176D 3	Strauss,R: Die Aegyptische Helena	Detroit SO	Dorati	
D177D 3	Bach,JS: Organ Works vol 4		Hurford	[Argo]
D178D 3	Beethoven: Fidelio	CSO	Solti	
D181D 4	Handel: Jephtha	ASMF	Marriner	[Argo]
D182D 3	Beethoven: Piano Sonatas vol 1 (Nos 1-7)		Binns	[Oiseau Lyre]
D183D 3	Beethoven: Piano Sonatas vol 2 (Sonatas 8-15)		Binns	[Oiseau Lyre]
D184D 3	Beethoven: Piano Sonatas vol 3 (Sonatas 16-23)		Binns	[Oiseau Lyre]
D185D 3	Beethoven: Piano Sonatas vol 4 (Sonatas 24-32)		Binns	[Oiseau Lyre]
D186D 4	Le Chansonnier Cordiforme	Consort of Musicke Rooley		[Oiseau Lyre]
D187D 5	Dowland: Lute Music		Rooley etc	[Oiseau Lyre]
D188D 7	Shostakovich: String Quartets	Fitzwilliam Quartet		
D189D 3	Handel: Messiah	AAM	Hogwood	[Argo]
D190D 3	Schumann: Symphonies 1-4, Ov Scherzo&Finale	VPO	Solti	[SXLs]
D195D 2	Schubert: Violin Sonata D574,Sonatinas 1-3,Fantasie D934	Lupu (pno) Goldberg (vln)		
D207D 3	Bach,JS: Organ Works vol 5		Hurford	[Argo]
D210D 3	Massenet: Le Roi de Lahore	NPO	Bonynge	[digital]
D212D 3	Verdi: La Traviata	NPO	Bonynge Pavarotti Sutherland	[digital]
D213D 2	Shostakovitch: Symphony 7, Age of Gold Ballet Suite	LPO	Haitink	[digital]
D214D 2	Beethoven: String Quartets Op 59/1-3 ("Rasumovsky")	Gabrielli Quartet		
D216D 4	Haydn: Il Ritorno di Tobia	RPO	Dorati	
D219D 4	Rossini: William Tell	NPO	Chailly Freni Pavarotti	
D220D 3	Mozart: The Haydn Quartets	Esterhazy Quartet		[Oiseau Lyre]
D221D 2	Bruckner: Symphony 5	CSO	Solti	[digital]
D222D 6	Mozart: The Complete Piano Sonatas		Schiff	
D223D 5	Janacek: Piano and Chamber Works	London Sinfonietta Atherton		
D224D 2	Janacek: From the House of the Dead	VPO	Mackerras	
D225D 2	Strauss,J: Cinderella Ballet, Ritter Pasman Ballet Suite	NPO	Bonynge	[digital]
D226D 3	Bach,JS: Organ Works vol 6		Hurford	[Argo]
D227D 3	Bach,JS: Organ Works vol 7	Alban Singers Hurford		[Argo]
D228D 4	Bach,JS: Organ Works vol 8	St Johns Cambridge Hurford		[Argo]
D229D 2	Mahler: Symphony 2	CSO	Solti	[digital]
D230D 3	Bellini: La Sonnambula	NPO	Bonynge Sutherland Pavarotti	[digital]
D231D 2	Berg: Wozzeck	VPO	Dohnanyi	[digital]
D232D 3	Ponchielli: La Gioconda	NPO	Bartoletti	[digital]
D235D 3	Weber: Der Freischutz	BavSO	Kubelik Behrens Kollo	
D236D 2	Pavarotti's Greatest Hits	various	Pavarotti	[SET,SXL originals]
D237D 6	Dufay: Complete Secular Music	Mediaeval Ensemble of London Davies		[Oiseau Lyre]
D238D 2	Ward: Madrigals 1613, 4 Viol Fantasias 34,8,14	Consort of Musicke Rooley		[Oiseau Lyre]
D239D 4	Mozart: Violin Concertos (complete)	RPO	Weller Fujikawa (vln)	
D240D 3	Vivaldi: 4 Seasons, Gloria, 8 Concertos	ASMF	Marriner Loveday (vln)	[Argo]
D241D 3	Bach,JS: Suite 3, 6 Concertos, Cantata 170	ASMF	Marriner	[Argo]
D242D 3	Handel: Water Music,Fireworks Music,Organ Concerto,etc	ASMF	Marriner	[Argo]
D243D 3	Mozart: Symphonies 25, 29, Violin Concerto K216, etc	ASMF	Marriner Loveday (vln)	[Argo]
D244D 3	St-Saens: Piano Concertos 1-5 , etc	Philh/RPO/LPO Dutoit Rog■		
D245D 2	Vivaldi: L'Estro Armonico op 3	AAM	Hogwood	[Oiseau Lyre]
D246D 3	Tippett: King Priam	London Sinfonietta Atherton		[digital]
D247D 3	Strauss,J: Die Fledermaus	VPO	Karajan	[SET201-3 digitally remastered]
D248D 2	Berlioz: Childhood of Christ	Goldsbrough Orch Davis		[Argo from SOL60032-3]
D249D 4	Tchaikovsky: Symphonies 4-6, Manfred	Philh	Ashkenazy	[SXLs]
D250D 5	Wagner: Tristan und Isolde	Welsh NatOp Goodall		[digital]
D251D 5	Mozart: "Concert Arias for Soprano"	Vienna CO Fischer Te Kanawa etc		
D252D 2	Gay: The Beggar's Opera	NPO	Bonynge	[digital]
D254D 3	Ockeghem: Secular Music	Mediaeval Ensemble of London Davies		[Oiseau Lyre]
D255D 2	"Live from Lincoln Center" (Sutherland ,Pavarotti,Horne)	NY City Op Bonynge		[digital]
D256D 3	Handel: La Resurrezione	AAM	Hogwood Kirkby Partridge	[Oiseau Lyre]

D257D 2	Janacek: The Cunning Little Vixen	VPO	Mackerras	[digital]
D258D 12	Beethoven: Piano Sonatas (complete)		Ashkenazy	[SXLs]
D259D 3	Berlioz: Damnation of Faust	CSO	Solti	[digital]
D260D 2	Frescobaldi: Keyboard Music		Hogwood	[Oiseau Lyre]
D261D 2	Fitzwilliam Virginal Book (hlts)		Hogwood (hpsd,organ,etc)	[Oiseau Lyre]
D262D 2	Haydn: The Creation	CSO	Solti	[digital]
D263D 2	Haydn: Music for England	AAM	Hogwood Nelson (sop)	[Oiseau Lyre]
D264D 2	Mahler: Symphony 2	Ccgbw	Klemperer Ferrier Vincent	[1951 mono recording]
D266D 3	Violin Concs (Beethoven,Bruch,Chausson,St-Saens,Sibelius)	various	Kyung Wha Chung	[SXL, SXDL originals]
D267D 4	Mozart: Marriage of Figaro	LPO	Solti Te Kanawa	[digital]
D268D 2	Music at Court	AAM	Hogwood Elliot (ten)	[Oiseau Lyre]
D270D 3	Boito: Mefistofele	NPO	de Fabritiis Ghiaurov Pavarotti	[digital]
D271D 3	Piano Concertos (Tchaikovsky 1,Chopin 2,Schumann,etc)	various	Ashkenazy	[SXLs]
D272D 3	Rameau: Hyppolyte et Aricie	ECO	Lewis	[Argo from SOL286-8]
D273D 3	Verdi: I Masnadieri	Welsh Nat Op	Bonynge	[digital]
D274D 2	Mahler: Symphony 9	CSO	Solti	[digital]
D275D 2	Bach,JS: Goldberg Vns, Duets BWV 802-5		Schiff (pno)	[digital]
D276D 3	Janacek: Jenufa	VPO	Mackerras Soderstrom Randova	[digital]
D279D 2	Vivaldi: The Trial between Harmony and Invention	AAM	Hogwood	[Oiseau Lyre,digital]
D280D 3	Beethoven: String Quartets op 18/1-6	Gabrieli Quartet		[digital]
D281D 2	Mahler: Symphony 3	CSO	Solti Dernesch	[digital]
D282D 2	Chamber Music at Versailles, 1697-1747	AAM	Hogwood Nelson (sop)	[Oiseau Lyre]

Decca/Argo - the Haydn Series

During the 1970s Decca issued three major Haydn series. These came in a collection of box sets issued over a period of 7 years.

Therecord label is blue-grey with silver lettering and includes an outline sketch of the composer.

Haydn Symphony Series (Decca label)

The complete symphonies in 9 box sets plus 2 disc gatefold sets of the appendices and the 24 minuets, played by the Philharmonia Hungarica with Dorati

HDNA1-6	Haydn: Symphonies 1-19	Phun	Dorati
HDNB7-12	Haydn: Symphonies 20-35	Phun	Dorati
HDNC13-18	Haydn: Symphonies 36-48	Phun	Dorati
HDND19-22	Haydn: Symphonies 49-56	Phun	Dorati
HDNE23-26	Haydn: Symphonies 57-64	Phun	Dorati
HDNF27-30	Haydn: Symphonies 65-72	Phun	Dorati
HDNG31-34	Haydn: Symphonies 73-81	Phun	Dorati
HDNH35-40	Haydn: Symphonies 82-92	Phun	Dorati
HDNJ41-46	Haydn: Symphonies 93-104	Phun	Dorati
HDNK47-48	Haydn: The Minor Symphonies	Phun	Dorati
HDNW90-1	Haydn: 24 Minuets H IX: 16	Phun	Dorati

Haydn Quartet Series (Argo label)

The complete string quartets in 8 box sets played by the Aeolian Quartet

HDNL49-51	Haydn: The Early String Quartets Op 71 and Op 74	Aeolian Quartet
HDNM52-56	Haydn: The Early String Quartets	Aeolian Quartet
HDNP57-60	Haydn: String Quartets Op 76 & Op 77 & Op 103	Aeolian Quartet
HDNQ61-66	Haydn: String Quartets Op 9 & Op 17	Aeolian Quartet
HDNS67-69	Haydn: String Quartets Op 54 & Op 55	Aeolian Quartet
HDNT70-75	Haydn: String Quartets Op 20 & Op 64	Aeolian Quartet
HDNU76-81	Haydn: String Quartets Op 33 & Op 42 & Op 50	Aeolian Quartet
HDNV82-84	Haydn: String Quartets Op 3 & Op 51	Aeolian Quartet

Haydn Piano Sonata Series (Decca label)

The complete piano sonatas in 5 box sets played by the John McCabe

HDN100-2	Haydn: Piano Sonatas Vol 1	John McCabe
HDN103-5	Haydn: Piano Sonatas Vol 2	John McCabe
HDN106-8	Haydn: Piano Sonatas Vol 3	John McCabe
HDN109-11	Haydn: Piano Sonatas Vol 4	John McCabe
HDN112-15	Haydn: Piano Sonatas Vol 5	John McCabe

* * * * *

SXL2000 series

Label: The early Decca SXL2000 label is black with silver logo and lettering. In the top half of the label the word 'Decca' is in large type face (about 1.5 cms high letters), and above it is the 'ffss' logo. Just above the spindle hole there is a 1 cm wide silver band with the lettering "FULL FREQUENCY STEREOPHONIC SOUND". This label is often referred to as "wide band" and was in use up to 1968-9. Consequently, all of the SXL2000 series have earliest pressing labels like this.

In the earliest samples this "wide band" label also has a concentric groove of about 3 cms radius, or about 1 cm in from the label edge.

In late samples (often referred to as "narrow band") the label remains black, but with the following changes: The 'ffss' logo is no longer used; The silver band above the spindle reduces to ½ cm wide, and the word "DECCA" is now in 1 cm high lettering inside a rectangular box. The quality of these later pressings is very high. Indeed, many people (including the author) believe that they are often better than the early pressings because the quality of English vinyl was better in the late 60s than it had been in the late 50s to early 60s.

The very earliest in the Decca SXL2000 series have jackets with a blue border on the back. These are quite rare and are found only on the earliest copies of Deccas before about SXL2110.

Cat. No.	Work	Orch.	Artists	Refs
SXL2001	Tchaikovsky: Ov 1812/Capriccio Italien/Marche Slave	LSO	Alwyn	(CS6038 SDD112 SPA92) RM17
SXL2002	Beethoven: Piano Concerto 5	VPO	Knappertsbusch/Curzon	(CS6019 SPA334) RM14
SXL2003	Beethoven: Symphony 5/Egmont Ov	OSR	Ansermet	(CS6037, SDD105) RM14
SXL2004	Tchaikovsky: Symphony 6	VPO	Martinon	(CS6052 SDD138)
SXL2005	Dvorak: Symphony 5 (New World)	VPO	Kubelik	(CS6020 SDD128) RM15
SXL2006	Mendelssohn: Vln Conc/Bruch Vln Conc 1	LSO	Gamba Ricci	(CS6010 SPA88) RM16
SXL2007	La Boutique Fantasque	IPO	Solti	(CS6005 SDD109 SPA376) RM14
SXL2008	Overtures in HiFi	PCO	Wolff	(CS6015) RM15
SXL2009	Berlioz: Symphonie Fantasque	PCO	Argenta	(CS6025 SDD115) RM15
SXL2010	Beethoven Piano Concerto 4	VPO	Schmidt-Isserstedt/Backhaus	(CS6054) RM12
SXL2011	Stravinsky: Petrouchka	SRO	Ansermet	(CS6009 ECS819) RM15 TAS 42/83+ TASEC
SXL2012	Grieg: Peer Gynt Incidental Music	LSO	Fjeldstad	(CS6049 SDD111) RM19
SXL2013	Brahms: Symphony 1	VPO	Kubelik	(CS6016) RM14
SXL2014	Giordano: Andre Chenier (hlts)		Tebaldi Bastianini Monaco	
SXL2015	Tchaikovsky: Symphony 4	SRO	Argenta	(CS6048) RM12
SXL2016	This is Vienna	VPO	Knappertsbusch	(CS6014) RM10
SXL2017	Stravinsky: The Firebird	SRO	Ansermet	(CS6017 SDD246 ECS817) RM13
SXL2019	Vivaldi: 4 Seasons	StCO	Munchinger	(CS6044) RM13
SXL2020	Espana (Chabrier, Rimsky-Korsakov, Granados, Moszkowski)	LSO	Argenta	(CS6006 SDD216 ECS797) RM19 TASEC
SXL2021	Massenet: Le Cid/Meyerbeer Les Patineurs	IPO	Martinon	(CS6058 SDD139 SPA203) RM14
SXL2022-3	Lehar: The Merry Widow	VSop	Stoltz	(SDD113-4)
SXL2024	Chopin: Recital		Kempff	(CS6041 SDD177) RM14
SXL2025	Chopin: Sonata 2 (Funeral March)		Kempff	(CS6042 SDD195) RM14
SXL2026	Mendelssohn: Vln Conc/Bruch Scottish Fantasia	LPO	Boult Campoli	(CS6047 SDD110 ECS775) RM14
SXL2027	Debussy: Jeux/Dukas La Peri	OSR	Ansermet	(CS6043 SDD375) RM19
SXL2028	Schubert: Octet in Fmaj		Vienna Octet	(CS6051 SDD230) RM16
SXL2029	Tchaikovsky: Violin Concerto	LSO	Argenta Campoli	(CS6011 SPA183) RM16

Catalog	Work	Orchestra	Performers	Reissues
SXL2030	Sibelius: Song Recital	LSO	Flagstad Fjeldstad	(OS25005 SDD248 ECS794)
SXL2031-2	Wagner: Die Walkure Act III	VPO	Solti Flagstad Edelmann	
SXL2033	*			
SXL2034	Tchaikovsky Concert Fantasia/Rachmaninov PC 1	LPO	Boult Katin	(CS6055) RM12
SXL2035	Mozart: Marriage of Figaro (hlts)	VPO	Kleiber	
SXL2037	Bizet: Carmen/L'Arlesienne Suites	OSR	Ansermet	(CS6062 SDD141 ECS755) RM17
SXL2038	*			
SXL2039-41	Puccini: La Fanciulla del West	AdSC	Tebaldi Del Monaco	
SXL2042	Stravinsky: Rite of Spring	OSR	Ansermet	(CS6031 ECS818) RM13 TAS 38/157
SXL2043	Recital		Tebaldi	(no CS)
SXL2044	Chopin: Les Sylphides/Delibes	PCO	Maag	(CS6026 SDD221 ECS809) RM15
SXL2045	Schubert: Symphony 9	LSO	Krips	(CS6061 SPA467) RM18
SXL2046	Mozart: Eine Kleine Nachtmusik, Tchaikovsky Serenade	IPO	Solti	(CS6066) RM15
SXL2047	Strauss,J: Blue Danube	VPO	Krips	(CS6007, SDD133) RM15
SXL2048	Recital		Bergonzi	(no CS)
SXL2049	Great Sacred Songs		Flagstad	(SDD207)
SXL2050-3	Strauss, R: Arabella	VPO	Solti	
SXL2054-6	Puccini: Madame Butterfly		Serafin Tebaldi Bergonzi	
SXL2057	Stereo Frequency Test Record			(no CS)
SXL2058	Mozart: Cosi Fan Tutte (hlts)	VPO	Bohm	
SXL2059	Brahms: Symphony 2	VPO	Kubelik	(CS6004) RM14
SXL2060	Mendelssohn: A Midsummer Night's Dream	LSO	Maag Vyvyan Lowe	(CS6001 SDD159 SPA451) RM19 TAS 49
SXL2061	*			
SXL2062	Ravel: Ma Mere l'Oye/Debussy:Nocturnes.	SRO	Ansermet	(CS6023 SDD374 ECS815/ECS816) RM18
SXL2063	*			
SXL2064-5	Smetana Ma Vlast	VPO	Kubelik	(CSA2202 SDD161/2)
SXL2066	*			
SXL2067	Mendelssohn: Symphony 4/Schubert Symphony 5	IPO	Solti	(CS6065 SDD121) RM14
SXL2068	Wagner: Great Scenes from Wagner	VPO	Knappertsbusch George London	(SDD143 no CS)
SXL2069-72	Verdi: Forza del Destino		Molinari-Pradelli Tebaldi Monaco	
SXL2074-5	Wagner: Die Walkure Act I/etc.	VPO	Knappertsbusch Flagstad	(no CS)
SXL2076	Rachmaninov: Concerto 2	LSO	Solti Katchen	(CS6064 SDD181) RM14 SM86+
SXL2077	Sibelius Violin Concerto	LSO	Fjeldstad Ricci	(CS6067 SDD276 SPA398) RM15
SXL2078-80	Puccini: Turandot	AdSC	Erede Tebaldi, Del Monaco	
SXL2081	Chopin: Recital		Kempff	(CS6040) RM14
SXL2082	Strauss,J: Concert	VPO	Boskovsky	(CS6008) RM17
SXL2083	'Italy'		Giuseppi di Stefano	(no CS)
SXL2084-5	Coppelia	OSR	Ansermet	(CSA2201 SDD371/2 DPA581/2)
SXL2086	Rimsky-Korsakov: Scheherazade	PCO	Ansermet	(CS6018) RM15
SXL2087-90	Mozart: Marriage of Figaro	VPO	Kleiber	
SXL2091	Rodrigo: Guitar Concerto/Falla:Nights	NOS	Argenta Yepes	(CS6046 SDD446 SPA233) RM18 TASEC65
SXL2092-3	Tchaikovsky: Nutcracker Suite	OSR	Ansermet	(CSA2203 SDD378/9 SPA357)
SXL2094-6	Boito: Mephistopheles		Tebaldi Monaco	
SXL2097	Liszt: Piano Concertos 1/2	LPO	Argenta Katchen	(CS6033 SDD124 SPA318) RM14
SXL2098	Haydn: Symphonies 94/99	VPO	Krips	(CS6027) RM11
SXL2099	*			
SXL2100	Leimer: Piano Concerto	VPO	Leimer	(no CS)
SXL2101-3	Wagner: Das Rheingold	VPO	Solti	
SXL2104	Brahms: Symphony 3	VPO	Kubelik	(CS6022)
SXL2105	Ravel: Bolero/Falla: 3 Cornered Hat, Weber: Invn to the Dance	PCO	Wolff	(CS6077) RM13
SXL2106	Beethoven Piano Concerto 3	LSO	Gamba Katchen	(CS6096)
SXL2107-8	Tchaikovsky: Swan Lake	OSR	Ansermet	(CSA2204 SDD354/5 DPS603/4)
SXL2109	Tchaikovsky: Symphony 5	VPO	Krips	(CS6095) RM13
SXL2110	Schubert: Trout Quintet		Vienna Octet Curzon	(CS6090 SDD185) RM18
SXL2111	Operatic Recital (Puccini, Massenet, Gounod, etc)	AdSC	Patané Di Stefano	(no CS)

SXL2112	Weber: Overtures	OSR	Ansermet	(CS6074 ECS645) RM14
SXL2113	Rimsky Korsakov: Xmas Eve/Sadko/Dubinushka/etc.	OSR	Ansermet	(CS6036 SDD281) RM16
SXL2114	Tchaikovsky: Piano Concerto 1	LSO	Solti Curzon	(CS6100 SDD191)
SXL2115	Handel: Organ Concertos vol 1: op 4/1-4	Karl Richter		(CSA2302, SDD470-1)
SXL2116	Beethoven Symphony 4	OSR	Ansermet	(CS6070, SDD104) RM15
SXL2117-20	Mozart: Don Giovanni	VPO	Krips Siepi Della Casa Gueden	
SXL2121	Beethoven: Symphony 7	VPO	Solti	(CS6093) RM13
SXL2122	Great Tenor Arias	del Monaco		(no CS)
SXL2123	Puccini: Arias	Virginia Zeani		(no CS)
SXL2124	Beethoven: Symphony 5	VPO	Solti	(CS6092) RM14
SXL2125	Bach: Brandenburg Concertos 1/6	StCO	Munchinger	(CSA2301)
SXL2126	Bach: Brandenburg Concertos 2/5	St CO	Munchinger	(no CS)
SXL2127	Bach: Brandenburg Concertos 3/4	StCO	Munchinger	(no CS)
SXL2128	Adam: Giselle	PCO	Martinon	(CS6098 SDD125 SPA384) RM16
SXL2129-31	Verdi: Il Trovatore	Tozzi Tebaldi Monaco		
SXL2132	Rossini: Arias	Berganza		(no CS)
SXL2133	Lehar: Merry Widow (hlts)	VSOp	Stolz Gueden Loose	(no CS)
SXL2134	Berlioz: Various	PCO	Martinon	(CS6101 SDD217) RM15
SXL2135	Mozart: Symphonies 32/38	LSO	Maag	(CS6107 SDD122) RM14
SXL2136	Debussy: la Boite a Joujoux/Printemps	OSR	Ansermet	(CS6079 SDD293) RM20
SXL2137	*			
SXL2140	*			
SXL2141	Glazunov: The Seasons	PCO	Wolff	(CS6116) RM13
SXL2145	Songs from Norway	LSO	Fjeldstad Flagstad	(SDD209)
SXL2148	*			
SXL2150-2	Peter Grimes	ROHCG	Britten	
SXL2153	Tchaikovsky: Swan Lake (hlts)	OSR	Ansermet	(CS6127) RM18
SXL2154	Strauss,R; Also Sprach Zarathustra	VPO	Karajan	(CS6129 SDD175) RM12
SXL2155	Lalo: Symphonie Espagnole/Ravel Tzigane	OSR	Ansermet Ricci	(CS6134 ECS670) RM12
SXL2156	Schubert: Symphonies 2/8	VPO	Munchinger	(CS6131) RM12
SXL2157	Beethoven: Septet	Vienna Octet		(CS6132 SDD200) RM18
SXL2158	Beethoven: Quintet in Eflat for pno&wind/etc	Vienna Octet Panhoffer		(CS6063 SDD256) RM16
SXL2159	Operatic Arias	Sutherland		(no CS)
SXL2160-2	Tchaikovsky: Sleeping Beauty	OSR	Ansermet	(CSA2304 SPA358)
SXL2163	Vienna Carnival	VPO	Boskovsky	(CS6149) RM14
SXL2164	Ravel: Daphnis & Chloe	LSO	Monteux	(CS6147 SDD170) RM19
SXL2165	Beethoven: Symphony 3	VPO	Solti	(CS6145, SDD103) RM12
SXL2166	Tchaikovsky: Symphony 4	PCO	Wolff	(CS6150 SDD131)
SXL2167-9	Verdi: Aida.	VPO	Karajan Tebaldi Bergonzi TASEC44 TAS32/158+	
SXL2170-1	Puccini: La Boheme	Serafin Tebaldi Bergonzi		
SXL2172	Brahms PC 1	LSO	Monteux Katchen	(CS6151 SDD137 SPA385) RM14
SXL2173	Grieg: Piano Concerto/Franck: Symphonic Variations	LSO	Boult Curzon	(CS6157) RM16
SXL2174	Suppe: Overtures	VPO	Solti	(CS6146 SDD194) RM16
SXL2175	Puccini: Turandot (hlts)	Erebe		(no CS)
SXL2176	Rachmaninov: Rhaps on Paganini/Dohnanyi Varns	LPO	Boult Katchen	(CS6153 SDD428) RM15
SXL2177	Wolf-Ferrari: Music of Wolf-Ferrari	PCO	Nello-Santi	(CS6154 SDD452) RM16
SXL2178	Beethoven: Piano Concertos 1/2	VPO	Schmidt-Isserstedt Backhaus	(CS6099/6188)
SXL2179	Beethoven: Piano Concerto 5	VPO	Schmidt-Isserstedt Backhaus	(CS6156)
SXL2180-1	Puccini: Tosca	AdSC	Pradelli	
SXL2182	Rossini Overtures	PCO	Maag	(CS6089) RM16
SXL2183	Liszt: Recital	Peter Katin		(CS6106) RM16
SXL2184	Wagner: Tristan & Isolde excerpts	VPO	Knappertsbutsch Nilsson	(no CS)
SXL2185-6	Leoncavallo: Pagliacci	Molinari-Pradelli Del Monaco etc		
SXL2187	Handel: Organ Concertos Vol 2: op 4, op 5, op 6, op 7/1-2	Karl Richter		(CSA2302, SDD470-1)
SXL2188	Stravinsky Song of the Nightingale/Pulcinella	OSR	Ansermet	(CS6138 SDD136 ECS776) RM16

Catalog	Title	Orchestra	Artist	Reference
SXL2189	Britten: 4 Sea Interludes/Nocturne	ROHCG	Britten Pears	(CS6179) RM19
SXL2190	Beethoven: Piano Concerto 3	VPO	Schmidt-Isserstedt Backhaus	(CS6094) RM14
SXL2191	Recital of lute songs	Bream	Peter Pears	
SXL2192	Boito: Mefistofele	AdSC	Serafin	
SXL2193	Beethoven: Symphony 6	OSR	Ansermet	(CS6160 SDD106) RM13
SXL2194	Paganini: 24 Caprices	Ricci		(CS6163 ECS803) RM16
SXL2195	Mussorgsky: Pictures at an Exhibition	OSR	Ansermet	(CS6177 SPA229) RM13
SXL2196	Mozart: Serenata Notturna K329/Notturno for 4 Orchs	LSO	Maag	(CS6133 SDD171 ECS740 SPA550) RM19
SXL2197	Bizet:Carmen Fantasie, Sarasate: Zigeunerweisen, St-Saens	LSO	Gamba Ricci	(CS6165 SDD420 ECS808) RM16
SXL2198	Philharmonic Ball	VPO	Boskovsky	(CS6182) RM18
SXL2199	The Instruments of the Orchestra	Malcolm Sargent		(no CS)
SXL2200	Die Schone Mullerin	Pears	Britten	(no CS)
SXL2201	Handel: Organ Concertos Vol 3: op 7/3-6	Karl Richter		(CSA2302, SDD470-1)
SXL2202	Puccini: Madame Butterfly highlights	AdSC	Serafin	(no CS)
SXL2204	Bach: The Musical Offering	StCO	Munchinger	(CS6142 SDD310) RM15
SXL2205	Bach: English Suite 6, French Suite 5, Preludes & Fugues	Backhaus		(no CS)
SXL2206	Brahms: Symphony 4	VPO	Kubelik	(CS6170) RM13
SXL2207	Vaughan Williams Symphony 8	Philh	Boult	(CS6078) RM16
SXL2208-10	Giordano: Andre Chenier	AdSC	Gavazeni	
SXL2211	Fauré: Requiem	OSR	Ansermet	(no CS)
SXL2212	Ravel: L'Enfants et Les Sortilege	OSR	Ansermet	(no CS SDD168)
SXL2213	Italian Opera Recital	Cesare Siepi (bass)		(no CS)
SXL2214	Mozart: Piano Concerto 27/Sonata 11	VPO	Bohm Backhaus	(CS6141 SDD116) RM10
SXL2215-7	Mozart: The Magic Flute	VPO	Bohm	
SXL2218	Prokofiev Peter and the Wolf	LSO	Katchen Henderson Graffman Lillie	(CS6187) RM18
SXL2219	Bach Organ Recital	Richter		(CS6172) RM14
SXL2220	Mozart Symphonies 41/35	IPO	Krips	(CS6081, SDD178)
SXL2221	Rimsky-K Tale of Tsar Saltan/Russian Easter Festival	OSR	Ansermet	(CS6012 SDD282) RM16
SXL2222	Brahms: piano Recital	Backhaus		(CS6021) RM13
SXL2223	Schumann: Symphonies 1/4	LSO	Krips	(no CS)
SXL2224	Mahler Kindertotenlieder/Fahrenden Gesellen	VPO	Boult Flagstad	(SDD215)
SXL2225-7	Ponchielli: La Gioconda	MMF	Gavazzeni	
SXL2228	Beethoven: Symphony 2/Leonora 2 Ov	OSR	Ansermet	(CS6184, SDD102) RM14
SXL2229	Mendelsshohn: Midsmr Nights drm/Schubert Rosamunde	OSR	Ansermet	(CS6186) RM13
SXL2230	Wagner: Das Rheingold/Die Walkure highlights	VPO	Solti	(no CS)
SXL2231	Ravel: String quartet/Prokofiev String quartet	Carmirelli Qt		(CS6174) RM15
SXL2232	Searle: Symphony 1/Seiber: Elegy etc	Melos CO LPO Boult Seiber		(CS6196) RM18
SXL2233	Mozart: Concert Arias, Haydn: Scena di Berenice	Haydn Orch Newstone Vyvyan		(no CS)
SXL2234	Bach/Handel arias	LPO	Boult Ferrier	(no CS)
SXL2235	Beethoven Symphony 7/Fidelio Ov	OSR	Ansermet	(CS6183 SDD107 SPA237) RM12
SXL2236	Brahms: Piano Concerto 2	LSO	Ferencsik Katchen	(CS6195 SDD223) RM14
SXL2237	Stravinsky: Symphony in C/Symph in 3 movements.	OSR	Ansermet	(CS6190, SDD239) RM14
SXL2238	Mozart: Horn Concertos	LSO	Maag Tuckwell	(CS6178) RM19
SXL2239	All Time popular favs	VPO	Knappertsbusch	(CS6192)
SXL2240	Recital (Bartok, Stravinsky, Prokofiev, Hindemith)	Ricci		(CS6193) RM15
SXL2241	Beethoven Sonatas 21 (Waldstein)/23 (appassionata)	Backhaus		(CS6161)
SXL2242	Verdi: Aida excerpts	VPO	Karajan Tebaldi Bergonzi	(no CS)
SXL2243	Albeniz: Iberia/Turina: Danzas Fantasticas	OSR	Ansermet	(CS6194 SDD180) RM16
SXL2244	Beethoven Symphony 3	OSR	Ansermet	(CS6189)
SXL2245	Classical Indian Music introduced by Menuhin			(CS6213) RM20
SXL2246	Mendelssohn: Symphony 3/Fingal's Cave	LSO	Maag	(CS6191 SDD145 SPA503) RM20 TAS44/178
SXL2247	Cimarosa: Il Maestro di Capella/other arias	Corena (bass)		(no CS)
SXL2248	Puccini: La Boheme highlights	AdSC	Serafin	(no CS)
SXL2249	Hungarian/Slavonic Dances (Brahms/Dvorak)	VPO	Reiner	(CS6198 SDD123 SPA377) RM17
SXL2250	Strauss (arr Dorati) Graduation Ball etc	VPO	Boskovsky	(CS6199 SDD127) RM14

Cat. No.	Title	Performer(s)	Reissues
SXL2251	Arias of the 18th Century (Gluck, Cherubini, Handel)	Teresa Berganza	(no CS)
SXL2252	Bizet: Jeux D'Enfants/Ibert: Divertissement/etc	PCO Martinon	(CS6200 SDD144 ECS782) SM67/138++
SXL2253-5	Mascagni: Cavalleria/Leoncavallo: Pagliacci	Acad di St Cec ilia Serafin	
SXL2256	The Art of the Prima Donna v1	Sutherland	(CSA2213)
SXL2257	The Art of the Prima Donna v2	Sutherland	(CSA2213)
SXL2258	Puccini: Tosca hlts	AdSC Pradelli Tebaldi	(no CS)
SXL2259	Bach, J.S: Italian Concerto/etc	George Malcolm	(CS6197 SDD272) RM17
SXL2260	Falla: El Amor Brujo/Retablo De Maese Pedro	OSR Ansermet/Argenta	(CS6028 SDD134) RM20
SXL2261	Strauss,R: Till Eulenspiegel/Death&Transfiguration	VPO Karajan	(CS6211 SDD211) RM16
SXL2262	Beethoven: Diabelli Variations	Katchen	(CS6203)
SXL2263	French Overtures	OSR Ansermet	(CS6205 SDD192 ECS827) RM16
SXL2264	Britten: Spring Symphony	ROHCG Britten	(no CS)
SXL2265	Corelli: Concerto Grosso 8/etc	StCO Munchinger	(CS6206) RM16
SXL2266	Rossini Overtures (Magpie, Barber, Semiramide, Tell, Ladder)	LSO Gamba	(CS6204) RM14
SXL2267	Puccini: Fanciulla del West excerpts	AdSC Capuana	(no CS)
SXL2268	Rimsky-Korsakov: Scheherazade/Borodin Polv Dances	OSR Ansermet	(CS6212 ECS735) RM15
SXL2269	Tchaikovsky: Romeo & Juliet ov/Strauss Don Juan	VPO Karajan	(CS6209) RM15
SXL2270	Mozart: Eine Kleine Nachtmusik/Musical Joke/etc	StCO Munchinger	(CS6207 ECS686) RM17
SXL2271	Recital (Rossini, Donizetti, Mozart, Bellini)	Graziella Sciutti	(no CS)
SXL2272	Mozart: Haffner Serenade K250	VPO Munchinger	(CS6214 SDD198) RM13
SXL2273	Ravel: Daphnis & Chloe/Alborado/Tombeau/Valses	OSR Ansermet	(CS6210) RM12
SXL2274	Beethoven: Symphony 9	OSR Ansermet	(CS6143 SDD108 SPA328) RM14
SXL2275	Bizet Symphony in C	OSR Ansermet	(CS6208 SDD231) RM16
SXL2276	Mahler: Symphony 4	Ccgbw Solti Stahlman	(CS6217) RM14
SXL2277	Stravinsky: Les Noces/Sym of Psalms	OSR Ansermet	(CS6219 SDD238) RM12
SXL2278	Franck: Piano Quintet	Vienna Philharmonic Quartet Curzon	(CS6226 SDD277) RM14
SXL2279	Tchaikovsky: Violin Conc/Dvorak Violin Conc	LSO Sargent Ricci	(CS6215 SDD126 SPA398)
SXL2280	Offenbach: Gaite Parisienne	ROHCG Solti	(CS6216) RM16
SXL2281-2	Mascagni: Cavalleria Rusticana	AdSC Serafin Simionato Del Monaco	(no CS)
SXL2283	Lars-Erik Larsson: Pastoral Suite op. 19, Little March, Wiren: Serenade op. 11	Stockholm SO Westerberg	(Only ever issued in Sweden)
SXL2284	Haydn: Symphonies 100/83	VPO Munchinger	(CS6230)
SXL2285	Tchaikovsky: Scenes from Swan Lake	Ccgbw Fistoulari	(CS6218) RM17
SXL2286	Mozart: Quartets K499/K589	Vienna Philharmonic Qt	(CS6231) RM16
SXL2287	Debussy: Images/Ravel: Pavane/Stravinsky	OSR Ansermet	(CS6225 SDD425) RM13
SXL2288	"1001 Nights" (Johann Strauss, Josef Strauss, Ziehrer)	VPO Boskovsky	(CS6232)
SXL2289	Dvorak: Symphony 9 in Eminor	VPO Kertesz	(CS6228 SPA87) RM17
SXL2290	Mozart: Divertimenti K136/K334	Vienna Octet	(no CS, SDD251)
SXL2291	Franck: Symphony, Le Chasseur Maudit	OSR Ansermet	(CS6222)
SXL2292	Prokofiev: Classical Symphony/Borodin/Glinka	OSR Ansermet	(CS6223) RM13
SXL2293	Encores	Katchen	(CS6235 SPA110)
SXL2294	Xmas with Leontyne Price	VPO Karajan Price	(no CS)
SXL2295	"Operetta Evergreens" (Lehar, Kalman, Strauss, Stolz, etc)	Gueden	(no CS)
SXL2296	Falla: Three Cornered Hat	OSR Ansermet Berganza	(CS6224 SDD321) RM19
SXL2297	Brahms: Clarinet Quintet/Wagner Adagio	Vienna Octet	(CS6234) RM16
SXL2298	Britten: Cello Sonata, Debussy: Cello Sonata, Schumann: Fünf Stücke im Volkston, Debussy: Cello Sonata	Rostropovich Britten	(CS6237) RM16
SXL2299	The Art of Oda Slobodskaya	LSO Fistoulari Slobodskaya	(no CS)
SXL2300-1	Bach: Orchestral Suites	StCO Munchinger	(CSA2206 SDD386-7 DPA589/90)
SXL2302	Handel: Water Music/Fireworks Music	LSO Szell	(CS6236 SDD169) RM19
SXL2303	Fauré: Pelleas & Melisande/Debussy	OSR Ansermet	(CS6227 SDD388) RM16
SXL2304	On the wings of song	ROHCG Downes Resnik	(no CS)
SXL2305	Holst: The Planets	VPO Karajan	(CS6244) RM15
SXL2306-7	Prokofiev Rome&Juliet/Cinderella	OSR Ansermet	(CS6240/6242 SPA226)
SXL2308	Tchaikovsky: Nutcracker/Grieg Peer Gynt	VPO Karajan	(CS6420)
SXL2309	Britten: Peter Grimes hlts	ROHCG Britten	(no CS)

SXL2310	Schumann: Dichterliebe		Waechter Brendel	(no CS)
SXL2311	Frank Martin: Concerto for 7 wind Insts etc	OSR	Ansermet	(CS6241) RM18
SXL2312	Debussy: Prelude L'Apres Midi/Ravel Pavanne etc	LSO	Monteux	(CS6248 SDD425) RM15
SXL2313	Herold/Lanchberry: La Fille Mal Gardee	ROHCG	Lanchberry	(CS6252) RM20 TAS 31,40+,73++ TASEC
SXL2314	Otello (hlts)	VPO	Karajan Del Monaco	
SXL2315	Donizetti: Lucia di Lammermoor (hlts)	AdSC	Pritchard Sutherland	
SXL2316	Handel: Messiah (hlts)	LSO	Boult	

SWL 10" series

These were the first stereo 10" discs introduced in Great Britain and were issued from late 1961, being mainly cheaper reissues from 12" SXL originals (I have shown the SXL numbers cross referenced). The entire series was deleted October 1st 1967.

Labels: The label is identical with the mono BR series –blue with silver lettering.

SWL8001	Bach: Brandenburg Concertos 3, 5	StCO	Munchinger	(SXL2126-7)
SWL8002	Mendelssohn: Symphony 4 (Italian)	IPO	Solti	(SXL2067)
SWL8003	Mozart: Don Giovanni (hlts)	VPO	Krips Della Casa etc	(SXL2117-20)
SWL8004	Puccini: madama Butterfly (hlts)	AdSC	Serafin Tebaldi Bergonzi	(SXL2054-6)
SWL8005	Tchaikovsky: Serenade for String Orch	IPO	Solti	(SXL2046)
SWL8006	Mozart: Symphony 41	LSO	Krips .	(SXL2220)
SWL8007	Grieg: Peer Gynt Suite	LSO	Fjeldstad	(SXL2012)
SWL8008	Beethoven: Piano Concerto 1	VPO	Schmidt-Isserstedt Backhaus	(SXL2178)
SWL8009	Delibes: Coppelia (hlts)	OSR	Ansermet	(SXL2084-5)
SWL8010	Tchaikovsky: The Nutcracker (hlts)	OSR	Ansermet	(SXL2092-3)
SWL8011	Mozart: Horn Concertos 2, 4	LSO	Maag Tuckwell	
SWL8012	Grieg: Piano Concerto	LSO	Fjeldstad Curzon	(SXL2173)
SWL8013	Schumann: Symphony 1 ("Spring")	LSO	Krips	(SXL2223)
SWL8014	Smetana: Vltava, From Bohemia's Woods and Fields	VPO	Kubelik	(SXL2064-5)
SWL8016	Beethoven: Piano Sonatas 14 ("Moonlight"), 8 ("Pathetique")		Backhaus	(SXL2190)
SWL8017	Mozart: Flute Concerto 2, Haydn: Trumpet Concerto	OSR	Ansermet	
SWL8018	Beethoven: Piano Sonatas Op 28/26, op 81a ("Les Adieux")		Backhaus	
SWL8019	Prokofiev: Peter and the Wolf	LSO	Henderson Lillie	(SXL2218)
SWL8020	Bizet: Carmen suites	OSR	Ansermet	(SXL2037)
SWL8021	Tchaikovsky: Violin Concerto	LSO	Sargent Ricci	(SXL2279)
SWL8022	Schumann: Piano Concerto	VPO	Wand Backhaus	
SWL8023	Chopin: Recital (Scherzo 3, Impromptu 1, etc)		Kempff	(SXL2024)
SWL8024	Mozart: Clarinet Concerto	LSO	Maag De Peyer	(SXL2238)
SWL8025	Britten: Nocturne Op 60	LSO	Britten	(SXL2189)
SWL8026	Waltzes from Swan Lake, Nutcracker, Sleeping Beauty, etc	OSR	Ansermet	
SWL8027	Schumann: Carnaval	OSR	Ansermet	
SWL8500	Beethoven: Piano Sonatas Op 109, Op 111		Backhaus	
SWL8501	Verdi: Arias from Aida and Otello	VPO	Karajan Tebaldi	(SXL2167-9 & SET209-11)
SWL8502	Stravinsky: Petrushka	IPO	Maazel	
SWL8503	Britten: Cello Sonata, Debussy: Cello Sonata	Rostropovich Britten		(SXL2098, SXL2298)
SWL8504	Debussy: Images, Ravel: Pavane, Stravinsky	OSR	Ansermet	(SXL2287)
SWL8505	Rimsky-Korsakov: Snow Maiden Suite	OSR	Ansermet	(SXL2176)
SWL8506	Verdi: Arias (La Traviata, Rigoletto, Ernani, etc)	ROHCG	Molinari-Pradelli Sutherland	(SXL2257 & SXL2159)
SWL8507	Haydn: Canzonettes, Britten: 6 Holderlin Fragments	Britten	Pears	
SWL8508	Handel: Messiah (choruses)	LSO	Boult	(SET218-20)
SWL8519	Mozart: Sinfonia Concertante K364	MPO	Kondrashin D Oistrakh Oistrakh	(SXL6088)
SWL8521	Chopin: Piano Concerto 2	LSO	Ashkenazy	(SXL6174)

SXL6000 series

Label: The early Decca SXL6000 labels are black with silver logo and lettering. In the top half of the label the word 'Decca' is in large type face (about 1.5 cms high letters), and above it is the 'ffss' logo. Just above the spindle hole there is a 1 cm wide silver band with the lettering "FULL FREQUENCY STEREOPHONIC SOUND". This label is often referred to as "wide band" and was in use up to 1968-9. Consequently, most of the SXL6000 series up to around SXL6450 have earliest pressing labels like this. Having said that, with some SXL6000s it is very hard to find the earliest label - for example SXL6000.

Up to about SXL6365 this "wide band" label also has a concentric groove of about 3 cms radius, or about 1 cm in from the label edge.

After SXL6450, the label remains black, but with the following changes: The 'ffss' logo is no longer used; The silver band above the spindle reduces to ½ cm wide, and the word "DECCA" is now in 1 cm high lettering inside a rectangular box. This label is often referred to as "narrow band". The quality of these later pressings is very high. Indeed, many people (including the author) believe that they are often better than the early pressings because the quality of English vinyl was better in the late 60s than it had been in the late 50s to early 60s.

Cat. No.	Title	Orchestra	Artist	Notes
SXL6000	Khachaturian Spartacus	VPO	Khachaturian	(CS6322) TASEC65
SXL6001	Khachaturian Symphony 2 'The Bell'	VPO	Khachaturian	(CS6323) TAS 39/152 TASEC65
SXL6002	Adam: Giselle	VPO	Karajan	(CS6251)
SXL6003	Honegger: Xmas Cantata/Symphony for strings	OSR	Ansermet	
SXL6004	Bach: Suites 2/3	OSR	Ansermet	(SDD129 ECS754)
SXL6005	Spanish/Italian Songs		Berganza	
SXL6006	Holst: Hymn of Jesus	Philh	Boult	(CS6324) TASEC 65
SXL6007	Folk Songs	Britten	Pears	
SXL6008	Verdi: Rigoletto (hlts)	AdSC	Sanzogno	
SXL6009	Handel: Messiah (choruses)	LSO	Boult McCarthy	
SXL6010	Handel: Messiah (hlts)	LSO	Boult Sutherland Bumbry	
SXL6011	Puccini: Manon Lescaut (hlts)	AdSC	Tebaldi Monaco	
SXL6012	Leoncavallo: Pagliacci/Cavalleria Rusticana	AdSC		
SXL6013	Verdi: Un Ballo in Maschera (hlts)	AdSC	Solti	
SXL6014	Beethoven: Diabelli Variations		Backhaus	Doubtful - possibly issued only as LXT6014
SXL6015-6	Strauss,J: Die Fledermaus	VPO	Karajan	
SXL6017	Cilea: Adriana Lecouvrer (hlts)	AdSC		
SXL6018	Shostakovich: Symphony 5	OSR	Kertesz	(CS6327 CSA2306 SDD179 ECS767)
SXL6020	Haydn: Symphonies 82, 86	OSR	Ansermet	(CSA2306)
SXL6021	Haydn: Symphonies 83, 87	OSR	Ansermet	(CSA2306 SDD183)
SXL6022	Haydn: Symphonies 84, 85	OSR	Ansermet	(CSA2306)
SXL6023	Brahms: Piano Concerto 1	LSO	Szell Curzon	(CS6329)
SXL6024	Bohemian Rhapsody	IPO	Kertesz	(CS6330 SPA202)
SXL6025	Beethoven: Fidelio, Leonore 1, 2, 3	IPO	Maazel	(CS6328)
SXL6026	Bartok: Divertimento for Strings, Vivaldi	Moscow CO	Barshai	(CS6332 SDD417)
SXL6027	Saint-Saens Symphony 3	OSR	Ansermet	(CS6331 SPA228)
SXL6028	Grieg/Schumann: Piano Concertos	IPO	Kertesz Katchen	(CS6336 SDD422)
SXL6029	Great Strauss Waltzes	VPO	Boskovsky	
SXL6030	The best of Tebaldi		Tebaldi	
SXL6031	Organ Recital		Ake Leven	(Not English Decca;only ever issued in Sweden)
SXL6032	The Art of Advocacy		Norman Birkett	

SXL6033	Verdi: Opera excerpts	ROHO	Quadri Nilsson	
SXL6034	*			
SXL6035	Hindemith VC/Bruch Scottish Fantasy	LSO	Horenstein Oistrakh	(CS6337 SDD465)
SXL6036	Borodin: Quartet 2, Shostakovich: Quartet 8	Borodin Quartet		(CS6338 ECS795 SDD156)
SXL6037	Schubert: Lieder	Prey		
SXL6038	Russian and Italian Bass Arias	LSO	Downes Ghiaurov	
SXL6039	Lortzing: Zar und Zimmermann, Der Waffenschmied (hlts)	VV	Gueden	
SXL6040	Strauss: Waltzes from the Vienna Woods	VPO	Boskovsky	(CS6340)
SXL6041	Brahms: Sonata in Fmin Op 5, etc	Curzon		(CS6341)
SXL6042	"Kirsten Flagstad in Memoriam" (Die Walkure, Rheingold, Wesendonck Songs)	Flagstad Knappertsbusch Solti London etc		
SXL6043	Dvorak: Quintet in A, Schubert Quartet 12	Vienna Phil Qt Curzon		(CS6357)
SXL6044	Dvorak: Symphony 8	LSO	Kertesz	(CS6358)
SXL6045	Mozart: Arias	Berganza		
SXL6046	Sibelius/Strauss,R: Songs	Krause		
SXL6047	*			
SXL6048	*			
SXL6049	Mozart: Wind Music V3	LWS	Brymer	(CS6346)
SXL6050	Mozart: Wind Music V1 (Snd K375, Divs K166, K213)	LWS	Brymer	(CS6347)
SXL6051	Mozart: Wind Music V2 (Snd K388, Divs K186, K253)	LWS	Brymer	(CS6348)
SXL6052	Mozart: Wind Music V4 (Divs K240, K252, K196e)	LWS	Brymer	(CS6349)
SXL6053	Mozart: Wind Music V5 (Divs K270, K289, K227, K411)	LWS	Brymer	(CS6350)
SXL6054	Mozart: Clarinet Concerto, Flute.& Harp Concertos	VPO	Munchinger	(SDD155 CS6352)
SXL6055	Mozart: Divertimento K287, M.Haydn: Div in Gmaj	Vienna Octet		(CS6353)
SXL6056	Mozart Symphonies 33, 39	VPO	Kertesz	(CS6354)
SXL6057	Rachmaninov: Piano Concerto 3	LSO	Fistoulari Ashkenazy	(CS6359)
SXL6058	Tchaikovsky: Piano Concerto 1	LSO	Maazel Ashkenazy	(CS6360)
SXL6059	Brahms: Symphony 1	OSR	Ansermet	
SXL6060	Brahms: Symphony 2, Tragic Overture	OSR	Ansermet	
SXL6061	Brahms: Symphony 3, St Anthony Variations	OSR	Ansermet	
SXL6062	Brahms: Symphonies 4, Academic Festival Overture	OSR	Ansermet	
SXL6063	Beethoven: Sonatas 17, 28		Backhaus	(CS6365)
SXL6064	Beethoven: Sonatas 12, 18		Backhaus	(CS6366)
SXL6065	Ravel Bolero/La Valse/Dukas/Honegger	OSR	Ansermet	(CS6367)
SXL6066	Stravinsky Baiser de la Fee	OSR	Ansermet	(CS6368 SDD244)
SXL6067	Mozart: Symphony 41/Haydn: Symphony 103	VPO	Karajan	(CS6369)
SXL6068	Great scenes from Aida	ROHCG	Pritchard Nilsson	
SXL6069	Schubert Schwanengesang	Prey		
SXL6071	*			
SXL6072	*			
SXL6073-4	Command Performance	LSO	Bonynge Sutherland	
SXL6075	Italian Arias	ROH	Downes Crespin	
SXL6076	Liszt: Sonata in Bmin/Liebestraum 3/etc	Curzon		(CS6371)
SXL6077	Birgit Nilsson sings German Opera	Nilsson		
SXL6078	'After the Opera' (Piano Improvistaions)	Herbert Holm		
SXL6079	Verdi: Scenes from Falstaff	NSOL	Downes	
SXL6080	Handel: Alcina (hlts)	LSO	Bonynge Sutherland Berganza	
SXL6081	Berlioz: Les Nuits d'Ete/Ravel Schrzd	OSR	Ansermet Crespin	
SXL6082	Beethoven Piano Concertos 2/4	LSO	Gamba Katchen	(CS6374 SDD228)
SXL6083	Operatic Recital	Robert Merrill		
SXL6084	Sibelius: Symphony 1/Karelia	VPO	Maazel	(CS6375) TAS 44/166
SXL6085	Tchaikovsky: Symphony 5	VPO	Maazel	(CS6376)
SXL6086	Schubert: Symphonies 4/5	VPO	Munchinger	(CS6378 ECS762 SDD172)
SXL6087	Mozart Clarinet Quintet K581/Divertimento K247	Members of Vienna Octet		(CS6379 SDD289)
SXL6088	Mozart: Sinfonia Concertante K364/etc	MPO	Kondrashin David & Igor Oistrakh	(CS6377)
SXL6089	Schubert: Symphony 9	VPO	Kertesz	(CS6381)

Cat. No.	Work	Orchestra	Artist(s)	Notes
SXL6090	Schubert: Symphony 8	VPO	Kertesz	(CS6382)
SXL6091	Mozart: Symphony 36/Nachtmusik	VPO	Kertesz	(CS6383 SDD480)
SXL6092	Schubert Death & the Maiden	VPO Quartet		(CS6384 SDD254)
SXL6093	Haydn: Quartets Op 32/Op 3 #5/Op 76 #2	Janacek Quartet		(CS6385 SDD285)
SXL6094	Ansermet conducts Wagner	OSR	Ansermet	(CS6386)
SXL6095	Sibelius: Symphony 4/Tapiola	OSR	Ansermet	(CS6387)
SXL6096	Beethoven: Symphonies 1/8	OSR	Ansermet	(CS6388, SDD101)
SXL6097	Beethoven: Sonatas 1/5/6/7		Backhaus	(CS6389)
SXL6098	Frank Martin: In Terra Pax	OSR	Ansermet	
SXL6099	Rachmaninov: Piano Concerto 2/etc	MPO	Kondrashin Ashkenazy	(CS6390)
SXL6100	Sibelius: Symphony 2	OSR	Ansermet	(CS6391)
SXL6101	Bach,J.S: Harpscd Conc 1/2	StCO	Munchinger Malcolm	(CS6392)
SXL6102	Pergolesi: Concertinos 1-4	StCO	Munchinger	(CS6393 SDD318)
SXL6103	Dvorak: Quartets 2/6	Janacek Quartet		(CS6394)
SXL6104	Pergolesi: Concertinos 5/6/etc	StCO	Munchinger	(CS6395 SDD319)
SXL6105	Brahms: Op 76/116		Katchen	(CS6396)
SXL6106	Spanish and Latin American Songs by Luigi Alva			
SXL6107	Strauss,R: Lieder		Prey Moore	
SXL6108	Mozart: Horn Concertos	LSO	Maag Tuckwell	(CS6403 SDD364)
SXL6109	Beethoven: Piano Concerto 5	LSO	Gamba Katchen	(CS6397 SDD225)
SXL6110	Britten: Serenade Op 31/Young Persons Guide	LSO	Britten	(CS6398)
SXL6111	Bartok: Miraculous Mandarin, Music for Str Perc & Celesta	LSO	Solti	(CS6399) TAS v72++
SXL6112	Mozart: Flute Concerto 2/Bach/Gluck	LSO	Monteux Claude Monteux	(CS6400 SDD427)
SXL6113	Mahler: Symphony 1	LSO	Solti	(CS6401)
SXL6114	Operatic Recital (Giordano, Verdi, Mascagni, Puccini)	ROHCG	Downes Prevedi (tenor)	
SXL6115	Dvorak: Symphony 7 in Dminor	LSO	Kertesz	(CS6402
SXL6116	Handel: Julius Caesar (hlts)	NSOL	Bonynge Sutherland	
SXL6118	Brahms: Complete Piano Works Vol 2		Katchen	(CS6404)
SXL6119	Mussorgsky: Bare Mt/Khovanchina/Glinka	OSR	Ansermet	(CS6405)
SXL6120	Prokofiev: Symphony 5	OSR	Ansermet	(CS6406 SD389)
SXL6121	Bartok: Dance Suite/Two Portraits/Rumanian Dances	OSR	Ansermet	(CS6407)
SXL6122	Puccini: Il Tabarro	MMF	Gardelli	
SXL6123	Puccini: Suor Angelica	MMF	Gardelli	
SXL6124	Puccini: Gianni Schicchi	MMF	Gardelli	
SXL6125	Sibelius: Symphony 2	VPO	Maazel	(CS6408) TAS 44/166
SXL6126	See LXT6126 (believed mono only)			
SXL6127	Verdi: La Traviata (hlts)	MMF	Pritchard	
SXL6128	Bellini: La Sonnambula (hlts)	MMF	Bonynge Sutherland	
SXL6129	Brahms: Complete Piano Works Vol 3		Katchen	(CS6410)
SXL6130	Mozart: Sonata for 2 pianos, Schumann: Andante&Vns for 2 pianos, 2 Cellos&Horn		Ashkenazy Frager Tuckwell	(CS6411)
SXL6131	Mozart: Complete Dances & Marches Vol 1	VME	Boskovsky	(CS6412)
SXL6132	Mozart: Complete Dances & Marches Vol 2	VME	Boskovsky	(CS6413)
SXL6133	Mozart: Complete Dances & Marches Vol 3	VME	Boskovsky	(CS6414)
SXL6134	Strauss,R: Don Juan/Tod und Verklarung	VPO	Maazel	(CS6415)
SXL6135	Schubert: Sonata in D Op 53/Impromptus		Curzon	(CS6416)
SXL6136	Kodaly: Hary Janos/Dances of Galanta	LSO	Kerte	(CS6417)
SXL6137	Pas de Deux	LSO	Bonynge	(CS6418)
SXL6138	Britten: Cello Sym & Orch, Haydn: Cello Concerto	ECO	Britten Rostropovich	(CS6419)
SXL6139	Verdi Choruses	AdSC		
SXL6140	Italian and German Arias	AdSC		
SXL6141	Respighi: Pines & Fountains of Rome	OSR	Ansermet	(SPA227)
SXL6142	Wagner: Siegfried (hlts)	VPO	Solti Windgassen	
SXL6143	Chopin: 4 Ballades & 3 Nouvelles Etudes		Ashkenazy	
SXL6144	"Duets of Love & Passion" (Samson&Delilah,Otello,Aida,etc)	ROHCG	Downes McCracken (tenor) Warfield (mezzo)	
SXL6146	Strauss,R: Der Rosankavelier (hlts)	VPO	Varviso	

SXL6147	Russian and French Arias	LSO Downes Ghiaurov	
SXL6148	Beethoven: Quartets Op 74/Op 95	Weller Quartet	
SXL6149	Recital	Marylin Horne	
SXL6150	Mozart: Divertimento K205, March K290, Cassation	Vienna Octet	(SDD325)
SXL6151	Brahms: String Quartets Op.51 nos 1/2	Weller Quartet	(SDD322)
SXL6152	Operatic Recital	Philh de Fabritiis Tebaldi	
SXL6153	Pergolesi: Stabat Mater	Orchestra Rossini di Napoli Caracciolo	
SXL6154	Bellini: I Puritani (hlts)	MMF Bonynge	
SXL6155	Strauss,J: Die Fledermaus (hlts)	VPO Karajan	
SXL6156	Bizet: Carmen (hlts)	OSR Schippers	
SXL6157	Tchaikovsky: Symphony 4	VPO Maazel	
SXL6158	Music for Two Pianos	Eden Tamir	
SXL6159	Tchaikovsky: Symphony 1	VPO Maazel	
SXL6160	Brahms: Complete Piano Works Vol 4	Katchen	
SXL6161	Schubert/Schumann: Goethe Lieder	Prey Engel	
SXL6162	Tchaikovsky: Symphony 2	VPO Maazel	
SXL6163	Tchaikovsky: Symphony 3	VPO Maazel	
SXL6164	Tchaikovsky: Symphony 6	VPO Maazel	
SXL6165	Ansermet conducts Berlioz	OSR Ansermet	
SXL6166	Ansermet conducts Mendelssohn	OSR Ansermet	
SXL6167	Debussy: Ansermet conducts Debussy (La Mer etc)	OSR Ansermet	
SXL6168	Chabrier: Rhapsody Espana/etc	OSR Ansermet	(SPA204)
SXL6169	Dvorak: Symphony 8	VPO Karajan	
SXL6170	Beethoven Complete Music for Wind Band	LWS Brymer	
SXL6171	Stravinsky: Renard/Scherzo a la Russe/Mavra	OSR Ansermet	(SDD241)
SXL6172	Brahms: Symphony 2	VPO Kertesz	
SXL6173	Schubert: String Quintet in C/Trio in B	Vienna Philharmonic Qt	
SXL6174	Bach: Keyboard Concerto 1/Chopin: Piano Concerto 2	LSO Zinman Ashkenazy	
SXL6175	Britten: Cantata Misericordum Op 69	LSO Pears Fischer-Dieskau	
SXL6176	Neapolitan Songs	New SO Pattacini Di Stefano	
SXL6177	"Decca Classical Stereo Sampler Album"	1965 sampler album	
SXL6178	Wagner: Tristan & Isolde Love duet	VPO Solti Nilsson	
SXL6179	Viotti: Violin Concerto 3/Boccherini: Symphony in C	Napoli Orch Caracciolo Prencipe	(CS6445)
SXL6180	Lidholm: Rites/Rosenberg: Ov "Marionettes"/etc	LSO Ehrling Leygraf (piano)	
SXL6181	The Art of Michelangeli	Michelangeli	
SXL6182	Haydn: Quartets 1, 2, 3	Weller Quartet	(SDD278)
SXL6183	Haydn: Quartets 4, 5, 6	Weller Quartet	(SDD278)
SXL6184	Mendelssohn/Bruch VCs	Fruhbeck de Burgos	(SDD443)
SXL6185	"Songs from the Land of the Midnight Sun"	Nilsson	
SXL6186	Schubert: Symphonies 3/6	VPO Munchinger	
SXL6187	Tchaikovsky: Swan Lake/Sleeping Beauty (hlts)	VPO Karajan	
SXL6188	Adam: Le Diable a Quatre	LSO Bonynge	
SXL6189	Beethoven: Piano Concerto 1/etc	LSO Gamba Katchen	(SDD227)
SXL6190	Arias from Verdi Operas	Various Sutherland	
SXL6191	Handel: Arias	Various Orchs Sutherland	
SXL6192	"Joan Sutherland sings Bellini"	LSO Bonynge Sutherland	
SXL6193	"Joy to the World"	Philh Bonynge Sutherland	
SXL6194	Piano Recital (Ravel, Rameau, Franck)	Varda Nishry	
SXL6195	Jenny Lind Songs	Soderstrom Eyron (piano)	
SXL6196	Berg: String Qt Op 3/Shostakovich:String Qt 10	Weller Qt.	
SXL6197	Mozart:Complete Dances & Marches Vol 4	VME Boskovsky	
SXL6198	Mozart: Complete Dances & Marches Vol 5	VME Boskovsky	
SXL6199	Mozart: Complete Dances & Marches Vol 6	VME Boskovsky	
SXL6200	The voice of Winston Churchill		
SXL6201	McCracken on Stage		

SXL6202	Bruckner: Symphony 9	VPO	Mehta	
SXL6203	Prokofiev: The Stone Flower (hlts)	OSR	Varviso	
SXL6204	Ravel: Daphnis & Chloe	OSR	Ansermet	(ECS824 SPA230) TASEC65
SXL6205	Schumann: Symphony 2/Manfred Ov	OSR	Ansermet	(ECS759)
SXL6206	Tchaikovsky: Romeo & Juliet/Hamlet	VPO	Maazel	
SXL6207	Pfitzner: Eichendorff/Wolf: Morike Lied	Prey		
SXL6208	Britten: Sinfonietta Op 1/Hindemith: Octet	Vienna Octet		
SXL6209	Bartok: Piano Concerto 3/Ravel: Piano Concerto	LSO	Kertesz Katchen	
SXL6210	Rossini: Italian in Algiers (hlts)	MMF	Varviso	
SXL6212	Bartok: Concerto for Orchestra	LSO	Solti	TAS65/176++
SXL6213	Schumann: Sym 3/Mendelssohn: Midsmr Nights Drm	LSO	de Burgos	(ECS760)
SXL6214	Schumann: Fantasia in Cmaj/Etudes Symphoniques	Ashkenazy		
SXL6215	Chopin: Scherzo Op 54/Nocturne Op 62/Ravel/Debussy	Ashkenazy		
SXL6217	Brahms: Complete Piano Works Vol 5	Katchen		
SXL6218	Brahms: Complete Piano Works Vol 7	Katchen		(CS6158)
SXL6219	Brahms: Complete Piano Works Vol 6	Katchen		
SXL6220	Wagner: Gotterdammerung (hlts)	VPO	Solti	
SXL6221	Nancy Tatum: recital	VOO	Quadri	
SXL6225	Mozart: Symphonies 40/41	Philh	Giulini	
SXL6226	Haydn: Symphonies 22/90	OSR	Ansermet	
SXL6227	Bruckner 4	LSO	Kertesz	(SDD464)
SXL6228	Brahms: Complete Piano Works Vol 8	Katchen		
SXL6230	Stravinsky: Pulcinella (complete)	OSR	Ansermet	
SXL6231	Lehar: Der Zarewitsch/Graf von Luxembourg (hlts)	VV		
SXL6232	Beethoven: Symphony 3	VPO	Schmidt-Isserstedt	
SXL6233	Beethoven: Symphony 9	VPO	Schmidt-Isserstedt	
SXL6234	Recital		Del Monaco	
SXL6235	Favourite Ovs of the 19th Century	LSO	Bonynge	
SXL6236	Sibelius: Symphonies 5/7	VPO	Maazel	TAS 44/166
SXL6237	"Decca Stereo Sampler Album 1966"	various		
SXL6238-41	Vienna Chamber Music Festival	Vienna Octet Curzon Boskovsky		
SXL6242-4	Invitation to a Strauss Festival	VPO	Boskovsky	
SXL6245	Folk songs and Spirituals	Felicia Weathers (soprano)		
SXL6246	Mozart: Complete Dances & marches (vol 7)	VPO	Boskovsky	
SXL6247	Mozart: Complete Dances & marches (vol 8)	VPO	Boskovsky	
SXL6248	Mozart: Complete Dances & marches (vol 9)	VPO	Boskovsky	
SXL6249	Recital (Verdi, Wagner, Beethoven, Cherubini)	Vienna Op Quadri Gwyneth Jones		
SXL6251	Easter Sunday in Rome 1966 (Mass celebrated in St Peters Square by Pope Paul VI)			
SXL6252	Mozart: Quintet K452/Beethoven: Quintet Op 16	London Wind Soloists Ashkenazy		
SXL6253	Dvorak: Symphony 6 in Dmajor	LSO	Kertesz	
SXL6254	Shield: Rosina	LSO	Bonynge	
SXL6255	Songs of Noel Coward	Sutherland		
SXL6256	New Year's Concert	VPO	Boskovsky	
SXL6257	Dvorak: Symphony 4 in Dminor	LSO	Kertesz	
SXL6258	Mozart: Quartets K575/K590	Weller Quartet		(SDD330)
SXL6259	Mozart: Piano Concertos K271/K246	LSO	Kertesz Ashkenazy	
SXL6260	Schubert: Sonatas D664/D784	Ashkenazy		
SXL6261	Closing scenes from Salome and Gotterdammerung	VPO	Solti Nilsson	
SXL6262	Operatic Arias	Geraint Evans		
SXL6263	"Romantic Russia" (Borodin: Prince Igor/Glinka: Russlan)	LSO	Solti	(SPA127)
SXL6264	Britten: School Concert	Boys of Downside School Britten		
SXL6265	Pettersson: Symphony 2	Swedish RSO Westerberg		
SXL6266	Bach,J.S: Cantatas 45/105	OSR	Ansermet	
SXL6267	Operatic recital	Pilar Lorengar		
SXL6268	Pizzetti: Pisanella/Concerto dell'Estate	OSR	Gardelli	

SXL6269	Glazunov: Ansermet Conducts Glazunov	OSR	Ansermet	(ECS642)
SXL6270	Beethoven: Symphony 7/Prometheus Ov	VPO	Abbado	
SXL6271	Rossini: Barber of Seville (hlts)	Rossini di Napoli	Varviso	
SXL6272	Bach: St Matthew Passion (hlts)	StCO	Munchinger	
SXL6273	Dvorak: Symphony 5 in Fmajor	LSO	Kertesz	
SXL6274	Beethoven: Symphony 4,Consecration of the House Ov	VPO	Schmidt-Isserstedt	
SXL6275	Mozart: Complete Dances and Marches Vol 10	VPO	Boskovsky	
SXL6276	Beethoven: Fidelio (hlts)	VPO	Maazel McCracken	
SXL6277-80	Not issued. Note that LXT6277-80 was never issued in stereo			
SXL6281	Still: Elegie for baritone Chorus & Small Orch, Concerto for Strings, Rubbra: Inscape Ste for Chor&Orch	Jaques Orch	Fredman	
SXL6282-4	Vienna Philharmonic Festival 2 (Brahms,Strauss,Mozart,etc)	VPO	Karajan	
SXL6285	Strauss: Horn Concertos	LSO	Kertesz Tuckwell	
SXL6286	Prokofiev: Romeo&Juliet/Chout	LSO	Abbado	
SXL6287	Falla: El Amor Brujo/etc	Philh	de Burgos	
SXL6288	Dvorak: Symphony 1	LSO	Kertesz	
SXL6289	Dvorak: Symphony 2	LSO	Kertesz	
SXL6290	Dvorak: Symphony 3/Hussite Ov	LSO	Kertesz	
SXL6291	Dvorak: Symphony 9 in Eminor/Othello Ov	LSO	Kertesz	TAS78/140+
SXL6292-5	Vienna Philharmonic Festival 3 (Wagner,Schubert,Sibelius,etc)	VPO	Karajan	
SXL6296	"Munchinger Miniatures"	StCO	Munchinger	
SXL6297	Mozart: Piano Concertos 20/25	StCO	Munchinger Katchen	
SXL6298	Liszt: Les Preludes/Wagner Preludes to Lohengrin/Parsifal	VPO	Mehta	
SXL6299	Verdi/Puccini: Arias	VOO	Quadri Felicia Weathers	
SXL6300	Beethoven: Sonatas 4, 25, 31	Backhaus		
SXL6301	Mozart: Sonatas K282,K283,K330,K332/Rondo K511	Backhaus		
SXL6302	Ansermet conducts Lalo	OSR	Ansermet	
SXL6303	Brahms: Sonata for 2 Pianos St-Saens: Vns for 2 Pianos on a theme by Beethoven	Eden	Tamir	
SXL6304	Strauss,R: Le Bourgeois Gentilhomme Rosankavalier (hlts)	VPO	Maazel Boskovsky Gulda Brabec	
SXL6305	Boito: Mefistofele (hlts)	Rome Opera		
SXL6306	Recital by Elena Suliotis (Verdi and Donizetti)	Rome Op	Fabritiis Suliotis	
SXL6307	Oskar Werner reading Poems by Goethe, Schiller			
SXL6308	Prokofiev: Scythian Suite/Prodigal Son	OSR	Ansermet	(CS6538)
SXL6309	Brahms: Piano Concerto 2	LSO	Mehta Ashkenazy	
SXL6310	Chausson: Symphony in B/Franck	OSR	Ansermet	(SDD451)
SXL6311	Tchaikovsky: Suite number 3	OSR	Ansermet	
SXL6312	Tchaikovsky: Suite 4 (Mozartiana)/Respighi: Rossiniana	OSR	Ansermet Ricci	
SXL6313	"What Everyone Should Know About Music"	OSR	Ansermet	
SXL6314	"Sibelius Songs"		Tom Krause	
SXL6315	"Madrigals to 3,4,5, and 6 parts, by John Wylbye"	Wilbye Consort directed Peter Pears		
SXL6316	Britten: Les Illuminations, Vns on a Theme of Frank Bridge	ECO	Britten	
SXL6318	Music for 4 Harpsichords	ECO	Leppard Malcolm Aveling Parsons Preston	
SXL6319	Spohr: Nonet/Double Quartet	Vienna Octet members		
SXL6320	"Romantic Overtures" (Weber, Schumann, Schubert)	VPO	Munchinger	
SXL6321	Brahms: Violin Sonatas Op 78/100/108	Katchen Suk		
SXL6322	Brahms: Piano Concerto 2	Bohm	Bacchaus	TAS 49/145 TAS78/146+
SXL6323	Tchaikovsky: Symphony 4	LAPO	Mehta	
SXL6324	Stravinsky: Petrushka/Circus Polka	LAPO	Mehta	
SXL6325	Schoenberg Verklarte Nacht/Scriabin Poem of Ecstasy	LAPO	Mehta	(CS6552)
SXL6326	Operatic recital (Weber, Beethoven, Wagner)	Vienna Op	Bernet James King	
SXL6327	"The Heroic Baritone" (Mozart, Wagner, etc)	Vienna Op	Tom Krause	
SXL6328	Moussorgsky: Pictures at an Exhibition (orch & piano versions)	LAPO	Mehta Askenazy	
SXL6329	Beethoven: Symphony 6	VPO	Schmidt-Isserstedt	
SXL6330	Mozart: Serenade 4	VME	Boskovsky	
SXL6331	Mozart/Haydn/Dittersdorf/Vanhal St Quartets	Weller Quartet		

Decca SXL6000 series

SXL6332	New Year's Concert	VPO	Boskovsky	
SXL6333	Song Recital	Crespin	Wustman	
SXL6334	Chopin: 4 Scherzi, Prelude Op 45, Barcarolle Op 60		Ashkenazy	
SXL6335	Beethoven: Sonata Op 106-Hammerklavier		Ashkenazy	
SXL6336	Recital of American Songs	Tatum	Parsons	
SXL6337	Bach,J.C: 6 Symphonies	LWS	Brymer	(SDD424)
SXL6338	Haydn: Seven Wind Divertimenti	LWS	Brymer	
SXL6339	Gluck: Don Juan (complete ballet)	ASMF	Marriner	
SXL6340	Brahms: Serenade 1	LSO	Kertesz	
SXL6341	Romantic Songs by Rossini, Bellini, Donizetti	Marimpietri	Benelli	
SXL6342	Rachmaninov: Symphony 2	OSR	Kletzki	
SXL6343	Berlioz: Symphonie Fantastiqie	OSR	Ansermet	
SXL6344	Dances of Old Vienna (Schubert/Strauss/etc)	VPO	Boskovsky	
SXL6345	Arias from French Operas		Marylin Horne	
SXL6346	Prokofiev: Sonatas 7 & 8/etc		Ashkenazy	
SXL6347	Schubert: 18 Songs	Krenn	Moore	
SXL6348	Dvorak: Concert Overtures	VPO	Kertesz	
SXL6349	Recital		Marylin Horne	
SXL6350	Bizet: Symphony in C/L'Arlesienne Suites	OSR	Gibson	
SXL6351	20th Century Violin Sonatas (Prokofiev, Milhaud, Debussy)	Voicou	Haas	
SXL6352	Borodin: Sym 2/Tchaikovsky: Francesca da Rimini	OSR	Varviso	
SXL6353	Mozart: Piano Concertos 6/20	LSO	Ketesz Ashkenazy	
SXL6354	Mozart: Piano Concertos K488/K491	LSO	Kertesz Curzon	(CS6580)
SXL6355	Albeniz: Suite ESpanola	Philh	Fruhbeck de Burgos	
SXL6356	Schumann: Symphonies 3/4	VPO	Solti	
SXL6357	Bartok: Sonata for 2 Pianos & Percussion/Poulenc	Eden	Tamir	(CS6583)
SXL6358	Beethoven: Piano Sonatas 9,11,20		Backhaus	
SXL6359	Beethoven: Sonatas 2,10,19		Backhaus	
SXL6360	Handel: Overtures & Sinfonias	ECO	Bonynge	
SXL6361	Strauss,R: Lieder	Weathers	G.Fischer	
SXL6362	"Decca Stereo Sampler Album 1968"			
SXL6363	Mendelssohn: Symphonies 3/4	LSO	Abbado	
SXL6364	Sibelius: Symphonies 3/6	VPO	Maazel	
SXL6365	Sibelius: Symphony 4/Tapiola	VPO	Maazel	TAS 44/138
SXL6366	Mozart: Divertimenti 1/2	VME	Boskovsky	
SXL6367	Strauss,R: Don Quixote	VPO	Maazel Brabec Staar	
SXL6368	Brahms: Serenade 2/Dvorak Serenade for Wind	LSO	Kertesz	
SXL6369	Handel: 12 Grand Concertos Op 6, Vol 1, nos 1-4	ASMF	Marriner	
SXL6370	Handel: 12 Grand Concertos Op 6 Vol 2	ASMF	Marriner	
SXL6371	Handel: 12 Grand Concertos Op 6 Vol 3	ASMF	Marriner	
SXL6372	Mozart: Symphony 40/Serenata Notturna	ECO	Britten	
SXL6373	Beethoven: Piano Sonata Op 111, 6 Bagatelles Op 126, etc		Katchen	
SXL6374	Berwald: Sinfonie Singulaire	LSO	Ehrling	
SXL6375	Weber/Vivaldi: Bassoon Concs/Hummel/L Mozart	OSR	Ansermet	
SXL6376	Verdi Arias	ROHO	Downes G.Jones	
SXL6377	Arias by Verdi & Donizetti		Pavarotti	
SXL6378	Recital of Messiaen and Liszt		Jean-Rodolphe Kars	
SXL6379	Strauss,R: Also Sprach Zarathustra	LAPO	Mehta	TAS 30+ 43 66 TASEC
SXL6380	Tchaikovsky: Symphony 5	IPO	Mehta	
SXL6381	Dvorak: Symphony 7	IPO	Mehta	
SXL6382	Strauss,R: Ein Heldenleben	LAPO	Mehta	TAS 30/141+ 43/159
SXL6383	Overtures of Old Vienna	VPO	Boskovsky	
SXL6384	"Madrigals by Thomas Weelkes"	Wilbye Consort	Pears	
SXL6385	Haydn/JC Bach: Harpsichord Concerti	ASMF	Marriner Malcolm	
SXL6386	Brahms: Song of Destiny/Rinaldo	Philh	Abbado	

SXL6387	Brahms: Piano Trios 1/3		Suk Katchen Starker
SXL6388	Copland: Lincoln Portrait/Kraft: Conc for 4 Percussion	LAPO	Mehta
SXL6389	Brahms: Hungn Dances 1-10,Dvorak: Slavonic Dances Op 46	Eden	Tamir
SXL6390	Schonberg: Variations Op 31/Symphony Op 9	LAPO	Mehta
SXL6391	Britten: Songs and Proverbs of William Blake	Pears	Fischer-Dieskau
SXL6392	Bach,J.S: Cantatas 101/130	OSR	Ansermet
SXL6393	Britten: Suite for Cello/2nd Suite for Cello		Rostropovich
SXL6394	Honegger: Symphonies 3/4	OSR	Ansermet
SXL6395	Lalo: Scherzo for Orch/Magnard: Symphony 3	OSR	Ansermet
SXL6396	Beethoven: Symphonies 5/8	VPO	Schmidt-Isserstedt
SXL6397	Bach,J.C: Sinf Conc in C/Sinfonia in Eb/Salieri	ECO	Bonynge
SXL6398	Janacek: Sinfonietta	LSO	Abbado
SXL6399	Rachmaninov: Symphony 3/Mussorgsky: Bare Mt	OSR	Kletzki
SXL6400	Bach,J.S: Magnificat in Dmaj/Cantata 10	StCO	Munchinger
SXL6401	Respighi: The Birds/Pines of Rome/Fountains of Rome	LSO	Kertesz
SXL6402	Mozart: Symphonies 31/32/35	StPh	Munchinger
SXL6403	Stravinsky: Rite of Spring/5 Easy Pieces/etc	Eden	Tamir
SXL6404	Mendelssohn: Midsummer Nights Dream	Philh	De Burgos
SXL6405	English Music for Strings	ECO	Britten
SXL6406	Russian Rarities (Glière, Stravinsky, Gretchaninov)	LSO	Bonynge
SXL6407	Burgmüller: La Péri	LSO	Bonynge
SXL6408	Franck: Sonata/Brahms: Trio for Violin,Horn&Piano	Perlman	Tuckwell Ashkenazy
SXL6409	Mozart: Masonic Funeral Music	LSO	Kertesz
SXL6410	'Salute to Percy Grainger'	ECO	Britten Pears
SXL6411	Prokofiev: Piano Conc 3/Ravel: Left Hand Conc	LSO	Kertesz Katchen
SXL6413	Britten: A Charm of Lullabies & Folk Songs	Greevy	Hamburger
SXL6414	Mendelssohn Sextet/Borodin Quintet	Vienna Octet	(SDD410) TAS 44/138
SXL6415	Piano Recital (Liszt, Chopin, etc)		Davis
SXL6416	Beethoven: Piano Sonatas 3, 13, 24		Backhaus
SXL6417	Beethoven: Piano Sonatas 16, 22, 27		Backhaus
SXL6418	Schubert: Symphony 8, Von Einem: "Philadelphia Symphony"	VPO	Krips
SXL6419	J Strauss II: Vienna Imperial	VPO	Boskovsky
SXL6420	Mozart: Serenades 3/13	VPO	Boskovsky
SXL6421	Wagner: "The Golden Ring" (hlts)	VPO	Solti.
SXL6422	French Opera Overtures	Philh	Bonynge
SXL6423	Beethoven: String Quartet Op 127, Haydn: Quartet Op 103	Weller Quartet	
SXL6424	Songs for Children		Gueden
SXL6426	Bridge: Cello Sonato/Schubert: Arpeggione	Britten Rostropovich	
SXL6427	Schubert: Symphony 9	StCO	Munchinger
SXL6428	Songs by Tchaikovsky and Britten	Vishnevskaya Rostropovich	
SXL6429	Verdi: Operatic Recital	Monte Carlo Rescigno Del Monaco	
SXL6430	Baroque Flute Sonatas (Handel, Telemann, Vinci, Loeillet, etc)	Pepin (flute) Viala (cello) Leppard (hpsd)	
SXL6431	Sibelius: Symphony 4/etc	Finnish RSO Berglund	
SXL6432	Sibelius: Tapiola/Kokkonen: Symphony 3	Finnish RSO Berglund	
SXL6433	Sibelius: Symphony 5	Helisnki PO Panula	
SXL6434	Sibelius: Finlandia, Legends	Helisnki PO Panula	
SXL6435	Delius: Piano Concerto, Debussy	LSO	Gibson Kars
SXL6436	Beethoven: Dances & Romances	VME	Boskovsky
SXL6437	Beethoven: Symphonies 1/2	VPO	Schmidt-Isserstedt
SXL6438	Beethoven: Creatures of Prometheus	IPO	Mehta
SXL6439	Mozart: Piano Sonatas K310, K576		Ashkenazy
SXL6440	Bloch: Schelomo/Voice in the Wilderness	IPO	Mehta
SXL6441	Gabrielli: Sonatas and Canzonas	StCO	Munchinger
SXL6442	Strauss, R: Sinfonia Domestica	LAPO	Mehta
SXL6443	"Great Scenes from Verdi"	LSO	Abbado Ghiaurov

SXL6444	Stravinsky: Rite of Spring/etc	LAPO	Mehta
SXL6445	Lutoslawski: Conc for Orchestra,Hindemith: Mathis der Maler	OSR	Kletzki
SXL6446	Mahler: Kindertotenlieder, Wagner: Wesendonk Lieder	RPO	Lewis Horne
SXL6447	Beethoven: Symphony 7	VPO	Schmidt-Isserstedt
SXL6448	Tchaikovsky: Fantasy Ov Romeo&Juliet/1812	LAPO	Mehta
SXL6449	Britten: Serenade for Horn, Tenor & Strings,Les Illuminations	LSO	Britten Tuckwell
SXL6450	Britten: YPGO/Variations on a Theme of Frank Bridge	LSO	Britten
SXL6451	"Arias from Italian Opera"	Berlin Deutsch Oper	Domingo
SXL6452-61	See SXLA6452 box set		
SXL6462	Kreutzer: Grand Septet/Berwald	Vienna Octet members	
SXL6463	Dvorak: Quintet/Spohr: Quintet	Vienna Octet members	
SXL6464	Beethoven: Quintet Op 29/Sextet Op 81b	Vienna Octet	
SXL6465	Beethoven: Egmont (complete incidental music)	VPO	Szell
SXL6466	Grieg: Nocturne/Sonata/Mendelssohn: Capriccio/etc		De Larrocha
SXL6467	Recital of Spanish Music		De Larrocha
SXL6468	Welsh Music for Strings	ECO	Atherton
SXL6469	Prokofiev: Symphonies 1/3	LSO	Abbado
SXL6470-5	See SXLB6470 box set		
SXL6476-80	See SXLC6476 box set		
SXL6481	Schubert: String Quintet in C/Quartettsatz	Weller Quartet	(SDD441)
SXL6482	Saint-Saens: Symphony 3	LAPO	Mehta
SXL6483	Schubert: Symphony 4/5	VPO	Kertesz
SXL6484	Concert (Schubert/Brahms/etc)	Eden/Tamir (pianos)	
SXL6485	Liszt Recital		Pascal Rogé
SXL6486	Schumann: Symphony 1/Ov, Scherzo & Finale Op 52	VPO	Solti
SXL6487	Schumann: Symphony 2/Ov Julius Caesar	VPO	Solti
SXL6488	Ravel: Daphnis & Chloe	LAPO	Mehta
SXL6489	Bruckner: Symphony 4	LAPO	Mehta
SXL6490	"Mozart & Haydn Discoveries"	Vienna Haydn Orch	Fischer-Dieskau
SXL6491	Nielsen: Symphony 5	OSR	Kletzki
SXL6493	Tchaikovsky/Sibelius: Violin Concertos	LSO	Previn Chung
SXL6494	Bruckner: Symphony 1	VPO	Abbado
SXL6495	"Happy New Year"	VPO	Boskovsky
SXL6496	Handel: Ovs to Semele/Julius Caesar/etc	ECO	Bonynge
SXL6497	Kodaly: Psalmus Hungaricus/Peacock Variations	LSO	Kertesz
SXL6498	"Luciano Pavarotti Sings Tenor Arias"		Pavarotti
SXL6499	Mozart: Serenade 1	VPO	Boskovsky
SXL6500	Mozart: Divertimento K63/Cassation K99	VME	Boskovsky
SXL6501	"Arias from Forgotten Operas"	OSR	Bonynge Tourangeau
SXL6502	Schubert Piano Recital	Jean-Rodolphe Kars	
SXL6503	Beethoven: Piano Concerto 3/32 Vns	LSO	Foster Lupu
SXL6504	Schubert: Pno Sonata op 143/Brahms: Rhapsody 1/3 Intermezzi		Lupu
SXL6505	Bruckner: Symphony 3	VPO	Bohm
SXL6506	Schubert & Schumann Lieder	Krenn	Werba
SXL6507	Janacek: Taras Bulba/Lachian Dances	LPO	Huybrechts
SXL6508	"Ashkenazy Plays Liszt"	Ashkenazy	
SXL6510	Dvorak: Symphonic Variations/Golden Spinning Wheel	LSO	Kertesz
SXL6512	Britten: Violin Concerto /Piano Concerto	ECO	Britten Richter
SXL6513	Hoddinott: Clarinet Concerto/Mathias: Piano Conc 3	LSO	Atherton
SXL6514	Lieder Recital (Schubert, Schumann, Brahms, Wolf, Strauss)	Jungwirth (bass)	Brenn (piano)
SXL6515-21	See SXLD6515 box set		
SXL6522	Schumann: Lieder Recital		Talvela
SXL6523	Beethoven: Eroica Vns/Schubert: Moments Musicaux		Curzon
SXL6524	"Christmas Festival"	Philh	Tebaldi
SXL6525	Recital (Mozart, Beethoven, Strauss, etc)		Lorengar

Catalog	Work	Orchestra	Conductor/Artist	Reference
SXL6526	"Welcome to the New Year"	VPO	Boskovsky	
SXL6527	Scriabin: Prometheus/Piano Concerto	LPO	Maazel Ashkenazy	
SXL6528	Falla: Nights in the Gardens of Spain, Chopin: Piano Conc 2	OSR	Comissiona De Larrocha	
SXL6529	Holst: The Planets	LAPO	Mehta	TAS73/141+++, TASEC73
SXL6530	Recital (Tchaikovsky, Borodin, Glinka, etc)		Ghiaurov	
SXL6531	"Eighteenth Century Overtures"	ECO	Bonynge	
SXL6532	Prokofiev: Violin Concerto 1/Glazunov: Violin Conc	OSR	Stein Sivo	
SXL6533	Suk: Srnd for Strings/Wolf: It Srnd/Strauss	StCO	Munchinger	
SXL6534	Rossini: Stabat Mater	LSO	Kertesz	
SXL6535	Liszt: Battle of the Huns/Mazeppa/Orpheus	LAPO	Mehta	SM69/150
SXL6536	Bach,CPE: Conc for Flute/Cimarosa: Conc for 2 Flutes	StCO	Munchinger Nicolet	
SXL6537	Operatic and Operetta Recital	VV	Bauer-Thiessel Farr (sop)	
SXL6538	Pettersson: Symphony 7	Stockholm PO	Dorati	
SXL6539	Mozart: Symphony 40/Schubert: Symphony 8	ECO	Britten	
SXL6540	Handel: Messiah (hlts)	ECO	Bonynge Sutherland	
SXL6541	Ballet Music from French Opera	LSO	Bonynge	
SXL6542	Sibelius: Finlandia/Pohjola's Daughter/etc	OSR	Stein	
SXL6543	Dvorak: Symphonic Poems	LSO	Kertesz	
SXL6544	Schmidt: Symphony 4	VPO	Mehta	
SXL6545	Bach: Concerto in Italian Style/French St 6/etc	Alicia de Larrocha		
SXL6546	Schumann: Kreisleriana/Allegro/Romance/Novelette		de Larrocha	
SXL6547	"Romantic Cello Concertos" (Auber, Massenet, etc)	OSR	Bonynge Silberstein	
SXL6548	Italian Operatic recital	Vienna Volksper	Santi Chiara	
SXL6549	Beethoven: Symphony 8	VPO	Krips	
	Schubert: Symphony 8	VPO	Abbado	
SXL6550	Varese: Arcana/Ionisation	LAPO	Mehta	
SXL6551	"French Music for 2 Pianos" (Poulenc, Satie)	Eden	Tamir	
SXL6552	Schubert: Symphonies 1/2	VPO	Kertesz	
SXL6553	Schubert: Symphonies 3/6	VPO	Kertesz	
SXL6554	Rachmaninov: Piano Concertos 1/2	LSO	Previn Ashkenazy	
SXL6555	Rachmaninov: Piano Concerto 3	LSO	Previn Ashkenazy	
SXL6556	Rachmaninov: Piano Concerto 4	LSO	Previn Ashkenazy	
SXL6557	Vivaldi: 4 Seasons	StCO	Munchinger	
SXL6558-61	See SXLE6558 box set			
SXL6562	Tchaikovsky: Manfred Symphony	VPO	Maazel	
SXL6563	Shostakovich: Symphonies 1/9	OSR	Weller	
SXL6564	Britten: String Quartets 1/2	Allegri Quartet		
SXL6565-7	See SXLF6565 box set			
SXL6568	"Hits from the Hollywoord Bowl"	LAPO	Mehta	
SXL6569	Elgar: Symphony 1	LPO	Solti	
SXL6570	Hoddinott: Symphony 3	LSO	Atherton	TASEC 44
SXL6571	Berlioz: Symphonie Fantastique	CSO	Solti	
SXL6572	"New year in Vienna"	VPO	Boskovsky	
SXL6573	Bruch: Violin Concerto 1/Scottish Fantasia	RPO	Kempe Chung	
SXL6574	Tchaikovsky: Symphony 4	Nat SO	Dorati	
SXL6575	Chopin: Sonata 2 ("Funeral March"), Nocturnes, Mazurka, Grande Valse Brillante		Ashkenazy	
SXL6576	Beethoven: Piano Sonatas 8, 14, 21		Radu Lupu	
SXL6577	"French and Spanish Songs"		Marylin Horne	
SXL6578	Recital (Schubert, Schumann, Wolf, Strauss)		Marylin Horne	
SXL6579	Recital of Italian Songs	Tebaldi	Bonynge (piano)	
SXL6580	Schubert: Sonata D960, Impromptu 6		Curzon	
SXL6581	Strauss,R: Don Juan, Rossini: Ov Barber of Seville, Wagner: Ov Meistersinger, Beethoven: Ovs Egmont, Leonora 3	CSO	Solti	
SXL6582	Stravinsky: The Firebird/Symphony in C	OSR	Segal	
SXL6583	Rachmaninov: Symphony 1	OSR	Weller	

SXL6584	Marylin Horne sings Rossini	RPO	Lewis Horne	
SXL6585	Operatic Duets (Leoncavallo, Verdi, Cilea, Ponchielli,etc)	OSR	Guadagno Tebaldi Corelli	
SXL6586-7	Albeniz: Iberia/etc		De Larrocha	
SXL6588	Offenbach: Le Papillon ballet	LSO	Bonynge	
SXL6589	Brahms: Cello Sonata 2/PianoTrio 2	Starker	Katchen Suk	
SXL6590	Schubert: Schwanengesang	Krause	Gage (pno)	
SXL6592	Elgar: Enigma Variations/Ives: Symphony 1	LAPO	Mehta	
SXL6594-7	See SXLG6594 box set			
SXL6598	Operatic and Operetta Arias (Mozart, Nicolai, Verdi, etc)	VV	Bauer-Theussel Farr (sop)	
SXL6599	Khachaturian: Piano Concerto/Franck: Sym Vns	LPO	De Burgos De Larrocha	
SXL6600	Janacek: Glagolitic Mass	RPO	Kempe	
SXL6601	Walton/Stravinsky: Violin Concertos	LSO	Previn Chung	
SXL6602	Schubert: Piano Sonata in Gmaj Op 78		Ashkenazy	
SXL6603	Beethoven: Piano Sonatas Op 57 ("Appassionata")/Op 10/3		Ashkenazy	
SXL6604	Rachmaninov: Etudes-Tableaux Op 39/etc		Ashkenazy	
SXL6605	Verdi: Aria Recital	ROHCG	Santi Chiara	
SXL6606	Hoddinott: Symphony 5/etc	RPO	Davis	TASEC
SXL6607	Mathias: Dance Ov/Harp Concerto/etc	LSO	Atherton	
SXL6608	Britten: Journey of the Magi/Who are these Children?/etc	Britten	Pears	
SXL6609	"Great Scenes from Italian Opera"	LPO	Varviso	
SXL6610-3	See SXLH6610 box set			
SXL6614	Mozart: Serenade 7	VME	Boskovsky	
SXL6615	Mozart: Serenade 9	VME	Boskovsky	
SXL6616	Mozart: Symphonies 29/35	VPO	Kertesz	
SXL6617	Mozart: Symphonies 25/40	VPO	Kertesz	
SXL6618	Rachmaninov: Music for 2 Pianos (6 duets op11, Fantasy op 5)	Eden	Tamir (pianos)	
SXL6619	"Songs My Mother Taught Me"	Philh	Bonynge Sutherland	
SXL6620-2	Prokofiev: Romeo and Juliet	Clvlnd	Maazel	TAS 6/185+ TASEC 44
SXL6623	Rachmaninov: Symphony 2	LPO	Weller	
SXL6624	Grieg: Piano Concerto/Schumann: Piano Concerto	LSO	Previn Lupu	
SXL6625	The Art of Hotter		Hotter Parsons	
SXL6626	Bach,JS: St John Passion (hlts)	ECO	Britten	
SXL6627	Tchaikovsky: Francesca da Rimini/Hamlet/Voyevode	NSO	Dorati	
SXL6628	Vivaldi: Concerti for Strings		Lucerne Festival Baumgartner	
SXL6629	"18th Century Arias"	NPO	Bonynge Tebaldi	
SXL6630	Beethoven: Piano Sonatas 31/32		Ashkenazy	
SXL6631	Kodaly: Hari Janos (hlts)	LSO	Kertesz	
SXL6632	Beethoven: Violin Sonatas 2\9 (Kreutzer)	Perlman	Ashkenazy	
SXL6633	Nielsen: Symphony 4	LAPO	Mehta	
SXL6634	Strauss,R: Don Quixote	LAPO	Mehta	
SXL6635-6	Delibes: Sylvia	Philh	Bonynge	
SXL6637	Operatic Arias (Verdi, Gounod, Massenet, Meyerbeer, Bizet, etc)	ROHCG	Matheson Rouleau (bass)	
SXL6638	Bach,JC: Sinfonias Op 18 Nos 1,3,5	StCO	Munchinger	
SXL6639	Madrigals by Wilbye, Gibbons, Tomkins		Wilbye Consort Pears (director)	
SXL6640	Britten: 3 Cantatas	LSO	Britten Pears Fischer-Dieskau	
SXL6641	Britten: Sinfonia da Requiem/Cello Symphony	LSO	Britten	
SXL6642	Schumann: Kreisleriana/Humoresque		Ashkenazy	
SXL6643	Virtuoso Overtures (Mozart/Rossini/Weber/Wagner/etc)	LAPO	Mehta	
SXL6644-8	See SXLJ6644 box set			
SXL6649	Tenor Arias (Pagliacci, Turandot, Faust, Tosca, etc)		Pavarotti	
SXL6650	"Pavarotti in Concert"		Pavarotti	
SXL6651	Beethoven: Piano Concerto 1/etc	CSO	Solti Ashkenazy	
SXL6652	Beethoven: Piano Concerto 2/etc	CSO	Solti Ashkenazy	
SXL6653	Beethoven: Piano Concerto 3/'Les Adieux' Sonata	CSO	Solti Ashkenazy	
SXL6654	Beethoven: Piano Concerto 4/Leonora Ov	CSO	Solti Ashkenazy	

SXL6655	Beethoven: Piano Concerto 5/Egmont Ov	CSO	Solti Ashkenazy	
SXL6656	Wagner: Tristan,Mastersingers,Lohengrin,Flying Dutchman	VPO	Stein	
SXL6657	Berg: Lulu/Strauss,R: Salome	VPO	Dohnanyi	
SXL6658	Recital (Rosenkavalier, William Tell, Boheme, etc)		Pavarotti	
SXL6659	"Popular Russian Songs"		Ghiaurov	
SXL6660-4	See SXLK6660 box set			
SXL6665-7	See SXLM6665 box set			
SXL6668	Prokofiev: Romeo and Juliet (hlts)	Clvlnd	Maazel	
SXL6669	Mozart: Rondo K485/Sonata K331/Fantasia K475		De larrocha	
SXL6670	Mozart: Divertimenti 7/11		Boskovsky	
SXL6671-2	Bruckner: Symphony 8	LAPO	Mehta	
SXL6673	Beethoven: Symphony 7/Egmont Ov	LAPO	Mehta	
SXL6674	Ravel: Sonatine, Valses Nobles et Sentimentale, Tombeau de Couperin		Pascal Rogé	
SXL6675	Brahms: Symphony 1	VPO	Kertesz	
SXL6676	Brahms: Symphony 2	VPO	Kertesz	
SXL6677	Brahms: Symphony 3	VPO	Kertesz	
SXL6678	Brahms: Symphony 4	VPO	Kertesz	
SXL6679	Mahler: Lieder Eines Fahrenden Gesellen, 4 Songs from Des Knaben Wunderhorn	CSO	Solti Minton	
SXL6680	Ravel: Concerto for Left Hand/etc	LPO	Foster De Larrocha	TAS 9/96+
SXL6681	Bruckner: Symphony 2	VPO	Stein	
SXL6682	Bruckner: Symphony 6	VPO	Stein	
SXL6683	Falla: Piano Music		De Larrocha	
SXL6684	Rossini: Barber of Seville/Berlioz/Beethoven/etc	CSO	Solti	
SXL6686-7	Bruckner: Symphony 5	VPO	Maazel	
SXL6688-9	Tchaikovsky: The Nutcracker	NPO	Bonynge	
SXL6690	Operatic Recital		Caballe	
SXL6691	Stravinsky: Rite of Spring	CSO	Solti	TASEC65 SM69/144++ Wilkinson
SXL6692	"New Year's Concert" (1973)	VPO	Boskovsky	
SXL6693	Chopin: Piano Concerto 2/etc	LSO	Zinman Ashkenazy	
SXL6694	Tchaikovsky: Romeo & Juliet/The Tempest	NSO	Dorati	
SXL6695	Nielsen: Symphony 3 (Sinfonia Espansiva)	LSO	Huybrechts	
SXL6696	Brahms: Hungarian Dances/Dvorak: Slavonic Dances	LSO	Boskovsky	
SXL6697	Rachmaninov: The 2 Suites for 2 Pianos		Ashkenazy Previn	
SXL6698	Mozart: Piano Concertos K414 & K467	ECO	Segal Lupu	
SXL6699	Anthony Milner: Roman Spring/etc	London Sinfonia Atherton		
SXL6700	Ravel: Gaspard de la Nuit/Pavane/etc		Pascal Roge	
SXL6701	"Straussiana"	NPO	Bonynge	
SXL6702	Prokofiev: Symphonies 1/7	LPO	Weller	
SXL6703	Ravel: Daphnis and Chloe	Clvlnd	Maazel	
SXL6704	"Waltzes by Emile Waldteufel"	NPO	Gamley	
SXL6705	Scriabin: Piano Sonatas 3,4,5,9		Ashkenazy	
SXL6706	Beethoven: Piano Sonatas Pathetique, Waldstein, Les Adieux		Ashkenazy	
SXL6707	Auber: Marco Spada	LSO	Bonynge	
SXL6708	Liszt: Paraphrases	Eden and Tamir (2 pianos)		
SXL6709	Liszt: Mephisto Waltz/Tasso	OdP	Solti	
SXL6710	Chopin: Etudes Op 1 & Op 25		Ashkenazy	
SXL6711	"The Magic of Lehar" (Arias from Operettas)	VV	Paulik Holm Krenn	
SXL6712	Kodaly: Vol 1	PHun	Dorati	
SXL6713	Kodaly: Hary Janos/Symphony in C	PHun	Dorati	
SXL6714	Kodaly: Peacock Variations/Summer Evening/Hungn Rondo	Phun	Dorati	
SXL6715	Ravel: Miroirs, Jeux D'Eau, Ma Mère L'Oye		Pascal Rogé	
SXL6716	Mozart: Piano Concerto for 2 Pianos K365, Piano Concerto for 3 Pianos K242	ECO	Barenboim Ashkenazy Fou Ts'Ong	
SXL6717	Works for Horn and Piano		Tuckwell Ashkenazy	
SXL6718	Rachmaninov: Songs Vol 1		Soderstrom Ashkenazy	

SXL6719	"Darwin - Song for a City"	RPO	Bonynge Sutherland
SXL6720	Rachmaninov: Symphony 3/The Rock	LPO	Weller
SXL6721	Bach,J.S: Partita 2 in Dmin/Sonata 3 in Cmaj		Chung
SXL6722	Schubert: Songs	Pears	Britten
SXL6723	Elgar: Symphony 2	LPO	Solti
SXL6724	Mozart: Divertimento 17		Boskovsky
SXL6725	"Great Galloping Gottschalk" (Piano Music of Louis Moreau Gottschalk)		Ivan Davis (piano)
SXL6726	Ballet Music from Verdi Operas	Clvlnd	Maazel
SXL6727	George Gershwin: Cuban Ov, Rpsdy in Blue, American in Paris	Clvlnd	Maazel
SXL6728	Brahms: Piano Concerto 1	LPO	De Waart Lupu
SXL6729	Schubert: Symphony 9	IPO	Mehta
SXL6730	Bartok: Concerto for Orchestra/Hungarian Pictures	IPO	Mehta
SXL6731	Rimsky-Korsakov: Scheherazade	LAPO	Mehta
SXL6732	Berlioz: Harold in Italy	IPO	Mehta
SXL6733	Chopin: 24 Preludes Op 28, Berceuse Op 57		de Larrocha
SXL6734	"Favourite Spanish Encores" (Albeniz, Granados, etc)		de Larrocha
SXL6735	Stravinsky: The Rite of Spring	VPO	Maazel
SXL6736	Beethoven: Violin Sonatas 4, 5 ("Spring")	Perlman	Ashkenazy
SXL6737	'Concertos in Contrast' (Weber/Haydn/Vivaldi/etc)	LAPO	Mehta
SXL6738	Art of Hotter II	Hotter	Parsons
SXL6739	Schubert: Piano Sonata in Dmaj Op 53		Ashkenazy
SXL6740	"New year's Eve Concert live from Vienna"	VPO	Boskovsky
SXL6741	Schubert: Piano Sonata Gmaj D894, 2 Scherzi D593		Lupu
SXL6742	Debussy: Iberia/Nocturnes	National SO of Washington	Dorati
SXL6743	Wagner: Siegfried's Funeral March, Valkyries, Rhine Journey	NSO	Dorati
SXL6744-5	Mahler: Symphony 2	VPO	Mehta
SXL6746	Rachmaninov: Piano Concerto 3	LSO	Previn De larrocha
SXL6747	Mozart: Trinitatis Mass K167, Haydn	VPO	Munchinger
SXL6748	Schubert: Rosamunde Inc Music	VPO	Munchinger
SXL6749	Strauss,R: Zarathustra/Don Juan/Till	CSO	Solti
SXL6750	Dvorak: Symphony 8/The Wood Dove	LAPO	Mehta
SXL6751	Dvorak: Symphony 9/Carnival Ov	LAPO	Mehta
SXL6752	Strauss: Alpine Symphony	LAPO	Mehta
SXL6753	Ives: Variations on 'America'/Symphony 2/etc	LAPO	Mehta
SXL6754	Tchaikovsky: Symphony 5	CSO	Solti
SXL6755	Bach,J.C: Sinfonias 2,4,6/Telemann: Don Quichotte	StCO	Munchinger
SXL6756	Schumann: Fantasia Op 17/Liszt: Sonata in Bmin		De Larrocha
SXL6757	Concertos from Spain	RPO	De Burgos
SXL6758	Dvorak & Suk: Serenades for Strings	StCO	Munchinger
SXL6759	St-Saens: Violin Conc 3/Vieuxtemps: Violin Conc 5	LSO	Foster Chung
SXL6760	Beethoven: Symphonies 1/8	CSO	Solti
SXL6761	Beethoven: Symphony 2/Ov Egmont	CSO	Solti
SXL6762	Beethoven: Symphony 5/Leonora Ov	CSO	Solti
SXL6763	Beethoven: Symphony 6	CSO	Solti
SXL6764	Beethoven: Symphony 7/Coriolan Ov	CSO	Solti
SXL6765	Massenet: Songs	Tourangeau (mezzo)	Bonynge (piano)
SXL6766	"Grieg Favourites" (Holberg Suite, etc)	NPO	Boskovsky
SXL6767	Prokofiev: Piano Concertos 1/2/Overture	LSO	Previn Ashkenazy
SXL6768	Prokofiev: Piano Concerto 3/Classical Symphony	LSO	Previn Ashkenazy
SXL6769	Prokofiev: Piano Concertos 4/5	LSO	Previn Ashkenazy
SXL6770	Dukas: Symphony in C/Sorcer's Apprentice	LPO	Weller
SXL6771	Schubert: Piano Sonatas: Amaj D959/Ab maj D557		Radu Lupu
SXL6772	Rachmaninov: Songs vol 2	Soderstrom	Ashkenazy
SXL6773	Prokofiev: Violin Concertos 1/2	LSO	Previn Chung

Catalog	Work	Orchestra	Artist	Notes
SXL6774-5	Bach,J.S: Brandenburg Concertos 1-6	ECO	Britten	
SXL6776	Delibes: Coppelia & Sylvia (hlts)	OSR	Bonynge	
SXL6777	Prokofiev: Symphony 6	LPO	Weller	TASEC98
SXL6778	Bach,J.S: St John Passion (hlts)	StCO	Munchinger	
SXL6779	Mahler: Symphony 1	IPO	Mehta	
SXL6781	"Pavarotti sings Sacred Music"		Pavarotti	
SXL6782	Overtures: Verdi/Beethoven/Berlioz/Glinka/etc	Clvlnd	Maazel	
SXL6783	Brahms: Symphony 1	Clvlnd	Maazel	
SXL6784	Mozart: Fantasia K397,Sonatas K311,K330, Haydn		De Larrocha	
SXL6785	Recital (Granados, Goyescas)		De Larrocha	
SXL6786	Brahms: Vns & Fugue on theme by Handel, Fantasias		Pascal Rogé	
SXL6787	Prokofiev: Symphony 5	LSO	Weller	
SXL6788	Britten: Songs	Pears	Ellis	
SXL6789	Beethoven: Violin Sonatas Op 12 No 3/Op 30 No 3		Perlman Ashkenazy	
SXL6790	Beethoven: Violin Sonatas Op 12 No 1/Op 96		Perlman Ashkenazy	
SXL6791	Beethoven: Violin Sonatas Op 30 Nos 1/2		Perlman Ashkenazy	
SXL6792	Romanzas de Zarzuelas	Barcelona	Caballe	
SXL6793	Britten: Folk Song Arrangements	Pears	Osian Ellis (harp)	
SXL6794	Schubert: Variations D603, Grand Duo in Cmaj D812	Eden	Tamir (pianos)	
SXL6795	Ellgar: Enigma Variations/Cockaigne Ov/London Town	CSO	Solti	
SXL6796	Brahms: Symphony 1	VPO	Mehta	TAS 43/159+
SXL6797	Brahms: Piano Concerto 1	IPO	Mehta Rubinstein	
SXL6798	Paganini: Violin Concerto 1	IPO	Mehta Belkin	
SXL6799	Schubert: Symphonies 3, 5	IPO	Mehta	
SXL6800	Berlioz: Romeo and Juliet (orch excerps)	VPO	Maazel	
SXL6801	Chopin: Piano Works Vol 2		Ashkenazy	
SXL6802	Bartok: Violin Concerto 2	LPO	Solti Chung	
SXL6803	Kodaly: Missa Brevis, Pange Lingua	Brighton Fest Chorus	Heltay	
SXL6804	Beethoven: Piano Sonatas op 10/1, op 10/2, op 28		Ashkenazy	
SXL6805	Recital (Carmen, Falstaff, Fledermaus, Walkure, etc)		Regina Resnik	
SXL6806-7	Mahler: Symphony 5/Adagio from Sym 10	LAPO	Mehta	(CSA2248)
SXL6808	Beethoven: Piano Sonatas 2 & 3		Ashkenazy	
SXL6809	Beethoven: Piano Sonatas 28 & 30		Ashkenazy	
SXL6810	Chopin: Piano Works Vol 3		Ashkenazy	
SXL6811	Bernstein Candide/Copland App Spring/Gershwin	LAPO	Mehta	
SXL6812	Massenet: Le Cid/Meyerbeer	NPO	Bonynge	TAS 25/95
SXL6813	Ravel: Bolero/Debussy: La Mer/Faun Prelude	CSO	Solti	
SXL6814	Tchaikovsky: Symphony 6	CSO	Solti	
SXL6815	Bartok: Rhapsody for Piano & Orch/Piano Concerto 1	LSO	Weller Rogé	
SXL6816	Bartok: Piano Concertos 2/3	LSO	Weller Roge	
SXL6817	"Prosit! 150 Years of Josef Strauss"	VPO	Boskovsky	
SXL6818	Mendelssohn: Symphonies 1, 5 ("Reformation")	VPO	Dohnanyi	
SXL6819	Schumann: Symphonies 1/4	VPO	Mehta	
SXL6820	"Classics for Brass Band" (Elgar, Holst, Ireland)	Grimethorpe Colliery Band	Elgar Howarth	
SXL6821	Tchaikovsky: The Nutcracker	NPO	Bonynge	
SXL6822	Respighi: Feste Romane	Clvlnd	Maazel	
SXL6823	Franck: Symphony in D	Clvlnd	Maazel	
SXL6824	Bach,J.S: The Musical Offering	StCO	Munchinger	
SXL6825	Operatic Recital (Verdi, Mascagni, Puccini, Catalani, etc)	Barcelona SO	Caballe	
SXL6826	"Grand Opera Choruses" (Wagner,Verdi, Beethoven,etc)	VPO	Solti,Maazel,Karajan,etc	
SXL6827	Massenet Scenes Alsaciennes/Scenes Dramatiques/etc	NPO	Bonynge	
SXL6828	Operatic Duets	NPO	Bonynge/Sutherland/Pavarotti	
SXL6829	Beethoven: Symphony 3	CSO	Solti	
SXL6830	Beethoven: Symphony 4/Weber: Ov Oberon	CSO	Solti	
SXL6831	Brahms: Intermezzi Op 118, Op 119, Op 79		Lupu	

SXL6832	Rachmaninov: Songs Vol 3	Soderstrom Ashkenazy	
SXL6833	Mozart: Symphonies 34/39	IPO Mehta	
SXL6834	Brahms: Symphony 2/Tragic Overture	Clvlnd Maazel	
SXL6835	Brahms: Symphony 3/Haydn Variations	Clvlnd Maazel	
SXL6836	Brahms: Symphony 4/Academic Festival Ov	Clvlnd Maazel	
SXL6837	Bruckner: Te Deum/Mass 2 in Emin	VPO Mehta	
SXL6838	Shostakovich: Symphony 10	LPO Haitink	
SXL6839	Operatic Recital (Verdi, Donizetti, Puccini, Rossini)	Various Pavarotti	
SXL6840	Mussorgsky: Pictures at an Exbn, Tchaikovsky: Piano Conc 1	LSO Maazel Ashkenazy	
SXL6841	Opera Recital (Aida, Turandot, Lombardi, Butterfly, etc)	LSO Gardelli Sass	
SXL6842	Elgar: Violin Concerto	LPO Solti Chung	TAS 43/157
SXL6843	Overtures: Oberon,Scala di Seta,Traviata, Midsmr Nts Dream	IPO Mehta	
SXL6844	Mozart : Sym 40,Serenade K525 (Eine Kleine Nachtmusik)	IPO Mehta	
SXL6845	Schubert: Symphonies 4/8	IPO Mehta	
SXL6846	Respighi : Ancient Airs and Dances Suites 1-3	LPO Jesus Lopez-Cobos	
SXL6847	Britten: Phaedra/Prelude & Fugue for Strings	ECO Britten Pears	
SXL6848	Elgar: Pomp&Circumstance Marches/Cockaigne/etc	LPO Solti	
SXL6849	Shostakovich: Suite on Poems of Michelangelo Op 145	Ashkenazy	
SXL6851	St-Saens: Introduction & Rondo Capriccioso, Havanaise, Chausson: Poème, Ravel: Tzigane	RPO Dutoit Chung	
SXL6852	Prokofiev: Symphony 3/Scythian Suite	LPO Weller	
SXL6853	Tchaikovsky: Manfred Symphony	NPO Ashkenazy	
SXL6854	Tchaikovsky: Violin Concerto, Valse Scherzo	Philh Ashkenazy Belkin	
SXL6855	Debussy: Piano Works Vol 1	Rogé	
SXL6856	Wagner: Ovs Dutchman, Tannhauser, Mastersingers, Tristan	CSO Solti	
SXL6857	Tchaikovsky: Suite 3	VPO Maazel	
SXL6858	Operatic Recital (Bizet, Donizetti, Bellini, Verdi, Puccini)	Various Pavarotti	
SXL6859	Recital (Faust, Boris, Onegin, Barber of Seville, Boheme, etc)	Ghiaurov	
SXL6860	Wagner: Tannhauser,Mastersingers (hlts)	VPO Solti	
SXL6861	Schumann: Piano Concerto, Intro&Allegro Op 134,Intro&Allegro Op 92	LSO Segal Ashkenazy	
SXL6862	Albinoni: Adagio/Pachelbel: Kanon/Gigue	StCO Munchinger	
SXL6863	Liszt: Symphonic Poems Prometheus/Les Preludes/etc	LPO Solti	
SXL6864	Operatic recital	Chiara	
SXL6865	Mozart: Piano Sonatas K332, K545, K576, Bach,JS: Beloved Jesu	de Larrocha	
SXL6866	Granados: Songs (Collection de Tonadillas)	De Larrocha Lorengar	
SXL6867	Strauss,J: Graduation Ball	VPO Dorati	
SXL6868	Scriabin: Piano Sonatas 2, 7, 10	Ashkenazy	
SXL6869	Rachmaninov: Songs Vol 4	Soderstrom Ashkenazy	
SXL6870	Neapolitan Songs	Various Pavarotti	
SXL6871	Beethoven: Piano Sonatas 17 & 18	Ashkenazy	
SXL6872	"Salute to Percy Grainger"	ECO Bedford	
SXL6873	Berlioz: Harold in Italy	Clvlnd Maazel	
SXL6874	Rimsky-Korsakov: Scheherazade	Clvlnd Maazel	
SXL6875	Prokofiev: Symphony 5	Clvlnd Maazel	
SXL6876	Weber: Symphony 1/Overtures	VPO Stein	
SXL6877	Chopin: The Complete Piano Works Vol 9	Ashkenazy	
SXL6878	Kodaly: Hymn of Zrinyi, Psalm 114, Laudes Organi	Brighton Fest Ch Luxon	
SXL6879	Mozart: Symphonies 25/29	ECO Britten	
SXL6880	"Star Wars": Star Wars, Planets, Zarathustra	LAPO Mehta	
SXL6881	Mozart: Piano Concertos K453, K467	Philh Ashkenazy	
SXL6882	Bartok: Miraculous Mandarin	VPO Von Dohnanyi	
SXL6883	Stravinsky: Petruchka	VPO Dohnanyi	
SXL6884	Tchaikovsky: Symphony 5	Philh Ashkenazy	
SXL6885	Suites from 'Star Wars' and 'Close Encounters'	LAPO Mehta	
SXL6886	Beethoven: Piano Concerto 4, Piano Sonatas Op 49/1 & 49/2	IPO Mehta Lupu	

SXL6887	Mozart: Piano Concertos 25/27	LPO	Solti de Larrocha
SXL6888	Falla: 7 Popular Spanish Songs	Caballé	
SXL6889	Beethoven: Piano Sonatas 13, 14, 16	Ashkenazy	
SXL6890	Brahms: Symphony 4	CSO	Solti
SXL6891	Schubert: Symphony 6, Ov Die Zauberharfe, etc	IPO	Mehta
SXL6892	Schubert: Symphonies 1, 2	IPO	Mehta
SXL6893	Britten: String Quartets 2, 3	Amadeus Qt	
SXL6894	Tchaikovsky: Symphony 6	RPO	Kord
SXL6895	Tchaikovsky: Capriccio Italien/Marche Slave	DSO	Dorati
SXL6896	"Rhapsody!" (Dvorak, Enesco, Ravel, Liszt)	DSO	Dorati
SXL6897	Bartok: Suite 1/Two Pictures	DSO	Dorati
SXL6898	Mahler: Songs of a Wayfairer/5 Ruckert Songs	LAPO	Mehta Horne
SXL6899	Beethoven: Piano Concerto 5	LAPO	Mehta De Larrocha
SXL6900	"Songs for Children"	Ashkenazy Soderstrom	
SXL6901	Grieg: Peer Gynt	RPO	Weller
SXL6902	Brahms: Symphony 3, Academic Festival Ov	CSO	Solti
SXL6903	Bizet: L'Arlesienne Suites 1&2, Jeux d'Enfants	Clvlnd	Maazel
SXL6904	Debussy: Nocturnes/Iberia/Jeux	Clvlnd	Maazel
SXL6905	Debussy: La Mer, Scriabin: Poem of Ecstacy	Clvlnd	Maazel
SXL6906	Shostakovich: Symphony 15	LPO	Haitink
SXL6908	Prokofiev: Symphony 4/Russian Overture	LPO	Weller
SXL6909	"Overture" (Nicolai, Wolf, Weber, etc)	NPO	Adler
SXL6910	Schubert: Piano Sonata D784, Impromptu 4 D899, Schumann		Alicia de Larrocha
SXL6911	Chopin: Piano Music vol 14 (Sonata 1,Mazurkas, Waltzes, etc)		Ashkenazy
SXL6912	Sibelius: Pelleas et Melisande/The Tempest	OSR	Stein
SXL6913	Tchaikovsky: Symphony 1, Marche Slave Ov	LAPO	Mehta
SXL6919	Tchaikovsky: Symphony 4	Philh	Ashkenazy
SXL6921	Recital (Norma,Traviata,Giocanda,Trovatore,etc)	NPO	Gardelli/Sass
SXL6922	Chopin: The Complete Piano Works Vol 5	Ashkenazy	
SXL6923	Operatic Recital (Mozart, Puccini), Verdi, Falla, Wagner)	LPO	Jesus Lopez Cobos Lorengar
SXL6924	Brahms: Symphony 1	CSO	Solti
SXL6925	Brahms: Symphony 2, Tragic Ov	CSO	Solti
SXL6926	Rachmaninov: Symphonic Dances op 45, Russian Rhapsody	Ashkenazy Previn (pianos)	
SXL6927	Shostakovich: Symphony 4	LPO	Haitink
SXL6928	Debussy: Piano Works vol 3 (Preludes, Childrens Corner)		Rogé
SXL6929	Beethoven: Sonatas 11 & 12	Ashkenazy	
SXL6930	Wagner: Operatic Arias (Rienzi, Tristan, Walkure, Tannhauser)	NPO	Bonynge Sutherland
SXL6931	Schubert: Piano Sonatas D845, D157		Lupu
SXL6932	Massenet: Cigalle/Valse de Lente	NPO	Bonynge
SXL6933	Mozart: Arias (Figaro, Flute, Exsultate Jubilate, etc)	NPO	Bonynge Sutherland
SXL6935	Spanish Songs (Granados, Falla, Albeniz, Rodrigo, etc)	Caballé	Zanetti (piano)
SXL6936	Recital (Vivaldi, Pergolesi, Giordani, etc)		Caballe
SXL6937	Bartok: Piano Concertos 2/3	LPO	Solti/Ashkenazy
SXL6938	Berlioz: Symphonie Fantastique	VPO	Haitink
SXL6940	Rachmaninov: Songs Vol 5	Soderstrom Ashkenazy	
SXL6941	Tchaikovsky: Symphony 6	Philh	Ashkenazy	TAS 26/279
SXL6942	Operatic Recital (Puccini, Mascagni, Mozart, Rossini)	NPO	Mitchell (sop)
SXL6943	"To my Friends" (Wolf, Brahms, Grieg, Loewe)	Schwarzkopf Parsons (piano)	
SXL6944	Franck: Violin Sonata in Amaj/Debussy: Violin Sonata	Chung	Lupu
SXL6945	Prokofiev: Symphony 2/Love of 3 Oranges Suite	LPO	Weller
SXL6946	Bruckner: Symphony 6	CSO	Solti
SXL6947	Mozart: Piano Concertos K459, K491	Philh	Ashkenazy
SXL6949	Scarlatti: 7 Sonatas, Soler: 6 Sonatas		de Larrocha
SXL6950	Guitar Recital (Albeniz, Villa-Lobos, Paganini, etc)		Carlos Bonell
SXL6951	Mozart: Piano Sonatas K282, K310		De Larrocha

SXL6952	Bach: Keyboard Concerto BWV1056, Haydn, Mozart	London Sinfonietta	Zinman de Larrocha (piano)
SXL6953	Sibelius : Violin Concerto, etc	Philh	Ashkenazy Belkin (violin)
SXL6954	Mendelssohn : Symphony 3, etc	VPO	von Dohnanyi
SXL6955	Tchaikovsky: Piano Concerto 1, Rococo Variations	LAPO	Dutoit Chung (piano) Chung (cello)
SXL6956	Chabrier: Espana, Falla: 3 Cornered Hat, Rimsky-Korsakov	LAPO	López-Cobos
SXL6957	Debussy: Piano Works vol 2 (Images, L'Isle Joyeuse, etc)		Pascal Rogé
SXL6959	Strauss,R: Alpine Symphony	BavRSO	Solti
SXL6960	Beethoven: Piano Sonatas op 2, op 10		Ashkenazy
SXL6961	Beethoven: Piano Sonatas 4, 9, 10		Ashkenazy
SXL6962	Beethoven: Piano Sonatas 22, 24, 25, 27		Ashkenazy
SXL6963	Elgar: Falstaff, Overture: In the South	LPO	Solti
SXL6964	Bartok: Five Songs op 16, Liszt: Songs	Sass (sop)	Schiff (piano)
SXL6965	Elgar: Cello Concerto, Tchaikovsky: Rococo Variations	Clvlnd	Maazel Harrell
SXL6966	Rimsky-Korsakov: Concert	Clvlnd	Maazel
SXL6968	Liszt: Années de Pèlerinage Italie		Pascal Rogé (piano)
SXL6969	Brahms: Handel Variatons, Reger: Telemann Variaitons		Bolet (piano)
SXL6970	Duets (Norma, Figaro, etc)	NPO	Magiera Freni Scotto
SXL6971	Verdi Arias (Aida, Otello, Ernani, Ballo)	IPO	Mehta Price (sop)
SXL6972	Tchaikovsky: Songs vol 1		Söderström Ashkenazy
SXL6973	Sibelius: 4 Legends from the Kalevala	OSR	Stein
SXL6974	Mussorgsky: Songs & Dances of Death, etc,Rachmaninov: Song		Talvela (bass) Gothoni (bass)
SXL6975	St-Saens: Orch Works (Danse Macabre,Rouet D'Omphale,etc)	Philh	Dutoit
SXL6976	Schumann: Symphony 2, Overture: Genoveva	VPO	Mehta
SXL6977	Beethoven: Ov Leonora 3, Rimsky-K, Rossini, Tchaikovsky	IPO	Mehta
SXL6978	Rachmaninov: Piano Concerto 2, Schumann: Piano Concerto	RPO	Dutoit de Larrocha
SXL6979	Brahms: Cello Sonatas 1, 2	Harrell	Ashkenazy
SXL6980	Granados: Danzas Espanolas, sets 1-4		de Larrocha
SXL6981	Chopin: Piano Works vol 15 (Polonaises, 3 Ecossaises, etc)		Ashkenazy
SXL6982	Mozart: Piano Concertos K482, K382	Philh	Ashkenazy
SXL6983	Borodin: String Quartets 1, 2		Fitzwilliam Quartet
SXL6984	Puccini: Tosca (hlts)	NPO	Rescigno Pavarotti
SXL6985	Wolf: Penthesilea: Der Corregidor Suite	OSR	Stein
SXL6986	Mascagni: Cavalleria Rusticana, Leoncavallo: Pagliacci (hlts)	NPO	Pavarotti
SXL6987	Mozart: Marriage of Figaro (hlts)	VPO	Karajan Cotrubas Tomova-Sintow
SXL6988	"Music of my Country" – arias from Zarzuelas	Barcelona SO	Garcia-Navarro Domingo
SXL6989	Mozart: Piano Quartets K478, K493	Musikverein Qt	Previn
SXL6990	Beethoven: Violin Sonatas op 24 (Spring), op 47 (Kreutzer)	Perlman	Ashkenazy [from SXL6736/SXL6632]
SXL6991	Operatic Duets (Donizetti, Verdi, Bellini)	Various	Bonynge Sutherland Pavarotti
SXL6994	Beethoven: Piano Sonatas op 13, op 49/1, op 49/2, op 57		Ashkenazy
SXL6995	Chopin: Piano Works vol 7 (Sonata 2,Mazurkas,Polonaises,etc)		Ashkenazy
SXL6996	Rachmaninov: Piano Sonata 2 op 36, Etudes Tableaux 1-8		Ashkenazy
SXL6997	Mozart: Piano Works (Sonatas K333, K457, K545, etc)		Schiff
SXL6998	Brahms: Clarinet Quintet op 115, Wolf: Italian Serenade		Fitzwilliam Quartet Hacker (clarinet)
SXL6999	Mozart: Concert Arias	Vienna CO	Fischer te Kanawa
SXL7000	Mozart: Soprano Concert Arias	Vienna CO	Fischer Gruberova (sop)
SXL7001	Mozart: Concert Arias	Vienna CO	Fischer Berganza
SXL7004	Schoenberg: Variations op 31, Brahms: St Anthony Variations	CSO	Solti
SXL7007	Mozart: Piano Concertos K466, K595	ECO	Britten Curzon
SXL7008	St-Saens: Piano Concertos Op 22, op 44	RPO	Dutoit Rogé
SXL7010	Mozart: Piano Concertos K450, K451		Ashkenazy (K450 is digital)
SXL7011	Beethoven: Piano Sonata op 106 (Hammerklavier), etc		Ashkenazy
SXL7012	Beethoven: Piano Sonatas op 13, op 27, op 57		Ashkenazy
SXL7013	Italian Song Recital	Philh	Gamba Pavarotti

Decca Headline HEAD series

Between 1974 and 1980 Decca issued the HEAD series of new recordings of contemporary music, many of them being world premiere recordings.

Label: HEAD labels are the same as the later SXL6000 labels but are red in place of black.

HEAD 1-2	Messiaen: La Transfiguration de Notre Seigneur Jésus Christ	Wahington Nat SO Dorati etc
HEAD 3	Contemporary Vocal Works (Lutoslawski, Berkeley, Bedford)	London Sinf cond by composers
HEAD 4	Takemitsu: Keyboard Works	Roger Woodward (kbd)
HEAD 5	Henze: Music for Viola and 22 Players, Violin Conc 2	London Sinf Henze
HEAD 6	Gerhard: The Plague	Wahington Nat SO Dorati etc
HEAD 7	Birtwistle: Verses for Ensembles, Nenia: Death of Orpheus, The Fields of Sorrow	London Sinf Atherton etc
HEAD 8	Musgrave: Horn Concerto, Concerto for Orch	SNO Musgrave Tuckwell
HEAD 9	Cage: Sonatas and Interludes for Prepared Piano	John Tilbury (pno)
HEAD10	Dallapiccola: Il Prigionero	Wahington Nat SO Dorati etc
HEAD11	Gerhard: Astrological Series – Libra, Gemini, Leo, Concertante for Violin and Piano	London Sinf Atherton etc
HEAD12	Ligeti: Melodien for Orch, Double Concerto, etc	London Sinfonietta Atherton
HEAD13	Xenakis: Synaphai, Aroura, Antikhthon	NPO Howarth
HEAD14	Modern Music for Brass Band	Grimethorpe Colliery Band Howarth
HEAD15	Berio: A-Ronne, Cries of London for 8 voices	Swingle II directed by Berio
HEAD16	Shukur: Works for Oud	Salman Shukur (oud)
HEAD18	"Transit" Brian Fernyhough	London Sinfonietta Howarth
HEAD19-20	Henze: Voices	London Sinfonietta Henze etc
HEAD21	Maxwell-Davies: Symphony	Philh Rattle
HEAD22	Panufnik: Sinfonia Mistica	LSO Atherton
HEAD23	Nordheim: Greening, Doria, Epitaffio	RPO Per Dreier etc
HEAD24-5	Birtwistle: Punch and Judy	London Sinf Atherton etc

Decca London (1958-64)

Cat.	Work	Orch	Conductor/Soloist	SXL
CS6001	Mendelssohn: A Midsummer Night's Dream	LSO	Maag	(SXL2060) TAS 38/157+ 49/144
CS6004	Brahms: Symphony 2	VPO	Kubelik	(SXL2059)
CS6005	La Boutique Fantasque	IPO	Solti	(SXL2007)
CS6006	Espana	LSO	Argenta	(SXL2020) TAS 42/83++ TASEC
CS6007	Strauss,J: Blue Danube	VPO	Krips	(SXL2047)
CS6008	Strauss,J: Concert	VPO	Boskovsky	(SXL2082)
CS6009	Stravinsky: Petrouchka	OSR	Ansermet	(SXL2011) TAS 42/83+ TASEC 44
CS6010	Mendelssohn: Vln Conc/Bruch Vln Conc 1	LSO	Gamba Ricci	(SXL2006)
CS6011	Tchaikovsky: Violin Concerto	LSO	Argenta Campoli	(SXL2029)
CS6012	Rimsky-Korsakov: Russian Easter Festival etc	OSR	Ansermet	(SXL2221)
CS6013	Debussy: Images pour Orchestre	OSR	Argenta	(No SXL)
CS6014	This is Vienna	VPO	Knappertsbusch	(SXL2016)
CS6015	Overtures in HiFi	PCO	Wolff	(SXL2008)
CS6016	Brahms: Symphony 1	VPO	Kubelik	(SXL2013)
CS6017	Stravinsky: The Firebird	OSR	Ansermet	(SXL2017)
CS6018	Rimsky-Korsakov: Scheherazade	PCO	Ansermet	(SXL2086)
CS6019	Beethoven: Piano Concerto 5	VPO	Knappertsbusch Curzon	(SXL2002)
CS6020	Dvorak: Symphony 5	VPO	Kubelik	(SXL2005)
CS6021	Brahms: piano Recital	Backhaus		(SXL2222)
CS6022	Brahms: Symphony 3	VPO	Kubelik	(SXL2104)
CS6023	Ravel: Ma Mere l'Oye/Debussy:Nocturnes	OSR	Ansermet	(SXL2062) TAS 38/157
CS6024	Debussy: La Mer, Prelude/Ravel: Rapsodie Espagnol	OSR	Ansermet	(No SXL, SDD214)
CS6025	Berlioz: Symphonie Fantastique	PCO	Argenta	(SXL2009)
CS6026	Chopin: Les Sylphides/Delibes	PCO	Maag	(SXL2044) TAS 13/91+
CS6027	Haydn: Symphonies 94/99	VPO	Krips	(SXL2098)
CS6028	Falla: El Amor Brujo/Retablo De Maese Pedro		Ansermet/Argenta	(SXL2260)
CS6029	Halffter Sinfonietta	NOS	Argenta	(No SXL)
CS6030	Brahms: Academic Festival/Tragic ovs/Haydn Varns	VPO	Knappertsbusch	(No SXL)
CS6031	Stravinsky: Rite of Spring	OSR	Ansermet	(SXL2042) TAS 38/157
CS6032	Dvorak: Serenade for strings Israel	Philh	Kubelik	(No SXL)
CS6033	Liszt: Piano Concertos 1/2	LPO	Argenta Katchen	(SXL2097)
CS6034	Stravinsky Apollon Musagete	OSR	Ansermet	(No SXL, SDD243 ECS822)
CS6035	Stravinsky: Capriccio - Magaloff	OSR	Ansermet	(No SXL)
CS6036	Rimsky Korsakov: Xmas Eve/Sadko/Dubinushka/etc	OSR	Ansermet	(SXL2113)
CS6037	Beethoven: Symphony 5/Egmont Ov	OSR	Ansermet	(SXL2003)
CS6038	Tchaikovsky: Ov 1812/Capricci Italien/Marche Slave	LSO	Alwyn	(SXL2001)
CS6039	Coll: Virtuos Showpieces	Ricci		(No SXL)
CS6040	Chopin: Recital	Kempff		(SXL2081)
CS6041	Chopin: Recital	Kempff		(SXL2024)
CS6042	Chopin: Sonata 2 (Funeral March	Kempff		(SXL2025)
CS6043	Debussy: Jeux/Dukas La Peri	OSR	Ansermet	(SXL2027)
CS6044	Vivaldi: 4 Seasons	StCO	Munchinger	(SXL2019)
CS6046	Rodrigo: Guitar Concerto/Falla:Nights	NOS	Argenta Yepes	(SXL2091)
CS6047	Mendelssohn: Vln Conc/Bruch Scottish Fantasia	LPO	Boult Campoli	(SXL2026)
CS6048	Tchaikovsky: Symphony 4	OSR	Argenta	(SXL2015 ECS742)
CS6049	Grieg: Peer Gynt Incidental Music	LSO	Fjelstadt	(SXL2012)
CS6050	Falla 3 Cornered hat/Turina: Sinfonietta	NOS	Argenta	(No SXL)
CS6051	Schubert: Octet in Fmaj	Vienna Octet		(SXL2028)
CS6052	Tchaikovsky: Symphony 6	VPO	Martinon	(SXL2004)
CS6053	Beethoven: Ovs Coriolan/Egmont/Leonora 3/Fideli	VPO	Munchinger	(No SXL)
CS6054	Beethoven Piano Concerto 4	VPO	Schmidt-Isserstedt Bacchaus	(SXL2010)
CS6055	Tchaikovsky Concert Fantasia/Rachmaninov Piano Conc 1	LPO	Boult Katin	(SXL2034)
CS6058	Massenet: Le Cid/Meyerbeer Les Patineurs	IPO	Martinon	(SXL2021)

Cat. No.	Work	Orchestra	Conductor/Soloist	SXL/Notes
CS6059	Prokofiev Violin Concertos 1/2	OSR	Ansermet Ricci	(No SXL, ECS746)
CS6060	Haydn: Sonatas 34/48/52/Andante/Fantasia		Backhaus	(No SXL)
CS6061	Schubert: Symphony 9	LSO	Krips	(SXL2045)
CS6062	Bizet: Carmen etc	OSR	Ansermet	(SXL2037)
CS6063	Beethoven: Quintet in Eflat for pno&wind/etc	Vienna Octet		(SXL2158)
CS6064	Rachmaninov: Concert 2	LSO	Solti Katchen	(SXL2076)
CS6065	Mendelssohn: Symphony 4/Schubert Symphony 5	IPO	Solti	(SXL2067)
CS6066	Mozart: Eine Kleine.../Tchaikovsky Serenade	IPO	Solti	(SXL2046)
CS6067	Sibelius Violin Cpncerto	LSO	Fjelstad Ricci	(SXL2077)
CS6070	Beethoven Symphony 4	OSR	Ansermet	(VICS1102)
CS6074	Weber: Overtures	OSR	Ansermet	(SXL2112)
CS6077	Invitation t the Dance	PCO	Wolff	(SXL2105)
CS6078	Vaughan Williams Symphony 8	Philh	Boult	(SXL2207)
CS6079	Debussy: la Boite a Joujoux/Printemps	OSR	Ansermet	(SXL2136)
CS6080	Haydn: Symphonies 96/104	VPO	Munchinger	(No SXL)
CS6081	Mozart Symphonies 41/35	IPO	Krips	(SXL2220)
CS6082	Schumann: Pian Concerto/Weber: Konzertstuck	VPO	Gulda Andreae	(No SXL)
CS6083	Dvorak: Symphony 2	VPO	Kubelik	(No SXL)
CS6084	Paganini: Violin Conc/Saint-Saens Violin Conc	LSO	Gamba Campoli	(No SXL, ECS663 SPA183)
CS6085	Coll: Bach/Scarlatti/Schumann/Chopin/Brahms		Katin	(No SXL)
CS6086	Bartok: Concert for Orchestra	OSR	Ansermet	(No SXL, ECS578)
CS6087	Coll: Operatic highlights vol 5	LSO	Gamba	(No SXL)
CS6088	Grieg: Holberg suite/Mozart: Petits Riens	StCO	Munchinger	(No SXL)
CS6089	Rossini Overtures	LSO	Maag	(SXL2182)
CS6090	Schubert Trout Quintet		Curzon etc	(SXL2110)
CS6091	Haydn: Trumpet Concerto/Mozart Flute Conc 2/etc	OSR	Ansermet Pepin Leloir	(No SXL)
CS6092	Beethoven: Symphony 5	VPO	Solti	(SXL2124)
CS6093	Beethoven Symphony 7	VPO	Solti	(SXL2121)
CS6094	Beethoven: Pian Concert 3	VPO	Schmidt-Isserstedt Backhaus	(SXL2190)
CS6095	Tchaikovsky: Symphony 5	VPO	Krips	(SXL2109)
CS6096	Beethoven Piano Concerto 3	LSO	Gamba Katchen	(SXL2106)
CS6097	Tchaikovsky: Nutcracker suites 1/2	OSR	Ansermet	(SXL2092/3,CSA2203 has whole ballet))
CS6098	Adam: Giselle	PCO	Martinon	(SXL2128) TAS(SM) 61/127++
CS6099	Beethoven: Pian Concertos 1/2	VPO	Schmidt-Isserstedt Backhaus	(SXL2178)
CS6100	Tchaikovsky: Pian Concert o 1	LSO	Solti Curzon	(SXL2114)
CS6101	Berlioz: Various	PCO	Martionon	(SXL2134)
CS6102	Pipe Organ Favourites		Rees	(No SXL)
CS6106	Liszt: Recital		Peter Katin	(SXL2183)
CS6107	Mozart: Symphonies 32/38	LSO	Maag	(SXL2135)
CS6108	Tchaikovsky: Symphony 6	OSR	Ansermet	(No SXL, SPA221)
CS6109	Mozart: Quintet for piano & winds, Trio K498	Vienna Octet		(No SXL)
CS6110	Brahms: Symphony 1	VPO	Krips	(No SXL)
CS6111	Respighi: Pines of Rome/Casella/La Gara	AdSC	Previtalli	(No SXL)
CS6112	Frescobaldi-Ghedini: Quattro Pezzi/Petrassi	AdSC	Previtalli	(No SXL)
CS6116	Glazunov: The Seasons	PCO	Wolff	(SXL2141)
CS6117	Tchaikovsky: Symphony 5	PCO	Solti	(No SXL)
CS6118	Tchaikovsky: Symphony 2	PCO	Solti	(No SXL)
CS6119	Chausson: Symphony	PCO	Denzler	(No SXL)
CS6120	Beethoven: Symphonies 1/8	OSR	Ansermet	(No SXL)
CS6121	Coll: Operatic highlights vol 2	LSO	Gamba	(No SXL)
CS6126	Borodin: Symphonies 2/3/Prince Igor Overture	OSR	Ansermet	(No SXL, ECS576) TASEC TAS58/137++
CS6127	Tchaikovsky: Swan Lake (hlts)	OSR	Ansermet	(SXL2153)
CS6128	Delibes: Coppelia	OSR	Ansermet	(SXL2084/5)
CS6129	Strauss,R; Als Sprach Zarathustra	VPO	Karajan	(SXL2154)
CS6130	Albeniz: Navarra/Guridi: 10 Basques Dances/Turina	NOS	Argenta	(No SXL)

CS6131	Schubert: Symphonies 2/8	VPO	Munchinger	(SXL2156)
CS6132	Beethoven: Septet	Vienna Octet		(SXL2157)
CS6133	Mozart: Serenata Notturna K329/Notturn for 4 Orchs	LSO	Maag	(SXL2196)
CS6134	Lal Symphonie Espagnole/Ravel Tzigane	OSR	Ansermet	(SXL2155)
CS6138	Stravinsky Song of the Nightingale/Pulcinella	OSR	Ansermet	(SXL2188)
CS6139	Massenet: Scenes Alsaciennes/Scenes Pittoreaques	PCO	Wolff	(No SXL, ECS772/773)
CS6140	Tchaikovsky: Suite 3	PCO	Boult	(No SXL, ECS766)
CS6141	Mozart Pian Concert 27/Sonata 11	VPO	Bohm Backhaus	(SXL2214)
CS6142	Bach: The Musical Offering	StCO	Munchinger	(SXL2204)
CS6143	Beethoven: Symphony 9	OSR	Ansermet	(SXL2274)
CS6145	Beethoven: Symphony 3	VPO	Solti	(SXL2165)
CS6146	Suppe: Overtures	VPO	Solti	(SXL2174)
CS6147	Ravel: Daphnis & Chloe	LSO	Monteux	(SXL2164)
CS6148	Breton Andalusian Scenes etc	NOS	Argenta	(No SXL)
CS6149	Coll: Vienna Carnival	VPO	Boskovsky	(SXL2163)
CS6150	Tchaikovsky: Symphony 4	PCO	Wolff	(SXL2166)
CS6151	Brahms: Piano Concerto 1	LSO	Monteux Katchen	(SXL2172)
CS6152	Preludes and Intermezzi from Zarzuelas	NOS	Argenta	(No SXL)
CS6153	Rachmaninov: Rhapsody on Paganini/Dohnanyi Varns	LPO	Boult Katchen	(SXL2176)
CS6154	Wolf-Ferrari: Music of Wolf-Ferrari	PCO	Nello-Santi	(SXL2177)
CS6156	Beethoven: Pian Concert 5	VPO	Schmidt-Isserstedt Backhaus	(SXL2179)
CS6157	Sym Varns	LSO	Boult Curzon	(SXL2173)
CS6158	Brahms: Variations on THemes of Handel, Paganini	Katchen		(SXL6218)
CS6159	Bartok: Music for SP&C/Beethoven: Qt op 133	OSR	Ansermet	(No SXL)
CS6160	Beethoven: Symphony 6	OSR	Ansermet	(SXL2193)
CS6161	Beethoven Sonatas 21 (Waldstein)/23 (appassionata)	Backhaus		(SXL2241)
CS6163	Paganini: 24 Caprices	Ricci		(SXL2194)
CS6165	Coll: Sarasate/Saint-Saens recital	LSO	Gamba Ricci	(SXL2197)
CS6169	Mozart: Div op 11/Schubert: Dances	StCO	Munchinger	(No SXL)
CS6170	Brahms Symphony 4	VPO	Kubelik	(SXL2206)
CS6172	Bach: Organ Recital	Richter		(SXL2219)
CS6173	Bach: BWV 544/542 Chorale preludes		Richter	(No SXL)
CS6174	Ravel: String quartet/Prokofiev String quartet	Carmirelli Qt		(SXL2231)
CS6177	Mussorgsky: Pictures at an Exhibition	OSR	Ansermet	(SXL2195)
CS6178	Mozart: Horn Concertos	LSO	Maag Tuckwell	(SXL2238)
CS6179	Britten: 4 Sea Interludes/Nocturne	Britten Pears		(SXL2189)
CS6181	Schumann: Piano Concerto/Waldscenen	VPO	Backhaus Ward	(No SXL, but issued on SWL 10" and SDD201)
CS6182	Coll: Philharmonic Ball	VPO	Boskovsky	(SXL2198)
CS6183	Beethoven Symphony 7/Fideli Ov	OSR	Ansermet	(SXL2235)
CS6184	Beethoven: Symphony 2/Leonora 2 Ov	OSR	Ansermet	(SXL2228)
CS6185	Delibes: Coppelia/Sylvia	OSR	Ansermet	(No SXL)
CS6186	Mendelsshohn: Midsummer Nights dream, Schubert: Rosamunde	OSR	Ansermet	(SXL2229)
CS6187	Prokofiev Peter and the Wolf	LSO	Henderson Katchen Graffman	(SXL2218)
CS6188	Beethoven: Piano Concerto 2	VPO	Schmidt Isserstedt	(SXL2178)
CS6189	Beethoven Symphony 3	OSR	Ansermet	(SXL2244)
CS6190	Stravinsky: Symphony in C/Symph in 3 movements.	OSR	Ansermet	(SXL2237)
CS6191	Mendelssohn: Symphony 3/Fingal's Cave	LSO	Maag	(SXL2246) TAS44/178
CS6192	All Time popular favourites	VPO	Knappertsbusch	(SXL2239)
CS6193	Recital	Ricci		(SXL2240)
CS6194	Albeniz: Iberia/Turina: Danzas Fantasticas	OSR	Ansermet	(SXL2243)
CS6195	Brahms: Piano Concerto 2	LSO	Ferencsik Katchen	(SXL2236)
CS6196	Searle: Symphony 1/Seiber: Elegy etc	Melos CO LPO	Boult Seiber	(SXL2232)
CS6197	Bach,J.S: Italian Concerto/etc	George Malcolm		(SXL2259)
CS6198	Coll: Hungarian/Slavonic Dances (Brahms/Dvorak)	VPO	Reiner	(SXL2249)
CS6199	Strauss (arr Dorati) Graduation Ball etc	VPO	Boskovsky	(SXL2250)

Catalog	Work	Orchestra	Conductor/Artist	SXL
CS6200	Bizet: Jeux D'Enfants/etc	PCO	Martinon	(SXL2252)
CS6201	Bach: Chaconne/Vivaldi&Pilau: Guitar Concertos	NOS Yepes	Alonso	(No SXL)
CS6202	Halffter: Raps Portuguesa/Turina: Raps Sinfonica	NOS Sorian	Alonso	(No SXL)
CS6203	Beethoven: Diabelli Variations		Katchen	(SXL2262)
CS6204	Rossini: Overtures	LSO	Gamba	(SXL2266)
CS6205	French Overtures	OSR	Ansermet	(SXL2263)
CS6206	Corelli: Concert Gross 8/etc	StCO	Munchinger	(SXL2265)
CS6207	Mozart: Concert	StCO	Munchinger	(SXL2270)
CS6208	Bizet: Symphony in C	OSR	Ansermet	(SXL2275)
CS6209	Tchaikovsky: Rome & Juliet ov/Strauss: Don Juan	VPO	Karajan	(SXL2269)
CS6210	Ravel: Daphnis & Chloe	OSR	Ansermet	(SXL2273)
CS6211	Strauss,R: Death & Transfiguration/Salome/Till Eulenspiegel	VPO	Karajan	(SXL2261)
CS6212	Rimsky-Korsakov: Scheherazade/Borodin Polv Dances	OSR	Ansermet	(SXL2268)
CS6213	Classical Indian Muisc introduced by Menuhin			(SXL2245)
CS6214	Mozart: Haffner Serenade K250	VPO	Munchinger	(SXL2272)
CS6215	Tchaikovsky: Violin Concerto/Dvorak Violin Concerto	LSO	Sargent Ricci	(SXL2279)
CS6216	Offenbach: Gaite Parisienne	ROHCG	Solti	(SXL2280)
CS6217	Mahler: Symphony 4	Ccgbw	Solti	(SXL2276)
CS6218	Tchaikovsky: Scenes from Swan Lake	Ccgbw	Fistoulari	(SXL2285)
CS6219	Stravinsky: Les Noces/Sym of Psalms	OSR	Ansermet	(SXL2277)
CS6220	Franck: Organ works		Demessieux	(No SXL)
CS6221	Franck: Organ works		Demessieux	(No SXL)
CS6222	Franck: Symphony	OSR	Ansermet	(SXL2291)
CS6223	Prokofiev: Classical Symphony/Borodin	OSR	Ansermet	(SXL2292)
CS6224	Falla: Three Cornered Hat	OSR	Ansermet Berganza	(SXL2296)
CS6225	Debussy: Children's Ballet/Symphonic Suite	OSR	Ansermet	(SXL2287)
CS6226	Franck: PianoQuintet	Curzon	Vienna Philharmonic Quartet	(SXL2278)
CS6227	Fauré: Pelleas & Melisande/Debussy	OSR	Ansermet	(SXL2303)
CS6228	Dvorak: Symphony 9 in Eminor	VPO	Kubelik	(SXL2289)
CS6230	Haydn: Symphonies 100/83	VPO	Munchinger	(SXL2284)
CS6231	Mozart: Quartets K499/K589	Vienna Philharmonic Quartet		(SXL2286)
CS6232	Coll: 10001 Nights	VPO	Boskovsky	(SXL2288)
CS6234	Brahms: Clarinet Quintet/Wagner Adagi o	Vienna Octet		(SXL2297)
CS6235	Encores		Katchen	(SXL2293)
CS6236	Handel: Water Music/Fireworks Msuic	LSO	Szell	(SXL2302)
CS6237	Recital		Rostropovich Britten	(SXL2298)
CS6240	Prokofiev Rome&Juliet	OSR	Ansermet	(SXL2306)
CS6242	Prokofiev Cinderella	OSR	Ansermet	(SXL2307)
CS6241	Frank Martin Concert for 7 wind Insts etc	OSR	Ansermet	(SXL2311)
CS6243	Bach: Suites 2/3	OSR	Ansermet	(SXL6004)
CS6244	Holst: The Planets	VPO	Karajan	(SXL2305)
CS6245	Wagner: Ovs: Flying Dutchman/Tannhauser/Rienzi	VPO	Solti	(SET227)
CS6246	Beethoven: Sonatas 30/32		Backhaus	(No SXL)
CS6247	Beethoven: Sonatas 15/26		Backhaus	(No SXL)
CS6248	Debussy: Prelude L'Apres Midi/Ravel Pavanne etc	LSO	Monteux	(SXL2312)
CS6249	Brahms: Symphony 3/Tragic Ov	VPO	Karajan	(No SXL)
CS6251	Adam: Giselle	VPO	Karajan	(SXL6002)
CS6252	Herold/lanchberry: La Fille Mal Gardee	ROHCG	Lanchberry	(SXL2313) TAS 31/12,40/158+ TASEC44
CS6324	Holst: Hymn of Jesus/Perfect Fool	LPO	Boult	(SXL6006)
CS6325	Stravinsky: Etudes/Suites 1,2, etc from Fairy's Kiss	OSR	Ansermet	(No SXL)
CS6327	Shostakovich: Symphony 5	OSR	Kertesz	(SXL6018)
CS6328	Beethoven: Fidelio, Leonore 1/2/3	IPO	Maazel	(SXL6025)
CS6332	Bartok: Divertimento/Vivaldi: Violin Concerto	Moscow Ch Orch	Barshai	(SXL6026)
CS6337	Hindemith VC/Bruch Scottish Fantasy	LSO	Horenstein Oistrakh	(SXL6035, SDD465)
CS6338	Borodin: Quartet 2/Shostakovich: Quartet 8	Borodin Quartet		(SXL6036)

Decca London series

CS6339	Glinka: Russlan&Ludmilla/Stravinsky: Petruchka st	IPO	Maazel	(No SXL)
CS6341	Brahms: Sonatas Op 117/2, Op 119/3	Curzon		(SXL6041)
CS6345	Respighi: Pines & Fountains of Rome	OSR	Ansermet	(SXL6141)
CS6346	Mozart: Wind Music V3	LWS	Brymer	(SXL6049)
CS6347	Mozart: Wind Music V1 (Snd K375/Divs K166/K213)	LWS	Brymer	(SXL6050)
CS6348	Mozart: Wind Music V2 (Snd K388/Divs K186/K253)	LWS	Brymer	(SXL6051)
CS6349	Mozart: Wind Music V4 (Divs K240/K252/K196e)	LWS	Brymer	(SXL6052)
CS6351	Mozart: Wind Music V5 (Divs K270/K289/K196f)	LWS	Brymer	(SXL6053)
CS6352	Mozart: Wind Music V5 (Divs K270/K289/K196f)	LWS	Brymer	(SXL6054)
CS6353	Mozart: Divertimento K287/Haydn Div in Gmaj	Vienna Octet		(SXL6055)
CS6354	Mozart Symphonies 33/39	VPO	Kertesz	(SXL6056)
CS6356	Rodrigo: Fantasia/Ohana: Concert	NOS	de Burgos Yepes	(No SXL)
CS6357	Dvorak: Quintet in A/Schubert Quartet 12	Vienna Phil Qt Curzon		(SXL6043)
CS6358	Dvorak: Symphony 8	LSO	Kertesz	(SXL6044)
CS6359	Rachmaninov: Piano Concerto 3	LSO	Fistoulari Ashkenazy	(SXL6057)
CS6360	Tchaikovsky: Piano Concerto	LSO	Maazel Ashkenazy	(SXL6058)
CS6365	Beethoven: Sonatas 17/28	Backhaus		(SXL6063)
CS6366	Beethoven: Sonatas 12/18	Backhaus		(SXL6064)
CS6367	Ravel Bolero/La Valse/Dukas/Honegger	OSR	Ansermet	(SXL6065)
CS6368	Stravinsky: Fairy's Kiss	OSR	Ansermet	(SXL6066)
CS6369	Mozart: Symphony 41/Haydn: Symphony 103	VPO	Karajan	(SXL6067)
CS6370	Britten: Quartet 2 in C/Fricker: Quartet 2	Amadeus Quartet		(No SXL,ZRG5372)
CS6371	Liszt: Sonata in Bmin/Liebestraum/etc	Curzon		(No SXL)
CS6374	Beethoven: Piano Concertos 2/4	LSO	Gamba Katchen	(SXL6082)
CS6375	Sibelius: Symphony 1	VPO	Maazel	(SXL6084)
CS6376	Tchaikovsky: Symphony 5	VPO	Maazel	(SXL6085)
CS6377	Mozart: Sinfonia Conc etc	MPO	Kondrashin Oistrakh	(SXL6088)
CS6378	Schubert: Symphonies 4/5	VPO	Munchinger	(SXL6086)
CS6379	Mozart: Quintet for Clarinet & Strings/etc	Vienna Octet Boskovsky		(SXL6087)
CS6381	Schubert: Symphony 9	VPO	Kertesz	(SXL6089)
CS6382	Schubert: Symphony 8/etc	VPO	Kertesz	(SXL6090)
CS6383	Mozart: Symphony 36/Eine Kleine Nachtmusik/etc	VPO	Kertesz	(SXL6091)
CS6384	Schubert: Quartets 10/14	Vienna Phil Quartet		(SXL6092)
CS6385	Haydn: Quartets 18/39/77	Janacek Qt		(SXL6093)
CS6386	Wagner: Meistersinger Ov/Parsifal Prelude etc	OSR	Ansermet	(SXL6094)
CS6387	Sibelius: Symphony 4/Tapiola	OSR	Ansermet	(SXL6095)
CS6388	Beethoven: Symphonies 1/8	OSR	Ansermet	(SXL6096)
CS6389	Beethoven: Sonatas 1/5/6/7	Backhaus		(SXL6097)
CS6390	Rachmaninov: Piano Concertos 2/3/Etudes	MPO	Kondrashin Ashkenazy	(SXL6099)
CS6391	Sibelius: Symphony 2	OSR	Ansermet	(SXL6100)
CS6392	Bach: Hpsd Concertos 1/2	StCO	Munchinger Malcolm	(SXL6101)
CS6393	Pergolesi: Concertinos 1-4	StCO	Munchinger	(SXL6102)
CS6394	Dvorak: Quartets 2/6	Janacek Qt		(SXL6103)
CS6395	Pergolesi: Concertinos 5/6/etc	StCO	Munchinger	(SXL6104)
CS6396	Brahms: Op 76/116	Katchen		(SXL6105)
CS6397	Beethoven: Piano Concerto 5/Egmont	LSO	Gamba Katchen	(SXL6109)
CS6398	Britten: Young Person's Guide/Serenade	LSO	Britten Tuckwell	(SXL6110)
CS6399	Bartok: Miraculous Mandarin/Music for Strings, Perc&Celeste	LSO	Solti	(SXL6111)
CS6400	Bach: Suite 2 for Flute & Strings/etc	LSO	Monteux Monteux	(SXL6112)
CS6401	Mahler: Symphony 1	LSO	Solti	(SXL6113)
CS6402	Dvorak: Symphony 7	LSO	Kertesz	(SXL6115)
CS6403	Mozart: Horn Concerti	LSO	Maag Tuckwell	(SXL6108)
CS6404	Brahms: Op 117-119	Katchen		(SXL6118)
CS6405	Mussorgsky: Bare Mt/Khovantchina/Glinka:	OSR	Ansermet	(SXL6119)
CS6406	Prokofiev: Symphony 5	OSR	Ansermet	(SXL6120)

CS6407	Bartok: Dance Suite/Rumanian Folk Songs/2 Portraits	OSR	Ansermet	(SXL6121)
CS6408	Sibelius: Symphony 2	VPO	Maazel	(SXL6125)
CS6409	Tchaikovsky: Symphony 6	VPO	Maazel	(SXL6164)
CS6410	Brahms: Sonatas OP 1/2	Katchen		(SXL6129)
CS6411	Mozart,Schumann: Music for 2 Pianos/etc	Ashkenazy Frager		(SXL6130)
CS6412	Mozart: Dances & Marches	VME	Boskovsky	(SXL6131)
CS6413	Mozart: Dances & Marches	VME	Boskovsky	(SXL6132)
CS6414	Mozart: Dances & Marches	VME	Boskovsky	(SXL6133)
CS6415	Strauss: Death & Transfiguration/Don Juan	VPO	Maazel	(SXL6134)
CS6416	Schubert: Sonata Op 53/Impromptus in Aflat/Gflat	Curzon		(SXL6135)
CS6417	Kodaly: Hari Janos/Dances of Galanta/etc	LSO	Kertesz	(SXL6136)
CS6418	'Pas de Deux'	LSO	Bonynge	(SXL6137)
CS6419	Britten: Symphony for Cello/Haydn: Cello Concerto	ECO	Britten Rostropovich	(SXL6138)
CS6420	Grieg: Peer Gynt (hlts)/Tchaikovsky: Nutcracker St 1	VPO	Karajan	(SXL2308)
CSA2201	Delibes: Coppelia	OSR	Ansermet	(SXL2084/5)
CSA2202	Smetana: Ma Vlast	VPO	Kubelik	(SXL2064/5)
CSA2203	Tchaikovsky: Nutcracker Suite	OSR	Ansermet	(SXL2092/3)
CSA2204	Tchaikovsky: Swan Lake	OSR	Ansermet	(SXL2107-8)
CSA2205	Bruckner: Symphony 5/Wagner: Gotterdamerung exts	VPO	Knappertsbusch	(No SXL)
CSA2206	Bach: Orchestral suites	StCO	Munchinger	(SXL2300-1)
CSA2213	The Art of the Prima Donna v1	Sutherland		(SXL2256)
CSA2213	The Art of the Prima Donna v2	Sutherland		(SXL2257)
CSA2228	Mahler: Symphony 5	CSO	Solti	(SET534-5)
CSA2248	Mahler: Symphonies 5, 10 (Adagio)	LAPO	Mehta	(SXL6806-7)
CSA2301	Bach: Brandenburg Concertos 1/6	StCO	Munchinger	(SXL2125)
CSA2302	Handel: Organ Concertos	Karl Richter		(SXL2115)
CSA2302	Handel: Organ Concertos Vol 2	Karl Richter		(SXL2187)
CSA2302	Handel: Organ Concertos Vol 3	Karl Richter		(SXL2201)
CSA2303	Chopin: Mazurkas (complete)	Magaloff		(No SXL)
CSA2304	Tchaikovsky: Sleeping Beauty	OSR	Ansermet	(SXL2160-2)
CSA2305	Chopin: Piano Works	Kempff		(No SXL)
CSA2306	Haydn: Symphonies 82-87	OSR	Ansermet	(SXL6020-22)
CSA2307	Music of the Strauss Family	VPO	Boskovsky	(No SXL)
CSA2401	Beethoven: Piano Concerti	OSR	Schmidt-Isserstedt	(No SXL)
CSA2402	Brahms: Symphonies 1-4, Academic Ov, Tragic Ov, Haydn Vns	OSR	Ansermet	(SXL6059-62)

* * * * *

Decca Argo (ZNF, ZRG)

People started collecting Argos only recently. This is surprising since there are many beautiful orchestral recordings on the Argo label. Argo is not a reissue label.

Record numbers: There are 3 record number series: ZNF, ZRG, and ZK. The very earliest Argos have ZNF numbers, and these are amongst the earliest stereo records, though there are very few of them. The great majority of Argos have ZRG numbers. Finally, there is the ZK series. These are reissues of the very early ZNF and ZRG records, and usually having exactly the same music, layout, and notes. The best example is ZK-1 Noye's Fludde, which is simply a later form of the original ZNF-1 record.

Labels: The early ZNF label is black with silver lettering, and has the word "ARGO" inside an oval shaped surround at the 12 o'clock position on the label. This is generally called the "oval logo". Slightly later issues of the ZNF records have the word "Argo" inside a rectangular box, again at the 12 o'clock position.

The ZRG label is the same except that the label colour is olive green. (By the way, the RG monos have a dark blue label). In the case of ZRG, up to around ZRG650 the earliest issues have the "oval logo" label. After that the earliest label has the rectangular surround.

The list: The list of Argo ZRG records is believed to be complete.

Number	Title	Performers
ZDA19-20	Tippett: A Child of our Time, Midsummer Marriage (hlts)	RLPO Pritchard etc
ZNF 1	Britten: Noye's Fludde	ECO Del Mar
ZNF 2	"Sixty Years of Motoring: The Sounds of Motor Cars"	Raymond Baxter (narrator)
ZNF 4	Homage to Shakespeare	
ZNF 5	Williamson: The Happy Prince	ASMF etc
ZNF 6	Holst: Choral hymns from the Rig Veda, Savitri	ECO Baker
ZNF 8-10	Cavalli: L'Ormindo	LPO Leppard etc
ZNF11-12	Cavalli: La Calisto	LPO Leppard Glyndebourne Chorus etc
ZNF15	Stravinsky: The Soldier's Tale	Ensemble cond Zalkowich Glenda Jackson (narr)
ZRG 501	"Airs by Handel"	ASMF Leppard Bernadette Greevy
ZRG 503	Liszt: Fantasia & Fugue/Prelude & Fugue	Preston
ZRG 504	Handel: Bass Arias	ASMF Ledger Robinson (bass)
ZRG 505	Pergolesi: Magnificat, Vivaldi: Gloria in Dmaj	ASMF Willcocks
ZRG 506	Rossini: String Sonatas 1,3,5,6	ASMF Marriner
ZRG 507	Howells: Motet on the Death of President Kennedy	Collegium Royale Kings Cambridge Willcocks
ZRG 511	Evensong for Ascensiontide	St John's College Cambridge Guest
ZRG 512	Holst: Songs/Part Songs/etc	Purcell Singers Holst Pears
ZRG 515	Haydn: Harmonienmesse	ASMF St Johns College (Camb) Choir Guest
ZRG 522	Harp recital (Mozart, Handel, Beethoven, Albéniz, etc)	Robles
ZRG 523	Choral Recital (Bruckner, Schoenberg, Debussy, Messiaen)	John Alldis Choir Alldis
ZRG 524	Mozart: Exsultate Jubilate	ASMF Marriner Spoorenberg (sop)
ZRG 527	Schubert: Part Songs	Elizabethan Singers Halsey
ZRG 528	English Organ Music (Elgar, Bridge, Britten, etc)	Preston
ZRG 529	Williamson: Julius Caesar Jones	Finchley Childrens Music Group Andrewes
ZRG 530-3	"The Living Tradition" (Music from Himalayas,Rumania,Middle East, etc)	
ZRG 535	Tippett: Symphony 2	LSO Davis
ZRG 536	Maw: Chamber Music, Rawsthorne: Quintet for Wind&Piano	London Music Group
ZRG 541	Handel: Chandos Anthems	ASMF/KCC Willcocks

ZRG 542	Haydn: Heiligenmesse	ASMF St Johns College (Ca mb) Choir Guest
ZRG 543	Haydn: Trumpet Concerto/Horn Concerto	ASMF Marriner Tuckwell
ZRG 544-5	Milton: Poems Directed by George Rylands	various readers
ZRG 550	A Meditation for Christ's Nativity	St Johns Cambridge Guest
ZRG 553	Gerhard: Concerto for Orchestra/Rawsthorne	BBCSO Del Mar
ZRG 554	Mozart: 3 Divs for Strings/Serenata Notturna	ASMF Marriner
ZRG 555	Lawes: Consort Music	Elizabethan Consort of Viols Dart
ZRG 557	"Eton Choir Book"	Purcell Consort Burgess
ZRG 558	Davy: St Matthew Passion	Purcell Consort Burgess
ZRG 560-1	"The Living Tradition" (Music from Andalucia, Turkey)	
ZRG 563	Handel: Ode for St Cecilia's Day	ASMF KCC Willcocks
ZRG 565	Maw: String Quartet, Wood: String Quartet	Aeolian Quartet
ZRG 566	"To Entertain a King" (Music for Henry 8th)	Musica Reservata Morrow
ZRG 569	Mendelssohn: Octet/Boccherini: Cello Quintet	ASMF Marriner
ZRG 570	Victoria: Requiem Mass/etc	Ch of St John's College Cambridge Guest
ZRG 571	Brahms: Motets and Chorale Preludes	New English Singers Preston
ZRG 572	Songs & Dances by Dowland, East, Holborne	Musica Reservata/Purcell Consort of Voices Morrow
ZRG 573	Elgar: Introduction & Allegro/Serenade/Elegy/etc	ASMF Marriner
ZRG 574	Debussy: Trio for Harp, Flute & Viola/Ravel/Bax	Delme Quartet
ZRG 575	Stravinsky: Pulcinella/Apollon Musagete	ASMF Marriner
ZRG 576	"Voices and Brass"	Philip Jones Brass Ensemble Leppard
ZRG 577	Arne: Conc in Gmin/E Bach: Concerto in Cmin	ASMF Marriner Malcolm (hpsd)
ZRG 578	Palestrina: Veni Sponsa Christi	St Johns Cambridge Guest
ZRG 584	Tchaikovsky: Serenade for Strings, Souvenir de Florence	ASMF Marriner
ZRG 585	Baroque Trumpet Concertos	ASMF Marriner Wilbraham (trumpet)
ZRG 590	"Glad Tidings" (Baroque Xmas Music)	London String Pl PJBE Norrington
ZRG 594	Mozart: Four Early Symphonies K112,K114,K124,K128	ASMF Marriner
ZRG 596	Music to Entertain Queen Victoria	Purcell Consort Burgess
ZRG 597	Music of Prince Albert	Purcell Consort Burgess
ZRG 598	Haydn: Creation Mass	ASMF Choir of St Johns College Cambridge Guest
ZRG 601	Music for Trumpet&Cornetto	Various Don Smithers (trumpet&cornetto)
ZRG 602	"A Florentine Festival - Music for Ferdinand de Medici"	Musica Reservata
ZRG 603	Rossini: String Sonatas 2&4/Donizetti: String Qt	ASMF Marriner
ZRG 604	Strauss,R: Metamorphosen/Wagner: Siegfried Idyll	ASMF Marriner
ZRG 605	Mendelssohn:Concerto for 2 Pianos,Conc for Piano&Strings	ASMF Marriner Ogdon Lucas
ZRG 606	Messiaen: Harawi-Chant d'Amour et de Mort	Barker (sop) Johnson (pno)
ZRG 607	Partsongs by Delius & Elgar	Louis Halsey Singers Halsey
ZRG 620	Victoria: O Quam Gloriosum	St Johns Cambridge Guest
ZRG 621	Italian & English Church Music (Britten,Purcell,Howells,etc)	St Johns Cambridge Guest
ZRG 622	Lutyens: Quincunx, Maw: Scenes & Arias	BBCSO Del Mar
ZRG 631	Haydn: Organ Concerto,Michael Haydn: Duo Concertante	ASMF Marriner Preston (organ)
ZRG 632	Couperin: La Reine Des Coeurs	George Malcolm
ZRG 633	Messiaen: Les Corps Glorieux, Le Banquet Celeste	Preston (organ)
ZRG 634	Haydn: Mass in Time of War	ASMF St Johns Coll Cambridge Guest
ZRG 635	Berlioz: Songs for Chorus	Schütz Choir Norrington
ZRG 638	Bedford: Music for Albion Moonlight, Lutyens: And Suddenly its Evening	BBCSO Carewe Manning (sop) BBCSO Handt (tenor)
ZRG 639	Schütz: The Resurrection	Schütz Choir/Elizabethan Consort of Viols/London Sackbuts Norrington Tilney (hpsd)
ZRG 640	Treasures of the English Baroque (Blow, Arne, Croft, etc)	
ZRG 642	Florentine Music of the 14th Century	EMCL Munrow
ZRG 643	"The Triumphs of Oriana"	Purcell Cosnort/London Sackbut Ens/Eliz Consort of Viols Burgess
ZRG 644	"Strings & Brass" - music by Gabrielli, Vivaldi, etc	ASMF Marriner PJBE
ZRG 645	Gesualdo: Motets, Monteverdi: Motets	Monteverdi Choir Gardiner
ZRG 646	Music of the Waits	Various
ZRG 649	Walton: Facade	London Sinfonietta Walton Ashcroft Scofield
ZRG 650-1	Messiaen: Vingt Regards Sur L'Enfants Jesus	Ogdon

ZRG 652	Elizabethan Words & Music	Purcell Consort Burgess Brett (spkr)
ZRG 653	Mozart: Symphonies 23/24/26/27	ASMF Marriner
ZRG 654	Vivaldi: The 4 Seasons	ASMF Marriner Loveday (vln)
ZRG 655	"Just Brass"	Philip Jones Brass Ensemble
ZRG 656	Crosse: Changes	LSO&Chorus Del Mar
ZRG 657	Bartok: Music for Strings Perc & Celeste	ASMF Marriner
ZRG 658	"Lo, Country Sports"	Elizabethan Consort of Viols Burgess
ZRG 659	Ceremonial Tudor Church Music (Byrd,Weelkes)	Elizabethan Consort of Viols/London Sackbuts Burgess
ZRG 660	Rainier: String Trio: Quanta, Rawsthorne: Clarinet Quartet	London Oboe Quartet/Aeolian Quartet King (clar)
ZRG 661	Recital (Handel, Boyce, Arne, etc)	ASMF Marriner Tear
ZRG 662	O Sacrum Convivium (Langlais,Duruflé,Fauré,Messiaen,etc)	St Johns Cambridge Guest
ZRG 663	Hindemith: Organ Sonatas 1-3	Preston (organ)
ZRG 664	Songs by Beethoven&Brahms	Shirley-Quirk Isepp (pno)
ZRG 665	Messiaen: Visions de L'Amen	Ogdon Lucas (pianos)
ZRG 666	Schütz: Cantate Domino	Schütz Choir Norrington
ZRG 667	Chansons	Elizabethan Consort Burgess
ZRG 668	Monteverdi: Madrigals	Purcell Consort Burgess
ZRG 669	Trumpet Concertos (Hummel, L. Mozart,Albrechtsberger)	ASMF Marriner Wilbraham (trumpet)
ZRG 670	Dvorak: Serenade for Strings/Grieg: Holberg Suite	ASMF Marriner
ZRG 671	Schütz: The Christmas Story	Schütz Choir Norrington
ZRG 672	"Radcliffe Quartets" 1969 (Forbes,Maconchy,Sherlaw,etc)	Allegri Quartet
ZRG 673	Music of the Crusades	EMCL Munrow
ZRG 674	Stravinsky: Capriccio, Shostakovich : Piano Concerto 1	ASMF Marriner Ogdon
ZRG 675	English Virginal Music (Byrd,Gibbons,etc)	Tilney (hpsd)
ZRG 676	Nicholas Maw: Sinfonia, Sonata for Strings and 2 Horns	ECO Del Mar
ZRG 677	Mozart: Coronation Mass	ASMF Marriner
ZRG 679	Mozart: Eine Kleine Nachtmusik, Sinfonia Concertante	ASMF Marriner
ZRG 680	Tippett: Concerto for String Orch/Fantasia/etc	ASMF Marriner
ZRG 681	Dunstable: Chansons, Josquin des Pres: Chansons	Purcell Consort Burgess
ZRG 682	Williamson: Chamber and Vocal Works	Gabrieli String Quartet/Nash Ens Cantelo (sop) Williamson (pno)
ZRG 685	Bliss: Intro & Allegro, Tippett, Previn, etc	Leics Schools SO Previn/Bliss
ZRG 686	Handel Ballet Music	ASMF Marriner
ZRG 687-8	Bach,J.S: 4 Suites for Orchestra	ASMF Marriner
ZRG 689	Schütz: St Matthew Passion	Schütz Choir Norrington
ZRG 690	Palestrina: Assumpta Est Maria, Missa Brevis	St Johns Cambridge Guest
ZRG 691	Hoddinott:Vocal&Chamber Works, Tate: Vocal Works	Cardiff Festival Players Lockhart
ZRG 692	Janacek: Diary of One Who Disappeared	Tear Ledger
ZRG 693	Music at Magdalen vol 1	Magdalen College Oxford/Eliz Consort Viols Rose
ZRG 694	Piano works by Johnson and Messiaen	Johnson (pno)
ZRG 695	Works for Cello (Rachmaninov,Hoddinott,Banks)	Isaac (cello) Tryon (pno)
ZRG 696	V Williams: Tallis Fantasia, Lark Ascending, Greensleeves	ASMF Marriner
ZRG 697	Handel: Fireworks Music, Water Music	ASMF Marriner
ZRG 698	Monteverdi: Madrigals	Schütz Choir Norrington
ZRG 699	Messiaen: Poèmes Pour Mi,Chants de Terre et de Ciel	Barker (sop) Johnson (pno)
ZRG 701	Gerhard: Symphony 4, Violin Concerto	BBCSO Davis Neaman (vln)
ZRG 702	Sessions: Rhapsody for Orchestra/Symphony 8/etc	London Sinfonietta Prausnitz
ZRG 703	Messiaen: Poemes Pour Mi/etc	BBCSO Boulez
ZRG 704	Composers at the Piano (Musgrave,Williamson,R.R.Bennett)	Performed by the composers
ZRG 705	Mozart: Div K334, Notturno for 4 Orchestras	ASMF Marriner
ZRG 706	Mozart: Symphonies 25/29	ASMF Marriner
ZRG 707	Tchaikovsky: Songs	Tear (tenor) Ledger (pno)
ZRG 708	Mussorgsky: Songs	Luxon (bar) Willison (pno)
ZRG 710	Bruckner: Mass in Emin	Schütz Choir PJBE Norrington
ZRG 711	Walton: Sonata for Strings, Prokofiev: Visions Fugitives	ASMF/Marriner
ZRG 712	Maxwell-Davies: Points and Dances	Fires of London Davies
	Fantasia on Taverner	Philh Groves

ZRG 713	Szymanowski: Piano Works	Jones (pno)
ZRG 714	Bridge: String Quartets 3, 4	Allegri Qt
ZRG 715	Fricker: Violin Concerto op 11, Banks: Violin Concerto	RPO Del Mar Neaman
ZRG 716	Mendelssohn: "Hear My Prayer"	Schütz Choir Norrington Palmer (sop)
ZRG 717	"Golden Brass"	Philip Jones Brass Ensemble
ZRG 718	Schumann: Liederkreise	Tear Ledger
ZRG 719	Bizet: Symphony in C/Prokofiev: Classical Sym	ASMF Marriner
ZRG 720	Stravinsky: Mass, Poulenc: Motets	London Sinfonietta Preston
ZRG 721	Liszt: Concerto Pathetique, Schumann: Andante & Variations, 6 Canonic Studies	Ogdon Lucas
ZRG 722	Music at Magdelen vol 2	Magdalen College Choir Bernard Rose
ZRG 724	Purcell: Ceremonial Music	ECO Choir of St Johns Cambridge Guest
ZRG 725	Walton: Jubilate, The Twelve, Litany, Missa Brevis, etc	Chistchurch Cathedral Choir Preston
ZRG 726	Musgrave: Clarinet Concerto/etc	Philh Del Mar De Peyer Tuckwell
ZRG 727	Delius: Cello Sonata, etc, Prokofiev: Cello Sonata op 119	Isaac (cello) Jones (pno)
ZRG 728	"The Triumphs of Maximillian I"	EMCL Munrow
ZRG 729	Mozart: Violin Concerto K216, Concertone K190	ASMF Marriner Loveday (vln) Brown (vln) Kaine (vln)
ZRG 730	Rachmaninov: Songs	Tear Ledger (pno)
ZRG 731	"Classics for Brass" (Strauss, Grieg, Poulenc, Dukas, etc)	Philip Jones Brass Ensemble
ZRG 732	V Williams: Songs	Robert Tear Ledger (pno)
ZRG 733-4	Vivaldi: L'Estro Armonico	ASMF Marriner
ZRG 735	Music of Lassus	Choir of Christ Church Oxford Preston
ZRG 737	Britten: Nocturne for Tenor, 7 Obbligato Insts & Strings op 60, Mahler: Lieder Eines Fahrenden Gesellen	ASMF Marriner Robert Tear
ZRG 739	Beethoven: Mass in Cmaj	ASMF Choir of St Johns,Camb Guest
ZRG 740	Christopher Tye: Euge Bone Mass, Western Wynde Mass	KCC Willcocks
ZRG 741	Busoni: Elégies op 70, Balet-Scene 4 op 33	Jones (pno)
ZRG 742	Clerambault:Livre d'Orgue-Suites du Premier et Deuxieme Ton	Weir (organ)
ZRG 743	Rawsthorne: Chamber Works	Cardiff Festival Ensemble
ZRG 744	Roberday: Fugues & Caprices for Organ	Gillian Weir
ZRG 745	Stanley: Organ Voluntaries	Elwyn Jones (organ)
ZRG 746	"The Amorous Flute"	Munrow
ZRG 747	Connolly: Vocal & Chamber Works	various
ZRG 748	Goehr: String Quartet op 23, Piano Trio op 20	Allegri Quartet/Orion Trio
ZRG 749	Berkeley & Bush: Chamber Works	Soloists inc Bean,Brymer,Civil
ZRG 750	Wood: String Quartets op 13, op 4, etc	Dartington String Quartet
ZRG 752	Gerhard: Symphony 1/Dances from Don Quixote	BBCSO Dorati
ZRG 753	Skalkottas: Instrumental Music	Melos Ensemble
ZRG 754	Britten: Prelude & Fugue, Schonberg: Suite for String Orch/etc	RPO Del Mar
ZRG 755	Weill: Symphonies 1/2	BBCSO Bertini
ZRG 756	Messiaen: Chronochromie	BBCSO Dorati
ZRG 757	Contemporary Music (Busoni, Dallapiccola, etc)	Philh/ECO Prausnitz
ZRG 758	Bennett: Calendar, Maxwell-Davies: Leopardi Fragments, etc	Melos Ensemble Carewe
ZRG 759	Birtwistle: Tragoedia, Crosse: Concerto da Camera, Wood: 3 Piano Pieces	Melos Ensemble Downes
ZRG 760	Bruckner: Motets, Liszt: Missa Choralis	St Johns College (Camb) Choir Guest
ZRG 761	Hoddinott: Violin Sonata 3, Piano Sonata 6, McCabe: String Trio op 37	Cardiff Ensemble Barton (vln) Jones (pno)
ZRG 762	Hindemith: Sonata for Cello & Piano/Kodaly	Isaac Jones
ZRG 763	Schoenberg: Verklarte Nacht/Webern/Hindemith	ASMF Marriner
ZRG 765	The Warwickshire Lad	Martin Best Consort
ZRG 766	Handel: Chandos Anthems 2, 5	ASMF Kings Cambridge Willcocks
ZRG 767	Blow: Coronation Anthems/Symphony anthems	ASMF KCC Willcocks
ZRG 768	Scarlatti: Stabat Mater	Schütz Choir of London Norrington
ZRG 769	"Composers of Wales" (Thomas:7 Songs for Tenor&Harp,etc)	Saunders (piano) Bennett (Harp) Bowen (tenor) Price (sop)
ZRG 770	Hoddinott:Vln Sonata op 63, Divertimento op 32, Septet op 10	Nash Ensemble

ZRG 771	Mathias: Chamber Works	Gabrieli Quartet Nash Ensemble
ZRG 772	Daniel Jones: String Quartet 9, String Trio, Sonata for 3 Unaccompanied Kettledrums	Gabrieli Quartet Fry (kettledrums)
ZRG 773-5	Corelli: Concerti Grossi Op 6	ASMF Marriner
ZRG 776-8	Bach,JS: Orgelbuchlein BWV 599-644, etc	Hurford (organ)
ZRG 780	German Hpsd Music 1685-1730 (Bach,Pachelberl,etc)	Tilney
ZRG 781	Dvorak : Mass in D	Christ Church, Oxford Chorus Preston
ZRG 782	Christmas at St Johns	Choir of St Johns Cambridge Guest
ZRG 783	Organ Recital (Bach,Buxtehude,etc)	Hurford (Dutch Organ at Eton College)
ZRG 784	Liszt: Organ Works	Planyavsky (Melk Monastery, Austria)
ZRG 785	Choral Works 'Day by Day'	Choir of School of St Mary&St Anne Harris
ZRG 786	Bliss: Piano Sonata, Lambert: Elegiac Blues, Piano Sonata	Gillespie (pno)
ZRG 787	Duruflé: Requiem	Choir of St Johns Cambridge George Guest
ZRG 788	Contemporary Songs (Crosse,Berkeley, Dickinson)	M.Dickinson (mezzo) P.Dickinson (pno)
ZRG 789	"Five Centuries at St George's"	Choir of St George's Chapel Windsor
ZRG 790	Birtwistle: The Triumph of Time	BBCSO Boulez
ZRG 791	Dallapiccola & Shaw: Works	London Sinfonietta BBC Singers
ZRG 792	Suk: Serenade for Strings, Strauss,R/Janacek	LACO Marriner
ZRG 793	Renaissance Vocal Music (Josquin des Pres, Susato, etc)	Musica Reservata Parrott Morrow
ZRG 794	Ives: Trio for Violin,Cello&Piano, Copland: Quartet for Piano & Strings	Cardiff Festival Ensemble
ZRG 795	Lassus: choral recital	Christ Church Oxford Preston
ZRG 799	Stravinsky: Symphony of Psalms/Canticum Sacrum	Philip Jones Brass Ensemble
ZRG 800-1	Vivaldi: La Stravaganza	ASMF Marriner
ZRG 803	Strauss,R: Deutsche Motette op62, Der Abend op34/1, Hymne op34/2	Schütz Choir of London Norrington
ZRG 804	Poulenc: Chansons	Palmer (sop) Constable (pno)
ZRG 805	"Homage to Kreisler"	Holmes (vln) Walker (pno)
ZRG 806	Organ Recital (Bach, Byrd, Buxtehude, etc)	Hurford
ZRG 807	Organ Recital (Franck, Mathias, Langlais, etc)	Hurford
ZRG 808	Debussy: Nocturnes, Rachmaninov: Symphonic Dances op 45	Shasby McMahon (pianos)
ZRG 809	Reger: Piano Quartet op 133, Strauss,R: Piano Quartet op 13	Cardiff Fest Ensemble
ZRG 810	Crosse: Purgatory	Royal Northern College of Music
ZRG 811	Stainer: Choral& Organ Works	Magdalen College Oxford Bernard Rose
ZRG 812	Camilleri: Missa Mundi	Weir (RFH Organ)
ZRG 813	Music for Brass (Addison,Dodgson,Bennett,etc)	Philip Jones Brass Ensemble
ZRG 814	Song Recital (Chopin, Liszt)	Tear Ledger (pno)
ZRG 815	Fauré: Songs	Palmer (sop) Constable (pno)
ZRG 817-8	Handel: Israel in Egypt	ECO Preston
ZRG 820	Bach,J.S: Concertos: for 3 violins/Violin&Oboe/Flute	ASMF Marriner
ZRG 821	Bach,J.S: Concertos: for Oboe D'Amore/Violin, etc	ASMF Marriner
ZRG 823	"Renaissance Brass"	Philip Jones Brass Ensemble
ZRG 824	Hoddinott: Concertino for Orch & Viola	Philh Atherton
ZRG 825	Schubert: Mass in Eflat	ASMF Choir of St Johns Cambridge Guest
ZRG 827	Lieder Recital (Mendelssohn, Weber)	Tear Ledger (pno) Walker (guitar)
ZRG 828	Corelli: Christmas Concerto/etc	ASMF Marriner
ZRG 829	Bach,JS: Masses in Gmin, Gmaj	Richard Hickox Singers & Orch
ZRG 831	Purcell: Verse Anthems	St Johns Cambridge Guest
ZRG 832	Greene: Anthems	St Albans Choir Hurford
ZRG 833	"Songs of Leisure and Love"	Alban Singers Hurford
ZRG 834	Ravel: Songs	Palmer (sop)
ZRG 835	Organ Recital (Bach, Buxtehude, Bull, Grigny)	Hurford
ZRG 836	Telemann: Don Quichotte Suite/Concertos	ASMF Marriner
ZRG 837	Telemann: Overtures	ASMF Marriner
ZRG 838	Finzi: Earth Air and Rain, Butterworth: A Shropshire Lad	Luxon Willison
ZRG 839	Vivaldi: Concerti for Wind & Strings	ASMF Marriner

ZRG 840	Vivaldi: Concertos for Wind and Strings	ASMF Marriner
ZRG 841	Fauré: Messe de Requiem/Cantique de Jean Racine	Choir of St Johns Cambridge ASMF George Guest
ZRG 842	Britten: Phantasy Quartet op 2, 6 Metamorphoses after Ovid	Hurwitz Major Simpson Francis
ZRG 843-4	Bach,JS: Chorale Preludes	Alban Singers Hurford (organ)
ZRG 845	Barber: Adagio for Strings, Ives: Symphony 3, Copland: The Quiet City/etc	ASMF Marriner
ZRG 846	Early English Music (Appleby, Davy, Mason, Preston)	Magdalen College Oxford Rose
ZRG 847	Schütz: Motets, Monteverdi: Sestina	Schütz Consort & Choir of London Norrington
ZRG 848	Tchaikovsky: Sernade for Strings,Dvorak:Serenade for Strings	ASMF Marriner
ZRG 850	Bononcini: Stabat Mater, Caldara: Crucifixus,Lotti: Crucifixus	Philomusica of London St Johns Cambridge Guest
ZRG 851	"Divertimento"	Philip Jones Brass Ensemble
ZRG 852	Stanford: Motets, C.Wood: Anthems	Magdalen College Oxford Rose
ZRG 853	Bach,CPE: Magnificat in Dmaj W215	KCC ASMF Ledger
ZRG 854	Bach,JS: Magnificat, Vivaldi: Magnificat	ASMF Ledger
ZRG 855	"The King Shall Rejoice and other Chapel Royal Anthems"	St Johns Cambridge Guest
ZRG 856	V Williams: Romance/Jacob: 5 Pieces/etc	ASMF Marriner Reilly (harmonica)
ZRG 857	Choral and Organ Works (Bassano,Gabrieli)	Magdalen College Oxford Rose
ZRG 858	Byrd: Mass for 5 Voices, Mass for 4 Voices	Christchurch Oxford Preston
ZRG 859	"Music from Venice" (Gabrielli,Groce,Monteverdi,etc)	Magdelen College Oxford cond Rose
ZRG 860	Butterworth:A Shropshire Lad,Banks of Green Willow, Britten: Frank Bridge Variations	ASMF Marriner
ZRG 862	Copland: Old American Songs, 12 Poems of Emily Dickinson	Tear Ledger (pno)
ZRG 864	Organ Recital (Widor, Vierne, Dupre, etc)	Weir (Hexham Abbey)
ZRG 866	Orch Works (Albinoni, Pachelbel, Purcell, Bononcini)	Richard Hickox Orch Hickox
ZRG 867	Haydn: Mariazellar Mass/Little Organ Mass/etc	ASMF Guest
ZRG 869	Schubert: Mass in Aflat	ASMF St Johns Cambridge Guest
ZRG 870	"Fanfare"	Philip Jones Brass Ensemble
ZRG 871	Choral Works (Elgar, Rachmaninov, Bruckner, Verdi, etc)	Christ Church Oxford Preston
ZRG 872	Handel: Messiah (hlts)	ASMF Marriner
ZRG 873	Bach,JS: Masses in Fmaj, Amaj	Richard Hickox Singers & Orch
ZRG 874	Boyce: Symphonies 1-8	ASMF Marriner
ZRG 875	Delius: Paradise Garden, Summer Night on the River, etc	ASMF Marriner
ZRG 876	Mozart: Requiem	ASMF Marriner Cotrubas Watts
ZRG 877	Scandinavian Music (Grieg,Sibelius,Nielsen,Wiren)	ASMF Marriner
ZRG 878	Poulenc: Concert Champetre, Organ Concerto	ASMF Brown Malcolm
ZRG 879	Handel: Messiah (hlts)	ASMF Marriner
ZRG 880	Mozart: Violin Concertos K216, K218	ASMF Brown
ZRG 881	V Williams: Conc Grosso/Concerto for Oboe & Strings/etc	ASMF/Marriner
ZRG 882	Mathias: Clarinet Concerto/Elegy for a Prince/etc	NPO Atherton
ZRG 883	Poulenc: Mass in Gmaj/Exultate Deo	St John's Cambridge Guest
ZRG 885	Mussorgsky: Pictures at an Exhibition	Philip Jones Brass Ensemble
ZRG 886-7	Handel: Acis & Galatea	ASMF Marriner
ZRG 888	Handel: Organ Concertos	ASMF Marriner Malcolm
ZRG 889	St-Saens: Mass for 4 Voices op 4	Worcester Cathedral Massey
ZRG 890	Samuel Sebastian Wesley: Choral Music	Worcester Cathedral Choir cond Donald Hunt
ZRG 892	Psalms of Consolation and Hope	St Johns Cambridge Guest
ZRG 893-4	Rossini: Petite Messe Solennelle	London Chamber Choir Heltay
ZRG 895	"Easy Winners"	Philip Jones Brass Ensemble
ZRG 896	Finzi: Dies Natalis/etc	LSO Hickox
ZRG 897	Tomkins: Musica Deo Sacra (hlts)	Magdalen College Ocford Rose
ZRG 898	"Baroque Brass"	Philip Jones Brass Ensemble
ZRG 899	Maw: Life Studies	ASMF Marriner
ZRG 900	Anonymous: The Play of Daniel	Pro Cantione Antiqua & Londini Consort
ZRG 902	Academy Encores (Handel,Bach,Haydn,Mozart)	ASMF Marriner
ZRG 903	Scarlatti: St Cecilia Mass	St Johns Cambridge Guest etc
ZRG 904	Respighi: Trittico Botticelliano, etc	London Chamber Choir Heltay

ZRG 905	Harmonica Concertos by Villa-Lobos, Arnold, Benjamin	LSO Atherton Reilly (harmonica)
ZRG 906	"Modern Brass"	Philip Jones Brass Ensemble
ZRG 907	Bennett: Spells, Aubade	Philh Bach Choir Willcocks/Atherton
ZRG 909	Finzi: In Terra Pax/Introit/Magnificat	London Sinfonia Hickox
ZRG 910	Mozart: Flute Concertos K313, K314	ECO Malcolm Bennett (flute)
ZRG 911	Mozart: Wind Serenades K375, K388	London Sinfonietta Pay
ZRG 912	"Festive Brass"	Philip Jones Brass Ensemble
ZRG 913	Pergolesi: Stabat Mater, Concertino Armonico 2	St Johns Cambridge Guest
ZRG 914	Christmas from Clare College, Cambridge	Cambridge Rutter
ZRG 915	Pergolesi: Miserere 2 in Cmin	Magdalen College Oxford Rose
ZRG 916	Schubert: Mass in Cmaj D961, etc	London Sinfonietta Atherton
ZRG 917-8	Haydn: Stabat Mater	London Chamber Choir Heltay
ZRG 919	Mozart: Serenade 10 K361	London Sinfonietta Atherton
ZRG 920	Spohr: Clarinet Concertos 1 & 2	London Sinfonietta Atherton Pay (clarinet)
ZRG 921	De Falla: Master Peter's Puppet Show/etc	LSO Rattle
ZRG 922	Blake: Violin Concerto, In Praise of Krishna	Philh/Northern Sinfonia Del Mar Blake Brown (vln)
ZRG 923	Italian Airs & Dances	London Early Music Group Tyler
ZRG 924	Mozart: Mass K258, Vesperae Solennes de Confessore K339	St Johns Cambridge Guest
ZRG 925	Lieder Recital (Beethoven, Schubert, Schumann, Wolf, etc)	Luxon (bar) Willison (pno)
ZRG 926	Mendelssohn: Symphonies 3, 4	ASMF Marriner
ZRG 928	Romantic Brass (Mendelssohn, Dvorak, Glazunov, etc)	Philip Jones Brass Ensemble
ZRG 929	Beethoven: Violin Concerto	ASMF Marriner Brown
ZRG 930	Harp Concertos (Handel,Boieldieu,Dittersdorf)	ASMF Brown Robles
ZRG 931	"Greensleeves" (Folk Song Arrangements)	ASMF Marriner
ZRG 932	La Battaglia (Byrd, Handel, Kuhnau, etc)	PJBE
ZRG 933	Mozart: Vesperae de Dominica K321, Litaniae de Venerabili	St Johns Cambridge Guest
ZRG 934	Delius: Appalachia, Sea Drift	RPO Hickox Shirley-Quirk
ZRG 935	Copland: Appalachian Spring, Music for Movies	London Sinfonietta Howarth
ZRG 936	Bartok: Violin Concerto 2	Philh Rattle Brown
ZRG 937	Berg: Chamber Concerto, Stravinsky: Agon Ballet	London Sinfonietta Atherton
ZRG 938	Duruflé:Mass op 11 'Cum Jubilo',Langlais:Mass 'Salve Regina'	PJBE Hickox
ZRG 939-40	Handel: Organ Concertos vols 1&2	ASMF Marriner Malcolm (organ)
ZRG 941	Handel: Organ Concertos vol 3	ASMF Marriner Malcolm (organ)
ZRG 942	Handel: Organ Concertos 13-16	ASMF Marriner Malcolm (organ)
ZRG 943	Bach,JS:Popular Organ Works (inc Toccata & Fugue in Dmin)	Hurford
ZRG 944	Chopin: Mazurkas, Preludes & March Funebre	Robles (harp)
ZRG 945	British Orch Music (Elgar,Delius,Butterworth,Warlock,etc)	ASMF Marriner
ZRG 946	Britten: Canticles	Pears Britten (pno) Ellis (harp)
ZRG 947	Britten: Cantata Academica,Cantata Misericordum,etc	LSO/KCC Britten/Willcocks
ZRG 948	Bach,JS: Orch Suites 2, 3	ASMF Marriner
ZRG5145-6	Lewis Carroll: Alice in Wonderland	directed by D Cleverdon
ZRG5148	"Music for the Feast of Xmas"	Choir of Ely Cathedral Renaissance Singers
ZRG5149	Victoria: Responsories for Tenebrae	Westminster Cathedral Choir George Malcolm
ZRG5151	Tudor Church Music by Orlando Gibbons	KCC Willcocks
ZRG5152	"Hear My Prayer" (Choral Recital)	St Johns Cambridge Guest
ZRG5160-3	Shakespeare: The Merchant of Venice	Members of the Marlowe Society directed by G Rylands
ZRG5164-7	Shakespeare: Measure for Measure	Members of the Marlowe Society directed by G Rylands
ZRG5168-71	Shakespeare: King John	Members of the Marlowe Society directed by G Rylands
ZRG5172-4	Shakespeare: Two Gentlemen of Verona	Members of the Marlowe Society directed by G Rylands
ZRG5175-7	Shakespeare: Macbeth	Members of the Marlowe Society directed by G Rylands
ZRG5179	V Williams: G Minor Mass/Britten: A Ceremony of Carols	Canterbury Cathedral
ZRG5180-1	Lewis Carroll: Alice Through the Looking Glass	directed by D Cleverdon
ZRG5186	Palestrina: Missa Aeterna Christi Munera	Renaissance Singers Michael Howard
ZRG5187	Austrian Classical Marches (Beethoven,Schubert,Berg,etc)	Boston Concert Band Eric Simon

ZRG5190	"A Festival of Lessons and Carols"	KCC Willcocks
ZRG5200-3	Shakespeare: Romeo and Juliet	Members of the Marlowe Society directed by G Rylands
ZRG5204-7	Shakespeare: A Winters Tale	Members of the Marlowe Society directed by G Rylands
ZRG5208-11	Shakespeare: Henry 4th Part 1	Members of the Marlowe Society directed by G Rylands
ZRG5212-5	Shakespeare: Henry 4th Part 2	Members of the Marlowe Society directed by G Rylands
ZRG5216-8	Shakespeare: The Tempest	Members of the Marlowe Society directed by G Rylands
ZRG5221-2	Kenneth Grahame: The Wind in the Willows	Goolden Shelley etc
ZRG5226	Byrd: Mass for 5 Voices/Ave Verum Corpus/etc	KCC Willcocks
ZRG5227-9	Malory: Le Morte d'Arthur (hlts)	Directed by J Barton
ZRG5234	Bach,J.S: Motet Jesu, Priceless Treasure	KCC Willcocks
ZRG5237	Thomas Weelkes & Thomas Tallis: Tudor Church Music	St Johns Cambridge Guest
ZRG5240	"A Procession with Carols"	KCC Willcocks
ZRG5247	Recital (Purcell, Blow, Boyce, etc)	Salisbury Cathedral Choir Dearnley
ZRG5249	"Tudor Church Music by Thomas Tomkins"	Magdelen College, Oxford Rose
ZRG5250-2	Shakespeare: Midsummer Nights Dream	Members of the Marlowe Society directed by G Rylands
ZRG5253-5	Shakespeare: Timon of Athens	Members of the Marlowe Society directed by G Rylands
ZRG5256-60	Shakespeare: Hamlet	Members of the Marlowe Society directed by G Rylands
ZRG5261-4	Shakespeare: Henry 5th	Members of the Marlowe Society directed by G Rylands
ZRG5265-8	Shakespeare: Cymbeline	Members of the Marlowe Society directed by G Rylands
ZRG5270-2	Bach,J.S: St John Passion	Philomusica of London Willcocks
ZRG5277	Britten: Three Canticles	Britten Tuckwell Pears
ZRG5280-3	Shakespeare: King Lear	Members of the Marlowe Society directed by G Rylands
ZRG5284-6	Shakespeare: 12th Night	Members of the Marlowe Society directed by G Rylands
ZRG5287-8	"The Hollow Crown" (The Kings&Queens of England)	Royal Shakespeare Production directed by J Barton
ZRG5289	Shakespeare excerpts Royal Shakespeare Company	
ZRG5290	Dowland: Ayres for 4 Voices	Golden Age Singers
ZRG5300-2	Shakespeare: Much Ado About Nothing	Members of the Marlowe Society directed by G Rylands
ZRG5303-6	Shakespeare: Henry 8th	Members of the Marlowe Society directed by G Rylands
ZRG5307-10	Shakespeare: Antony and Cleopatra	Members of the Marlowe Society directed by G Rylands
ZRG5311-2	Shakespeare: The Comedy of Errors	Members of the Marlowe Society directed by G Rylands
ZRG5313-5	Shakespeare: Love's Labour's Lost	Members of the Marlowe Society directed by G Rylands
ZRG5316	John Taverner: Tudor Church Music	KCC Willcocks
ZRG5318	Choral Works by Batten and Dering	Peterborough Cathedral Choir Stanley Vann
ZRG5320	Stainer: The Crucifixion	Ch of St Johns Cambridge Guest
ZRG5322	Bach,JS: St John Passion (hlts)	Philomusica/KCC Willcocks
ZRG5325	Haydn: Nelson Mass	LSO/KCC Willcocks
ZRG5326	Wind Quintets by Seiber, Gerhard, Fricker, Arnold	London Wind Quintet (Morris Sutcliffe Walton Brooke Civil)
ZRG5327	Maxwell-Davies: O Magnum Mysterium	Cirencester Maxwell-Davies
ZRG5328	Fricker: 12 Studies for Piano op38, Musgrave, Rawsthorne	Parikian (violin) Crowson (piano)
ZRG5329	Walton: String Quartet/Maconchy: String Quartet	Allegri Quartet
ZRG5333	"On Christmas Night"	LSO Willcocks
ZRG5339	Franck: Chorale 2, Pièce Héroique, Messiaen: L'Ascension	Simon Preston (organ)
ZRG5340	20th Century Church Music (Britten,Walton,Ireland,etc)	St Johns Cambridge Guest
ZRG5348-50	Shakespeare: The Taming of the Shrew	Members of the Marlowe Society directed by G Rylands
ZRG5354-6	Shakespeare: All's Well that Ends Well	Members of the Marlowe Society directed by G Rylands
ZRG5357-60	Shakespeare: Titus Andronicus	Members of the Marlowe Society directed by G Rylands
ZRG5361	Handel: Organ Concertos Vol 1	Jean-Francosi Paillard CO Marie-Claire Alain
ZRG5362	Byrd: Mass in 3 Parts/Mass in 4 Parts	KCC Willcocks
ZRG5363	Duruflé: Requiem	Lamoureux Orch Duruflé
ZRG5364	Rameau: Concertos for Strings	Jean Francois Paillard CO Paillard
ZRG5365	Evensong for Ash Wednesday	KCC Willcocks
ZRG5366	Telemann: Concertos for Flute/Oboe/Viola/etc	Munich Pro Arte Orch Redel
ZRG5367	Bach,JS: Cantata Ich Hatte Viel Bekummernis	Schütz Orch & Choir Werner
ZRG5369	Handel: Coronation Anthems	ECO/KCC Willcocks
ZRG5371	Evensong of Feast of Translation of St Edward the Confessor	Westminster Abbey McKie

ZRG5372	Britten: String Quartets, Fricker: String Quartet 2	Amadeus Quartet
ZRG5375	Handel: Organ Concertos Vol 2	JF Paillard CO Marie Claire Alain
ZRG5376	Charpentier: Midnight Mass for Christmas	Jean Francois Paillard Chamber Orch
ZRG5377	Handel: Organ Concertos 9, 10, 11, 12	Jean Francois Paillard CO Paillard Alain (organ)
ZRG5378	Lully: Suite of the Symphonies from Amadis, Mouret	Jean Francois Paillard CO Paillard
ZRG5379	Handel: Organ Concertos 13-16	Jean Francois Paillard CO Paillard Alain (organ)
ZRG5386-8	Shakespeare: Henry 6th Part 1	Members of the Marlowe Society directed by G Rylands
ZRG5389-92	Shakespeare: Henry 6th Part 2	Members of the Marlowe Society directed by G Rylands
ZRG5393-6	Shakespeare: Henry 6th Part 3	Members of the Marlowe Society directed by G Rylands
ZRG5398	Palestrina: Stabat Mater/etc	KCC Willcocks
ZRG5399	"Sing Nowell" (Carols by Contemporary Composers)	Elizabethan Singers Halsey
ZRG5400	Handel: Concertos for Wind & Strings Op 3	ASMF Marriner
ZRG5405	Hymns for All Seasons	St Johns Cambridge Guest
ZRG5406	"English Cathedral Music"	St Johns Cambridge Guest
ZRG5407-10	Shakespeare: Richard 3rd	Members of the Marlowe Society directed by G Rylands
ZRG5411-3	Shakespeare: Pericles	Members of the Marlowe Society directed by G Rylands
ZRG5414-7	"Rhyme and Rhythm" (Poetry&Song for Children)	Michael Hordern Spike Milligan etc
ZRG5418	20th Century English Songs (Ireland,Bridge,Bennett,Rainier)	Pears Britten (pno) Dickson (cello)
ZRG5419	Bach,JS: 6 Chorales, Mozart: Fantasias K608, K594	Preston (organ)
ZRG5420	Reubke: The 94th Psalm/Reger	Simon Preston
ZRG5421-2	Bach,JS: The Art of Fugue	Philomusica of London Malcolm
ZRG5423	Choral Recital (Tallis, Byrd, Stanford, Parry, etc)	St Michaels College,Tenbury Nethsingha
ZRG5424	Britten: Part Songs	Elizabethan Singers Halsey
ZRG5425	Hamilton:Cello Sonata,etc, Lutyens:String Quartet 6	Dartington String Quartet etc
ZRG5426	Gardner, Joubert, Lutyens, Naylor	John Alldis Choir Alldis R.R.Bennett (pno)
ZRG5430	Milhaud: Cantatas, Poulenc: 4 Motets, Lauds of St Anthony	Stephen Caillat CO Caillat
ZRG5434	"Ireland,Mother Ireland" (Irish Songs&Ballads)	Radio Eirann SO etc Doyle
ZRG5436	Tallis: Tudor Church Music ("Spem in Alium", etc)	KCC Willcocks
ZRG5439	"English Songs" (Tippett, Britten, Warlock, Grainger, etc)	Pears Britten (piano)
ZRG5440	Britten: Missa Brevis/Rejoice inthe Lamb	Choir of St Johns Cambridge Guest
ZRG5442	Handel Concertos for Oboe and Strings	ASMF Marriner Lord (oboe)
ZRG5443	English Mediaeval Songs	Tear (tenor) Ellis (harp)
ZRG5444	Purcell: Music for the Chapel Royal	St Johns College (Camb) Choir Guest
ZRG5446	"Sir Christmas" (carols newly composed and arranged)	Elizabethan Singers Halsey
ZRG5447	Messiaen: La Nativite du Seigneur	Preston (organ)
ZRG5447	Messiaen: La Nativite du Seigneur	Preston (organ)
ZRG5448	Organ Recital	Preston (organ)
ZRG5450	"A Festival of Lessons & Carols"	Recorded Kings College Cambridge, Xmas Eve 1964
ZRG5457	"Harp Music of Spain"	Marisa Robles
ZRG5458	"Harp Music of France"	Marisa Robles
ZRG5459	Irish Songs	Radio Eirann Light Orch
ZRG5460	Let Erin Remember (choral works with 2 soloists)	Radio Eirann Light Orch Doyle
ZRG5467	Mendelssohn: String Symphonies	ASMF Marriner
ZRG5468-9	Yeats: Noh Plays (Japanese Dance Drama)	Various
ZRG5470-2	Shaw: St Joan	directed by S Butler
ZRG5475	"Instrumental Music"	Tuckwell De Peyer
ZRG5479	Tallis: Tudor Church Music vol 2 (Lamentations of Jeremiah)	Kings Cambridge Willcocks
ZRG5489	Rawsthorne: String Quartets 1-3	Alberni Quartet
ZRG5490	Handel: Coronation Anthems	ASMF Willcocks
ZRG5491-2	Rameau: Works for Harpsichord	George Malcolm
ZRG5494	Monteverdi: Mass in 4 Parts/etc	Ch of St Johns Cambridge Guest
ZRG5495	Holst: 6 Medieval Lyrics/7 Part Songs Op 44	ECO Imogen Holst
ZRG5496	English Folk Song Recital	Elizabethan Singers Halsey
ZRG5497	Holst: 4 Songs for Voice and Violin/etc	Purcell Singers Imogen Holst Pears Brainin
ZRG5498	Haydn: Concertos for Horn	ASMF Marriner Tuckwell

ZRG5499	Contemporary Carols	Elizabethan Singers Halsey
ZRG5500	Haydn: Theresa Mass	ASMF St Johns College (Camb) Choir Guest
ZRG5501	Handel: Arias	ASMF Leppard Greevy (alto)

Decca L'Oiseau-Lyre

Again, people started collecting these records only recently, and again L'Oiseau-Lyre is not a reissue label.

Labels: There is very little variation in the Oiseau-lyre label over the years, other than the fact that the earliest issues have the "groove" characteristic of all Deccas, being about 7 cms diameter. The colour is darkish green. The earlier labels also have the word "London" at 6 o'clock.

The list: The list of Decca L'Oiseau-Lyre records is believed to be complete.

SOL250	Schoenberg: Serenade for Septet&Bass Voice op 24	Melos Ensemble Maderna Case (bass)
SOL251	Couperin: Les Nations	Jacobean Ensemble directed by Thurston Dart
SOL252-4	Mozart: Piano Sonatas K279-284,K309-K311,K330,K331	Balsam (piano)
SOL255	Masters of Early Keyboard Music vol 5 (works of John Bull)	Dart (hpsd)
SOL256-7	Berlioz: Beatrice & Benedict	LSO Davis
SOL258-60	Mozart: Piano Sonatas K332,K333,K457,K570,K545,K576,etc	Balsam (piano)
SOL261-2	Bach,J.S: Goldberg Variations	Malcolm
SOL263	Monteverdi: Magnificat etc	London Carmelite Priory Malcolm
SOL264	Recital (Albinoni, Handel, Telemann, etc)	ASMF Marriner
SOL265	Stravinsky: Cantata and Mass	ECO/St Anthony Singers Davis
SOL266	Mozart: Symphonies 28, 38	ECO Davis
SOL267	Prokofiev: Quintet Op 39, Shostakovich: Quintet Op 57	Melos Ensemble
SOL268	Brahms & Schumann: Lieder	Watts (alto) Parsons (pno)
SOL269	Palestrina: Two Masses (Sine Nomine, Ecce Ego Joannes)	London Carmelite Priory McCarthy
SOL270	Victoria: Motets&Masses	London Carmelite Priory McCarthy
SOL271	Weber: Piano Sonatas op 49, op 70	d'Arco (pno)
SOL272	Schumann: Fantasiestuke op 12, Sonata in Gmin op 22	d'Arco (pno)
SOL273	Haydn: Piano Sonatas vol 1 (46,18,28,22)	Balsam (pno)
SOL274	Haydn: Piano Sonatas vol 2 (Nos 6, 30, 31, 38)	Balsam (pno)
SOL275	Haydn: Piano Sonatas vol 3 (Nos 20, 23, 40, 48)	Balsam (pno)
SOL276	Recital for Strings (Telemann, Vivaldi, etc)	ASMF Marriner
SOL277	Italian Concertos by Vivaldi, Cherubini, Corelli, etc	ASMF Marriner
SOL278	Spohr: Violin Concertos 8, 9	Symphony Orch Beck
SOL279	18th Century Flute Concertos	ASMF Claude Marriner
SOL280	Bach,J.S: Cantatas 56, 82	ASMF Marriner Shirley-Quirk
SOL282	Berg: 4 Pieces for Clarinet&Piano op 5	de Peyer Crowson (pno)
SOL283	Choral Works by Palestrina & Victoria	London Carmelite Priory McCarthy
SOL284	Beethoven: Serenade Op 25, Weber: Trio Op 63	Melos Ensemble
SOL285	Mozart: Piano Quartets K478, K493	Pro Arte Quartet
SOL286-8	Rameau: Hyppolytus & Aricia	ECO Lewis
SOL289	Fauré: Piano Quartet Op 15, Piano Trio Op 120	Pro Arte Piano Quartet
SOL290	Hummel: Septet Op 74, Quintet Op 87	Melos Ensemble
SOL291-2	Bach,JS: French Suites 1-6	Isabelle Nef (hpsd)
SOL293	Schumann: Frauenliebe und Leben, Wolf: Lieder	Watts (alto) Parsons (pno)
SOL294	Purcell: The Indian Queen	ECO Mackerras
SOL295	Bach,J.S: Cantatas 159, 170	ASMF Marriner Baker Tear
SOL296	Busoni: Violin Sonatas op 29, op36a	Bress (vln) Johnsson (pno)
SOL297	Rameau:Instl suite from Le Temple de la Gloire, Gretry	ECO Leppard

SOL298	French Song Recital	Melos Ensemble Baker
SOL299	Vocal Music by Monteverdi	ECO Leppard
SOL300	Couperin: Apotheose de Lully, Charpentier: Suite from Medea	ECO Leppard
SOL301	Lully: Pieces de Symphonie	ECO Leppard
SOL302	Rameau: 2nd Instrumental Suite from "Le Temple de la Gloire"	ECO Leppard
SOL303	Leclair: Scylla et Glaucus St, Destouches: St from opera Issé	ECO Leppard
SOL304	Berlioz: Vocal & Choral Music	ECO Davis Pashley (sop)
SOL305	Berlioz: Vocal Works	Monteverdi Choir Gardiner
SOL306-7	Clementi: Piano Sonatas	Crowson (pno)
SOL308	Harp Music of 19th & 20th centuries	Osian Ellis
SOL309	Harp Recital (Bach, Handel, etc)	Osian Ellis
SOL310	Machaut: La Messe de Notre Dame	Purcell Choir Burgess
SOL311	Tallis & Byrd: Cantiones Sacrae 1575 vol 1	Cantores in Ecclesia Howard
SOL312	Tallis & Byrd: Cantiones Sacrae 1575 vol 2	Cantores in Ecclesia Howard
SOL313	Tallis & Byrd: Cantiones Sacrae 1575 vol 3	Cantores in Ecclesia Howard
SOL314	Brahms: Trio in Eflat maj, Schubert, Schumann	Melos Ensemble
SOL315	Stanley: Concertos op 2	Hurwitz CO Hurwitz
SOL316	Chausson: Piano Quartet op 30, Martinu: Piano Quartet 1	Richards Piano Quartet
SOL317	Bach, JC: Symphonies	ECO Davis
SOL318	Avison: Concertos op 6 nos 1,2,6,8,9,12	Hurwitz Chamber Ensemble
SOL319	Purcell, Handel, Bach: Trio Sonatas	Goldsborough Ensemble
SOL320	Brahms: Piano Quintet Op 60, Schumann: Piano Quartet Op 47	Pro Arte Quartet
SOL321	Rameau: Hyppolytus & Aricia (hlts)	ECO Lewis
SOL322	Berlioz: hlts from Beatrice & Benedict,L'Enfance du Christ	LSO/Goldsborough Orch Davis
SOL323	Song&Lieder Recital (Handel,Scarlatti,Schubert,Faure,Quilter)	Burrows (ten) Constable (pno)
SOL324	Songs of Love and Sentiment	Burrows (ten) Constable (pno)
SOL325	Renaissance Instrumental Duets	Rooley (lute) Tyler (lute etc)
SOL326	Organ Recital (Tournemire, Demessieux, St-Saens)	Kynaston (Hereford Cathedral)
SOL327	Lieder Recital (Schumann & Mahler)	Reynolds (mezzo) Parsons (pno)
SOL328	"The Leaves be Greene" (Renaissance English Music)	Consort of Musicke Hill (tenor)
SOL329	Courtly Pastimes (Songs & Dances)	St Georges Canzona Southcott
SOL330	Renaissance Dances by Phalese and Susato	Musica Aurea Woltèche
SOL331	Maconchy: Ariadne, Walton: Songs	ECO Leppard Harper
SOL332	French Court Music of the 13th Century	Musica Reservata Beckett
SOL333	Motets (Gabrieli, Schutz, Monteverdi)	Louis Halsey Singers Halsey
SOL334	"O Vilanella" (16th Century Italian Popular Music)	Consorte of Musicke Rooley
SOL335	Organ Recital (Brahms,Mozart,Reubke,Bonnet)	Herrick (Coventry Cathedral)
SOL336	My Lute Awake: Lute Recital	Anthony Rooley James Tyler (lutes)
SOL337	Tallis: Choral Works	Cantores in Ecclesia Howard
SOL338-9	Palestrina: The Song of Songs	Cantores in Ecclesia Howard
SOL340-1	Bach,JS: Motets & Organ Works	Louis Halsey Singers Halsey Lumsden (organ)
SOL342	Mathias: Organ Works	Herrick (Hereford Cathedral)
SOL343	Organ Recital (Franck, Maneri, Jongen, Robinson, etc)	Robinson (Chester Cathedral)
SOL344	Reizenstein: Piano Quintet,Sonatina for Oboe&Piano, etc	Melos Ensemble
SOL345	Song Recital (Bellini,Donizetti,Verdi,Rossini,etc)	Price (sop) Lockhart (pno)
SOL346	Mathias: Harp Concerto, Dance Overture, etc	LSO Atherton Ellis (harp)
SOL347	Carissimi: Historia di Jonas, Cavalli:Missa pro Defunctis	Louis Halsey Singers Halsey
SOL348	Reizenstein: Violin Sonatas op 20, op 46, etc	Gruenberg Wilde
SOL349	Guitar Recital	Walker (guitar)
SOL350-1	Mendelssohn:Organ Sonatas op 65/1-6,Preludes&Fugues op 37/1-3	Fisher (Chester Cathedral)
SOL352	Widor: Suite Latine, 3 New Pieces op 87	Parker-Smith (Organ of Coventry Cathedral)
SOL60001	Handel: Music from Alcina, Jephtha, Esther&Rodrigo	Philomusica of London Lewis Sutherland
SOL60002	Purcell: Trumpet Sonata, 3 Pieces, Chacony in Gmin, etc	Philomusica of London Lewis
SOL60003	Bach,JS: Cantatas 53, 54, 200	Philomusica of London Dart

SOL60004	Haydn: Symphonies 46, 52	Haydn Orch Newstone
SOL60005-6	Bach,J.S: Brandenburg Concertos 1-6	Philomusica of London Dart
SOL60007	Bach,JS: Concerto for Flute, Violin & Harpsichord, etc	Philomusica of London Dart (hpsd)
SOL60008-9	Purcell: King Arthur	London Philomusica Dart
SOL60010	Handel: Water Music	London Philomusica Dart
SOL60011-12	Handel: Acis and Galatea	Philh Boult Pears Sutherland
SOL60013	Handel: Conc for Harp & Lute, Harp Conc, Conc Grosso in C	Philomusica of London Jones
SOL60014	Couperin: Les Nations	Jacobean Ensemble Dart Marriner (violin)
SOL60015	Beethoven: Septet	Melos Ensemble
SOL60016-7	Bach,JS: Cello Suites	Clément (cello)
SOL60018	"Four 18th Century Flute Quartets" (Viotti, Bach, etc)	Rampal (flute)
SOL60019	"The Royal Brass Music of King James I"	Consort Dart
SOL60020	Mozart: Clarinet Trio K498, Weber: Grand Quintetto Op 34	Melos Ensemble
SOL60021-3	Mozart: Piano Works	Balsam (pno)
SOL60024	Rameau: Orchestral Music from the Operas and Ballets	Lamoureux Orch de Froment
SOL60025-6	Handel: L'Allegro ed Il Penseroso	Philomusica of London Willcocks
SOL60027	Bach,JS: Cantata 147	Collegium Musicum Thomas
SOL60028	Clarinet Recital (Weber,Debussy,etc)	De Peyer Preedy (pno)
SOL60029	Mozart: Divertimentos K247, K251	ECO Davis
SOL60030	Mozart: Concertone for 2 Vlns Oboe & Cello, Haydn: Sym 84	ECO Davis
SOL60031	17th Century Motets (Buxtehude, Couperin, Purcell, Schutz)	Pears Malcolm
SOL60032-3	Berlioz: Childhood of Christ	Goldsborough Orch Davis
SOL60034	Folk Song Recital	Brown (tenor) Williams (guitar)
SOL60035	Weber: Clarinet Concerto, Spohr: Clarinet Concerto 1	LSO Davis De Peyer
SOL60036	18th Century Shakespearean Songs	ECO Leppard Cantelo
SOL60037	Britten: Cantata Academica	LSO Malcolm
SOL60038	Froberger: Keyboard Works	Dart (clavichord)
SOL60039	Bach: French Suites	Dart
SOL60040	Plainsong: Responsories, Hyms, Antiphons, etc	London Carmelite Priory McCarthy
SOL60041	Boyce: 6 Overtures	Lamoureux Orch Lewis
SOL60042	Anerio: Missa pro Defunctis	London Carmelite Priory Malcolm
SOL60043-4	Mozart: Violin Sonatas	Kroll Balsam (pno)
SOL60045	Concertos by Corelli, Torelli, Handel, etc	ASMF Marriner
SOL60046	Handel: 3 Italian Cantatas	ECO Leppard Watts
SOL60047	Purcell: Dido & Aeneas	ECO Lewis Baker
SOL60048	Ravel: Intro & Allegro, Debussy, Roussel, etc	Melos Ensemble
SOL60049	Mozart: Symphonies 33, 36	ECO Davis
SOL60050	Stravinsky: Dumbarton Oaks, Conc in D, Danses Concertantes	ECO Davis
SOL60051	Osian Ellis: Songs with Harp	Ellis (voice & harp)
SOL60052	Roussel: Piano Works	Petit (pno)

Decca Reissue Labels

With the increasing rarity of original Decca SXLs many collectors are turning to the Decca reissue labels. In much the same way as RCA reissued most of the LSC shaded dogs on the VICS label in the late 60s, Decca reissued many of the greatest early Decca recordings from around 1966 on three principal labels:

"**Ace of Diamonds**" (numbers like SDDnnn). This label was used mainly for reissues of the earlier SXLs as well as a few which had never before been issued in stereo, an example of the latter being the HP LIST Britten Prince of the Pagodas. The sound of this record is as fine as anything Decca ever produced, so we can certainly expect great sound from this label. The labels on these records are white with black lettering. The earliest (before about SDD200) have "**Full Frequency Range Recording**" around the perimeter of the label. The earliest of these records come from 1965, only a few years after the originals were deleted, and using the same stampers.

The "**World of the Great Classics**" label (blue labels with numbers like SPAnnn). These were mainly used to reissue those recordings made by Decca for RCA during the earlier agreement between these two companies which concluded around 1962. These recordings were originally issued as RCA LSC shaded dogs. An example is the HP LIST SPA122 Sibelius Symphony 5, which is a reissue of the original RCA LSC2405.

The '**Eclipse**' label (numbers like ECSnnn). These are just like the SPA series - mainly Decca reissues of original RCAs or of Decca Londons which were never issued on SXL.

Stereo Treasury. These were issued in America and are the equivalent of England's "Ace of Diamonds" records. The numbers are STS15nnn and the record jackets are thick cardboard like the American Londons. You will find the stampers just the same as the early "Ace of Diamonds".

What is really important about all these reissue labels is that if you study the stamper code in the vinyl of these reissue series you can see that they often used the same plates as were used for the original SXL issues. So with these records we get close to the original sound quality but without the high price premium.

The lists: The list of Ace of Diamonds is now believed to be complete. The lists of Eclipse and SPA "The World Of" are not intended to be complete 100% listings. However, they do list most of the orchestral records, and **all** of the orchestral records that I have come across.

Ace of Diamonds

SDD101	Beethoven Symphonies 1/8	OSR	Ansermet	(SXL6096)
SDD102	Beethoven Symphony 2/Leonora no 2 Ov	OSR	Ansermet	(SXL2228 ECS739)
SDD103	Beethoven Symphony 3	OSR	Ansermet	(SXL2165)
SDD104	Beethoven Symphony 4/Coriolan Ov	OSR	Ansermet	(SXL2116)
SDD105	Beethoven Symphony 5/Egmont Ov	OSR	Ansermet	(SXL2003)
SDD106	Beethoven: Symphony 6/Prometheus Ov	OSR	Ansermet	(SXL2193)
SDD107	Beethoven Symphony 7/Fidelio Ov	OSR	Ansermet	(SXL2235 SPA237)
SDD108	Beethoven: Symphony 9	OSR	Ansermet	(SXL2274 SPA328)
SDD109	Rossini-Respighi: La Boutique Fantasque	IPO	Solti	(SXL2007 SPA376)
SDD110	Mendelssohn: Violin Conc/Bruch: Scottish Fantasia	LPO	Boult Campoli	(SXL2026 ECS775)
SDD111	Grieg: Peer Gynt Incidental Music	LSO	Fjelstadt	(SXL2012 SPA421)
SDD112	Tchaikovsky 1812 Ov/Capriccio Italien/Marche Slave	LSO	Alwyn	(SXL2001)
SDD113-4	Lehar: The Merry Widow	VSop	Stolz Gueden Loose	(SXL2022-3)
SDD115	Berlioz: Symphonie Fantastique	PCO	Argenta	(SXL2009)
SDD116	Mozart: Piano Concerto 27/Sonata 11	VPO	Bohm Backhaus	(SXL2214 CS6141) RM10
SDD117	Brahms: Symphony 1	VPO	Kubelik	(SXL2013)
SDD118	Brahms: Symphony 2	VPO	Kubelik	(SXL2059)
SDD119	Brahms: Symphony 3	VPO	Kubelik	(SXL2104)
SDD120	Brahms: Symphony 4	VPO	Kubelik	(SXL2206)
SDD121	Mendelssohn: Italian Symphony/Schubert: Symphony 5	IPO	Solti	(SXL2067)
SDD122	Mozart: Symphony 32/Symphony 38	LSO	Maag	(SXL2135)
SDD123	Hungarian/Slavonic Dances (Brahms/Dvorak)	VPO	Reiner	(SXL2249 SPA377)
SDD124	Liszt: Piano Concertos 1/2	LPO	Argenta Katchen	(SXL2097 SPA318)
SDD125	Adam: Giselle	PCO	Martinon	(SXL2128 SPA384)
SDD126	Tchaikovsky: Violin Conc/Dvorak Violin Conc	LSO	Sargent Ricci	(SXL2279 SPA398)
SDD127	Strauss (arr Dorati) Graduation Ball etc	VPO	Boskovsky	(SXL2250)
SDD128	Dvorak: Symphony 5 (New World)	VPO	Kubelik	(SXL2005)
SDD129	Bach: Suites 2/3	OSR	Ansermet	(SXL6004)
SDD130	Schubert: Symphonies 2, 8 ("Unfinished")	VPO	Munchinger	(SXL2156)
SDD131	Tchaikovsky: Symphony 4	PCO	Wolff	(SXL2166)
SDD132	Operetta Evergreens	Vienna Opera Orch Stolz Gueden		
SDD133	Strauss,J: Blue Danube	VPO	Krips	(SXL2047)
SDD134	Falla: El Amor Brujo/Retablo De Maese Pedro	NOS/Argenta & OSR/Ansermet		(SXL2260)
SDD135	Recital of Folk Songs	Voges (alto) Parsons (piano)		
SDD136	Stravinsky Song of the Nightingale/Pulcinella	OSR	Ansermet	(SXL2188 ECS776)
SDD137	Brahms: Piano Concerto 1	LSO	Monteux Katchen	(SXL2172 SPA385)
SDD138	Tchaikovsky: Symphony 6	VPO	Martinon	(SXL2004)
SDD139	Massenet: Le Cid/Meyerbeer: Les Patineurs	IPO	Martinon	(SXL2021)
SDD140	Chopin: Ballade 3,Andante Spianato,Grande Polonaise Brillante		Kempff	(SXL2081)
SDD141	Bizet: Carmen & L'Arlesienne Suites	OSR	Ansermet	(SXL2037 ECS755)
SDD142	Tchaikovsky: Symphony 5	VPO	Krips	(SXL2109)
SDD143	Wagner: Great Scenes from Wagner	VPO	Knappertsbusch George London	(SXL2068)
SDD144	Bizet: Jeux D'Enfants/Ibert: Divertissement/etc	PCO	Martinon	(SXL2252)
SDD145	Mendelssohn: Symphony 3/Fingal's Cave	LSO	Maag	(SXL2246 SPA503)
SDD146	Operatic Recital (Donizetti, Verdi)	PCO	Santi Sutherland	(SXL2159)
SDD147	"Music in London 1670-1770"	ECO	Hurwitz	No SXL
SDD148	Marin Marais: Suite 1 in Dmin, Suite from "Alcide"	Jean Louis Petit Chamber Orch		
SDD149	Rameau: Suite in D for Trumpets and Orch, Suite Les Paladins	Jean Louis Petit Chamber Orch		
SDD150	"Karajan Bon Bons" (Nutcracker, Sleeping Beauty, etc)	VPO	Karajan	
SDD151	Rimsky Korsakov: Scheherazade	OSR	Ansermet	(SXL2268)
SDD152	d'Auvergne: Les Troquers	Jean-Louise Petit Chamber Orchestra		
SDD153	Schubert: Symphony 9	LSO	Krips	(SXL2045)
SDD154	Fauré: Requiem	OSR	Ansermet	(SXL2211)

SDD155	Mozart: Clarinet/Flute Concertos	VPO	Munchinger	(SXL6054)
SDD156	Borodin: Quartet 2, Shostakovich: Quartet 8	Borodin Quartet		(SXL6036)
SDD157	Schumann: Symphonies 1, 4	LSO	Krips	(SXL2223)
SDD159	Mendelssohn: Midsummer Nights Dream	LSO	Maag	(SXL2060 SPA451)
SDD160	Lully: Bruits de Trompettes, Sinfonies pour les Patres	Jen-Louis Petit CO		
SDD161-2	Smetana: Ma Vlast	VPO	Kubelik	(SXL2064-5)
SDD163	Unaccompanied Choral Works (Byrd, Lassus, Palestrina, etc)	Bourne Singers		
SDDR164	Piano Recital (Liszt,Chopin,Bach)	Ferrucio Busoni		(from the Duo-Art piano roll)
SDD165	Chopin recital	Ignace Jan Paderewski		(from the Duo-Art piano roll)
SDDR166	Piano recital (Paderewski, Liszt, Chopin))	Ignace Jan Paderewski		(from the Duo-Art piano roll)
SDDR167	Piano Recital by Prokofiev (from Piano Roll 78s)			
SDD168	Ravel L'Enfants et Les Sortilege	OSR	Ansermet	(SXL2212)
SDD169	Handel: Water Music/Fireworks Music	LSO	Szell	(SXL2302)
SDD170	Ravel: Daphnis and Chloe	LSO	Monteux	(SXL2164)
SDD171	Mozart: Serenata Notturna K329/Notturno for 4 Orchs	LSO	Maag	(SXL2196 ECS735)
SDD172	Schubert: Symphonies 4/5	VPO	Munchinger	(CS6378 SXL6086 ECS762)
SDDR173	Piano Recital		Cortot	(from the Duo-Art piano roll)
SDD174	Haydn: Symphonies 94, 99	VPO	Krips	(SXL2098)
SDD175	Strauss,R: Zarathustra	VPO	Karajan	(SXL2154)
SDD176	Mozart: Concert	LSO	Pritchard Berganza	
SDD177	Chopin: Recital	Kempff		(SXL2024 CS6041) RM14
SDD178	Mozart: Symphonies 41, 35	IPO	Krips	(SXL2220)
SDD179	Shostakovich: Symphony 5	OSR	Kertesz	(SXL6018 ECS767)
SDD180	Albeniz Iberia	OSR	Ansermet	(SXL2243)
SDD181	Rachmaninov: Piano Concerto 2/Balakirev: Islamey	LSO	Solti Katchen	(SXL2076)
SDD182	Haydn: Symphonies 82, 86	OSR	Ansermet	(SXL6020)
SDD183	Haydn: Symphonies 83/87	OSR	Ansermet	(SXL6021)
SDD184	Haydn: Symphonies 84/85	OSR	Ansermet	(SXL6022)
SDD185	Schubert: The Trout Quintet	Vienna Octet Curzon		(SXL2110)
SDD186-7	Bach: Brandenburg Concertos	StCO	Munchinger	(SXL2125-7)
SDD188	Tchaikovsky: Concert Fantasia, Rachmaninov: Piano Conc 1	LPO	Boult Katin	(SXL2034)
SDD189	Honegger: Xmas Cantata, Symphony for strings	OSR	Ansermet	(SXL6003)
SDD191	Tchaikovsky: Piano Concerto 1	LSO	Solti Curzon	(SXL2114 CS6100)
SDD192	French Overtures (Lalo/Herold/Offenbach/Auber)	OSR	Ansermet	(SXL2263 ECS827)
SDD193	"Teresa Berganza sings Arias of the 18th Century"	ROHCG	Gibson Berganza	(SXL2251)
SDD194	Suppe: Overtures	VPO	Solti	(SXL2174)
SDD195	Chopin: Sonata 2 (Funeral March)	Kempff		(SXL2025 CS6042) RM14
SDD196	Choral Recital (Byrd,Praetorius,Palestrina,Victoria,etc)	Ambrosian Singers		
SDD197	Britten: 6 Hoelderlin Fragments, Haydn: 6 Canzonettes, etc	Britten	Pears	
SDD198	Mozart: Haffner Serenade (complete)	VPO	Munchinger	(SXL2272)
SDD199	V Williams: Symphony 8, Partita for Double String Orchestra	LPO	Boult	(SXL2207)
SDD200	Beethoven: Septet	Vienna Octet		(SXL2157)
SDD201	Schumann: Piano Concerto/Waldscenen	VPO	Wand Backhaus	(CS6181)
SDD202-4	Franck: Organ Works played at Organ of La Madeleine,Paris	Jeanne Demessieux		
SDD205	Tchaikovsky: Srnd for Strings/Dvorak: Srnd for Strings	IPO	Solti	(SXL2046, LW5332)
SDD206	Spanish and Italian Songs		Berganza	(SXL6005)
SDD207	Great Sacred Songs	LPO	Boult Flagstad	(SXL2049)
SDD208	Mozart: Cosi fan Tutte (hlts)	VPO	Bohm	(SXL2058)
SDD209	Songs from Norway	LSO	Fjelstadt Flagstad	(SXL2145)
SDD210	"Animals in Music"		Varda Nishry (piano)	
SDD211	Strauss,R: Till Eulenspiegel/Death&Transfiguration	VPO	Karajan	(SXL2261)
SDD212	Wagner: Wesendonck Lieder	VPO	Knappertsbusch Flagstad	
SDD213	Handel: Giulio Cesare (Arias)	NSOL	Bonynge Sutherland	(SXL6116)
SDD214	Debussy: La Mer/Ravel: Rapsodie Espagnol	OSR	Ansermet	(CS6024)
SDD215	Mahler Kindertotenlieder/Fahrenden Gesellen	VPO	Boult Flagstad	(SXL2224)

SDD216	Espana	LSO	Argenta	(SXL2020 ECS797)
SDD217	Berlioz: Ovs Corsaire/Damn.of Faust/Carnaval Romain	PCO	Martinon	(SXL2134)
SDD218	Mozart: Magic Flute (hlts)	VPO	Bohm	(SXL2215-7)
SDD219	Guitar Recital (Dowland, Ravel, Albeniz, Villa-Lobos, etc)	Sérgio & Eduardo Abreu		
SDD221	Chopin: Les Sylphides/Delibes	PCO	Maag	(SXL2044 ECS809)
SDD222	Aria Recital (Carmen,Die Walkure,Trovatore,Don Carlo, etc)	ROHCG	Downes Resnik	(SXL2304)
SDD223	Brahms: Piano Concerto 2	LSO	Ferencsik Katchen	(SXL 2236 CS6195) RM14
SDD224	"Teresa Berganza sings Rossini"		Berganza	(SXL2132)
SDD225	Beethoven: Piano Concerto 5	LSO	Gamba/Katchen	(SXL6109)
SDD226	Beethoven: Piano Concerto 3/Rondo in Bflat	LSO	Gamba Katchen	
SDD227	Beethoven: Piano Concerto 1/Choral Fantasia	LSO	Gamba Katchen	(SXL6189)
SDD228	Beethoven Piano Concertos 2/4	LSO	Gamba Katchen	(SXL6082)
SDD229	Beethoven: Diabelli Variations		Katchen	(SXL2262)
SDD230	Schubert: Octet	Vienna Octet		(SXL2028)
SDD231	Bizet Symphony in C/etc	OSR	Ansermet	(SXL2275)
SDD232	Beethoven: Symphony 7	VPO	Karajan	(SB2087, LDS2348)
SDD233	Mozart: Symphony 40, Haydn: Symphony 104	VPO	Karajan	(SB2092, LSC2347)
SDD234	Sibelius: Symphony 2	LSO	Monteux	(SB2070, LSC2342)
SDD235	In Honour of St Hubert (Hubert's Mass, etc)	Wiener Waldhorn Verein		
SDD236	Organ Recital from Liverpool Met Cathedral	Demessieux		
SDD237	Mozart: Marriage of Figaro (hlts)	VPO	Kleiber	(SXL2035)
SDD238	Stravinsky: Symphony of Psalms/Sym in 3 movements	OSR	Ansermet	(SXL2277)
SDD239	Stravinsky: Symphony in C, Symphonies of wind instruments	OSR	Ansermet	(SXL2237)
SDD240	Stravinsky: Petrushka/Les Noces	OSR	Ansermet	
SDD241	Stravinsky: Renard/Mavra/Scherzo a la Russe	OSR	Ansermet	(SXL6171)
SDD242	Stravinsky: Concerto for Piano & Orch/etc	OSR	Ansermet	(LXT5154,1st time in stereo)
SDD243	Stravinsky: Apollon Musagetes/Rite of Spring	OSR	Ansermet	(CS6034 ECS822)
SDD244	Stravinsky: The Fairy's Kiss (complete)	OSR	Ansermet	(SXL6066)
SDD245	Stravinsky: Pulcinella	OSR	Ansermet	(SXL6230)
SDD246	Stravinsky: The Firebird	OSR	Ansermet	(SXL2017 ECS817)
SDD247	Stravinsky: The Fairy's Kiss/The Soldier's Tale	OSR	Ansermet	
SDD248	Sibelius Songs	LSO	Fjelstadt Flagstad	(SXL2145 ECS794)
SDD249	Brahms: Clarinet Quintet, /Wagner: Adagio	Vienna Octet		(SXL2297)
SDD250	Dvorak: String Quartets Op 34/Op 96	Janacek Quartet		(SXL6103)
SDD251	Mozart: Divertimentos K334/K136	Vienna Octet		(SXL2290)
SDD252	Opera Arias for Baritone (Rossini,Verdi,Donizetti,Puccini,etc)	Ettore Bastianini		
SDD253	Works for Solo Violin (Paganini, Weiner)	Stanley Weiner (violin)		
SDD254	Schubert: Death and the Maiden Quartet/etc	Vienna Phil Quartet		(SXL6092)
SDD255	Elgar: Pomp&Circ/Things to Come/etc	LSO	Bliss	(SB2026, LSC2257)
SDD256	Beethoven: Quintet in Eflat for pno&wind/etc	Vienna Octet Panhoffer		(SXL2158) RM16
SDD257	Tchaikovsky: Swan Lake (hlts)	OSR	Ansermet	(SXL2107/8)
SDD258	Bach: Organ Works	Karl Richter		(SXL2219)
SDD259	"The Vienna of Johann Strauss"	VPO	Karajan	
SDD260	Dvorak: Symphony 2	LSO	Monteux	(SB2155, LSC2489)
SDDA261-9	Brahms: The Complete Works for Piano		Katchen	
SDD270	Dvorak: Quintet in A, Schubert Quartet 12	Vienna Phil Qt Curzon		(SXL6043)
SDD271	Schumann: Pno Conc/Le Carnaval Ballet (orch Glazunov)	OSR Ansermet Lipatti		
SDD272	Bach: Italian Concerto/French St 5/etc	George Malcolm		(SXL2259)
SDD273	Arias and Duets (Mozart, Kelly, etc)	Abrams (sop) Klein (tenor) Alexander (pno)		
SDD274	"Brass Now and Then"	PJBE		
SDD275	Wilbye: Madrigals	Wilbye Consort Pears		(SXL6315)
SDD276	Sibelius: Violin Concerto	LSO	Fjelstad Ricci	(SXL2077 SPA398)
SDD277	Franck: Piano Quintet	Vienna Philharmonic Quartet Curzon		(SXL2278 CS6226) RM14
SDD278	Haydn: Quartets Op 33/1-3	Weller Quartet		(SXL6182)
SDD279	Haydn: Quartets Op 33/4-6	Weller Quartet		(SXL6183)

Catalog	Work	Orchestra	Conductor/Artist	Original
SDD280	Mozart: "Figaro for Wind Instruments"	London Wind Soloists	Brymer	
SDD281	R-Korsakov: Dubinushka/Sadko/Russian Easter/etc	OSR	Ansermet	(SXL2113)
SDD282	R-Korsakov: Tale of Tsar Saltan/Snow Maiden/etc	OSR	Ansermet	(SXL2221)
SDD283	Brahms: Symphony 1	VPO	Karajan	(SB2086, LDS2351)
SDD284	Brahms: Symphony 3, Tragic Ov	VPO	Karajan	(SXL6282)
SDD285	Haydn: Quartets Op 32/Op 3 #5/Op 76 #2	Janacek Quartet		(SXL6093)
SDD286	Bach and Handel Arias	LPO	Boult Ferrier	(SXL2234)
SDD287	Operatic Arias	AdSC	Erede Tebaldi	(SXL2043)
SDD288	Aria Recital (Handel, Mozart)	Della Casa		(LXT5277,1st time in stereo)
SDD289	Mozart: Clarinet Quintet/Piano/Wind Quintet	Vienna Octet Panhoffer		(SXL6087)
SDD290	Mozart: Divertimenti K287, K247	Vienna Octet		(SXL6087/6055)
SDD291	Mozart: Quartets K499, K589	Vienna Phil Quartet		(SXL2286)
SDD292	Verdi: La Forza del Destino (hlts)	AdSC	Molinari-Pradelli	(SXL2069-72)
SDD293	Debussy: la Boite a Joujoux, Dukas: La Peri	OSR	Ansermet	(SXL2136)
SDDB294-7	Handel: 6 Conc Grossi Op3/12 Conc Grossi Op 6	ASMF	Marriner	
SDDC298-300	Invitation to a Strauss Festival	VPO	Boskovsky	
SDDD301-3	Tchaikovsky: Sleeping Beauty	OSR	Ansermet	
SDDE304-7	Beethoven: The 5 Piano Concerti	VPO	Stein Gulda	
SDD308	"Arias and Duets from Italian Opera"		Bergonzi	(SXL2048)
SDD309	Beethoven: String Quartets 10, 11	Weller Quartet		(SXL6148)
SDD310	Bach: The Musical Offering	StCO	Munchinger	(SXL2204)
SDD312	Mozart: Symphony 41, Haydn: Symphony 103	VPO	Karajan	(SB2092, LDS2347)
SDD313	"Italian Operatic Arias"	ROHCG	Crespin	(SXL6075)
SDD314	Debussy: The Martyrdom of St Sebastian	OSR	Ansermet	(LXT5024,1st time in stereo)
SDD315	Dvorak: String Quintet Op 97/String Sextet Op 48	Vienna Octet		
SDD316	Henk Badings: Octet, Egon Wellesz: Octet	Vienna Octet		
SDD317	"The Art of Bel Canto"	Various	Bonynge Sutherland	(SET268-9, SET 351, SET 352)
SDD318	Pergolesi: Concertinos 1-4	StCO	Munchinger	(SXL6102)
SDD319	Pergolesi: Concertinos 5/6/etc	StCO	Munchinger	(SXL6104)
SDD320	Franck: Symphony	OSR	Ansermet	(SXL2291)
SDD321	Falla: 3 Cornered Hat/etc	OSR	Ansermet	(SXL2296)
SDD322	Brahms: String Quartets Op.51 nos 1/2	Weller Quartet		(SXL6151)
SDD323	Schumann: Symphony 3, Mendelssohn: Midsmr Nts Drm Ov	LSO	De Burgos	(SXL6213)
SDD324	Recital (7 Spanish Popular Songs, 8 Basque Songs, 4 Spanish Songs)		Berganza	(SXL6005)
SDD325	Mozart: Divertimento K205, March K290, Cassation	Vienna Octet		(SXL6150)
SDD326	Mahler: Des Knaben Wunderhorn	LPO	Wyn Morris	(Delyse DS6077)
SDD327	Mahler: Das Klagende Lied	NPO	Morris	(Delyse DS6087)
SDD328-9	Guitar Recital	John Williams		
SDD330	Mozart: Quartets K575/K590	Weller Quartet		(SXL6258)
SDD331	Mozart: Symphony 38/Clarinet Concerto	LSO	Maag Peyer	(SXL2135/BR3057)
SDD332	Verdi: Il Trovatore (hlts)	Geneva	Erede Tebaldi Del Monaco	(SXL2129-31)
SDD333	Puccini: La Fanciulla del West (hlts)	AdSC	Tebaldi Del Monaco	(SXL2039-41)
SDD334	Puccini: Tosca (hlts)	AdSC	Tebaldi Del Monaco	(SXL2180-1)
SDD335	Mozart: Arias	ASMF	Marriner Spoorenberg	(ZRG 524)
SDD336	Bach,C.P.E: Symphony 2, Arne: Overture 1	ASMF	Marriner Malcolm	(ZRG 577)
SDDF337-9	Ansermet conducts Ravel	OSR	Ansermet	
SDD340	Michael Haydn: String Quintets in Gmaj & Fmaj	Vienna Philharmonic Quintet		(SXL6055)
SDDG341-6	Haydn: The Last 6 Masses	ASMF	St Johns Choir Guest	
SDDH347-51	Mozart: Dances & Marches	VME	Boskovsky	
SDD352	Sonatas for Violin and Piano (Ravel, Ysaye, Enescu)	Voicou	Stefanescu	
SDD353	Chopin: Waltzes		Katin	
SDD354-5	Tchaikovsky: Swan Lake	OSR	Ansermet	(SXL2107/8 DPA603/4)
SDD356-7	Bach: The Art of Fugue	Philomusica of London	Malcolm	(ZRG5421-2)
SDD358	Haydn: Symphonies 60, 67	Phun	Dorati	(HDNE23-6/HDNF27-30)
SDD359	Haydn: Symphonies 49,51	Phun	Dorati	(HDND19-22)

SDD360	Lute Songs (Dowland, Morley, etc)	Pears	Bream	(SXL2191)
SDD361	Mozart: Symphonies 40/41	VPO	Karajan	(Symphony 40: SB2092, LDS2347)
SDD362	Haydn: Symphonies 103 ("Drum Roll")/104 ("London")	VPO	Karajan	(SXL6067 and SB2092)
SDD363	"Christmas in Venice"	PJBE	Monteverdi Choir Gardiner	
SDD364	Mozart: Horn Concertos 1-4	LSO	Maag	(SXL6108)
SDD365	Organ Recital (Franck, Boellmann)	Ralph Davier		
SDD366	Organ Recital – Royal Albert Hall Organ	Ralph Davier		
SDD367	Bach: Organ Works	Ralph Davier (organ of Royal Albert Hall)		
SDD368	Recital of Songs and Arias (Purcell, Bach, Mahler, Ravel, etc)	Baker	(Argo and OSL originals)	
SDD369	Music to Entertain Queen Victoria	Purcell Consort of Soloists & Voices	(ZRG 596)	
SDD370	Albert, Prince of Saxe Coburg and Gotha - Songs	Purcell Consort of Soloists & Voices	(ZRG 597)	
SDD371-2	Delibes: Coppelia	OSR	Ansermet	(SXL2084/5 DPA581/2)
SDD373	Debussy: Images/Printemps	OSR	Ansermet	(SXL2136/SXL2287)
SDD374	Ravel: Ma Mere l'Oye/Debussy: Nocturnes	OSR	Ansermet	(SXL2062 ECS815)
SDD375	Debussy: Jeux/Nocturnes/Danse	OSR	Ansermet	(SXL2027/2062)
SDD376	Schubert: String Quintet, String Trio	VPO	Quartet	(SXL6173)
SDD377	Schubert: Part Songs	Watts	Tear	(ZRG 527)
SDD378-9	Tchaikovsky: The Nutcracker	OSR	Ansermet	(SXL2092/3 SPA357)
SDD380	Mozart: Requiem	Munich Bach Orch Richter Stader	(SMA56)	
SDD381	Organ Recital	John Turner		
SDD382	Mozart: Don Giovanni (hlts)	VPO	Krips	(SXL2117-20)
SDD383	Beethoven: Music for Wind Band	LWE	Brymer	(SXL6170)
SDD384	Bach: Cantatas 45, 105	OSR	Ansermet	(SXL6266)
SDD385	Pergolesi: Stabat Mater	Naples Rossini Orch Caracciolo	(SXL6153)	
SDD386-7	Bach,J.S: Orchestral Suites	StCO	Munchinger	(SXL2300/1)
SDD388	Debussy: Pelleas&Melisande/etc	OSR	Ansermet	(SXL2303)
SDD389	Mendelssohn: Octet/Rimsky-Korsakov: Quintet	Vienna Octet		
SDD390	Operatic Recital (Giordano,Puccini,Bizet,Massenet,Gounod)	AdSC	di Stefano	(SXL2111)
SDD391	"Great Tenor Arias"(Verdi,Meyerbeer,Puccini,Cilea,Giordano)	AdSC	Gavazzeni Bergonzi	(SXL2048)
SDD392	Rossini: Overtures Tell, Magpie, Barber, Bruschino, Ladder, etc	Philh	Gardelli	
SDDJ393-5	Invitation to a Ballet Festival	Various		
SDDK396-8	Ansermet conducts Debussy	OSR	Ansermet	
SDD399	Prokofiev: Symphonies 1/5	OSR	Ansermet	(SXL2292/6120)
SDD400	Holst : The Planets	VPO	Karajan	(SXL2305)
SDD401	Schumann: Vln Sonata op 105, Strauss,R: Vln Sonata op18	Sivó (vln) Buchbinder (pno)		
SDD402	Arias and Lieder (Bach, Schubert, Brahms)	Helen Watts (alto)		
SDD403	Organ Recital (All Sts Church, Clifton, Bristol, England)	Edward Fry		
SDD404	Organ Recital (St Monica's, Westbury on Trym, England)	Edward Fry		
SDDL405-9	Mozart: Complete Wind Music	LWS	Brymer	
SDD410	Mendelssohn: Sextet/Borodin: Quintet	Vienna Octet		(SXL6414)
SDD411	Corelli: Christmas Concerto, Pachelbel: Kanon, etc	StCO	Munchinger	(SXL2265/SET346)
SDD412	Haydn: Symphonies 90, 92	PHun	Dorati	(HDNH35-40)
SDD413	Haydn: Symphonies 73/74	PHun	Dorati	(HDNG31-4)
SDD414	Haydn: Symphonies 42/45	PHun	Dorati	(HDNC13-18)
SDD415	Haydn: Symphonies 51, 55	PHun	Dorati	(HDND19-22)
SDD416	Spohr: Nonet Op 31, Double Quartet Op 87	Vienna Octet		(SXL6319)
SDD417	Bartok: Divertimento for String Orch	Moscow	Barshai	(SXL6026)
SDD418	Leoncavallo: I Pagliacci (hlts), Mascagni: Cavalleria (hlts)	AdSC	Molinari-Pradelli	(SXL2253-5)
SDD419	Beethoven: Quintet Op 29/Sextet Op 81b	Vienna Octet		(SXL6464)
SDD420	Saint-Saens: Havanaise/Intr&Rondo/Sarasate/Bizet	LSO	Gamba Ricci	(SXL2197 ECS808 SPA550)
SDD421	Beethoven: Overtures Leonora 1, 2, 3, Fidelio	IPO	Maazel	(SXL6025)
SDD422	Grieg/Schumann: Piano Concertos	IPO	Kertesz Katchen	(SXL6028)
SDD423	Dvorak: Quintet Op 77, Spohr: Quintet Op 52	Vienna Octet		(SXL6463)
SDD424	Bach,J.C: 6 Symphonies	LWS	Brymer	(SXL6337)
SDD425	Ravel: Pavane/Rapsodie Espagnol	LSO	Monteux	(SXL2312/SXL2287)

Cat. No.	Work	Orchestra	Conductor/Artist	Source
SDD426	Wagner: higlights (Ring, Tristan, etc)	VPO	Knappertsbusch	(SXL2074-5, SXL2068)
SDD427	Mozart: Concerto/Bach: Suite 2/etc	LSO Monteux	Claude Monteux	(SXL6112)
SDD428	Rachmaninov: Rhaps on Paganini, Dohnanyi Nursery Vns	LPO	Boult Katchen	(SXL2176)
SDD429	Verdi: Falstaff (hlts)	NSOL	Downes	(SXL6079)
SDD430	Wagner: Die Walkure (hlts)	LSO	Leinsdorf Nilsson Vickers	(LDS6706)
SDD431	Haydn: Symphonies 88, 89	PHun	Dorati	(HDNH35-40)
SDDM432-4	Festival of Sacred Music	Various		
SDD435	French Piano Music		Cecile Ousset	
SDDN436-8	Festival of Light Classics		Stokowski Herrmann etc	
SDD439	Wagner: Flying Dutchman (hlts)	ROHO	Dorati Rysanek	(SER4535-7)
SDD440	Dvorak: Symphony 8	VPO	Karajan	(SXL6169)
SDD441	Schubert: String Quintet in C/Quartettsatz	Weller Quartet		(SXL6481)
SDD442	Beethoven: String Quartet op 127, Haydn: String Qt op 103	Weller Quartet		(SXL6423)
SDD443	Mendelssohn/Bruch: Violin Concertos	LSO	De Burgos	(SXL6184)
SDD444	English Piano Works (Ireland,Bax,Warlock,Moeran,etc)	John McCabe		
SDD445	Mozart: Sinfonia Concertante K364/etc	MPO	Kondrashin D&I Oistrakh	(SXL6088 CS6377)
SDD446	Falla: Nights in the Gardens of Spain/Granados	NOS	Argenta	(SXL2091 SPA233)
SDD447	Brahms: Cello Sonata op 38, Chopin, Dvorak, Schumann	May (cello)	Hamburger (pno)	
SDD448	Berwald: Piano Quintets	Vienna Philharmonic Quintet		
SDD449	Mozart: Sonatas for Keyboard and Flute	Schulz (flute)	Medjimorec (pno)	
SDD450	Haydn: 7 Divertimenti	LWS	Brymer	(SXL6338)
SDD451	Music for 4 Harpsichords (Bach, Malcolm, etc)	ECO	Leppard Malcolm etc	(SXL6318)
SDD452	Wolf-Ferrari: Music of Wolf-Ferrari	PCO	Nello-Santi	(SXL2177)
SDD453	Shostakovich: String Quartets 1,3	Gabrielli Quartet		
SDD454	Tchaikovsky: 1812, Romeo & Juliet, Sleeping Beauty, Swan Lake, Marche Slave	LSO	Stokowski	(PFS4181/4083/4189)
SDD455	"Debussy Fantasia" (La Mer,Engulfed Cathedral,L'Apres Midi)	LSO	Stokowski	(PFS4220/4095/OPFS3-4)
SDD456	Mussorgsky: Pictures at an Exhibition, Night on Bare Mt, Boris		Stokowski	(PFS4139/4181/4095)
SDD457	Haydn: Symphonies 26, 28	PHun	Dorati	(HDNB7-12)
SDD458	Haydn: Symphonies 29, 30	PHun	Dorati	(HDNB7-12)
SDD459	Lehar: Land of Smiles	Vienna Volksoper Lambrecht Di Stefano Koller		
SDD460	Lehar: Die Lustige Witwe (hlts)	VSOp	Stolz Gueden Loose	(SXL2022-3)
SDD461	Lehar: Der Zarewitsch, Graf von Luxemburg (hlts)	VSOp	Schönherr Gueden Kmennt	(SXL6231)
SDD462	Lortzing: Zar und Zimmermann, Der Waffenschmied (hlts)	VSOp	Ronnefeld Gueden Kmennt	(SXL6039)
SDD463	Organ Recital (Bach,Handel,Widor, etc at Norwich Cathedral)	Michael Nicholas		
SDD464	Bruckner: Symphony 4	LSO	Kertesz	(SXL6227)
SDD465	Bruch: Scottish Fantasy/Hindemith: Violin Concerto	LSO	Horenstein Oistrakh	(SXL6035)
SDD466	Vivaldi: Violin Concertos	Belgian CO Maes Volkaert (vln)		
SDD467	Sibelius: Tempest Suites 1 & 2, Scaramouche	Hungarian State SO Jussi Jalas		
SDD468	Haydn: Symphonies 20, 21, 22	PHun	Dorati	(HDNB7-12)
SDD469	Mendelssohn: String Quartet 4/4 Pieces Op 81	Gabrielli Quartet		
SDD470-2	Handel: Organ Concertos	Karl Richter		(SXL2115, 2187, 2201)
SDD473	Strauss,J: 1001 Nights	VPO	Boskowsky	(SXL2288)
SDD474	Strauss,J: "Champagne from Vienna"	VPO	Boskowsky	(SXL2163/SXL2082/SXL2198)
SDD475	Nielsen: Piano Music vol 1		McCabe (piano)	
SDD476	Nielsen: Piano Music Vol 2		McCabe (piano)	
SDD477	Brahms: Paganini Vns, Schumann: Carnaval op 9	Ousset (pno)		
SDD478	Beethoven: String Quartets Op 18/1, Op 18/2	Gabrielli Quartet		
SDD479	Dvorak: String Quartets Op 51/Op 105	Gabrielli Quartet		
SDD480	Mozart: Eine Kleine Nachtmusik/Symphony 36/etc	VPO	Kertesz	(SXL6091)
SDD481	"Great Soprano Arias"		Tebaldi	(SXL6629 etc)
SDD482	Haydn: The Paris Symphonies (82 & 83)	PHun	Dorati	(HDNH35-40)
SDD483	Haydn: The Paris Symphonies (84 & 85)	PHun	Dorati	(HDNH35-40)
SDD484	Haydn: The Paris Symphonies (86 & 87)	PHun	Dorati	(HDNH35-40)
SDD485	Beethoven (arr Sedlak): Fidelio, Mozart: Entfuhrung	LWS	Brymer	
SDD486	Ravel: Concerto in Gmaj/Concerto in Dmaj	LSO	Kertesz Katchen	(SXL6209/6411)

SDD487	Dvorak: String Quintet, Bagatelle Op 47	Vienna Philh Qt	
SDD488	Sibelius: 4 Legends from the Kalevala	Hungarian State SO Jussi Jalas	(not issued SXL)
SDD489	Sibelius: Finlandia, Kuolema, Scènes Historiques	Hungarian State SO Jussi Jalas	
SDD490	Bruckner: String Quintet, Intermezzo	Vienna Philh Quintet	
SDD491	Schmidt: Piano Quintet in Gmaj, Variations on a Theme	Vienna Philharmonic Quartet	
SDD492	Bizet: Carmen & L'Arlesienne Suites	Philh Munch	(PFS4127)
SDD493	Tchaikovsky: Symphony 5	NPO Stokowski	(PFS4129)
SDD494	Respighi: Fountains of Rome/Pines of Rome	NPO Munch	(PFS4131)
SDD495	Berlioz: Symphonie Fantastique	Philh Stokowski	(PFS4160)
SDD496	Rimsky-Korsakov: Scheherazade, Borodin: Polovtsian Dances	OSR Ansermet	(SXL2268)
SDD497	Britten: String Quartet Op 2, Bridge	Gabrielli Quartet	
SDD498	Brahms: Piano Sonata Op 5, Intermezzi Op 117, Op 119	Curzon	(SXL6041)
SDD499	Organ Recital on Organ of Canterbury Cathedral	Allan Wicks	
SDD500	Haydn: Symphonies 93/94	Phun Dorati	(HDNJ41-6)
SDD501	Haydn: Symphonies 95, 96	Phun Dorati	(HDNJ41-6)
SDD502	Haydn: Symphonies 97, 98	Phun Dorati	(HDNJ41-6)
SDD503	Haydn: Symphonies 99, 100	PHun Dorati	(HDNJ41-6)
SDD504	Haydn: Symphonies 101/102	PHun Dorati	(HDNJ41-6)
SDD505	Haydn: Symphonies 103/104	PHun Dorati	(HDNJ41-6)
SDD506	Sibelius: King Christian II Suite/Swan White Suite	Hungarian State SO Jussi Jalas	
SDD507	"The Surprising Soprano" (Song Recital)	Michael Aspinall Kenny (piano)	
SDD508	Schubert: Octet in Fmaj	Vienna Octet	
SDD509	Mozart: String Quartets K575, K590	Küchl Quartet	
SDD510	Schumann: String Quartet Op 41/1, Brahms: Quartet Op 67	Musikverein Quartet	
SDD512	Schubert: String Quartets 15 in G, 12 in Cmin	Gabrielli Quartet	
SDD513-8	Mozart: Sonatas for Piano & Violin	Lupu Goldberg	(13BB207-12)
SDD519	Schoenberg: Verklarte Nacht/Chamber Symphony 1	London Sinfonia Atherton	(SXLK6660-4)
SDD520	Schoenberg: Pierrot Lunaire, 3 Pieces for Chamber Orch	London Sinfonia Atherton	(SXLK6660-4)
SDD521	Haydn: Trios for Flute, Cello, Piano 28,29,30	Vienna Flute Trio	
SDD522	Brahms: Piano Concerto op 83	LGO Masur Ousset	
SDD523	Ibert: 3 Brief Pieces, Janacek, Hindemith, etc	Vienna Wind Soloists	
SDD524-5	Tchaikovsky: String Quartets 1, 2, 3	Gabrielli Quartet	
SDD526	Debussy: String Quartet op 10, Ravel: String Quartet	Orford Quartet	
SDD527	Janacek: String Quartets 1, 2	Gabrielli Quartet	
SDD528	Beethoven: Septet op 20, Trio op 11	Members of New Vienna Octet	
SDD529	Smetana: String Quartets 1 & 2	Gabrielli Quartet	
SDD530	Spanish Harpsichord Music	Jonathan Woods	
SDD531	Britten: Sinfonietta, 6 Metamorphoses, Hindemith	Vienna Octet	(SXL6208)
SDD532	Brahms: Piano Works Vol 1 (op 117, op 118, op 119)	Katchen	(SXL6105)
SDD533	Brahms: Piano Works Vol 2 (op 76, op 116)	Katchen	(SXL6118)
SDD534	Brahms: Piano Works Vol 3 (Sonatas in Cmaj/F# maj)	Katchen	(SXL6129)
SDD535	Brahms: Piano Works Vol 4 (Op 39, Op 79, Op 10)	Katchen	(SXL6160)
SDD536	Brahms: Piano Works Vol 5 (Hungarian Dances Vols 1 & 2)	Katchen	(SXL6217)
SDD537	Brahms: Piano Works Vol 6 (op 9, op 21/1, op 21/2)	Katchen	(SXL6219)
SDD538	Brahms: Piano Works Vol 7 (Handel & Paganini Variations)	Katchen Suk Starker	(SXL6218)
SDD539	Brahms: Piano Works Vol 8 (op 5, op 4)	Katchen	(SXL6228)
SDD540	Brahms: Piano Trios 1 & 3	Katchen Suk Starker	(SXL6387)
SDD541	Brahms: Piano Trio 2, Sonata 2	Katchen Suk Starker	(SXL6589)
SDD542	Brahms: Violin Sonatas 1, 2, 3	Katchen Suk	(SXL6323)
SDD543	Wolf: Italian Serenade, Kodaly: String Quartet 2, Suk	Musikverein Quartet	
SDD544	Mendelssohn: String Quartets in Eflat maj, Amin	Orford String Quartet	
SDD545	Wind Quintets by Cambini, Danzi, Rejcha	Vienna Wind Soloists	
SDD546	Haydn: Symphonies 43, 44	Phun Dorati	(HDNC13-18)
SDD547	Haydn: Symphonies 48, 49	PHun Dorati	(HDNC13-18, HDND19-22)
SDD548-50	Mozart: Piano Duos	Eden Tamir	

SDD551	Beethoven: String Quartets Op 95, Op 74 ("Harp")	Gabrielli Quartet	
SDD555	Wind Quintets by Francaix, Taffanel	Vienna Wind Soloists	
SDD558	Mozart: Clarinet Quintet K581, Clarinet Trio K498	Vienna Octet	
SDD559	Mozart: String Quartets K458, K428	Musikverein Quartet	
SDD560	Mozart: String Quartets K464, K465	Musikverein Quartet	
SDD561	Mozart: String Quartets K465, K499	Gabrielli Quartet	
SDD562	Mendelssohn: String Quintets op 18, op 87	Vienna Philh Quintet	
SDD563	Schubert: Impromptus D899, D935	Andras Schiff (piano)	
SDD564	Bach,JS: Italian Concerto, French Suite 5, French Overture	Schiff (piano)	
SDD565	Dvorak: String Quartets op 61, op 96	Gabrielli Quartet	
SDD566	Donizetti: Requiem	Pavarotti Cortez etc	
SDD567-8	Rossini: Petite Messe Solenelle	La Scala Gandolfi Freni Valentini	
SDD569	Verdi: Operatic Arias	Pavarotti Ricciarelli	
SDD570-2	Great Voices of the Verona Arena vols 1-3	Various	
SDD574	Handel: Julius Caesar (hlts)	NSOL Bonynge Sutherland Horne	(SXL6116)
SDD575	Brahms: Clarinet Quintet op 115, Weber	New Vienna Octet Peter Schmidl (clarinet)	
SDD577	Mozart: Divertimento K563, Duo for Violin&Viola K424	Küchl (violin) Staar (viola) Bartolomey (cello)	
SDD578	Operatic Arias & Duets	Orch dell'Ater Magiera Pavarotti Freni	
SDD579	Mozart: Serenade for 13 Wind instruments K361	Vienna Wind Soloists	

Ace of Diamonds Grand Opera series (GOS)

GOS501-3	Mozart: Magic Flute	VPO	Bohm	(SXL2215-7)
GOS509-1	Handel: Alcina	LSO	Bonynge	(SET232)
GOS525-7	Donizetti: La Favorita	MMF	Erede	(original issue)
GOS540-2	Stravinsky: The 4 ballets	OSR	Ansermet	(SXL2017, 2011, 2042, 6066)
GOS543-5	Mozart: Cosi Fan Tutte	VPO	Bohm	(LXT5107-9, original stereo issue)
GOS551-3	Tchaikovsky: Eugene Onegin	Belgrade NatOp	Danon	(original issue)
GOS554-7	Strauss,R: Die Frau Ohne Schatten	VPO	Bohm	(LXT5180-4, original stereo issue)
GOS558-9	Britten: Prince of the Pagodas	ROHCG	Britten	(LXT5336-7, original stereo issue)
GOS562-5	Borodin: Prince Igor	Belgrade NatOp	Danon	(original issue)
GOS566-7	Donizetti: L'Elisir d'Amore	MMF	Pradelli	(LXT5155-7, original stereo issue)
GOS568-70	Tchaikovsky: The Queen of Spades	Belgrade NatOp	Baranovich	(original issue)
GOS571-3	Strauss: Arabella	VPO	Solti Gueden	(SXL2050-3)
GOS574-6	Gluck: Alceste	Orch cond Jones	Flagstad	(LXT5273-6, original stereo issue)
GOS577-8	Wagner: Die Walkure Act 3, Todesverkundigung (Act 2)	VPO	Solti Flagstad	(SXL2031-2)
GOS581-2	Wagner: Die Walkure Act I, Gotterdammerung excerpts	VPO	Knappertsbusch	(SXL2074-5)
GOS583-4	Lehar: Giuditta	VSOp	Moralt Gueden	(original stereo issue)
GOS585-7	Mozart: Marriage of Figaro	VPO	Kleiber	(SXL2087-9)
GOS588-0	Mascagni: Cavalleria Rusticana, Leoncavallo: Pagliacci		Serafin	(SXL2253-5)
GOS591-3	Boito: Mefistofele	AdSC	Serafin	(SXL2094-6)
GOS594-6	Puccini: La Fanciulla del West	AdSC	Capuana	(SXL2039-41)
GOS597-9	Verdi: La Forza del Destino	AdSC	Molinari-Pradelli	(SXL2069-72)
GOS600-1	Giordano: Andrea Chenier	AdSC	Gavazzeni	(SXL2208-10)
GOS602-3	Honegger: King David	OSR	Ansermet	(original issue)
GOS604-6	Mozart: Don Giovanni	VPO	Krips	(SXL2117-9)
GOS607-8	Puccini: Manon Lescaut	AdSC	Molinari-Pradelli	(LXT2995-7, original stereo issue)
GOS609-11	Ponchielli: La Gioconda	MMF	Gavazzeni	(SXL2225-7)
GOS612-3	Puccini: Tosca	AdSC	Molinari-Pradelli	(SXL2180-1)
GOS614-6	Verdi: Il Trovatore	Geneva Orch	Erede	(SXL2129-31)
GOS617-8	Verdi: Requiem	VPO	Reiner	(LDS6091)
GOS619-21	Mussorgsky: Khovanshchina	Belgrade NatOp	Baranovich	(LXT5045-8, original stereo issue)
GOS622-4	Puccini: Turandot	AdSC	Erede	(SXL2078-80)
GOS625-7	"Italian Opera Festival"	Various		
GOS628-30	Bach,JS: St John Passion	Philomusica Kings College Choir Willcocks		(ZRG5270-2)
GOS631-3	Rossini: La Cenerentola	MMF	Fabritiis	(SET265-7)

GOS634-5	Mascagni: Cavalleria Rusticana, Operatic Arias	MMF	Erede Tebaldi Bjorling	(SB2021-2)
GOS636-8	"Grand Opera Festival"	Various		
GOSR639	Massenet: Thais	Orch&Chorus cond Etcheverry		(Vega VAL22/1-3)
GOS642-5	Rimsky-Korsakov: The Snow Maiden	Belgrade NatOp Baranovich		(LXT5193-7, original stereo issue)
GOS646-8	Glinka: A Life for the Tsar	Belgrade NatOp Danon		(LXT5173-6, original stereo issue)
GOS649-51	Boildieu: La Dame Blanche	Chorus & Orch Pierre Stoll		(Vega VAL23/1-3)
GOS652-4	Prokofiev: The Fiery Angel	Paris Op Bruck		
GOS655-7	Verdi: Rigoletto	AdSC	Sanzogno Sutherland	(SET224-6)
GOS658-9	Leoncavallo: Pagliacci, Italian Songs	AdSC	Molinari-Pradelli	(SXL2185-6)
GOS660-2	Verdi: Force of Destiny	AdSC	Previtali	(RCA SER4516-9)
GOS663-5	Donizetti: Lucia di Lammermoor	AdSC	Pritchard Sanzogno Sutherland	(SET212-4)
GOS666-8	"Grand Opera Gala"	Various		
GOS674-6	"Festival of French Opera"	Various		
GOS677-9	"Festival of German Opera"	Various		

Eclipse

ECS510	Tchaikovsky: Piano Conc 1, Rachmaninov: Piano Conc 2	LSO	Fistoulari Katchen	
ECS543	Rimsky-Korsakov: Antar, etc	OSR	Ansermet	(genuine stereo though labelled electronic)
ECS544	Dvorak: Symphony 7, Slavonic Dances	Hamburg SO Schmidt-Issersdedt		
ECS569	Tchaikovsky: Violin Concerto, Wieniawski: Violin Concerto 2	LPO	Boult Elman	(Electronic Stereo)
ECS571	Bruckner: Symphony 7	Ccgbw	Van Beinum	
ECS573	Rachmaninov: Sym 3/R-Korsakov: Russian Easter Ov	LPO	Boult	(LSC 2185)
ECS574	Haydn: Symphonies 94/101	VPO	Monteux	(LSC 2394)
ECS575	Tchaikovsky: Sleeping Beauty	LSO	Monteux	(LSC2177)
ECS576	Borodin: Symphonies 2/3	OSR	Ansermet	(CS6126) TEC
ECS578	Bartok: Conc For Orch, Frank Martin: Conc for 7 wind Insts	OSR	Ansermet	(CS6086)
ECS580	Shostakovich: Symphony 1/Age of Gold	LSO	Martinon	(LSC 2322)
ECS583	V Williams: A Sea Symphony	LPO	Boult	
ECS585	Paganini: Recital	Ricci	Persinger	
ECS586	Walton: Facade/Mam'zelle Angot	ROHCG	Fistoulari	(LSC 2285)
ECS590	Schubert: Wanderer Fantasy	Katchen		
ECS593	Prokofiev: Symphony 5	PCO	Martinon	(LSC2272)
ECS594	Rachmaninov: Symphony 2	LPO	Boult	(VICS1139)
ECS595	"Virtuoso Showpieces"		Ricci	(not issued SXL)
ECS596	Brahms: Symphony 2	VPO	Monteux	(VICS1055 SB2110 [not LSC])
ECS597	Prokofiev: Cinderella Suites	ROHCG	Rignold	(VICS1138)
ECS619	Prokofiev: Symphony 7/Overture Russe	PCO	Martinon	(LSC 2288)
ECS620-1	Chopin: The Mazurkas		Magaloff	
ECS627	Mendelssohn: Piano Concertos 1 & 2	LSO	Collins Katin	(not issued SXL)
ECS635	Mozart and Haydn Recital	Haydn Orch Newstone Jennifer Vyvyan		(not issied SXL)
ECS636	Tchaikovsky: Symphony 3/Suite 3	LPO	Boult	
ECS637	Berlioz Overtures Carnaval Romain, Corsaire, King Lear, etc	PCO	Wolff	
ECS638	Beethoven: Symphonies 1/8	VPO	Monteux	(LSC2491)
ECS639	"Campoli Encores" (Albeniz, Brahms, Schubert, etc)		Campoli	(Original issue)
ECS640	Chausson: Symphony/Honegger: Symphony 3	PCO	Denzler	
ECS641	Khachaturian: Violin Concerto/Glazunov	OSR	Ansermet Ricci	
ECS642	Glazunov: The Seasons/Balakirev: Thamar Sym Poem	OSR	Ansermet	(SXL6269)
ECS643	Brahms: Symphony 1	VPO	Krips	(not issued SXL)
ECS644	V Williams: Symphony 8	LPO	Boult	(SXL2207)
ECS645	Weber: Overtures	OSR	Ansermet	(SXL2112)
ECS658	Mendelssohn: Piano Trio No 1, Haydn	Valda Aveling Donald Weeks Dennis Nesbit		
ECS663	Saint-Saens: Violin Conc 3/Sarasate/etc	LPO	Gamba Campoli	(CS6084)
ECS665-7	Wagner: Flying Dutchman	Bayreuth Keilberth		

ECS670	Lalo: Symphonie Espagnole/Ravel: Tzigane	OSR	Ansermet	(SXL2155)
ECS671	Beethoven: Symphony 4/Ah Perfido	LSO	Monteux	(SXL2116)
ECS673	Roussel: Symphonies 3/4	OSR	Ansermet	Never issued on SXL
ECS674	Strauss: Till Eulenspiegel/Death and Transfiguration	VPO	Reiner	(LSC2077)
ECS677	Adam: Giselle	PCO	Wolff	(LSC2301)
ECS686	Mozart: Eine Kleine Nachtmusik/Divertimento 1	StCO	Munchinger	(SXL2270)
ECS695	Auber: Overtures	PCO	Wolff	
ECS696	Ravel: String Quartet, Prokofiev: String Quartet 2	Carmirelli Quartet		
ECS697	Mozart: Violin Concertos 3, 7	StCO	Munchinger Ferras	
ECS701	Brahms: Acad Fest Ov, Haydn Variations, Alto Rps, Tragic Ov	VPO	Knappertsbusch	
ECS702	Rachmaninov: The Isle of the Dead	PCO	Ansermet	
	Liszt: Mazeppa, Hamlet	PCO	Munchinger	
ECS703	Tchaikovsky: Symphony 2, Dukas: Sorcerer's Apprentice		Solti	(Original issue)
ECS714	Schubert: Symphony 9	Ccgbw	Krips	
ECS723	Beethoven: Piano Sonatas 30, 31, 32	Gulda		
ECS735	Rimsky-Korsakov: Scheherazade	OSR	Ansermet	(SXL2268)
ECS739	Beethoven: Symphony 2.Coriolan Ov	OSR	Ansermet	(SXL2228)
ECS740	Mozart: 4 Notturnos/Symphony 32	LSO	Maag	(SXL2196 SDD171)
ECS742	Tchaikovsky: Symphony 4/Liadov Russian Folksongs	OSR	Argenta/Ansermet	(Tchaikovsky on CS6048, Liadov original)
ECS746	Prokofiev: Violin Concertos 1/2	OSR	Ansermet Ricci	(CS6059) TEC
ECS750	Stravinsky: Rite of Spring	PCO	Monteux	(LSC 2085)
ECS754	Bach: Suites 2/3	OSR	Ansermet	(SXL6004 SDD129)
ECS755	Bizet: Carmen/L'Arlesienne Suite	OSR	Ansermet	(SXL2037 SDD141)
ECS756	Honegger: Pacific 231/Roussel/Spider's Banquest St	OSR	Ansermet	
ECS757	Borodin: Prince Igor/Pol Dances/Mussorgsky: Night on Bare Mt	OSR	Ansermet	
ECS758	Schumann: Symphonies 1, 4	LSO	Krips	(SXL2233)
ECS759	Schumann: Symphony 2/Ov Manfred	OSR	Ansermet	(SXL6205)
ECS760	Schumann: Sym 3/Mendelssohn: MidSmr Nts Drm Ov	LSO	De Burgos	(SXL6213)
ECS761	Schubert: Symphonies 2, 8 ("Unfinished")	VPO	Munchinger	
ECS762	Schubert: Symphonies 4/5	VPO	Munchinger	(CS6378 SXL6086)
ECS763	Schubert: Symphonies 3/6	VPO	Munchinger	
ECS766	Tchaikovsky: Suite 3	PCO	Boult	(CS6140)
ECS767	Shostakovich: Symphony 5	OSR	Kertesz	(SXL6018 SDD179)
ECS772	Massenet: Scenes Pittoreaques/Franck: Chasseur Maudit/Lalo: Rhapsody/Scherzo	PCO/Wolff		(Massenet on CS6139)
ECS773	Massenet: Scenes Alsaciennes/Charpentier: Italian Impressions	PCO	Wolff	(Massenet on CS6139)
ECS775	Mendelssohn: Violin Conc/Bruch Scottish Fantasia	LPO	Boult Campoli	(SXL2026 SDD110)
ECS776	Stravinsky: Pulcinella Suite/Song of the Nightingale	OSR	Ansermet	(SXL2188 SDD136)
ECS779	Dvorak: Symphony 2 (7)	LSO	Monteux	(LSC 2489)
ECS780	Mahler: Kindertotenlieder, Fahrenden Gesellen	VPO	Boult Flagstad	(SXL2224)
ECS781	Beethoven: Symphony 6, Prometheus Ov	OSR	Ansermet	
ECS782	Bizet: Jeux D'Enfants/Ibert: Divertissement/etc	PCO	Martinon	(SXL2252 SDD144)
ECS789	Sibelius: Symphony 2	LSO	Monteux	(LSC2342)
ECS790	Bach: Cantatas 130, 67, 101 (excerpts)	OSR	Ansermet	
ECS794	Sibelius Songs	LSO	Fjelstadt Flagstad	
ECS795	Borodin: Quartet 2/Shostakovich: Quartet 8	Borodin Quartet		(SXL6036 CS6338)
ECS797	Espana	LSO	Argenta	(SXL2020 SDD216)
ECS798	Brahms: Alto Rhapsody/etc	OSR	Ansermet Watts	Never issued SXL
ECS801	Bizet: Symphony in C/Jeux D'Enfants/etc	OSR	Ansermet	(SXL2252/SXL2275)
ECS803	Paganini: 24 Caprices	Ricci		(SXL2194)
ECS805	Fauré: Pavane/Masques/Pelleas/etc	NSOL	Agoult	(LSC2326 SPA111)
ECS806	Music of Gluck (Dance of the Spirits, Chaconne, Don Juan, etc)		Monteux, Gibson, Marriner, etc	
ECS807	Weber: Clarinet Concerto, Bassoon Concerto, Konzertstuck	VPO	De Peyer	
ECS808	St-Saens: Havanaise/Bacchanale/Danse Macabre/etc	LSO	Gamba Ricci	(SXL2197)
ECS809	Chopin: Les Sylphides/Delibes	PCO	Maag	(SXL2044 SDD221 ECS809)
ECS815	Ravel: Mother Goose/Valses/etc	OSR	Ansermet	(SXL2062 SDD374)
ECS816	Debussy: Nocturnes/Jeux/Danse	OSR	Ansermet	(SXL2027/SXL2062)

ECS817	Stravinsky: The Firebird	OSR	Ansermet	(SXL2017 SDD246)
ECS818	Stravinsky: Rite of Spring	OSR	Ansermet	(SXL2042)
ECS819	Stravinsky: Petruchka	OSR	Ansermet	(SXL2011)
ECS820	Stravinsky: Sym of Psalms/Sym in 3 mvmts	OSR	Ansermet	(SXL2237/SXL2277)
ECS821	Stravinsky: Symphony in C/Symphonies of wind insts	OSR	Ansermet	(SXL2237)
ECS822	Stravinsky Apollon Musagete/etc	OSR	Ansermet	(SDD243 CS6034)
ECS823	Mozart: Symphonies 33/39	VPO	Kertesz	
ECS824	Ravel: Daphnis & Chloe	OSR	Ansermet	(SXL6204 SPA230) TEC
ECS825	Mozart: Piano Concertos K466, K503	StCO	Munchinger Katchen	
ECS826	Wagner: Wesendock Lieder	VPO	Knappertsbusch Flagstad	(not issued SXL)
ECS827	French Overtures (Lalo/Offenbach/Auber/Herold)	OSR	Ansermet	(SXL2263 SDD192)
ECS828	Haydn: Symphonies 94, 99	VPO	Krips	(SXL2098)
ECS838	Rachmaninov: Symphony 3, Mussorgsky: Night on Bare Mt	OSR	Kletzki	

"World of" (SPA)

Most of these SPA reissues contain music extracted from a number of different original recordings and by a number of different orchestras and conductors. Consequently, in some cases I have not indicated an orchestra or conductor.

SPA 1	"The World of Mantovani"		Mantovani	
SPA 10	Strauss,J: Blue Danube, Pizzicato Polka, Roses from the South	VPO	Boskovsky	
SPA 30	"Oliver!"		Original recording of the London Musical	
SPA 36	"The World of Mantovani vol 2"		Mantovani	
SPA 54	"The Big Band World of Ted Heath"		Ted Heath and his Band	
SPA 55	"The World of Ballet" (Nutcracker, Swan Lake, etc)			
SPA 69	Beethoven: Piano Sonatas (Moonlight, Pathetique, Appassionata)		Backhaus	
SPA 70-1	Mahler: Symphony 3	Vienna Orch	Adler	(mono)
SPA 73	The World of Johann Strauss	VPO	Knappertsbusch	(SXL2016)
SPA 74	'The World of Benjamin Britten'	LSO	Britten	
SPA 87	Dvorak: New World Symphony	VPO	Kertesz	(SXL2289)
SPA 88	Mendelssohn/Bruch: Violin Concertos	LSO	Gamba Ricci	(SXL2006)
SPA 89	Rimsky Korsakov: Scheherazade	LSO	Monteux	(LSC2208)
SPA 90	Prokofiev: Peter and the Wolf, Classical Symphony	LSO	Sargent	
SPA 91	Finlandia'	LSO	Mackerras	(LSC 2336)
SPA 92	Overtures: William Tell/Fingal's Cave/Mdsmr Ngts Dream/etc			
SPA 97	"The World of Ballet vol 2" Extracts from Faust, Bartered Bride, etc			
SPA108	Tchaikovsky: Ov 1812/Capriccio Italien/Marche Slave	LSO	Alwyn	(SXL2001 SDD112)
SPA110	'Encores'		Katchen	(SXL2293)
SPA111	Debussy: Claire de Lune	Agoult LPSO		(ECS805 SPA111)
SPA113	Beethoven: Symphony 6	VPO	Monteux	(LSC2316)
SPA119	Tchaikovsky: Romeo & Juliet ov, Strauss: Don Juan	VPO	Karajan	(SXL2269)
SPA120	Handel: Water Music, Fireworks Music	LSO	Szell	(SXL2302)
SPA121	Elgar: Enigma variations/Brahms: Haydn Vns	LSO	Monteux	(LSC 2418)
SPA122	Sibelius: Symphony 5	LSO	Gibson	(LSC2405) TEC
SPA123	Beethoven: Symphony 3	VPO	Monteux	(VICS1036)
SPA125	"A Journey into Stereo Sound"			(SKL4001)
SPA127	'Solti Conducts...' Glinka: Russlan&Ludmilla/Borodin: Pol	LSO	Solti	(SXL6263)
SPA129	Bach: Brandenburg Conc 2, Suites 2, 3, Vivaldi, Gabrielli	StCO	Munchinger	
SPA152	Stravinsky: Petrouchka/Firebird Suite	PCO	Monteux	(SB2037)
SPA153	Mendelssohn: Midsummer Nights Drm,Schubert:Rosamunde	OSR	Ansermet	
SPA169	Rachmaninov: Piano Concertos 1 & 2	LSO	Davis Katin	
SPA170	Grieg: Peer Gynt Suite 1, Piano Concerto, Litolff: Scherzo			(SXL2012 etc)
SPA173	"March". A collection from some of the finest early SXL/RCA			(LSC2327 LSC2449)
SPA174	Dvorak: Carnival Ov/Albeniz: Iberia/Debussy: Nocturnes			

SPA175	Danse Macabre	NSOL	Gibson	(LSC2225)
SPA179	Spanish Guitar Music Yepes			
SPA182	Rimsky-Korsakov: Capriccio Espagnol/Ravel/Glinka/etc			
SPA183	Tchaikovsky/Paganini: Violin Concertos	LSO	Argenta Campoli	(SXL2029/CS6084)
SPA184	Suppe: Light Cavalry, Queen of Spades, Adam, Nicolai, etc	Agoult	Wolff	
SPA187	Ketelbey: The World of Albert Ketelbey	NSOL	Sharples	
SPA201	Vivaldi: 4 Seasons	StCO	Munchinger	(SXL2019)
SPA202	Bohemian Rhapsody (Vltava/Bartered Bride/Slavonic Dances)		Kertesz	(SXL6024)
SPA203	"Ballet Music from the Opera" Massenet: Le Cid		Martinon	(SXL2021 etc)
SPA204	Spain! (includes Bizet: Carmen,Chabrier: Espana)	OSR	Ansermet	(SXL6168)
SPA206	Tchaikovsky: Symphony 4	LSO	Szell	
SPA220	Bizet: Carmen/L'Arlesienne	ROHCG	Gibson/Morel	(LSC2327 LSC2449)
SPA221	Tchaikovsky: Symphony 6	OSR	Ansermet	(Not on SXL, CS6108)
SPA222	Berlioz: Symphonie Fantastique	VPO	Monteux	(LSC2362)
SPA223	Tchaikovsky: Symphony 5	PCO	Solti	
SPA224	Tchaikovsky: Swan Lake	ROHCG	Morel	(LSC2227)
SPA226	Prokofiev: Rome&Juliet/Cinderella	OSR	Ansermet	(SXL2306/7)
SPA227	Respighi: Pines & Fountains of Rome	OSR	Ansermet	(SXL6141)
SPA228	Saint-Saens: Symphony 3	OSR	Ansermet	(SXL6027)
SPA229	Mussorgsky: Pictures at an Exbn/Prokofiev: Lt Kije	OSR	Ansermet	(SXL2195)
SPA230	Ravel: Daphnis & Chloe	OSR	Ansermet	(SXL6204 ECS824)
SPA231	Debussy: La Mer/Clair de Lune/Petite Suite/Faune/etc			
SPA233	Rodrigo: Guitar Concerto/Falla:Nights	NOS	Argenta Yepes	(SXL2091 SDD446)
SPA237	Beethoven Symphony 7/Fidelio Ov	OSR	Ansermet	(SXL2235 SDD107)
SPA249	Beethoven: Pathetique Sonata, Bagatelle, Schubert, Liszt		Brendel	
SPA257	Mussorgsky: Night on Bare Mt/Borodin: Prince Igor	BPO	Solti	
SPA260	The World of the Trumpet (Haydn, Hummel, Vivaldi)	Various		
SPA261	The World of the Harpsichord		Malcolm	
SPA281	Borodin: Symphony 2	LSO	Martinon	(LSC2298)
SPA282	Sibelius: Symphony 2, Valse Triste	OSR	Ansermet	(SXL6100)
SPA312	Strauss,J: Fledermaus, Thunder&Lightning, Morning Papers, etc	VPO	Boskovsky	
SPA314	Delibes: Coppelia & Sylvia (hlts)	OSR	Ansermet	
SPA315	Brahms: Hungn Dance 5, Rhapsody 2, Acad Fest Ov, etc			
SPA317	Wagner: Tannhauser, Die Walkure, Gotterdammerung/etc VPO/Solti			
SPA318	Liszt: Piano Concertos 1/2	LPO	Argenta Katchen	(SXL2097 SDD124)
SPA326	Beethoven: Symphonies 5, 8	OSR	Ansermet	
SPA327	Beethoven: Symphony 7, Leionora 3 & Egmont Ovs	OSR	Ansermet	
SPA328	Beethoven: Symphony 9	OSR	Ansermet	(SXL2274 SDD108)
SPA334	Beethoven: Piano Concerto 5	VPO	Knappertsbusch Curzon	(SXL2002)
SPA347	Solti at the Opera	ROHCG	Solti	(LSC2313)
SPA357	Tchaikovsky Nutcracker (hlts)	OSR	Ansermet	(SXL2092/3 SDD378/9)
SPA358	Tchaikovsky: Sleeping Beauty	OSR	Ansermet	(SXL2160-2)
SPA375	Tchaikovsky & Dvorak: Serenades for Strings	IPO	Solti	
SPA376	Rossini-Respighi: La Boutique Fantasque/Dukas	IPO	Solti	(SXL2007 SDD109)
SPA377	Hungarian/Slavonic Dances (Brahms/Dvorak)	VPO	Reiner	(SXL2249 SDD123)
SPA378	Brahms: Symphony 1	OSR	Ansermet	
SPA379	Brahms: Symphony 2, Tragic Ov	OSR	Ansermet	
SPA380	Brahms: Symphony 3, Haydn Variations	OSR	Ansermet	
SPA381	Brahms: Symphony 4, Academic Fest Ov	OSR	Ansermet	
SPA382	Bach,JS: Brandenburg Concertos 1-3	StCO	Munchinger	
SPA383	Bach,JS: Brandenburg Concertos 4-6	StCO	Munchinger	
SPA384	Adam: Giselle	PCO	Martinon	(SXL2128 SDD125)
SPA385	Brahms: Piano Concerto 1	LSO	Monteux Katchen	(SXL2172 SDD137)
SPA392	Ravel: Daphnis & Chloe (excerpts)/Pavane/Rapsodie Espagnol			
SPA393	"World of the French Horn" Horn Concertos by Mozart,Haydn			

SPA397	Strauss,R: Zarathustra, Till Eulenspiegel	RPO	Lewis	
SPA398	Sibelius: Violin Concerto, Dvorak: Violin Concerto			(SXL2077/SXL2279)
SPA401	Beethoven: Piano Concertos 1, 2	VPO	Schmidt-Issersdtedt Backhaus	
SPA421	Grieg: Peer Gynt/etc	LSO	Fjelstadt	(SXL2012 SDD111)
SPA445	Rossini: William Tell/Thieving Magpie/Barber of Seville			
SPA451	Mendelsshohn: Midsummer Nights Dream	LSO	Maag	(SXL2060 SDD159)
SPA452	Beethoven: Piano Concerto 5	VPO	Schmidt-Isserstedt Backhaus	(SXL2179)
SPA458	Brahms Piano Concerto 2	LSO	Ferencsik Katchen	(SXL2236)
SPA467	Schubert: Symphony 9	LSO	Krips	(SXL2045)
SPA476	Mozart: Requiem	VPO	Kertesz	(SET302)
SPA487	Pas de Deux from Don Quixote, Swan Lake, Giselle, Nutcracker, etc			
SPA494	Respighi: Fountains of Rome/Pines of Rome	Philh	Munch	
SPA495	Mozart: Clarinet Concerto, Flute & Harp Concerto	VPO	Munchinger	
SPA503	Mendelsohn: Symphony 3/Fingal's Cave	LSO	Maag	(SXL2246 SDD145)
SPA505	Rachmaninov: Rhaps on Paganini, Piano Concerto 2		Katchen	(SXL2076, SXL2176)
SPA520	Britten: Young Person's Guide, Prokofiev: Peter & the Wolf	RPO	Dorati Sean Connery	
SPA521	Mahler: Symphony 1	RPO	Leinsdorf	
SPA522	Mozart: Symphony 40, Horn Concerto 4, etc	RPO	Foster Civil	
SPA525	Copland: Fanfare for the Common Man, Gershwin	LAPO	Mehta Katchen	
SPA536	Elgar: Enigma Variations/Pomp&Circ Marches	LSO	Monteux	
SPA537	Wagner: Valkyries, Siegfried's Journey, Funeral Music, Valhalla	LSO	Stokowski	
SPA549	Sibelius: Finlandia, Karelia Suite, Swan of Tuonela	Philh	various	
SPA550	Mozart: Serenata Notturna K329/Notturno for 4 Orchs	LSO	Maag	(SXL2196 SDD420)
SPA551	Ravel: Bolero/Rapsodie Espagnol/Bizet: Carmen Fantasie/etc			
SPA552	Mendelssohn: Ovs Fingal's Cave, Midsmr Nts Dream, Ruy Blas	OSR	Ansermet	

"World of" double albums

DPA503	Piano Concertos: Tchaikovsky, Rachmaninov, Grieg, Schumann		Gulda	Katin
DPA505	Violin Concertos by Mendelssohn, Bruch, Tchaikovsky, Sibelius	LSO	Fjelstad Ricci	
DPA507	"Favourite Opera" (Sutherland,Tebaldi, Krause, Della Casa, etc)			
DPA511	"Favourite Orch Music" (Fingals Cave, Bolero, Finlandia, Peer Gynt, etc)		Various	
DPA517	"Favourite Operatic Duets" (Boheme, Butterfly, Traviata, Tosca, etc)			
DPA521	Mozart: Flute Concerto, Clarinet Concerto, Horn Concerto 4	LSO	Monteux Claude Monteux, VPO Munchinger	
DPA531	Sibelius: Karelia St, Violin Concerto, Symphony 2	LSO	Gibson, LSO Fjelstad Ricci	(LSC2405, SXL2077)
DPA539	Dvorak: Symphony 9, Carnival Ov, Slavonic Dances, etc	Kertesz	Reiner	
DPA541	Mozart:Symphony 40,Piano Concerto 21,Clarinet Concerto,etc	VPO	Boskowsky etc	
DPA543	Strauss,R: Zarathustra, Don Juan, Till Eulenspiegel, 7 Veils	VPO	Karajan	
DPA545	Schubert: Symphony 8, Rosamunde, Trout Quintet	VPO	Schuricht VPO Monteux Vienna Octet Curzon	
DPA553	Brahms: Acad Fest Ov,Alto Rhaps,Haydn Vns,Hungn Dances	OSR	Ansermet LSO Monteux VPO Reiner	
DPA557	Mendelssohn:Fingal's Cave,Vln Conc, Italian Sym, Dream, etc	OSR	Ansermet and LSO Maag	
DPA559	Bizet: Carmen, L'Arlesienne, Symphony in C, Jeux D'Enfants	OSR	Ansermet	
DPA561	Ravel:Bolero,Goose,Daphnis,Valse,Pavane,Alborado,Rps Esp	OSR	Ansermet	
DPA565	Rachmaninov: Piano Conc 2, Paganini Rpsd, Sym 2, Vocalise	LSO	Solti Katchen	
DPA567	Grieg: Peer Gynt, Piano Concerto, Holberg Suite, etc	LSO	Fjelstadt & Kertesz Katchen	
DPA569	Tchaikovsky: The Nutcracker	OSR	Ansermet	(SXL2092-3)
DPA575	Smetana: Ma Vlast	VPO	Kubelik	
DPA581	Delibes: Coppelia	OSR	Ansermet	(SXL2084/5 SDD371/2)
DPA583	Brahms: German Requiem/Alto Rhapsody/etc	OSR	Ansermet	(SET333/4)
DPA589	Bach: Orchestral Suites	StCO	Munchinger	(CSA2206 SDD386-7 SXL2300-1)
DPA597	Handel: Water Music, Harp Concerto, Concerto Grosso, etc	Philomusica of London Dart		
DPA599	Beethoven: Symphony 9, Symphony 5	LPO	Stokowski	
DPA603	Tchaikovsky: Swan Lake	OSR	Ansermet	(SXL2107/8 SDD354/5)
DPA609	Vivaldi: 4 Seasons, etc	StCO	Munchinger	
DPA613	Berlioz:Symphonie Fantastique,Carnaval Romain,Nuits D'Ete	VPO	Monteux OSR Ansermet	
DPA619	Debussy: La Mer/Faun Prelude/Nocturnes/Iberia/etc	OSR	Ansermet	(SXL2062)

DPA629	"Music of Spain" (Carmen Fantasy etc)	LSO	Gamba	Ricci	(SXL2197)
DPA631	"Music of France"				

Brunswick Stereo SXA

Both the SXA40xx and SXA45xx series were introduced in 1962 although the former, consisting of only a few items, was complete within a few months. The latter series was complete by 1968.

The label: The label is purple with silver lettering. The word "stereophonic" is within a narrow band about 1cm above the spindle hole, and the word "Brunswick" in italic is about 1cm above that. As with all Decca pressings of this era the label has a groove around the label about 2.5cms diameter.

The list: The list is believed to be complete for all Brunswick stereo releases.

Note that I have only shown explicit mono cross references for the SXA40nn series. All the SXA45nn series have corresponding monos numbered AXA45nn.

SXA4001	The Play of Daniel (12th Century Musical Drama)	NY Pro Musica Orch Greenberg	[AXTL1086]
SXA4002	"Virtuosi,USA" (Paganini,Wieniawski,Bach)	Virtuosi,USA Vardi	[AXTL1093]
SXA4003	Bach,JS: Harpsichord Concertos BWV1061,1064,1065	Baroque CO Saidenberg	[AXTL1094]
SXA4004	Des Pres: Masses and Chansons	NY Pro Musica Motet Choir Greenberg	[AXTL1095]
SXA4005	Mozart: Sinfonia Concertante K364, etc	Aeterna CO Waldman J Fuchs (vln) L Fuchs (viola)	[AXTL1097]
SXA4006	Moussorgsky: Pictures at an Exhibition, Schumann: Carnaval op 9	Moiseiwitsch	[AXTL1098]
SXA4007	"Instrumental Music from Courts of Q Elizabeth&K James"	NY Pro Musica Greenberg	[AXTL1099]
SXA4501	"A Tribute to Kreisler" (works by Kreisler)	Ricci Smith (pno)	
SXA4503	Schumann: Kreisleriana op 16, Kinderscenen op 15, Romance in F op 28/2, Arabesque op 18	Moiseiwitsch (pno)	
SXA4506	Recorder Recital (Telemann,Veracini,Fesch,etc)	Brüggen (recorder) van Wering (hpsd)	
SXA4509	"Forty Fabulous Fingers" vol 2(Paganini,Bach,Paderewski,etc)	The Original Piano Quartet	
SXA4510	Guitar Recital (Castelnuovo-Tedesco,Sor,Frescobaldi,etc)	Segovia (guitar)	
SXA4511	Renaissance Festival Music	NY Pro Musica Greenberg	
SXA4513	Spanish Mediaeval Music (Alfonso X, El Sabio)	NY Pro Musica Greenberg	
SXA4514	"Forty Fabulous Fingers" vol 1(Milhaud,Liszt,St-Saens,etc)	The Original Piano Quartet	
SXA4515	Elizabethan and Jacobean Ayres,Madrigals&Dances	NY Pro Musica Greenberg	
SXA4516	Music of the Early German Baroque	NY Pro Musica Greenberg	
SXA4517	Mediaeval English Carols and Italian Dances	NY Pro Musica Greenberg	
SXA4518	Five Centuries of Song	The Abbey Singers	
SXA4520	Dawson: Negro Folk Symphony	American SO Stokowski	
SXA4521	"The Glory of Cremona" (Ricci plays 15 famous violins created by Stradivari, Amati, Guarneri, etc)	Ricci (vln) Pommers (pno)	
SXA4522	Senfl: Easter Mass, Songs	NY Pro Musica Greenberg	
SXA4523	Beethoven: Piano Sonatas op 27, op 81a	Moiseiwitsch (pno)	
SXA4524	Music of Shakespeare's Time (Morley,Byrd,Dowland,etc)	NY Pro Musica Greenberg	
SXA4525	"Meadowland and other Favourites" (Choral Hymns)	Don Cossack Choir Jaroff	
SXA4526	Walton: Facade	Oberlin directed by Dunn Gingold (narrator)	
SXA4527	Castelnuovo-Tedesco: Platero and I (2nd series), Ponce: Sonata Romántica	Segovia (guitar)	
SXA4528	Busoni: Indian Fantasy for Piano&Orch, Bortkievich:Piano Concerto 1	Vienna State Opera Strickland Mitchell (pno)	
SXA4529	Paganini:Violin Concerto op 7,St-Saens:Violin Concerto op 20	Cincinnati SO Rudolf Ricci	
SXA4530	Don Cossack Chorus	Don Cossack Chorus Jarov	
SXA4531	Harpsichord Recital (Scarlatti, Vivaldi, Couperin, Byrd)	Marlowe (hpsd)	
SXA4532	Guitar Recital (De Valera, Mompou, Tansman)	Segovia	
SXA4533-4	Haydn: The Creation	Musica Aeterna Waldman etc	

SXA4535	Guitar Recital (Milan,Visée,Haydn,Albéniz,Torróba,etc)	Segovia
SXA4536	The Renaissance Band (Praetorius, Isaac, Lassus)	NY Pro Musica Greenberg
SXA4537	Contemporary American Works for Harpsichord	Marlowe (hpsd)
SXA4538	Italian Madrigals & Haydn Part Songs	Abbey Singers Oelbaum (pno)
SXA4539	Early Italian baroque Music	NY Pro Musica Greenberg
SXA4540	Haydn: Symphonies 57, 86	Cincinnati SO Rudolf
SXA4541	Nielsen: Symphony 4, Ov: Maskarade	Cincinnati SO Rudolf
SXA4542	Mozart: Serenade K320 (Posthorn), Symphony 28	Cincinnati SO Rudolf
SXA4543	Haydn:Harpsichord Conc op 21,Bach,JS:Brandenburg Conc 5	Baroque CO Saidenberg Marlowe (hpsd)
SXA4544	"A Countess from Hong Kong" (Film Score)	
SXA4545	"Pages from the Notebook of Anna Magdalena Bach" (Bach's 2nd wife, a Bach family musical evening)	NY CO Bressler (ten)
SXA4546	Florentine Music (Andreas,Donatus,Isaak,Festa,Gherrardellus)	NY Pro Musica Davenport
SXA4547	Rieti: Harpsichord Concerto, etc	CO Baron Marlowe (hpsd)
SXA4548	Dvorak: Czech Suite op 39, Serenade op 44	Musica Aeterna Orch Waldman
SXA4550	Guitar Recital (Purcell,Handel,Bach,Scarlatti,etc)	Segovia

Telefunken Stereo SMA

The SMAseries (and the GMA mono discs within the same numbering series) were released between 1959 and 1967 at a cheaper price than any major rival.

The label: ?.

The list: ?

SMA 1	Beethoven: Symphony 3	Hamburg PO Keilberth
SMA 2	Beethoven: Symphony 5	Hamburg PO Keilberth
SMA 3	Tchaikovsky: Nutcracker Suite, Serenade in Cmaj	Belgian Nat RO Andre
SMA 4	Respighi: Pines of Rome, Fountains of Rome	Belgian Nat RO Andre
SMA 8	Ballet Suites Coppelia, Sylvia	Belgian RSO Andre
SMA 9	Dvorak: Cello Concerto	Hamburg Philh Keilberth Hoelscher
SMA 10	German Overtures (Weber, Gluck, Humperdinck, Nicolai)	Berlin State Rother
SMA 11	Dvorak: Slavonic Dances op 46 (1,3,4,6,8),op 72(1,2,4,7,8)	Bamberg SO Keilberth
SMA 13	French Ovs (Herold,Adam,Auber,Berlioz,Thomas)	Belgian Nat RO Andre
SMA 14	Borodin: Polovtsian Suites Liszt: Hungarian Rhapsodies 3 & 6 Enesco: Rumanian Rhapsody 1	
SMA 16	Mendelssohn:Midsummer Nights Dream,Schubert:Rosamunde	Berlin State Opera Orch Rother
SMA 17	Mozart: Symphonies 38 39	Bamberg SO Keilberth
SMA 19	Bruch: Violin Concerto 1,Spohr: Violin Concerto 8	Berlin SO Albert Field (vln)
SMA 20	Beethoven: Symphonies 1, 8	Bamberg SO Keilberth
SMA 22	Orchestral Concert (Falla,Ravel, Dukas)	Belgian RSO Andre
SMA 25	Strauss,J/Lehar: Operetta hlts	Various Rothenberger
SMA 26	Operetta Overtures (Fledermaus,Night in Venice, etc)	Berlin State Opera Rother
SMA 28	Wagner:Lohengrin (Preludes Acts 1&2), Meistersinger (Preludes Acts 1&2)	Hamburg Philh Keilberth
SMA 29	Haydn: Symphonies 85 101	Bamberg SO Keilberth
SMA 39	Mozart: Symphonies 40 41	Bamberg SO Keilberth
SMA 48	Beethoven: String Quartet op 127	Tatrai Quartet
SMA 56	Mozart: Requiem	Munich Bach Orch Karl Richter
SMA 83	Bruckner: Symphony 6	BPO Keilberth
SMA 87	Brahms: Symphony 2	BPO Keilberth
SMA 88	Beethoven: Symphony 7, Egmont ov	BPO Keilberth
SMA 89	Brahms: Symphony 3 Hungarian Dances	BPO Keilberth
SMA 90	Mozart: Symphonies 35, 36, 6 German Dances K509	Bamberg SO Keilberth
SMA 93	Marches from Europe	4th Air Force Band,Hamburg
SMA 95	"Operetta Highlights" (Zeller, Millöcker,Lehár, Fall)	various
SMA 97	Marches from Germany	Berlin Police Force Band
SMA100	Concert of Favourite Melodies (Gounod,Offenbach,Elgar,etc)	various
SMA102	Strassner: Baroque Suite on Jazz and Negro Spiritual Themes	Halberg Chamber Mus Soc Strassner
SMA103	Beethoven: Overtures Egmont, Leonora 3, Fidelio, Coriolan, Ruins of Athens	BPO Keilberth
SMA104	Bruckner: Symphony 9	Hamburg Philh Keilberth
SMA105	An Evening in Song (Operetta and Neoploitan Songs)	Schutz (tenor)
SMA106	Strauss,R: Orch excerpts from Salome, Rosenkavalier, etc	Bavarian SO Keilberth
SMA107	"Music by Moonlight" (Schumann,Liszt,Schubert,Sibelius,etc)	Orch cond by Müller-Lampertz
SMA109	"A Treasure Chest of Melodies" (Bizet,Tchaikovsky,Bruch,etc)	Bamberg SO Wöss
SMA109	"A Treasure Chest of Melodies" (Bizet,Tchaikovsky,Bruch,etc)	Bamberg SO Wöss
SMA110	"A Treasure Chest of Melodies" (Reznicek, Adam, etc)	Bamberg SO Wöss
SMA111	"Intermezzo" (Suppe,Komzak,J Strauss,Kalman,etc)	Bavarian Radio Orch Michalski

EMI

The list: Note that this list is believed to be complete for the early ASDnnn series, the Columbia SAX2nnn series, the later ASDnnnn series, and for the SLS box sets.

Labels: The earliest label for the "3 digit ASDs" is usually referred to as "white and gold". This is a white label with a gold surrounding circular band. The lettering is mixed gold and red. Above the spindle is the word STEREOPHONIC in gold, and above that is "HIS MASTER'S VOICE" in red. Above this is a picture of Nipper. The last record to use this label was ASD575.

The second label is usually referred to as "black and red dog", or "dog in semi circle". This is a predominantly red label, with predominantly black lettering. In the upper semi-circle there is a larger (and better) picture of Nipper, with "HIS MASTER'S VOICE" in white around the perimeter. This label is the second label for ASDs up to ASD575. It is the first label for "3 digit" ASDs after ASD575. It is also the first label for later "4 digit" ASDs up to somewhere around ASD2450-ASD2480. I have seen this label only on these numbers above ASD2450: ASD2453, ASD2454, ASD2455, ASD2458, ASD2459, ASD2462, ASD2465, ASD2466, ASD2468, ASD2470, ASD2477, ASD2478, ASD2483.

Pressings: I do not understand the engravings on the vinyl of EMI records and I don't know anyone who does. I would be very interested to hear from anyone who claims to be able to decipher these marks!

Abbreviations

BavSO	Bavarian Symphony Orchestra
BBCSO	BBC Symphony Orchestra
BFCO	Bath Festival Chamber Orchestra
BNSO	Bournemouth Sinfonietta
Bolshoi	Bolshoi Theatre Orchestra
BPO	Berlin Philharmonic Orchestra
BSOO	Berlin State Opera Orchestra
BRSO	Bavarian Radio Symphony Orchestra
BSO	Berlin Symphony Orchestra
CBSO	City of Birmingham Symphony Orchestra
Clvlnd	Cleveland Orchestra
CMI	Collegium Musicum Italicum
DrSt	Dresden Staatskapelle
EMCL	Early Music Consort of London
ENOC	English National Opera Company
FNRO	French National Radio Orchestra
Glynd	Glyndebourne
GSOpB	German State Opera Berlin
HO	Halle Orchestra
KCC	Choir of Kings College Cambridge
LACO	Los Angeles Chamber Orchestra
LGO	Leipzig Gewandhaus Orchestra
LenPO	Leningrad Philharmonic Orch
LenSO	Leningrad Symphony Orch
LMP	London Mozart Players
MCO	Moscow Chamber Orchestra
MFO	Menuhin Festival Orchestra
MPO	Moscow Philharmonic Orchestra
MRSO	Moscow Radio Symphony Orchestra
ONDF	Orchestre National de France
ODP	Orchestre de Paris
ONB	Orchestre National de Belgique
OROH	Orchestra of Rome Opera House
OTNO	Orchestra of the Theatre National de l'Opera
PO	Paris Opera
Philh	Philharmonia Orchestra (including New Philharmonia)
Phild	Philadelphia Orchestra
PTSO	Pittsburgh Symphony Orchestra
RLPO	Royal Liverpool Philharmonic Orchestra
RPO	Royal Philharmonic Orchestra
SOL	Sinfonia of London

USSR	USSR Symphony Orchestra
VSOp	Vienna State Opera
VV	Vienna Volksoper
WarPh	Warsaw Philharmonic Orchestra

Early EMIs (1958-1964)

ASD 251	Rimsky Korsakov: Scheherazade	RPO	Beecham
ASD 252	Bizet L'Arlesienne	RPO	Beecham
ASD 253	Tchaikovsky: Symphony 4	Philh	Silvestri
ASD 254	Beethoven Symphony 7	Philh	Cantelli
ASD 255	Ravel: Concerto in G/Rachmaninov: Conc 4	Philh	Gracis Michelangeli
ASD 256-7	Gilbert & Sullivan: The Mikado	Glynd	Sargent
ASD 258	Grieg: Peer Gynt	RPO	Beecham
ASD 259	Beecham Lollipops	RPO	Beecham
ASD 260	Sibelius: Symphony 1	BBCSO	Sargent
ASD 261	Tchaikovsky: Symphony 5	Philh	Silvestri
ASD 262	Balakirev: Islamey, Rimsky-Korsakov: Le Coq D'Or, etc	Philh	Goossens
ASD 263	Prokofiev: Classical Sym/Shostakovich Sym 1	Philh	Kurtz
ASD 264	Brahms Violin Concerto	BPO	Kempe Menuhin
ASD 265-6	Gilbert & Sullivan: The Gondoliers	Glynd	Sargent
ASD 267	Beethoven: Symphony 5/Leonora 3 Ov	BPO	Cluytens
ASD 268	Brahms Piano Concerto 2	Philh	Boult Kentner
ASD 269	Holst: Planets	BBCSO	Sargent
ASD 270	Strauss,R: Tod und Verk/Dance of 7 Veils	Philh	Rodzinski
ASD 271	Tchaikovsky: Swan Lake (suite)	Philh	Kurtz Menuhin
ASD 272	Grieg/Schumann Piano Concertos	Philh	Menges Solomon
ASD 273	Tchaikovsky: Symphony 6	Philh	Silvestri
ASD 274-7	Mozart: Marriage of Figaro	Glyndebourne	Gui
ASD 278	Mendelssohn/Tchaikovsky Violin Concertos	Philh	Silvestri Ferras
ASD 279	'Nights in Vienna' (Lehar/Strauss/Suppe/etc)	VPO	Kempe
ASD 280	Beethoven: Mass in C	RPO	Beecham
ASD 281	Falla: 3 Cornered Hat/Granados/Albeniz	RPO	Rodzinski
ASD 282-4	Haydn: The Seasons	RPO	Beecham Morrison Young
ASD 286	Handel: Water Music/Fireworks Music	RPO	Sargent
ASD 287	Beethoven Symphony 2/Ruins of Athens	RPO	Beecham
ASD 288	Tchaikovsky: Romeo&Juliet	RPO	Rodzinski
ASD 289	Tchaikovsky: Nutcracker (extracts)	Philh	Kurtz
ASD 290	Lalo: Sym Esp/S-Saens Intr & Rondo Capr	Philh	Goossens Menuhin
ASD 291	Handel: Airs	LSO	Sargent Lewis
ASD 294	Beethoven Piano Concerto 1/Sonata Op 90	Philh	Menges Solomon
ASD 295	Puccini: Gianni Schicchi	RomeOp	Santini Gobbi
ASD 296	Schubert: Symphony 8/Rosamunde	RPO	Kletzki
ASD 297	Falla: El Amor Brujo/Ravel: Rapsodie Espagnol	Philh	Vandernoot
ASD 298	Handel: Love in Bath	RPO	Beecham
ASD 299	S-Saens: Carnival of the Animals, Prokofiev: Peter & the Wolf	Philh	Kurtz Flanders(nar) TASEC
ASD 301	Grieg: Piano Concerto/Liszt: Piano Concerto 2	Philh	Vandernoot Czyffra
ASD 302	Operatic Arias (Italian, Czech, Russian Opera)	Philh	Susskind Joan Hammond
ASD 303	Sibelius: Symphony 5/Pohjola's Daughter	BBCSO	Sargent
ASD 304	'Popular Symphonic Movements'	VPO	Cluytens
ASD 307-10	Gounod: Faust	OTNO	Cluytens De Los Angeles (SLS753)
ASD 311	Beethoven: Symphony 7	RPO	Beecham
ASD 312	Bartok: Concerto for Orchestra	RPO	Kubelik
ASD 313	Stravinsky: Rite of Spring	Philh	Markevitch
ASD 314	Bruch: Violin COncerto/Lalo: Sym Espagnol	Philh	Susskind Ferras
ASD 315	Tchaikovsky: Piano Concerto 1	Philh	Vandernoot Czyffra
ASD 317/8	Liszt: Faust Symphony/Orpheus	RPO	Beecham
ASD 319-21	Weber: Der Freischutz	BPO	Keilberth Grümmer Prey
ASD 322	Schubert: Trout Quintet	Amadeus	Hephzibah Menuhin
ASD 323-4	Gilbert & Sullivan: Iolanthe	Glynd	Sargent

ASD 325	Schubert: Symphony 9	RPO	Kubelik
ASD 326	Strauss: Don Quixote/Till Eulenspiegel	BPO	Kempe
ASD 327	Bach,J.S: Brandenburg Concertos 1/2/3	Menuhin	BFCO
ASD 328	Bach,J.S: Brandenburg Concertos 4/5/6	Menuhin	BFCO
ASD 329	Delius: Florida Suite/Over the Hills/etc	RPO	Beecham
ASD 330	Overtures (Bartered Bride/Oberon/Hebrides/etc)	VPO	Kempe
ASD 331-3	Bizet: Carmen	FNRO	Beecham De Los Angeles
ASD 334	Mendelssohn/Bruch: Violin Concertos	Philh	Menuhin
ASD 335	Purcell Anthology	Various soloists	
ASD 336	Beethoven: Overtures (Leonora/Coriolan/Egmont/etc)	BPO	Kempe
ASD 337	Schubert: Lieder Recital	Fischer-Dieskau Engel	
ASD 338	Overtures: Hansel und Gretel/MidSmr Nts Dream/etc	Philh	Silvestri
ASD 339-41	Haydn Symphonies 99-104	RPO	Beecham
ASD 342	Bach,J.S: Cantata Arias	BPO	Forster Fischer-Dieskau
ASD 343	Rimsky-Korsakov: Tsar Saltan/etc	Philh	Kletzki
ASD 344	Mozart: Clarinet Concerto/Bassoon Concerto	RPO	Beecham Brymer
ASD 345	Schubert: Symphonies 3/5	RPO	Beecham
ASD 346	Bach,J.S: Violin/Double Concertos	BFCO	Menuhin Ferras
ASD 347	Brahms: Hungn Dances/Dvorak: Scherzo Capriccioso	RPO	Kubelik
ASD 348	Brahms: Symphony 2	RPO	Beecham
ASD 349	Beethoven: Symphony 6	RPO	Kubelik
ASD 350	Brahms: Symphony 1	BPO	Kempe
ASD 351-2	Mahler: Das Lied von der Erde/Sym 5 Adagio	Philh	Kletzki Dickie Fischer-Dieskau
ASD 353-4	Verdi: Requiem	OROH	Serafin
ASD 356	Wolf: Lieder Recital	Fischer-Dieskau Moore	
ASD 357	Delius: Brigg Fair/1st Cuckoo/etc	RPO	Beecham
ASD 358	Dvorak: Cello Concerto	RPO	Boult Rostropovich
ASD 359-61	Verdi: La Traviata	OROH	Serafin De Los Angeles (SLS757)
ASD 362	Wolf: Lieder Recital	Fischer-Dieskau Moore	
ASD 363	Wagner: Tannhauser/Gotterdammerung/etc (hlts)	BSOO	Konwitschny Grummer Frick
ASD 364-5	Gilbert & Sullivan: Yeomen of the Guard	Pro Arte	Sargent
ASD 366	Respighi: Fountains of Rome/Bartered Bride	Philh	Goossens
ASD 367-9	Vivaldi: Il Cimento dell 'armonia e dell 'invention	Virtuoisi di Roma Fasano	
ASD 370	Chopin: Piano Concerto 1	Philh	Kletzki Pollini
ASD 371	Tchaikovsky: Sleeping Beauty (suite)	Philh	Kurtz
ASD 372	Bach,J.S: Ov in French Style/Italian Concerto	Rosalyn Tureck	
ASD 373-5	Puccini: Madama Butterfly	OROH	Santini De Los Angeles
ASD 376	Orchestral Marches	Philh	Kurtz
ASD 377	Beethoven: Violin Concerto	VPO	Silvestri Menuhin
ASD 378	Wolf: Lieder Recital (Spanisches Liederbuch)	Fischer-Dieskau Moore	
ASD 379	Tchaikovsky: Symphony 5	BPO	Kempe
ASD 380	Dvorak: Symphony 5	BPO	Kempe
ASD 381-2	Gilbert & Sullivan: Pirates of Penzance	Pro Arte	Sargent
ASD 383	Christmas Carols	Royal Choral Society Sargent	
ASD 384	Love Duets	RPO	Tausky Hammond Charles Craig
ASD 385-7	Wagner: Flying Dutchman	Berlin Opera Konwitschny	(SLS 760)
ASD 388	Bizet: Symphony in C/Lalo: Symphony in G	FNRO	Beecham
ASD 389	Beethoven: 'Spring' & 'Kreutzer' Sonatas	Yehudi & Hephzibah Menuhin	
ASD 390	Tchaikovsky: Songs	Boris Christoff	
ASD 391-3	Vivaldi: L'Estro armonico	Virtuosi di Roma Fasano	
ASD 394-5	Strauss,J: Der Zigeunerbaron	VPO	Hollriser
ASD 396	Dvorak: Symphony 2	VPO	Silvestri
ASD 397	Bach: Contata No203, Handel: Arias		Fischer-Dieskau
ASD 398	Tchaikovsky: Symphony 4	VPO	Kubelik
ASD 399	Berlioz: Symphonie Fantastique	FNRO	Beecham TAS77/136+

ASD 400	Prokofiev: Love of 3 Oranges, Khachaturian: Gayaneh, Rimsky-Korsakov: Capriccio Espagnol	VPO	Silvestri
ASD 401	Stravinsky: Sym in 3 mvmts/Song of Nightingale	Philh	Silvestri
ASD 402-3	Dvorak: Slavonic Dances	BBCSO	Schwarz
ASD 404-5	Bach,J.S: Suites	BFCO	Menuhin
ASD 406	Brahms: Symphony 3/Tragic Ov	BPO	Kempe
ASD 407	Verdi: Arias (Falstaff, Rigoletto, Don Carlos)	BPO	Erede Gedda Fischer-Dieskau
ASD 408	Franck: Symphony	Philh	Silvestri
ASD 409-11	Haydn: The Creation	BPO	Forster (SLS762)
ASD 412	Gounod: Faust (hlts)	French Op	Cluytens
ASD 413	'The Fabulous De Los Angeles'	De Los Angeles Moore	
ASD 414	Bach: The Musical Offering	BFCO	Menuhin
ASD 415-6	Gilbert & Sullivan: HMS Pinafore	Pro Arte	Sargent
ASD 417	Rhapsodies for Orch (Liszt/Ravel/Enesco)	VPO	Silvestri
ASD 418	Schubert: Symphonies 3/4	VPO	Kubelik
ASD 419	Gilbert & Sullivan: Trial by Jury	Pro Arte	Sargent
ASD 420	Favourite Overtures (Rossini/Berlioz/etc)	RPO	Beecham
ASD 421	Strauss,R: Ein Heldenleben	RPO	Beecham
ASD 422	Borodin: Symphony 2/Plovtsian Dances	VPO	Kubelik
ASD 423	Mozart: Piano Trio K542/Ravel: Piano Trio	Menuhin Kentner et al	
ASD 424-5	Wolf: Goethe Lieder	Fischer-Dieskau Moore	
ASD 426	Beethoven: Symphony 3	BPO	Kempe
ASD 427	Mozart: Violin Concertos K 218, K219	PCO	Vandernoot Ferras
ASD 428	Tchaikovsky: Symphony 5	VPO	Kubelik
ASD 429	Bach: Violin Conc in E/Mozart: Violin Conc 5	LSO/RPO	Kubelik De Vito
ASD 430	Berlioz: Damnation of Faust (hlts)	Paris Opera	Cluytens
ASD 431	'Viennese Bon Bons'	BPO	Kempe
ASD 432	'More Beecham Lollipops'	RPO	Beecham
ASD 433	Beethoven: Symphony 6	BPO	Cluytens
ASD 434	Busoni: Chamber Fantasy/Liszt	Ogdon	
ASD 435	Rossini: Overtures (Tell, Semiramide, etc)	VPO	Sargent
ASD 436-8	Verdi: Rigoletto	MMF	Gavazzeni Bastianini
ASD 439	Delibes: Coppelia	Philh	Irving
ASD 440	Paganini: Violin Concertos 1/2	RPO	Erede Menuhin
ASD 443	Holst: The Perfect Fool/Walton: Facade/Britten	RPO	Sargent
ASD 444	Strauss,J: Die Fledermaus/Gypsy Baron (hlts)	VPO	Hollreiser
ASD 445-8	Wagner: Tannhauser	GSOpB	Konwitschny
ASD 449	Music from Bohemia (Dvorak/Weinberger/etc)	RPO	Kempe
ASD 450	Beethoven: Sonata 17/Schumann: Fantasia	Richter	
ASD 451	Mozart: Symphonies 36/38	VPO	Kubelik
ASD 452	Spanish Songs of the Renaissance	De Los Angeles	
ASD 453	Harpsichord recital (Bach/Couperin/etc)	Rosalyn Tureck	
ASD 454	Stainer: Crucifixion	Leeds Philh Ch Bardgett	
ASD 455	Shostakovich: Symphony 5	VPO	Silvestri
ASD 456	Operatic Recital (Wagner, Massenet, Verdi)	PO	Cluytens Rita Gorr
ASD 457	Bach: Cantatas 211/212 (Coffee & Peasant)	BPO	Forster Fiescher-Dieskau
ASD 458	Franck: Symphony in D minor	FNRO	Beecham
ASD 459	Duets	De Los Angeles Fischer-Dieskau Moore	
ASD 460	Mendelssohn: Midsmr Nights Dream, Humperdinck: Hansel & Gretel	RPO	Kempe
ASD 461	Brahms Symphony 4	RPO	Kempe
ASD 462	Tchaikovsky: Symphony 6	VPO	Kubelik
ASD 463	Music of India	Ravi Shankar	
ASD 464	'Czyffra Favourites'	Czyffra	
ASD 465	Gluck: Iphegenie en Tauride	PCO	Pretre Gedda Gorr
ASD 466	Overtures from Italian Operas	Philh	Serafin

ASD 467	Coleridge Taylor: Hiawatha	Philh	Sargent
ASD 468	Sibelius: Symphony 7/Pelleas & Melisande/Oceanides	RPO	Beecham
ASD 469	Song Recital	Di Stefano	
ASD 470	Dvorak: Symphony 8/Carnaval Ov	LPO	Silvestri
ASD 471	'Pearls of Viennese Operetta'	VPO	Loibner Rysanek
ASD 472	Sullivan: HMS Pinafore (hlts)	Pro Arte	Sargent
ASD 473	Mozart Violin Concertos 3/5	BFCO	Menuhin
ASD 474	Brahms: Violin Sonatas 1/2	Menuhin Kentner	
ASD 475	Schubert: Fantasie in Cmaj, Brahms: Piano Sonata 3	Menuhin Kentner	
ASD 476	Neapolitan Songs	Di Stefano	
ASD 477	Bach: Piano Recital	Rosalyn Tureck	
ASD 478	Schubert: Rosamunde/Gluck: Ballet Suite	VPO	Kempe
ASD 479	20th Century Spanish Songs	De Los Angeles Soriano	
ASD 480	Handel: The Gods Go A'Begging	RPO	Beecham
ASD 481	Schubert: Die Schone Mullerin	Fiescher-Dieskau Gerald Moore	
ASD 483	Mahler: Symphony 1	VPO	Kletzki
ASD 484-5	Sullivan: Patience	Pro Arte	Sargent
ASD 487	Sullivan: Operatic Highlights	Pro Arte	Sargent
ASD 488	Neapolitan Songs	Franco Corelli (tenor)	
ASD 489-90	Bach,J.S: Sonatas for Violin/Harpsd	Menuhin Gauntlett Malcolm	
ASD 491	Handel: Concerti Grossi Op 6 (7-11)	BFCO	Menuhin
ASD 492	Rachmaninov: Piano Concerto 2/Preludes	Philh	Pritchard Ogdon
ASD 493	Bruckner: Symphony 9	VPO	Schuricht
ASD 494	Kodaly: Hari Janos/Tchaikovsky/Gotovac	VPO	Kempe
ASD 495	Sullivan: Operatic Highlights	Pro Arte	Sargent
ASD 496	Poulenc: Les Biches/Dutilleux Le Coup/Milhaud	PCO	Pretre
ASD 497	Dohnanyi: Suite for Orch/Boutique Fantasque	RPO	Sargent
ASD 498	Music of India	Imrat Khan et al	
ASD 499	Bliss: Piano Concerto	Philh	Sargent Trevor Barnard
ASD 500	Bach: Concerto in D/Handel/Vivaldi	BFCO	Menuhin Goossens
ASD 501	Bach,J.S: Christmas Oratorio	LGO	Thomas
ASD 502	Bach,J.S: Oratorios 1 & 2	LGO	Thomas
ASD 503	Bach,J.S: Oratorios 3 & 4	LGO	Thomas
ASD 504	Bach,J.S: Oratorios 5 & 6	LGO	Thomas
ASD 505	Cantos de Espana	PCO	De Burgos De Los Angeles
ASD 506	Haydn: Symphony 45/Mozart: Srnds K525/K239	BFCO	Menuhin
ASD 507	Stravinsky: Pulcinella/Fairy's Kiss	Philh	Vandernoot
ASD 508	Vaughan Williams: Symphony 5	Philh	Barbirolli
ASD 509	Rimsky-K: Capr Esp/Moussorgsky/Borodin	RPO	Pretre
ASD 510	Beethoven: Violin Sonatas 7/10	Yehudi & Hephzibah Menuhin	
ASD 511	Stravinsky: Oedipus Rex	RPO	Davis
ASD 512	Tippett: Conc for Double String Orch, Prokofiev: Visions Fugitive	BFCO	Barshai
ASD 513	Glinka: Life for the Tsar/Gounod Faust	Philh	Kurtz
ASD 514	Schubert: Symphony 8/Mozart: Eine Kleine	VPO	Kubelik
ASD 515	Bruckner: Mass 3	BSO	Forster
ASD 516	Neapolitan Songs	Franco Corelli	
ASD 517	Poulenc: Concerto for 2 Pianos, Concert Champêtre	PCO	Pretre Poulenc Fevrier
ASD 518	'The Inimitable Sir Thomas'	RPO	Beecham
ASD 519	Hungarian, Slavonic and Polovtsian Dances	PCO	Silvestri
ASD 520	Schumann: Sonata 2/Papillons	Richter	
ASD 521	V Williams: Tallis,Greensleeves,Elgar: Intro & Allegro, Serenade	SOL	Barbirolli
ASD 522-4	Smetana: Bartered Bride	Bamberg SO Kempe	
ASD 525	Vienna Philharmonic on Holiday	VPO	Kempe
ASD 526-8	Bach: St John Passion	BSO	Forster
ASD 529	Italian Operatic Arias (Puccini, Bellini, Giordano)		Franco Corelli
ASD 530	A French Recital (Ravel, Duparc, Debussy)	PCO	Pretre De Los Angeles

ASD 531	Enescu: Violin Sonata 3/Debussy: Violin Sonata/Ravel: Tzigane	Ferras	Barbizet
ASD 532	Rimsky-Korsakov: Coq D'Or/Kabalevsky: Comedians	Philh	Kurtz
ASD 533	Mozart: Violin Concertos 4/6	BFCO	Menuhin
ASD 534	Bach,J.S: Hunting Cantata, Telemann: Canary Cantata	BSO	Forster Fischer-Dieskau
ASD 535	Wagner: Das Rheingold excerpts	State Opera Berlin	Kempe
ASD 536	An evening at the Proms	BBCSO	Sargent
ASD 537	Berlioz: Harold in Italy	Philh	Davis Menuhin
ASD 538	Liszt: Piano Recital	Kentner	
ASD 539	Music of India (vol 2)	Vilayat Khan	
ASD 540	Elgar: Symphony 1	Philh	Barbirolli
ASD 541	Sibelius En Saga/Finlandia/etc	VPO	Sargent
ASD 542	Franck: Sym Vns/Tchaikovsky: Piano Concerto 1	Philh	Barbirolli Ogdon
ASD 543	Verdi: La Traviata (hlts)	RomeOp	Serafin De Los Angeles Serafin
ASD 544	Schubert: Schwanengesang	Fischer-Dieskau Moore	
ASD 545	Falla: Nights in the Gardens of Spain	PCO	De Burgos Soriano
ASD 546	Piano Recital	Ogdon	
ASD 547	Songs of Glinka	Boris Christoff	
ASD 548	Elgar: Enigma variations/Cockaigne	Philh	Barbirolli
ASD 549	Brahms: Double Concerto/etc	Philh	Kletzki Ferras Tortelier
ASD 550	Gluck: Orfeo & Euridice (hlts)	BSO	Stein Prey
ASD 551/2	Schubert: Winterreise	Fischer-Dieskau Moore	
ASD 553	Wagner: Wesendonck Lieder etc	FNRO	Pretre Crespin
ASD 554	Corelli: Concerti Grossi	Virtuosi di Roma Fasano	
ASD 555	Wagner: Tannhauser (hlts)	Konwitschny Fischer-Dieskau et al	
ASD 556	Wagner: Flying Dutchman (hlts)	Konwitschny Fischer-Dieskau et al	
ASD 557	"A Castle Brühl Concert"	Cologne Soloists Ensemble	
ASD 558	Great Sopranos of our Time (Nilsson, Schwarzkopf, Callas, Sutherland, De Los Angeles)		
ASD 559	Shostakovich: Symphony 12	Philh	Pretre
ASD 560	Operatic recital (Handel, Weber, Wagner, Donizetti)	Klobucar (cond) Traxel	
ASD 561	Schubert: Wanderer Fantasy/Sonata in A	Richter	
ASD 562	Weber: Der Freischutz (hlts)	BPO	Keilberth
ASD 563-4	Sullivan: Ruddigore	Pro Arte	Sargent
ASD 565	Lieder Recital	Erika Koth	Engel
ASD 566	Tchaikovsky: Eugen Onegin (hlts)	BavSO	Zalinger Prey
ASD 567	Mozart: Sinfonia Concertante/Haydn: Concerto in C	BFCO	Barshai Menuhin
ASD 568	'More Carols'	Royal Choral Society Sargent	
ASD 569	Mozart: Missa Brevis K220/Palestrina	St Hedwig's Choir Forster	
ASD 570	Music of Spain	PCO	de Burgos
ASD 571	Massenet: Herodiade	Pretre	Crespin et al
ASD 572	Berg: Violin Concerto	PCO	Pretre Ferras
ASD 573	Brahms: Haydn Varns/Acad Fest Ov/Tragic Ov	Philh	Krips
ASD 574	Christoff sings 'Tsars and Kings'	PCO	Cluytens Boris Christoff
ASD 575	Mozart: Concerto for Flute&Harp/Telemann	Philh	Menuhin
ASD 576	Gluck: Alceste (hlts)	Paris Op	Pretre
ASD 577	Handel: Water Music	BFCO	Menuhin
ASD 578	Prokofiev: Symphony 5	Philh	Kletzki
ASD 579	Vivaldi Concertos	Virtuosi di Roma Fasano	
ASD 580-1	Nicolai: Merry Wives of Windsor	BavSO	Heger
ASD 582	Rimsky Korsakov: Tsar Saltan/Snow Maiden, Khachaturian	Philh	Kurtz
ASD 583	Poulenc: Stabat Mater/4 Motets	PCO	Pretre Crespin
ASD 584	Bloch: Violin Concerto	Philh	Kletzki Menuhin
ASD 585	Saint Saens: Symphony 3	PCO	Pretre
ASD 587	Brahms: Sextet 1	Menuhin Masters Aronowitz etc	
ASD 588	Rossini: Stabat Mater	BSO	Forster

Catalog	Work	Orchestra/Performer	Conductor/Artist
ASD 589	Gounod: Messe Solenelle	PCO	Hartemann
ASD 590	Bizet: Carmen highlights	FNRO	Beecham
ASD 591	Mozart: Violin Concertos 1/2	BFCO	Menuhin
ASD 592	Mozart: Violin Concerto 7/Concertone	BFCO	Menuhin
ASD 593	Schumann & R Strauss Lieder	Della Casa	Peschko
ASD 594	Strauss,R: Ariadne auf Naxos (hlts)	BPO	Erede
ASD 595	Mozart: Symphony 29/Haydn: Symphony 49	BFCO	Menuhin
ASD 596/7	Mahler: Symphony 9	BPO	Barbirolli
ASD 598	Handel: Concerto Grossi Op 6 Nos 3,6,10,12	BFCO	Menuhin
ASD 599	Religious Music	Franco Corelli	
ASD 600	Liszt: Sonata in Bmin/Hungarian Fantasia	Philh	Pritchard Ogdon
ASD 601	Carter: Piano Sonata/Double Concerto	Rosen	Kirkpatrick
ASD 602-3	Bruckner Symphony 8	VPO	Schuricht
ASD 604	Handel: Concerto Grossi Op 6 Nos 1,2,4,5	BFCO	Menuhin
ASD 605	Mozart: Clarinet Trio K498/Clarinet Quintet	Melos Ens	De Payer
ASD 606-7	Song and Operatic Recital	Philh	Erede Gobbi Moore
ASD 608	Falla: Three Cornered Hat	Philh	De Burgos De Los Angeles
ASD 609	Puccini: Madama Butterfly	Rome Opera	Santini
ASD 610/11	Elgar: Symphony 2/Falstaff	HO	Barbirolli
ASD 612	Schonberg: Suite for String Orch/etc	RPO	del Mar
ASD 613	Gerhard: Symphony 1/Dances from Don Quixote	BBCSO	Dorati
ASD 614	Bizet: Jeux D'Enfants/Lutoslawski/Rachmaninov	Vronsky & Babin (pianos)	
ASD 615	"Religious Works" (Scarlatti,Telemann,Couperin)	Fischer-Dieskau et al	
ASD 616	Recital: 'On Wings of Song' (Schubert,Bridge,Mendelssohn,etc)	Joan Hammond	Newton (piano)
ASD 617	Mozart: Symphonies 35, 41	VPO	Kubelik
ASD 618	Beethoven: Romances/Chausson/Wieniawski	Philh	Pritchard Menuhin
ASD 619	Thomas: Mignon (hlts)	Paris Opera	Hartemann
ASD 620	Brahms: Clarinet Quintet/Reger	Melos Ens	de Peyer
ASD 621	Tippett: Piano Concerto/Sonata 2	Philh	Davis Ogdon
ASD 622	Operatic Recital (Bellini, Verdi, Mozart, etc)	OROH	Ferraris Mirella Freni
ASD 623	Organ Works by Frescobaldi & Bach	Germani	
ASD 624	Bach,J.S: Easter Oratorio	SW German	Gonnenwein
ASD 625	Mendelssohn: Elijah (hlts)	RPO	Sargent
ASD 627	Mozart: Serenade K 250 (Haffner)	BFCO	Menuhin
ASD 628	Couperin: Apotheose de Lully, Apotheose de Corelli, etc	Toulouse CO	Auriacombe
ASD 629	Liszt: Piano Concerto 1/Todtentanz/Hungarian Fantasia	Philh	Vandernoot Czyffra
ASD 630	Brahms: Lieder Recital	Fischer-Dieskau Gerald Moore	
ASD 631	Telemann: Orchestral Music	MCO	Barshai
ASD 633	Bach,J.S: Flute Sonatas Vol 1	George Malcolm Elaine Shaffer	
ASD 635	Purcell: An Anthology Vol 1	Menuhin et al	
ASD 636	Tchaikovsky: Symphony 5	NPO	Pretre
ASD 637	Britten: Varns on theme of Bridge/Tippett	BFCO	Menuhin
ASD 639	Messiaen: Chronochromie/ Boulez: Le Soleil des Eaux	BBCSO	Dorati
ASD 640	Choral Music by Goehr/Maxwell Davies/etc	Melos Ens	
ASD 641	'Byrd and his Contemporaries'	KCC	Willcocks
ASD 642	20th C Spanish Piano Music (Falla/Rodrigo/etc)	Soriano	
ASD 643	Brahms: Sextet 2/Schubert: Trio in B	Menuhin et al	
ASD 644	Delius: Cello Concerto/Songs of Farewell	RPO	Sargent Du Pre
ASD 645	Hoddinott/Goehr/Birtwhistle/et al	Ogdon	
ASD 646	Tchaikovsky: Serenade for strings/Arensky Vns	LSO	Barbirolli
ASD 648-9	Dream of Gerontius	HO	Barbirolli
ASD 650	Schumann: Lieder	Fischer-Dieskau Moore	
ASD 651	A World of Song	SOL	De Burgos De Los Angeles
ASD 653	'From Christmas to Candlemas'	KCC	Willcocks
ASD 654	Strauss: Der Rosankavalier Suite/Stravinsky	Philh	Krips
ASD 655	Elgar: Cello Concerto, Sea Pictures	LSO	Barbirolli Du Pre Janet Baker

SAX: EMI Columbia (1958-1964)

EMI Columbia records are SAX (12" LPs) and SBO (10" LPs)

EMI Columbia Labels: The earliest label for the EMI Columbia SAX series is usually referred to as "blue and silver". This is a pale blue label covered with semi-circular hatching in silver. The lettering is in both silver and black. There is a silver coloured perimeter band. Surrounding the spindle is the word STEREOPHONIC in blue on a black background, and in italic script. Above that is "COLUMBIA" in black. Above this is the "magic note" logo - a pair of musical notes in a circle. This label was used for all the earliest issue of all up to SAX2500, and for none after SAX2538.

The second label is usually referred to as "black and red", or "black and red dog". This label is quite similar to the ASD second label, but with the Nipper picture replaced by a large "magic note" logo in white on a red background.

There is also a third, later label. This is a brighter red and the "magic notes" logo is in a rectangle.

Catalog	Work	Orchestra	Conductor/Artists
SAX2252	Beethoven: Piano Concerto 5	Philh	Ludwig Gilels
SAX2253	Debussy: Claire de Lune/Suk/Wieiawski	Oistrakh	Yampolsky
SAX2254-6	Verdi: Falstaff	Philh	Karajan Schwarzkopf Gobbi
SAX2257-8	Orff: Die Kluge	Philh	Sawallisch Schwarzkopf
SAX2259	Beethoven: Sonatas 9/10/13/14		Gieseking
SAX2260	Beethoven: Symphony 6	Philh	Klemperer
SAX2261	Mussorgsky: Pictures at an Exhibition	Philh	Karajan
SAX2262	Brahms: Symphony 1	Philh	Klemperer
SAX2263	Dvorak: Cello Concerto/Fauré: Elegie	Philh	Susskind Starker
SAX2264	Brahms Double Concerto/Tragic Ov	Philh	Galliera Fournier Oistrakh
SAX2265	Songs you Love		Schwarzkopf Moore
SAX2266-8	Rossini: Barber of Seville	Philh	Galliera Callas Gobbi
SAX2269-72	Strauss,R: Der Rosankavalier	Philh	Karajan Schwarzkopf Ludwig
SAX2274	Offenbach: Gaite Parisienne, Gounod: Faust, etc	Philh	Karajan
SAX2275	Dvorak: Symphony 5/Smetana: The Moldau	BPO	Karajan
SAX2276-7	Beethoven: Symphony 9	Philh	Klemperer
SAX2278	Mozart: Symphonies 25/40	Philh	Klemperer
SAX2279	Stravinsky: Firebird/Jeux d'enfants	Philh	Giulini
SAX2280	Sibelius: Symphony 2	Philh	Kletzki
SAX2281	Schubert: Trio in B flat Op 99		D Oistrakh Knushevitsky Oborin
SAX2282	Schumann: Cello Concerto/Tchaikovsky	Philh	Sargent Fournier
SAX2283	Schwarzkopf sings Operetta	Philh	Ackermann Schwarzkopf
SAX2284	Recital (Beethoven/Weber/Mozart)	Philh	Wallberg Nilsson
SAX2285	Tchaikovsky: Nutcracker/Swan Lake	Philh	Sawallisch
SAX2286-8	Puccini: Fanciulla del West		La Scala Matacic Nilsson
SAX2289	Bizet: L'Arlesienne Sts 1&2/Carmen St 1	Philh	Karajan
SAX2290-2	Cherubini: Medea		La Scala Serafin Callas
SAX2293	'Callas pertrays Verdi heroines'	Philh	Rescigno Callas
SAX2294	Opera Intermezzi (Puccini/Verdi/Leoncavallo)	Philh	Karajan
SAX2296	Wagner: Flying Dutchman, Die Walküre (hlts)	Philh	Ludwig Hotter Nilsson
SAX2297	Beethoven: Piano Concerto 5	Philh	Galliera Arrau
SAX2298-9	Donizetti: L'elisir d'Amore		La Scala Serafin Carteri Alva
SAX2300	Schwarzkopf portrays Romantic Heroines (Tannhauser, Freischutz, Lohengrin)		Schwarzkopf
SAX2302	Tchaikovsky: 1812/Berlioz/Sibelius	Philh	Karajan
SAX2303	Ravel: Daphnis St 2, Bizet: Carmen St 1, Respighi : Pines	Philh	Galliera
SAX2304	Mozart: Concerto 3/Prokofiev Concerto 2	Philh	Galliera Oistrakh
SAX2306	Tchaikovsky: Swan Lake/Sleeping Beauty (hlts)	Philh	Karajan
SAX2307	Brahms: Violin Concerto	Philh	Kondrashin Kogan
SAX2308-10	Handel: Messiah	RLPO	Sargent
SAX2315	Beethoven: Violin Concerto	FNRO	Cluytens Oistrakh
SAX2316-7	Donizetti: Lucia di Lammermoor	Philh	Serafin Callas
SAX2318	Beethoven: Symphonies 1/8	Philh	Klemperer
SAX2319	Walton: Belshazzar's Feast, Partita for Orch	Philh	Walton
SAX2320	Mad Scenes from Anna Bolena, Hamlet, Il Pirata	Philh	Rescigno Callas
SAX2321	Mahler: Fahrendedn Gesellen/Kindertotenlieder	Philh	Boult Ludwig
SAX2322	Dvorak: New World Symphony	Philh	Sawallisch
SAX2323	Tchaikovsky: Violin Concerto/Meditation	PCO	Silvestri Kogan
SAX2324	Verdi: Overtures	Philh/RPO	Serafin
SAX2327	Borodin: Prince Igor/Moussorgsky/Rimsky-K	Philh	Matacic
SAX2328	Brahms: Piano Concerto 2	BPO	Karajan Richter-Haaser
SAX2329	Lalo: Symphonie Espagnol/Tchaikovsky	Philh	Kondrashin Kogan
SAX2331	Beethoven: Symphony 2/Coriolan/Prometheus	Philh	Klemperer
SAX2332	Chopin 14 Waltzes		Malcuzynski
SAX2333	Goethe Lieder		Schwarzkopf Moore
SAX2335	Mozart: Piano Concertos 20/23	Philh	Boult Annie Fischer

SAX2336-7	Strauss,J: Die Fledermaus	Philh	Ackermann
SAX2338	Chopin: Polonaises		Malcuzynski
SAX2339	Tchaikovsky: Romeo & Juliet Ov/etc	Philh	Markevitch
SAX2340	Schumann: Frauenliebe und Leben, Brahms: Zigeunerlieder	Ludwig	Moore
SAX2341	Falla: 3 Cornered Hat/Ravel: Daphnis/etc	Philh	Giulini
SAX2342	Mendelssohn: Symphony 3/Hebrides Ov	Philh	Klemperer
SAX2343	Weber: Overtures	Philh	Sawallisch
SAX2344	Chopin: Piano Concerto 2/Fantaisie in Fmin	LSO	Susskind Malcuzynski
SAX2345	Mahler: Symphony 4	Philh	Kletzki Loose
SAX2346	Beethoven Piano Concerto 2	Philh	Galliera Arrau
SAX2347/8	'Klemperer conducts Wagner'	Philh	Klemperer
SAX2350	Brahms: Symphony 4	Philh	Klemperer
SAX2351	Brahms: Symphony 3/Academic Fest Ov	Philh	Klemperer
SAX2352	Beethoven: Archduke Trio		D Oistrakh Knushevitsky Oborin
SAX2353	Soprano Arias from Wagner and Verdi (Tannhauser, Walküre, Otello, Don Carlo)	Philh	Susskind Nordmo Lövberg
SAX2354	Beethoven: Symphony 4/Consn of the House	Philh	Klemperer
SAX2355	Rimsky-Korsakov: Capr Esp/Ravel: La Valse	Philh	Cluytens
SAX2356	Mozart: Symphonies 29/38	BPO	Karajan
SAX2357	Tchaikovsky: Symphony 4	BPO	Karajan
SAX2358	Mahler: Lieder	Ludwig	Moore
SAX2359-61	Ponchielli: La Gioconda	La Scala	Votto Callas
SAX2362	Brahms: Symphony 2/Tragic Overture	Philh	Klemperer
SAX2363	Schubert: Moments Musicaux/March in E/etc		Arrau
SAX2364	Beethoven: Symphony 3	Philh	Klemperer
SAX2365	Handel: Messiah (hlts)		Huddersfield Choral Society et al
SAX2366	Wolf: Aus dem Italienisch Liederbuch		Schwarzkopf Moore
SAX2367	Strauss,R: Don Juan/Till Eulenspiegel	Philh	Klemperer
SAX2368	Tchaikovsky: Symphony 6	Philh	Giulini
SAX2369-72	Mozart: Don Giovanni	Philh	Giulini Schwarzkopf
SAX2373	Beethoven: Symphony 5/Ov King Stephen	Philh	Klemperer
SAX2375	Prokofiev: Peter & Wolf/E Mozart: Toy Sym	Philh	Karajan Ustinov (nar)
SAX2376	Colaratura Arias (Lucia, Barber of Seville, Rigoletto, etc)	Philh	Davis Anna Moffo
SAX2377	Rossini/Verdi: Overtures	Philh	Giulini
SAX2378	Rossini: Overtures	Philh	Karajan
SAX2379	Sibelius: Symphony 2	Philh	Karajan
SAX2380	Tchaikovsky: Piano Conc 1/Weber: Konzertstuck	Philh	Galliera Arrau
SAX2381-4	Mozart: Marriage of Figaro	Philh	Giulini Schwarzkopf
SAX2385	Beethoven: Piano Sonatas 17/30		Richter-Haaser
SAX2386	Beethoven: Violin Concerto	PCO	Silvestri Kogan
SAX2387	Brahms: Piano Concerto 1	Philh	Giulini Arrau
SAX2388	Brahms: Violin & Piano Sonatas 1/2		Igor Oistrakh Ginzburg
SAX2389	Mozart: E Kleine Nachtmusik/Ave Verum Corpus	BPO	Karajan
SAX2390	Beethoven: Piano Sonatas Op 54/Op 57		Arrau
SAX2391	Albeniz: Asturias, Sevillanas, Serenade Espagnole, Tango, Granados: Allegro de Concierto, 3 Spanish Dances		Iturbi
SAX2392	Sibelius: Symphony 5/Finlandia	Philh	Karajan
SAX2393	Mendelssohn: Midsummer nights dream	Philh	Klemperer
SAX2394	Ravel: Piano Concerto in G/Conc for Left Hand	PCO	Cluytens Francois
SAX2395	Haydn: Symphonies 98/101	Philh	Klemperer
SAX2397	Schubert: Symphony 9	Philh	Klemperer
SAX2398	Mendelssohn: Symphony 4, Schumann: Symphony 4	Philh	Klemperer
SAX2399-2400	Leoncavallo: Pagliacci	La Scala	Matacic Gobbi Corelli
SAX2401	Chopin: Piano Sonata 3 in Bmin Op 58/Fantaisie in Fmin		Arrau
SAX2402	Schubert: Sonata in Bflat major D960		Annie Fischer

SAX2403	Beethoven: Piano Concerto 4	Philh	Kertesz Richter-Haaser
SAX2404	Philharmonia Promenade Concert	Philh	Karajan
SAX2405	Dvorak: New World Symphony, Carnaval Ov	Philh	Giulini
SAX2406	Mozart: Horn Concertos	Philh	Klemperer Civil
SAX2407	Beethoven: Piano Sonatas 27/29		Richter-Haaser
SAX2408/9	Bach,J.S: Brandenburg Concertos	Philh	Klemperer
SAX2410	'French Operatic Arias'	FNRO	Pretre Callas
SAX2411	Brahms: Violin Concerto	ONRF	Klemperer Oistrakh
SAX2412-4	Bellini: Norma	La Scala	Serafin Callas
SAX2415	Beethoven: Symphony 7	Philh	Klemperer
SAX2416	Tchaikovsky: Symphony 2	Philh	Giulinu
SAX2417	Weber: Overtures	Philh	Klemperer
SAX2418	Tchaikovsky: Capriccio Italien etc	La Scala	Matacic
SAX2419	Rossini-Respighi: La Boutique Fantasque	Philh	Galliera
SAX2420	Brahms: Symphony 1	Philh	Giulini
SAX2421	'Ballet Music from the Opera'	Philh	Karajan
SAX2422	Beethoven: Piano Concerto 5/Rondo in C	Philh	Kertesz Richter-Haaser
SAX2423	Strauss,R: Der Rosankavalier (hlts)	Philh	Karajan Schwarzkopf
SAX2424	Schubert: Symphony 8, Brahms: Haydn Variations	Philh	Giulini
SAX2426	Mozart: Piano Concertos 17/26	Philh	Kertesz Richter-Haaser
SAX2427-9	Mozart: Abduction from the Seraglio	RPO	Beecham
SAX2430-1	Brahms: German Requiem	Philh	Klemperer Schwarzkopf Dieskau
SAX2432	Bartok: Music for Strings Percussion & Celeste	BPO	Karajan
SAX2433	'The Hoffnung Astronautical Music Festival'		
SAX2434	Recital (Debussy: Children's Corner, etc; Ravel: Jeux D'Eau, etc)		Jose Iturbi
SAX2435	Beethoven: Piano Sonatas 18/32		Annie Fischer
SAX2436	Mozart: Symphonies 35/36	Philh	Klemperer
SAX2437	Strauss,R: Tod und Verklarung/Metamorphosen	Philh	Klemperer
SAX2438	Rossini: Barber of Seville (hlts)		Callas Gobbi et al
SAX2439	Overtures (Wagner/Weber/etc)	BPO	Karajan
SAX2441	Mahler: Symphony 4	Philh	Klemperer Schwarzkopf
SAX2442-3	Bizet: The Pearl Fishers	L'Opera Comique	Dervaux Gedda
SAX2444	Chopin: Sonatas 2/3		Malcuzynski
SAX2445	Poulenc: Gloria/Organ Concerto	FNRO	Duruflé
SAX2446-50	Bach,J.S: St. Matthew Passion	Philh	Klemperer Schwarzkopf
SAX2451-3	Beethoven: Fidelio	Philh	Klemperer Ludwig Vickers
SAX2454-5	Bruckner: Symphony 7	Philh	Klemperer
SAX2456	Orff: Die Kluge (hlts)	Philh	Sawallisch Schwarzkopf et al
SAX2457	Orff: Der Mond (hlts)	Philh	Sawallisch Christ et al
SAX2458	Tchaikovsky: Symphony 6	Philh	Klemperer
SAX2459	Walton: Symphony 2/Partita for Orch	Clvlnd	Szell
SAX2460	Weill: 3 Penny Opera (orch hlts)/etc	Philh	Klemperer
SAX2461	Dvorak: Symphony 8, Scherzo Capriccioso	Philh	Giulini
SAX2462	Brahms: Alto Rhaps/Wagner: Wesendconck Lieder	Philh	Klemperer Ludwig
SAX2463	Debussy: La Mer/Nocturnes	Philh	Giulini
SAX2464	'Klemperer Conducts More Wagner'	Philh	Klemperer
SAX2465	Chopin: Mazurkas		Malcuzynski
SAX2466	Brahms: Piano Concerto 2	Philh	Giulini Arrau
SAX2467	Strauss,R: Also Sprach Zarathustra/Till Eulenspiegel	Philh	Maazel
SAX2468	Mozart: Symphonies 38/39	Philh	Klemperer
SAX2469	Debussy: L'Isle Joyeuse/etc		Samson Francois
SAX2470-2	Mozart: "Haydn" String Quartets		Juilliard Quartet
SAX2473-4	Mahler: Symphony 2	Philh	Klemperer Schwarzkopf
SAX2475	Schumann: Symphonies 1/4	Clvlnd	Szell
SAX2476	Ravel: Orch Works V1: Daphnis & Chloe	PCO	Cluytens
SAX2477	Ravel: Orch Works V2: Bolero/Raps Esp	PCO	Cluytens

Catalog	Work	Performers
SAX2478	Ravel: Orch Works V3: Mother Goose	PCO Cluytens
SAX2479	Ravel: Orch Works V4: Tombeau/Alborado/Pavane	PCO Cluytens
SAX2480	Stravinsky: Serenade in A/Sonata Schoenberg: Suite op 25/ 2 Piano Pieces Op 33	Charles Rosen
SAX2481	Gedda in Paris	PCO Pretre Gedda
SAX2482	Cherubini: Medea (hlts)	Paris Op Pretre Gorr
SAX2483	Tchaikovsky: Romeo & Juliet, Francesca da Rimini	Philh Giulini
SAX2484	Moussorgsky-Ravel: Pictures at an Exhibition	Philh Maazel
SAX2485	Schumann: Piano Concerto/Liszt Piano Conc 1	Philh Klemperer Fischer
SAX2486	Mozart: Symphonies 40/41	Philh Klemperer
SAX2487	'The Red Army Ensemble'	Red Army Ensemble
SAX2488	Mahler: Symphony 10/Strauss: Death&Transfiguration	Clvlnd Szell
SAX2489	Arias from German Opera (Flute, Tannhauser, etc)	Berlin SO Stein Hermann Prey
SAX2490	"Szell conducts Russian music" (Borodin, Tchaikovsky, etc)	Clvlnd Szell
SAX2491	Ponchielli: La Gioconda (hlts)	La Scala Votto Callas et al
SAX2492	Debussy: 12 Etudes	Charles Rosen
SAX2493	Beethoven: Symphony 8/Schubert: Symphony 8	Clvlnd Szell
SAX2494	Tchaikovsky: Symphony 4	Philh Klemperer
SAX2495	Strauss,R: Don Quixote/Don Juan	Clvlnd Szell Fournier
SAX2496	Schumann: Symphony 2	Clvlnd Szell
SAX2497	Tchaikovsky: Symphony 5	Philh Klemperer
SAX2498	Brahms: Symphony 2	Philh Giulini
SAX2499-2500	Handel: Solomon	RPO Beecham
SAX2501	Strauss,R: Till Eulenspiegel/Dvorak: Symphony 7	Clvlnd Szell
SAX2502	Schubert: Sonata in Amaj/Mozart: Rondo in Amin	Charles Rosen
SAX2503	"Callas in Paris" (Berlioz, Bizet, Massenet, etc)	PCO Pretre Callas
SAX2504	Beethoven: Quartets 3/6	Drolc Quartet
SAX2505	Beethoven: Songs	Prey Moore
SAX2506	Schumann: Symphony 3, Manfred Ov	Clvlnd Szell
SAX2507	Prokofiev: String Qt 1/Tchaikovsky: String Qt 1	Kroll Quartet
SAX2508	Beethoven: Violin Concerto	Philh Leinsdorf Milstein
SAX2509	Chopin: Ballades 1-4	Malcuzynski
SAX2510	Beethoven: Symphony 7/Wagner: Tannhauser	Clvlnd Szell
SAX2511	Carl Loewe Ballads	Prey Weissenborn
SAX2512-3	Beethoven: Symphony 9/Wagner: Mastersingers Prelude	Clvlnd Szell
SAX2514	Schubert: Symphonies 5/8	Philh Klemperer
SAX2515	Rachmaninov: Piano Concerto 3	WarPh Rowicki Malcuzynski
SAX2516	Brahms: Symphony 3	Philh Giulini
SAX2517	Schubert: Symphony 9	Clvlnd Szell
SAX2518	Vivaldi: Violin Concerti (P234, P419, P88, P236)	Milstein Chamber Orchestra
SAX2519	Schubert: String Quartet 14/Haydn: Strinq Quartet Op 64,5	Kroll Quartet
SAX2520	Beethoven: String Qt 11/Hindemith: String Qt 3	Kroll Quartet
SAX2521	Chopin: 24 Preludes Op 28	Samson Francois
SAX2522	Schumann: Davidsbündlertänze	Charles Rosen
SAX2523	Beethoven: Piano Sonatas 16/18	Richter-Haaser
SAX2524	Mendelssohn: Symphony 4/Hebrides Ov/etc	Clvlnd Szell
SAX2525	Bach,J.S: St Matthew Passion Chorales	Philh Klemperer
SAX2526	Brahms: Piano Concerto 1	Clvlnd Szell Fleisher
SAX2527	Walton: Shakespeare Film Scores	Philh Walton
SAX2528	Franck: 4 Symphonic Poems/Le Chasseur Maudit/etc	ONB Cluytens
SAX2529	Haydn: Symphony 92/Mozart: Symphony 35	Clvlnd Szell
SAX2530	Beethoven: Quartets 4/5	Drolc Quartet
SAX2531	Sonatas for 2 Violins	Kogan Elizabeth Gilels
SAX2532	Debussy: La Mer/Ravel: Daphnis St 2/Pavane	Clvlnd Szell
SAX2533	Prokofiev: Piano Concertos 3/5	Philh Rowicki Francois
SAX2534	Brahms: Piano Concerto 2	Clvlnd Szell Fleisher

SAX2535	Schubert: String Quartet 15	Juilliard Quartet	
SAX2536	Strauss,R: Horn Concerto 1	Clvlnd	Szell Bloom
	Mozart: Clarinet Concerto	Clvlnd	Szell Marcellus
SAX2537	Berlioz: Symphonie Fantastique	Philh	Klemperer
SAX2538	Handel: Dettingen Te Deum	German Madrigal Choir	
SAX2539	Bohemian Carnival	Clvlnd	Szell
SAX2540	Callas sings Mozart, Weber, Beethoven	PCO	Rescigno Callas
SAX2541	Brahms: Piano Quintet Op 34	Juilliard Quartet Fleisher	
SAX2542	Beethoven: Ovs Leonora 1-3/Fidelio	Philh	Klemperer
SAX2543	Beethoven: Piano Concerto 3	Philh	Giulini Richter-Haaser
SAX2544	Mozart: Mass in C K427	SW German CO Gonnenwein	
SAX2545	Strauss,R: Sinfonia Domestica	Clvlnd	Szell
SAX2546	Mozart: Symphonies 31/34	Philh	Klemperer
SAX2547	Schumann: Symphony 3	Philh	Klemperer
SAX2548	Debussy: Jeux/Images Pour Orchestre	PCO	Cluytens
SAX2549	Beethoven: Symphony 6	Clvlnd	Szell
SAX2550	Verdi: Arias (Otello, Don Carlos, Araldo)	PCO	Rescigno Callas
SAX2551	Liszt, Bartok Recital		Charles Rosen
SAX2552	Mozart: Symphony 41/Beethoven: Symphony 5	Clvlnd	Szell
SAX2553	Mozart: Symphony 33/Div 2 K131	Clvlnd	Szell
SAX2554	Dvorak: Symphony 9	Philh	Klemperer
SAX2555	Britten: 4 Sea Intlds/Vns & Fugue on theme of Purcell	Philh	Giulini
SAX2556	Stravinsky: Fairy's Kiss/Mussorgsky: Pictures	Clvlnd	Szell
SAX2557	Beethoven: 33 Variations on a Waltz by Diabelli	Richter-Haaser	
SAX2558	Mendelssohn: Quartets 2/3	Juilliard Quartet	
SAX2559	Mozart: Don Giovanni (hlts)	Philh	Giulini Schwarzkopf
SAX2560	Rossini: Overtures (Cenerentola, Tancredi, Semiramide, Tell, etc)	Philh	Giulini
SAX2561	Beethoven: Piano Sonatas 3/22/26	Richter-Haaser	
SAX2562	Roussel: Bacchus & Ariadne etc	PCO	Cluytens
SAX2563	"Music of Old Russia" (Tchaikovsky: Valse Scherzo,		
	Rimsky-Korsakov: Fantasy on Russian Themes)	Orch cond Irving Milstein	
SAX2564	Rossini and Donizetti Arias	PCO	Rescigno Callas
SAX2565	Beethoven: Symphonies 1/2	Clvlnd	Szell
SAX2566	Bizet: L'Arlesienne Suites 1/2/Carmen: Suite 1	PCO	Cluytens
SAX2567	Schumann : Dichterliebe, 9 Lieder from Kerner Lieder	Prey	Engel
SAX2569	Bruckner: Symphony 4	Philh	Klemperer
SAX2570	Beethoven: Ovs Consec/Coriolan/Prometheus/etc	Philh	Klemperer
SAX2571	Haydn: Symphonies 88/104	Philh	Klemperer
SAX2572	Brahms: Symphony 3/Haydn Variations	Clvlnd	Szell
SAX2573	Mozart: Marriage of Figaro (hlts)	Philh	Giulini Schwarzkopf
SAX2574	Beethoven: Piano Sonatas Op 2/1 & Op 2/2	Richter-Haaser	
SAX2575	Barber: Piano Conc/Schuman: Song of Orpheus	Clvlnd	Szell Leonard Rose
SAX2576	Walton Vns Theme of Hindemith/Hindemith: Sym Vns	Clvlnd	Szell
SAX2577	Beethoven: Symphony 3	Clvlnd	Szell
SAX2578	Verdi: Falstaff (hlts)	Philh	Karajan Schwarzkopf Gobbi
SAX2579	Bach: Concerto for 2 Violins/Sonata in Cmaj		
	Vivaldi: Concerto Grosso Op 3/11	Milstein	Morini
SAX2580	Gounod: Romeo and Juliet (hlts)	Paris Op	Lombard Carteri Gedda
SAX2582	Bruckner: Symphony 6	Philh	Klemperer
SAX2583	Schumann: Kinderszenen/Kreileriana	Annie Fischer	
SAX2584	Schütz: Christmas Oratorio	Small Orch Hans Thamm	
SAX2587	Mozart: Overtures (Figaro/Giovanni/Magic Flute/etc)	Clvlnd	Szell
SAX2588	Stravinsky: Symphony in 3 mvmts/Pulcinella St	Philh	Klemperer
SAX2589	Wolf: "Songs from the Romantic Poets"	Schwarzkopf Moore	
SAX5251	Roussel: Symphonies 3/4	PCO	Cluytens

SAX5252	Handel: Concerto Grosso op 6/4,		[SBO2751]
	Mozart: Serenade 13, Symphony 25	Philh Klemperer	[SAX2278]
SAX5253	Bach: Arias from St Matthew Passion	Philh Klemperer Schwarzkopf	
SAX5254	Mozart: Violin Concertos 4/5	Philh Milstein	
SAX5255	Schubert: Sonatas in Amin D784, Cmin D958	Richter-Haaser	
SAX5256	Mozart: Symphony 29/33	Philh Klemperer	
SAX5257	Beethoven: Sonatas Hammerklavier/Op 110	Rosen	
SAX5258	Strauss,R: 4 Last Songs/etc	BRSO Szell Schwarzkopf	
SAX5259	Mozart: Serenade for 13 Wind Insts K361	London Wind Qt Klemperer	
SAX5260	Bartok: String Quartets 1, 2	Juilliard Quartet	
SAX5261	Bartok: String Quartets 3, 4	Juilliard Quartet	
SAX5262	Bartok: String Quartets 5, 6	Juilliard Quartet	
SAX5263	Bartok: Concerto for Orchestra/Janacek: Sinfonietta	Clvlnd Szell	
SAX5264	Vivaldi: Violin Concertos (P163, P228, P208, P195)	Chamber Orch Milstein	
SAX5265	Ravel: Rapsodie Espagnol, Pavane,		
	Falla: Love the Magician	Philh Giulini De Los Angeles	
SAX5266	Haydn: Symphony 100/102	Philh Klemperer.	
SAX5267	Virtuoso Piano Transcriptions (Chopin, Mendelssohn, Schubert, etc)	Rosen	
SAX5268	Lieder and Song Recital (Schubert, Schumann, Wolf, etc)	Schwarzkopf Moore	
SAX5269	Schumann: Symphony 1, Manfred Ov	Philh Klemperer	
SAX5271	Schubert: String Quartets 9, 13	Juilliard Quartet	
SAX5272	Schubert: Recital	Ludwig Parsons	
SAX5273	Chopin: Piano Concerto 2/Liszt: Piano Concerto 1	Philh Pritchard Rosen	
SAX5274	Recital (Schubert, St-Saens, Brahms, Ravel)	Ludwig Parsons	
SAX5275	Prokofiev: Violin Concertos 1/2	De Burgos/Giulini Milstein	
SAX5276	Franck: Symphony in Dmin	Philh Klemperer	
SAX5277	Wagner: Faust Ov, Rienzi Ov, Flying Dutchman Ov		
	Lohengrin Prelude, Mastersingers Ov	Clvlnd Szell	
SAX5278	Lyric Songs	Gedda Moore	
SAX5279	Brahms: Symphony 1	Clvlnd Szell	
SAX5280	Mozart: Symphony 28/Sinfonia Concertante K364, Figaro Ov	Clvlnd Szell	
SAX5281-2	Mahler: Symphony 9	Philh Klemperer	
SAX5283	Mahler: Symphony 4	Clvlnd Szell Raskin (soprano)	
SAX5284	Brahms: Symphony 2, Tragic Ov	Clvlnd Szell	
SAX5285	Bach: Violin Concertos 1/2/Vivaldi	Milstein with Chamber Orch	
SAX5286	Favourite Scenes from Otello, La Bohème, Eugene Onegin, etc	Schwarzkopf	
SAX5287	Mozart: Piano Concertos 24/27	Philh Kurtz Annie Fischer	
SAX5288-9	Bruckner: Symphony 5	Philh Klemperer	
SAX5290	Mozart: Piano Concerto 25, Serenade K388	Philh Klemperer Barenboim	
SAX5291	Debussy: Images Book 1 & 2/Estampes	Rosen	
SAX5292	Brahms: Symphony 4/Academic Fest Ov	Clvlnd Szell	
SAX5293	Mozart: Opera Arias (Flute,Figaro,Giovanni,Cosi)	DrSt Suitner Prey	
SAX5294	Bruckner: Symphony 3	Clvlnd Szell	
SBO2751	Handel: Concerto Grosso op 6/4, Mozart: Serenade K525	Philh Klemperer	
SBO2752	Beethoven: Piano Concerto 4	Philh Ludwig Gilels	
SBO2753	Beethoven: Concerto for Violin, Cello and Piano	Philh Sargent Oistrakh Oborin Knushevitsky	
SBO2754	Mozart: Opera Arias (Figaro, Giovanni, Cosi, Entfuhrung)	Philh Galliera Moffo	
SBO2756	Leoncavallo: Pagliacci (hlts)	La Scala Matacic Gobbi Corelli	
SBO2757	Red Army Ensemble vol 2		

* * * * *

Later EMIs (from about 1964)

There are a large number of these later EMIs, also sometimes called "ASD 4 digit" (ASDnnnn) to distinguish them from the earlier "ASD 3 digit" (ASDnnn) records. This booklet lists ASDs in this series from ASD2251 to ASD4415.

Labels: There are 5 different labels in this series. However, many people prefer to group the ASDnnn series and the ASDnnnn series together, in which case the earliest "white and gold" label, already described, can be thought of as the 1st label. Sticking to this scheme, the 5 labels within the ASDnnnn series are numbered 2nd, 3rd, 4th, 5th, 6th labels.

2nd label: This label has already been described under the ASDnnn series. The earliest pressings of records from ASD2251 up to around ASD2450 have exactly the same label as was described earlier and named either "black and red dog" or "dog in semi-circle".

3rd label: The 3rd, 4th, and 5th labels are all very similar. They all feature a dog in a small "postage stamp" rectangle at 12 o'clock on the label. On the 3rd label the inside of the rectangle is coloured. In addition, round the circumference of the label there is copyright lettering, but no solid white band, as is found on the later labels. This label was used up to around ASD2800.

4th label: On the 4th label the inside of the "postage stamp" is black and white, and there is a solid white band around the circumference of the label. This label was used up to around ASD3800.

5th label: On the 5th label the inside of the "postage stamp" is again coloured, just as it was on the 3rd label, but now there is a solid white band around the circumference of the label. This label was used up to around ASD4000.

6th label: The 6th label, introduced in the 1980s, sees a reversion to the style of the 2nd label, only this time the dog entirely fills the whole of the upper semi-circle of the label. This label is usually referred to as "Large Dog".

ASD2251	Schubert: Symphony 9	Halle	Barbirolli
ASD2252	Lehar: Merry Widow (hlts)	Philh	Matacic Schwarzkopf
ASD2254	Mozart: Piano Concertos Nos 14/19	BFCO	Menuhin Y.Menuhin
ASD2255	Bartok:Div for Strings/Stravinsky/Hindemith	BFCO	Menuhin
ASD2256	Mozart: Quintet K452/Beethoven: Quintet Op 16	Melos Ensemble	
ASD2257	Mussorgsky: Boris Godunov (hlts)	PCO	Cluytens (from SAN110-3)
ASD2258	Beethoven: The 2 Piano Trios Op 70	Menuhin Gendron Hephzibah Menuhin	
ASD2259	Elgar Violin Concerto	Philh	Boult Menuhin
ASD2260	Ravel: Sheherazade etc.	PCO	Pretre Los Angeles
ASD2261	Purcell: An Anthology - Volume 2	BFCO	Menuhin Joan Carlyle (sop)
ASD2262	Handel: Dixit Dominus	ECO	Willcocks KCC
ASD2263	Popular Schubert Songs	Fiescher-Dieskau Moore	
ASD2264	Westminster Abbey 1065 –1965 900th Anniversary Service		
ASD2265	Mozart: Cosi fan Tutte (hlts)	Philh	Bohm (from SAN103-6)
ASD2267	Bach,CPE: Concerto in D Minor, Bach,JS: Conc in A min	BFCO	Menuhin Malcolm
ASD2268	Bach: Flute Sonatas - Volume 2	Shaffer (flute) Malcolm (hpsd) Gauntlett (viola)	
ASD2269	Mozart: Symphony 40/Schubert: Symphony 5	MCO	Barshai
ASD2270	Marlowe: Dr Faustus	OUDS	Burton
ASD2271	Puccini: La Boheme (hlts)	Rome Opera Schippers	
ASD2272	Sibelius: Karelia Suite/Valse Triste	Halle	Barbirolli
ASD2273	Schubert: Recital (inc Wanderer, Auf dem Wasser)	Fischer-Dieskau Moore	
ASD2274	"Favourite Arias"	De Los Angeles	
ASD2275	Verdi: Arias (Macbeth, Ballo, Aida, Don Carlo, etc)	PCO	Pretre Crespin
ASD2276-7	Berlioz: Scenes from the Trojans	PCO	Prêtre
ASD2279	Orr: Symphony in 1 Mvmt, Musgrave: Tryptich for Ternor&Orch, Hamilton: Sinfonia for 2 Orchestras	SNO	Gibson
ASD2280	Mozart: Conc for 2 pianos/Conc 3 for 3 pianos		
ASD2281	Bartok: Violin Concerto 2/etc	Philh	Dorati Menuhin
ASD2282	Bizet: Carmen Hlts	Paris Op Pretre	
ASD2283	Liszt: Operatic Fantasies/Late Piano Works	PO	Ogdon
ASD2284	Bruckner: Symphony 3	VPO	Schuricht
ASD2285	Beethoven Violin Concerto	Philh	Klemperer Menuhin
ASD2286	Poulenc: Babar the Elephant	PCO	Pretre
ASD2287	"Mélodies" (Debussy, Ravel, Fauré, etc)	De Los Angeles Soriano	
ASD2288	Handel: Choruses from Messiah	Philh	Klemperer
ASD2289	Skalkottas: Octet/8 Variations on Greek Folk Tune/etc	Masters, Simpson, Gazelle	
ASD2290	"Sing Praises"	KCC	Willcocks
ASD2292	Elgar: Pomp & Circumstance Marches/Elegy/etc	Philh	Barbirolli
ASD2294	"West meets East" Enesco:Sonata 3	Menuhin Ravi Shankar (sitar)	
ASD2295	"Music from India"	Vilyat Khan & Bismallah Khan	
ASD2296	Poulenc:Bal Masque/Rapsodie Negre	PCO	Pretre
ASD2297	Haydn: Symphonies 26, 44, 48	BFCO	Menuhin
ASD2298	Panufnik: Sinfonia Sacra/Sinfonia Rustica	Monte Carlo Orch Panufnik	
ASD2299	Walton: Symphony 1	Philh	Sargent
ASD2300	Puccini: Tosca (hlts)	Pretre	Gobbi/Callas
ASD2301	Holst: The Planets	Philh	Boult
ASD2302	Bach: Cantata 82	Menuhin Janet Baker	
ASD2303	Haydn: Missa in Tempre Belli, etc	ECO	Willcocks
ASD2304	Indian Music	Shankar et al	
ASD2305	Bax: Tintagel/etc	LSO	Barbirolli
ASD2306	Poulenc: Piano Concerto/Aubade	PCO	Pretre
ASD2307	Rossini: Barber of Seville (hlts)	Glyndebourne Gui.	
ASD2308	Sibelius: Symphony 2/etc	Halle	Barbirolli
ASD2309	Mozart: "Music for the Archbishop" (Serenade K203, Divertimento K138, March K237)	BFCO	Menuhin
ASD2311	Elgar: The Music Makers/Parry	LPO	Boult Baker

ASD2312	"Music from India" vol 3			
ASD2313	Mozart: "2 Salzburg Divertimenti" (K287,K136)	BFCO	Menuhin	
ASD2314	Mozart: Magic Flute (hlts)	Philh	Klemperer	
ASD2315	Stravinsky: Rite of Spring/Prokofiev: Classical Sym	Philh	De Burgos	
ASD2316	Milhaud Creation/S-Saens	PCO	Pretre	
ASD2317	Recital (Schubert, Schumann, Brahms)	Bumbry Hokanson (piano)		
ASD2318	Mozart: Piano Concertos 20/23	ECO	Barenboim	
ASD2319	Mozart: Piano Quartets 1/2	Menuhin Fou Ts'Ong Gerhardt Cassado		
ASD2320	Strauss,R:Oboe Concerto/Duet Concertino	Berlin RO Rogner		
ASD2321-2	Stevenson: Passacaglia,Tippett: 1st Sonata, Ogdon: Theme & Variations	John Ogdon		
ASD2323	Bartok: Violin Concerto/Viola Concerto	Philh	Dorati Menuhin	
ASD2324	"Grand Opera Gala"	Callas, Schwarzkopf, De Los Angeles, etc		
ASD2325	Bruckner: 5 Motets/Brahms/Mozart/Wolf	Philh	Pitz	
ASD2326	Sibelius: Symphonies 5/7	HO	Barbirolli	
ASD2327	Mozart: Symphonies 39/40	ECO	Barenboim	
ASD2328	Schubert: Piano Quintet	Melos Ensemble		
ASD2329	V Williams: Symphony 6/The Lark Ascending	Philh	Boult	
ASD2330	Offenbach: Tales of Hoffmann (hlts)	Orch de Cons Cluytens Schwarzkopf		
ASD2331	Haydn & Boccherini: Cello Concertos	ECO	Barenboim Du Pre	
ASD2332	Tchaikovsky: Symphony 6	LSO	Horenstein	
ASD2333	Crosse: Concerto da Camera, Wood: 3 Piano Pieces, etc	Melos Ensemble Parikian		
ASD2334	Handel and Mozart Arias	ECO	Fischer Popp	
ASD2335	Strauss,R: Duets from Rosenkavalier	DrSt	Della Casa/Rothenberger	
ASD2336-7	Busoni: Piano Concerto	RPO	Revenaugh Ogdon	(SLS 776) TASEC
ASD2338	Mahler: Kindertotenlieder	HO	Barbirolli Baker	
ASD2339	Recital of Puccini Arias	Mirella Freni		
ASD2340	Charpentier: Midnight Mass for Xmas Eve	ECO	Willcocks	
ASD2341	Indian Music	Shankar		
ASD2342	Berlioz: Symphonie Fantastique	OdP	Munch	
ASD2343	Schubert: Symphonies 2/6	BFCO	Menuhin	
ASD2344	Janacek: Concertino/In the Mist/Youth Sextet	Melos Ensemble		
ASD2345	Borodin: Prince Igor - excerpts	Sofia National Opera Christoff		
ASD2346	Schoenberg Verklarte Nacht/Wagner Siegfried Idyll	ECO	Barenboim	
ASD2347	Bartok: Piano Concerto 3 Sonata for 2 Pianos & Percussion	Philh	Sargent Ogdon/Lucas	
ASD2348	Beethoven: Symphony 3	BBCSO	Barbirolli	
ASD2349	Schoenberg: Chamber Symphony,Webern: Cantata 1	Harper	Prausnitz	
ASD2350	Dvorak: Piano Quintet/"American" Quartet	Smetana Quartet		
ASD2351	"English Music for Strings"	BNSO	Del Mar	
ASD2352	Handel: Organ Concertos (1,5,13,14)	BFCO	Menuhin Preston	
ASD2353	Brahms: Piano Concerto 1	Philh	Barbirolli Barenboim	
ASD2354	Brahms: Horn Trio Op40, Piano Trio Op87	Civil	Menuhin Y Menuhin Gendron	
ASD2355	Ravel: Daphnis & Chloe (cplt)	Philh	Ambrosians De Burgos	
ASD2356	Elgar: Wand of Youth Suites 1,2,Chanson de Matin, etc	LPO	Boult	
ASD2357	Mozart: Piano Concertos 13/17	ECO	Barenboim	
ASD2358	Fauré: Requiem	Philh	Willcocks	
ASD2359	Giordano: Andre Chénier (hlts)	Rome Op Santini		
ASD2360	V Williams: London Symphony	HO	Barbirolli	
ASD2361	Rachmaninov: Piano Concerto 2/Paganini Rhapsody	Philh	Atzmon Anievas	
ASD2362	Brahms: Clarinet Sonatas	Barenboim De Peyer		
ASD2363	Rodrigo Conc de Aranjuez	Spanish NSO Diaz (guitar)		
ASD2364	German Opera Arias (Mozart, Wagner, Nicolai, Beethoven,etc)	Bavarian State Op Gedda		
ASD2365	Glazunov: Vln Conc/Dvorak Vln Conc	Philh	de Burgos Milstein	
ASD2366	Sibelius: Symphony 1/Pelleas & Melisande.	HO	Barbirolli	
ASD2367	Music of India vol 5		Ali Akbar Khan	

Catalog	Work	Orchestra	Artist	Notes
ASD2369	Satie: Parade/Gymnopedies 1/3/Relâche	PCO	Auriacombe	
ASD2370	V Williams: Tallis Fantasia/The Wasps/Elgar	BNSO	Silvestri	
ASD2371	Chopin: Music for Piano & Orch	PCO	Skrowaczewski/Weissenberg	
ASD2373	St-Saens: Samson et Dalila (hlts)	ONDF	Pretre	
ASD2374	Weber: Clarinet Quintet/Schumann: Fantasy Pieces	Melos Ensemble De Peyer		
ASD2375	V Williams: Symphony 4/Norfolk Rhapsody 1	Philh	Boult	
ASD2376/7	Mahler: Symphony 6	Philh	Barbirolli	
ASD2378	Gluck: Orfeo ed Euridice (hlts)	LGO	Neumann Bumbry	
ASD2379	Mozart: Symphonies 31/41	ECO	Barenboim	
ASD2381	Bach,J.S: Cantatas 80, 140	Consortium Musicum Gönnenwein		
ASD2382	Opera Duets	Various Artists		
ASD2384	Handel: Sonatas for Violin,Hpsd, Viola da Gamba	Menuhin Gauntlett Malcolm		
ASD2386	Schumann: Piano Quintet, Tchaikovsky: String Quartet 1	Smetana Quartet		
ASD2388	Busoni: Berceuse Elegaique/Dallapicola/etc	Philh	Prausnitz	
ASD2389	Satie: Piano Music (3 Gymnopedies/Piege de Meduse/etc)	Ciccolini		
ASD2390	Weill: Symphonies 1/2	BBCSO	Bertini	
ASD2391	Brahms: Alto Rhapsody/etc	Philh	Klemperer Ludwig	
ASD2393	V Williams: Pastoral Symphony/Fen Country	Philh	Boult	
ASD2394	Music from India	Banerjee (sitar) etc		
ASD2395	Verdi: Il Trovatore (hlts)	RomeOp	Schippers	(from SAN151-3)
ASD2396	Bach: Cantatas 79, 148, 149	Consortium Musicum Gonnenwein Baker		
ASD2397	Delius: Requiem	RPO	Davies	
ASD2399	Strauss,R: Songs (Zeuignung, Die Nacht, Allerseelen, etc)	Fischer-Dieskau Moore		
ASD2400	"Music of the 4 Countries"	SNO	Gibson	
ASD2401	Brahms: Symphony 1	VPO	Barbirolli	
ASD2402	Dvorak: String Quartet/Schubert: Quartettsatz	Smetana Quartet		
ASD2403	Puccini: Turandot (hlts)	Nilsson		
ASD2404	Elizabeth Schwarzkopf Song book Vol 2	Schwarzkopf Parsons		
ASD2406	"Soviet Army Chorus & Band on Parade"			Mdya
ASD2407	Sibelius: Violin Concerto/Belshazzar's Feast	Rozhdestvensky Oistrakh		Mdya
ASD2408	"Stars of the Bolshoi" (Vishnevskaya, Petrov, etc)	Bolshoi		Mdya
ASD2409	Shostakovich: Execn of Stepan Razin/Symphony 9	MPO	Kondrashin	Mdya
ASD2410	Prokofiev: Symphonies 1/7	MRSO	Rozhdestvensky	Mdya
ASD2411	Prokofiev: Concerto 3,Rachmaninov: Concerto 4	MRSO	Rozhdestvensky Petrov	Mdya
ASD2413	Brahms: Piano Concerto 2	Philh	Barbirolli Barenboim	
ASD2415	Zarzuela Songs	SNO	De Burgos De Los Angeles	
ASD2416	Liszt: Hungarian Rhapsody 15,Liebestraum 3,etc	Ogdon		
ASD2417	Schubert: Octet	Melos Ensemble		
ASD2420	Shostakovich: Symphony 10	USSR	Svetlanov	Mdya
ASD2421	Brahms: Symphony 2/Tragic Ov	VPO	Barbirolli	
ASD2422	V Williams: Sancta Civitas	LSO	Willcocks	TASEC65
ASD2423	Loewe: Ballads	Fischer-Dieskau Moore		
ASD2424	Mozart: Symphonies 39/40	ECO	Barenboim	
ASD2425	Music of India: Volume 7		Ustad Vilayat Khan	
ASD2426	Schubert: Symphonies 1/3	Menuhin Orch Menuhin		
ASD2427	Gerhard: Collages	BBCSO	Prausnitz	
ASD2429-30	Prokofiev: Cinderella (complete ballet)	MRSO	Rozhdestvensky	(SLS 779) Mdya
ASD2431	Lieder Recital (Schubert, Wolf, Richard Struass)	Baker	Moore	
ASD2432	Brahms: Symphony 3	VPO	Barbirolli	
ASD2433	Brahms: Symphony 4	VPO	Barbirolli	
ASD2434	Mozart: Piano Concertos 14/15	ECO	Barenboim	
ASD2435	Sullivan: Irish Symphony	RLPO	Groves	
ASD2436	Brahms: Cello Sonatas	Du Pre	Barenboim	
ASD2437	Delius: Songs of Sunset/Cynara	RLPh	Groves	
ASD2438	Nielsen: Wind Quintet/Berwald: Septet	Melos Ensemble		

Cat. No.	Work	Orchestra	Conductor/Artist	Notes
ASD2439-40	V Williams: Sea Symphony/The Wasps suite	LPO	Boult	
ASD2441	"The Music of Iannis Xenakis"		Pasquier, Penassou, etc	
ASD2442	Debussy La Mer/Nocturnes	Orch de Paris	Barbirolli	
ASD2443	Handel: Organ Concertos (4,6,8,10)	BFCO	Menuhin Preston	
ASD2444	Berlioz: Les Nuits d'Ete/Ravel Schrzd	Philh	Barbirolli Baker	
ASD2445	Operatic Recital	ROHCG	Gedda	
ASD2446	Music of India Volume 9		Bismallah Khan	
ASD2447	Shostakovich: Violin Concerto 2/Symphony 6	MPO	Kondrashin Oistrakh	Mdya
ASD2448	Bizet-Schedrin: Carmen	Bolshoi	Rozhdestvensky	Mdya
ASD2449	Bartok: Two Rhapsodies/Violin Concerto	BBCSO	Boulez Menuhin	
ASD2450	Poulenc: Sinfonietta/Suite francaise	ODP	Pretre	
ASD2451	Russian Opera Arias	Bolshoi	Vishnevskaya	Mdya
ASD2453	Puccini: Madama Butterfly (hlts)	Rome Opera	Bergonzi Scotto	
ASD2454	Schumann: Symphony 2	Philh	Klemperer	
ASD2455	Weber: Concerto/Rossini: Theme & Vns	Philh	De Burgos	
ASD2457	French and Italian Opera Arias	La Scala	Votto Freni	
ASD2458	V Williams Mystical Songs/Mass	Willcocks Kings College		
ASD2459	Schonberg Pelleas&Melisande	Philh	Barbirolli	
ASD2460	Music of India vol 11		Vilayat Khan	
ASD2462	Mozart: Sinf Concertante/Haydn: SinfConcertante	ECO	Barenboim	
ASD2463	Prokofiev Symphony 2	MRSO	Rozhdestvensky	Mdya
ASD2464	Shostakovich: String Quartet 1, Tchaikovsky: Souvenir de Florence (String Sextet)	Borodin Quartet	Rostropovich (cello) Talalyan (viola)	Mdya
ASD2465	Mozart: Piano Concertos 21/27	ECO	Barenboim	
ASD2466	Haydn: Cello Concerto/etc	LSO	Barbirolli Du Pre	
ASD2467	Honegger: Symphony 2/Messiaen: Exspecto	OTNO	Munch Baudo	
ASD2468	Handel: Two Italian Cantatas	ECO	Leppard Baker	
ASD2469	V Williams: Sym 8/Conc for 2 pianos.	Philh	Boult Vronsky Babin	
ASD2470	Messiaen: Quartet for the End of Time		Beroff Gruenberg De Peyer Pleeth	
ASD2471	Rachmaninov: Symphony 1	USSR	Svetlanov	Mdya
ASD2472	Khachaturian: Violin Concerto Prokofiev: Violin Concerto 1	MRSO MRSO	Khachaturian David Oistrakh RhozdestvenskyIgor Oistrakh	Mdya
ASD2473	Bellini And Donizetti Arias and Duets	Philh	Downes Gedda Freni	
ASD2474	Shostakovich: Symphony 8	USSR	Kondrashin	Mdya
ASD2475	Russian Opera and Cantata Arias	Bolshoi	Rozhdestvensky Arkhipova	Mdya
ASD2476	Bartok: Piano Concertos 1/3	Philh	Boulez Barenboim	
ASD2477	Delius: In a Summer Garden/Song Before Sunrise	HO	Barbirolli	
ASD2478	Schubert: Symphonies 4,5	BFCO	Menuhin	
ASD2480	Tchaikovsky: Symphony 1 Liadov: Kikimora/Polonaise in C	USSR	Ivanov	Mdya
ASD2481	Khachaturian: Piano Conc/Shostakovich: Piano Conc 1	MPO	Kondrashin	Mdya
ASD2482	Rachmaninov: Isle of Dead/Scriabin	USSR	Svetlanov	Mdya
ASD2483	Schubert: Moments Musiceaux/Schumann: Nachtstucke	Gilels		
ASD2484	Mozart: Piano Concertos 5/9	ECO	Barenboim	
ASD2485	Handel: Music for Royal Fireworks/etc	BFCO	Menuhin	
ASD2486	Sibelius: En Saga	LSO	Dorati	
ASD2487	V Williams: An Oxford Elegy/Flos Campi/etc	Willcocks Kings College		
ASD2488	Rachmaninov: Symphonic Dances	MPO	Kondrashin	Mdya
ASD2489	V Williams: Five Tudor Portraits	Philh	Willcocks Bach Choir	
ASD2490	Rimsky-Korsakov: Overtures May Night,Ivan the Terrible, Tchaikovsky: Symphony 2	USSR SO	Svetlanov	Mdya
ASD2491-2	Mahler: Symphony 7	Philh	Klemperer	(SLS 781)
ASD2493	Strauss,R: 7 Songs/Mozart: 4 Concert Arias	LSO	Brendel Schwarzkopf	
ASD2494	Sibelius Symphony 4	HO	Barbirolli	
ASD2495	Schubert: Symphony No8, Overtures	BFCO	Menuhin	
ASD2496	'Happy Birthday Sir John' (Purcell, Corelli, Bach, etc)		Barbirolli	

ASD2497	Ravel: Bolero/Rhapsodie Espagnol/Daphnis/Pavane	ODP	Munch	
ASD2498	Schumann/Saint-Saens: Cello Concertos	NPO	Barenboim Du Pre	
ASD2499	Tchaikovsky:Sym 3/Liadov:Enchanted Lake/Baba-Yaga	USSR SO Svetlanov		Mdya
ASD2500	Beethoven: Piano Concerto 5	Philh	Klemperer Barenboim	
ASD2501	Elgar: PianoQuintet/Concert Allegro	Allegri Qt Ogdon		
ASD2502	Elgar: Severn Suite/Nursery Suite/etc	RLPO	Groves	
ASD2506	Ravel: Intro.& Allegro/Francaix/Poulenc	Melos Ensemble		
ASD2508	Mozart: Don Giovanni (hlts)	Philh	Klemperer	
ASD2511-2	Shostakovich: Symphony 7/Kabalevsky: Cello Concerto 2	Leningrad PO Svetlanov Daniel Shafran		(SLS 784) Mdya
ASD2513	"Great Scenes and Arias from French Operas"	RPO	Mackerras Beverly Sills	
ASD2515	Beethoven: Creatures of Prometheus Ballet Music	FCO	Menuhin	
ASD2516	Berlioz: Trojans (hlts)	LSO	Gibson Baker	
ASD2517	Songs of Catalonia	De Los Angeles		
ASD2518/9	Mahler: Symphony 5	Philh	Barbirolli	
ASD2520	Rimsky-Korsakov: Scheherazade	USSR	Svetlanov	Mdya
ASD2521	Prokofiev: Alexander Nevsky,	USSR	Svetlanov	Mdya
	Rimsky-Korsakov: Song of Oleg the Wise	Bolshoi	Khaikin	
ASD2522	Glazunov: The Seasons	MRSO	Khaikin	Mdya
ASD2523	Scriabin: The Divine Poem (Symphony 3)	USSR SO Svetlanov		Mdya
ASD2524	Schubert: Trio 1 D898/Sonata D28	Menuhin Gendron		
ASD2525	Brahms: Violin Concerto	Clvlnd	Szell Oistrakh	[SLS786 (also issued separately)]
ASD2526	Brahms: Double Concerto	Clvlnd	Szell Oistrakh Rostropovich	[In SLS786 (not issued separately)]
ASD2528-30 as SLS 787				
ASD2531	Bartok: Concerto for Orch,			
	Kodaly: Dances of Galanta	CSO	Ozawa	
ASD2533	Bach: Magnificat/Bruckner: Te Deum	Philh	Barenboim	
ASD2534	Handel: Organ Concertos	BFCO	Menuhin Preston	
ASD2535	Beethoven: Symphony 6/Egmont Ov	Philh	Giulini	
ASD2536	Schubert: Trio 2 D929/Nocturne D897	Menuhin Gendron		
ASD2537	Beethoven: Symphony 7/Klemperer: Rameau Vns	Philh	Klemperer	
ASD2538	V Williams: Symphony 5/Serenade to Music.	LPO	Boult	
ASD2539	Rachmaninov: The Bells/etc	MPO	Kondrashin	Mdya
ASD2540	Rimsky-Korsakov: Sym 1/Glazunov: Sym 5	MRSO	Khaikin	Mdya
ASD2541	Mussorgsky: Boris Godunov - excerpts	Bolshoi	Melik-Pashaev	Mdya
ASD2542	Walton: Violin & Viola Concertos	Philh	Walton Menuhin	
ASD2543	Verdi: Aida (hlts)	Rome Op Mehta		[From SAN189-91]
ASD2544	Carnegie Hall Piano Recital, 1969 (Beethoven, Medtner, etc)		Gilels	
ASD2545	Rachmaninov: Symphony No2	Bolshoi	Svetlanov	Mdya
ASD2546	Mendelssohn: Piano Concertos 1, 2/Rondo Brillante	LSO	Ceccato Ogdon	
ASD2547	Schumann: Symphony 3	Philh	Klemperer	
ASD2548	Schubert: Symphony 9	Menuhin Fest Orch Menuhin		
ASD2549	"Portrait of the Artist" (Bach, Haydn, Mahler, Schubert, etc)	Fischer-Dieskau		
ASD2550	Beethoven: Piano Concerto 4	Philh	Klemperer Barenboim	
ASD2551	Modern British Piano Works (Rawsthorne,Goehr,Blake,etc)		Ogdon	
ASD2552	Franck: Symphony in Dmin	OdeP	Karajan	
ASD2553	Duets at QEH	Fischer-Dieskau J.Baker		
ASD2554	Brahms: Piano Concerto 2	ODP	Maazel Richter	
ASD2555	Brahms: 16 Songs	Christa Ludwig		
ASD2557	Prokofiev: Symphony 4/Schedrin: Conc for Orch	MRSO	Rozhdestvensky	Mdya
ASD2558	Tchaikovsky: Manfred	USSR	Svetlanov	Mdya
ASD2559	Portrait of the Artist		Christoff	
ASD2560	Beethoven: Symphonies 1/8	Philh	Klemperer	
ASD2561	Beethoven: Symphony 2/Leonora 2/Prometheus	Philh	Klemperer	
ASD2562	Beethoven: Symphony 3/Fidelio Ov	Philh	Klemperer	
ASD2563	Beethoven: Symphony 4/Egmont Inc Music	Philh	Klemperer	
ASD2564	Beethoven: Symphony 5/Coriolan Ov	Philh	Klemperer	[SAX2373]

ASD2565	Beethoven: Symphony 6/Leonora Ov 1	Philh	Klemperer	
ASD2566	Beethoven: Symphony 7/Cons of the House Ov	Philh	Klemperer	[SAX2415]
ASD2567-8	Beethoven: Symphony 9	Philh	Klemperer	[In SLS788 and SLS790 (Not issued separately)]
ASD2571	Beethoven: Piano Trios Nos 4/5	Barenboim Zukerman Du Pre		
ASD2572	Beethoven: Archduke Trio/Trio No. 7	Barenboim Zukerman Du Pré		
ASD2574	Nicolai Gedda: "Portrait of the Artist"	Gedda		
ASD2575	Klemperer: Symphony 2/String Quartet 7	Philh	Klemperer	
ASD2576	Tchaikovsky: Piano Concerto 1	OdeP	Karajan Weissenberg	
ASD2577	Chopin: 2 Polonaises, 4 Nocturnes, Ballade	Pollini		
ASD2578	Bellini and Donizetti Heroines	VV	Jalas Sills	
ASD2579	Beethoven: Piano Concerto 3	Philh	Klemperer Barenboim	
ASD2580	Fauré: Pelleas/Masques et Bergamasques	OTNO	Baudo	
ASD2581	V Williams: Symphony 9/Fant on old 104th	LPO	Boult Katin	
ASD2582	Beethoven Triple Concerto	BPO	Karajan Oistrakh Rostr Richter	
ASD2583	Mozart: Symphonies 33/36 (Linz)	ECO	Barenboim	
ASD2584	Handel: Coronation Anthems	MFO	Menuhin	
ASD2585	Shostakovich: Violin Concerto 1	MRSO	Kondrashin Kogan	Mdya
	Cello Concerto 1	MRSO	Rozhdestvensky Khomitser	
ASD2586	Roussel: Cello Concertino/Suite in F/Piano Concerto	ODP	Jacquillat	
ASD2587	Rachmaninov: Cello Sonatas/Chopin	Tortelier Ciccolini		
ASD2589	Brahms: Haydn Vns, Academic Festival Ov, Tragic Ov	VPO	Barbirolli	
ASD2590	Songs by Debussy, Fauré, Duparc	Baker	Moore	
ASD2591	Operatic Recital (Verdi, Belini, Ponchielli, Giordano)	Grace Bumbry		
ASD2592	Tchaikovsky: Symphony 4, Glinka: Jota Aragonesa	USSR SO Svetlanov		Mdya
ASD2593	Prokofiev: Cantata for the 20th Anniv of October Revolution	MPO	Kondrashin Petrov	Mdya
ASD2594	Tchaikovsky: Piano Trio in Amin Op 50	Menuhin Gendron Hephzibah Menuhin		
ASD2595	Verdi: Rigoletto (hlts)	Rome Op Molinari-Pradelli		
ASD2596/7	Shaporin: The Story of the Battle for the Russian Land,			
	Petrov: In Memory of the victims of the siege of Leningrad	Conductors: Svetlanov/Yansons		Mdya
ASD2598	Shostakovich: Symphony 12	Leningrad PO Mravinsky		Mdya
ASD2599	Tchaikovsky: Symphony 5	USSR	Svetlanov	Mdya
ASD2600	Howells: Hymnus Paradisi	Philh	Willcocks	
ASD2601	Beethoven: Songs	Gedda	Eyron (piano)	
ASD2602	West Meets East: Indian Music	Menuhin Shanker		
ASD2603	Satie: Piano Works - Volume 2		Ciccolini	
ASD2606	Berlioz: Romeo & Juliet	CSO	Giulini	
ASD2607	Arensky: Piano Concerto/Scriabin: Piano Concerto	MRSO	Khaikin	Mdya
ASD2608	Beethoven: Piano Concerto 2/Choral Fantasia	Philh	Klemperer Barenboim	
ASD2609	Mendelssohn: Elijah (hlts)	Philh	de Burgos	
ASD2610	Mozart: Serenade No13 K.525, Divertimento No7, Marches	ECO	Barenboim	
ASD2611	Portrait of an Artist		Rothenberger	
ASD2612	'Concertos for Cyril & Phyllis'	CBSO	Arnold Smith Sellick	
ASD2613	Strauss, R: Ein Heldenleben	LSO	Barbirolli	
ASD2614	Stravinsky: Petrouchka & Firebird Suites	CSO	Giulini	
ASD2615	Janet Baker Recital (Monteverdi & Scarlatti)	ECO	Leppard Baker	
ASD2616	Beethoven: Piano Concerto 1	Philh	Klemperer Barenboim	
ASD2617	Tchaikovsky: Symphony No6 Glinka: Kamarinskaya	USSR	Svetlanov	Mdya
ASD2618	Franck: Violin Sonata in A/Brahms: Violin Sonata 3	Oistrakh Richter		Mdya
ASD2619-21	Tchaikovsky: Swan Lake	MPO	Rozhdestvensky	(SLS795) Mdya
ASD2630	Rheinberger: Star of Bethlehem/Cornelius	Heger Streich		
ASD2631	V Williams: Sinfonia Antartica (7)	LPO	Boult	
ASD2632	Puccini: Arias	LSO	Mackerras Caballé	
ASD2633	Shostakovich: Symphony 14	MCO	Barshai	Mdya
ASD2634	"Elizabeth Schwarzkopf Song book Vol 3" (Schubert, Schumann, Chopin, Grieg, etc)			
ASD2635	Delius Appalachia/Brigg Fair	Halle	Barbirolli	
ASD2636	Prokofiev: Symphony 3/etc	MRSO	Rozhdestvensky	Mdya

ASD2637	Britten: St Nicholas	ASMF	Willcocks	
ASD2638	"Contrasts - The Lighter Elgar"	Northern Sinfonia Marriner		
ASD2639	Prokofiev: Symphony 6	MRSO	Rozhdestvensky	Mdya
ASD2640	Ippolitov-Ivanov: Caucasian Sketches/Mtsyry	MPO	Rozhdestvensky	Mdya
ASD2644	Haydn: String Quartets 67 ("Lark"), 39 ("Bird"), Schubert: Quartet 10	Smetana Quartet		
ASD2645	Tchaikovsky: Piano Concerto 2 (original version)	MRSO	Rozhdestvensky Zhukov	Mdya
ASD2646	Rachmaninov: Symphony No3 Mussorgsky: Khovantschina	MRSO	Svetlanov	Mdya
ASD2647	Bach,J.S: Concerto for 1 and 2 harpsichords	BFCO	Menuhin Malcolm Preston	
ASD2648	Sibelius: Symphonies 3/6	HO	Barbirolli	
ASD2649	Spanish & Sephardic Songs	De Los Angeles		
ASD2650	Brahms: Symphony 4	CSO	Giulini	
ASD2651	Strauss,R: Sonatina 1 in F/Suite in B flat	LSO	de Peyer	
ASD2652	Janacek: Sinfonietta/Lutoslawski: Conc for Orch	CSO	Ozawa	
ASD2653	Dvorak: Symphony 8	Clvlnd	Szell	
ASD2654	Kalinnikov: Sym 2/Liadov: Enchanted Lake/etc	USSR	Svetlanov	Mdya
ASD2655	Opera Choruses	Various Artists		
ASD2656	Poulenc: Suite Francaise/Novelettes/Nocturnes Mouvements Perpetuels/Pastourelle/Toccata/Valse	Tacchino		
ASD2660	Brahms: Symphony 3/Tragic Ov	LPO	Boult	
ASD2661	Beethoven: Mass in C	Philh	Giulini Baker etc	
ASD2662	Handel: Organ Concertos Nos 7, 11, 12	Menuhin Festival Menuhin Preston		
ASD2664	Russian Orchestral Works (Glinka, Rimsky, Borodin)	USSR SO Svetlanov		Mdya
ASD2667	Beethoven: Violin Concerto	Philh	Boult Suk	
ASD2668	Shostakovich: Symphony 5	USSR	Maxim Shostakovich	Mdya
ASD2669	Prokofiev: Love of 3 Oranges, "7 They Are 7", etc	MRSO	Rozhdestvensky	Mdya
ASD2670	Bartok: Music for SP&C/Div for Strings	ECO	Barenboim	
ASD2671	Beethoven: Chamber Works	Melos Ensemble		
ASD2672	Elgar: Crown of India Suite/Imperial March/etc	RLPO	Groves	
ASD2673	V Williams: Job, A Masque for Dancing	LSO	Boult	TASEC
ASD2688	Stars of the Bolshoi vol 2	Vishnevskaya, Arkhipova, Petrov, etc		Mdya
ASD2689	Borodin: Symphony 1,Liadov: From Days of Old, From the Book of Revelation, Musical Snuff-Box	USSR	Svetlanov	Mdya
ASD2690	Verdi: Otello (excerpts)	Philh	Barbirolli Fischer-Dieskau	
ASD2691-2	Mahler: Symphony 2	Philh	Klemperer	[In SLS806]
ASD2693/4	Sibelius: Kullervo Symphony	BNSO	Berglund	
ASD2695	"Klemperer conducts Wagner" (Rienzi, Dutchman, Tannhauser, Lohengrin)			
ASD2696	"Klemperer conducts Wagner" (Meistersinger, Tristan, Gotterdammerung, Lohengrin)			
ASD2697	Wagner: Das Rheingold/Tannhauser/Parsifal/Die Walkure	Philh	Klemperer	
ASD2698	V-Williams: Symphony 5/Tallis Fantasia	Philh	Barbirolli	
ASD2699	Vaughan Williams: Riders to the Sea/Magnificat	London Orch Nova Davies		
ASD2700	Borodin: Sym 2/Liadov: 8 Russian Folgsongs/Baba Yaga	USSR	Svetlanov	Mdya
ASD2701	Ravel: Piano Concerto/Prokofiev: Piano Concerto 3	OdP	Ozawa Weissenberg	
ASD2705	Brahms: Symphony 1	Philh	Klemperer	
ASD2706	Brahms: Symphony 2/Tragic Overture	Philh	Klemperer	
ASD2707	Brahms: Symphony 3/Academic Festival Overture	Philh	Klemperer	
ASD2708	Brahms: Symphony 4	Philh	Klemperer	
ASD2709	Shostakovich: Piano Conc 2/Ogdon: Piano Conc 1	RPO	Foster Ogdon	
ASD2710	Duets at RFH	Fischer-Dieskau J.Baker		
ASD2712	Massenet: Werther - excerpts	OdeP	Pretre de los Angeles Gedda	
ASD2713	Bach: Harpsichard Concertos	BFCO	Menuhin Malcom	
ASD2717	Glazunov: Symphony 8	MRSO	Svetlanov	Mdya
ASD2718	Shostakovich: Violin Sonata Op 134/Piano Trio Op 67	Oistrakh Richter Rostropovich		Mdya
ASD2719	Bruckner: Symphony 9	Philh	Klemperer	
ASD2720	Kalinnikov: Symphony 1/Liapounov: Piano Conc 2	MRSO	Khaikin	Mdya
ASD2721	Elgar: Sea Pictures	LSO	Barbirolli	

ASD2722	Mahler: Symphony 1	CSO	Giulini	
ASD2723	Great Operatic Duets	LSO	Mackerras Caballé Martí	
ASD2724	Wagner: Flying Dutchman (hlts)	Philh	Klemperer	
ASD2725	Beethoven: 2 Romances for Violin & Orch	ASMF	Marriner Suk	
ASD2726-9	Strauss: Der Rosenkavalier	Philh	Karajan	[In SLS810]
ASD2732	Mozart: Symphonies 40/41	BPO	Karajan	
ASD2737	Beethoven: Symphony 7	CSO	Giulini	
ASD2738	Tchaikovsky: Francesca da Rimini/Serenade	Philh/LSO	Barbirolli	
ASD2739	English Concert: G.Williams:Penillion	RPO	Groves	
ASD2740	V Williams: London Symphony/Norfolk Rhapsody	LPO	Boult	
ASD2741	Shostakovich: Symphony 4	MPO	Kondrashin	Mdya
ASD2743	Schubert: Symphony 8/Rosamunde Ov	RLPO	Groves	
ASD2744	Bartok: Piano Concerto 2/Prokofiev: Piano Concerto 5	ODP	Maazel Richter	
ASD2746	Brahms: Symphony 2/Alt Rhp	LPO	Boult Baker	
ASD2747	Shostakovich: Symphony 2	LenPO	Blazhkov	Mdya
ASD2748	Elgar: Symphony 1	Philh	Barbirolli	
ASD2749	Elgar: Symphony No2	HO	Barbirolli	
ASD2750	Elgar: Enigma variations	LSO	Boult	
ASD2751	Dvorak: Cello Concerto	CSO	Barenboim Du Pre	
ASD2752	Concerto for Sitar and Orchestra	LSO	Previn Ravi Shankar	
ASD2753	Saint-Saens: Carnival of the Animals/etc	CBSO	Fremaux	
ASD2754	Gershwin: Rhapsody in Blue/American in Paris	LSO	Previn	
ASD2755	Vainberg: Violin Concerto/Symphony 4	MPO	Kondrashin Kogan	Mdya
ASD2756	Rimsky Korsakov: Scheherazade Borodin:Polovtsian Dances	CSO	Ozawa	
ASD2757	Tchaikovsky: Swan Lake	MSO	Rozhdestvensky	Mdya
ASD2758	Prokofiev: Symphony 5	MSO	Rozhdestvensky	Mdya
ASD2759	Williamson: Violin Conc/Berkeley: Violin Conc	LPO	Boult Menuhin	
ASD2760	Schubert: Symphony 9	Clvlnd	Szell	
ASD2761	Scriabin: Symphony 1	USSR	Svetlanov	Mdya
ASD2762	Falstaff/Froissart/Intr&Allegro	Halle	Barbirolli	
ASD2763	Prokofiev: Chout/Shostakovich: Age of Gold	MRSO	Rozhdestvensky	Mdya
ASD2764	Elgar: Cello Concerto/Delius: Cello Concerto	LSO	Barbirolli Du Pré	
ASD2765	Shostakovich: Symphony 1,Prokofiev: Sinfonietta	MRSO	Aranovich	Mdya
ASD2766	Ravel: Tombeau, Rapsodie Esp, Alborado	OdP	Karajan	
ASD2770	Stravinsky: Music for Piano and Orch	ODP	Ozawa Beroff	
ASD2771	Tchaikovsky: Eugene Onegin (hlts)	Bolshoi	Rostropovich	Mdya
ASD2772	Piano Recital (Schumann, Chopin, Liszt, Debussy, etc)		Postnikova	Mdya
ASD2773	Grieg: Lyric Suite/Homage March/Peer Gynt	Halle	Barbirolli	
ASD2774	Bizet: Carmen (hlts)	Paris Opera	De Burgos Bumbry	
ASD2775	Tchaikovsky: Hamlet/The Tempest/etc	USSR	Svetlanov	Mdya
ASD2780	Mozart: 4 Horn Concertos/Concert Rondo/etc	ASMF	Marriner Tuckwell	
ASD2781	Shostakovich:Ballet Suites,Ov on Russian & Kirghiz Songs	Bolshoi	Maxim Shostakovich	Mdya
ASD2782	Paganini: Violin Conc no. 1	RPO	Perlman	
ASD2783	Bach,J.S: Violin/double concs.	ECO	Barenboim Perlman Zukerman	
ASD2784	Edward Heath Concert			
ASD2786	Walton: Facade	ASMF	Marriner	
ASD2787	Verdi: Arias Montserrat	RPO	Caballe	
ASD2788	Mozart: Requiem	ECO	Barenboim	
ASD2789-90	Brahms: German Requiem	Philh	Klemperer	[In SLS821]
ASD2791	Operatic Recital (Aida, Attila, I Lombardi, etc)	Callas		
ASD2793-6	Bach: St Matthew Passion	Philh	Klemperer	[In SLS827]
ASD2797-8	Puccini: Tosca	La Scala	Sabata	[in SLS825]
ASD2799	Mahler: Symphony 4	Philh	Klemperer Schwarzkopf	
ASD2800	Prokofiev: Alexander Nevsky	LSO	Previn	
ASD2801	Liadov: Enchanted Lake, Kikimora, baba Yaga, 8 Russian Folk Songs	USSR	Svetlanov	Mdya

ASD2802	Grieg & Schumann: Piano Concertos	Philh	Berglund Ogdon	
ASD2803	Sauguet: Cello Concerto, Tishchenko: Cello Concerto	MRSO	Rostropovich	Mdya
ASD2804	Delius: Paris (The Song of a Great City)	RLPO	Groves	
ASD2805	Shostakovich: Symphony 6/Sibelius: Symphony 7	LenPO	Mravinsky	Mdya
ASD2806	Mozart: Symphonies 29, 30, 34	ECO	Barenboim	
ASD2807	"Elizabeth Schwarzkopf Sings Operetta"	Philh	Ackermann Schwarzkopf	
ASD2808	Bruckner: Study Symphony in f	LSO	Shapirra	
ASD2809	Mendelssohn/Bruch: Violin Concertos	LSO	De Burgos Menuhin	
ASD2810	Goehr: Violin Concerto/Hamilton: Violin Concerto	RPO	Del Mar Parikian	
ASD2811	Verdi: La Forza del Destino (excerpts)	RPO	Gardelli Bergonzi Cappucilli	
ASD2812	Wagner: Lohengrin, Mastersingers, Tristan	Philh	Boult	
ASD2813	Tchaikovsky: Violin Concerto, Chausson: Poeme, St Saens: Introduction & Rondo Capriccioso	MPO	Rozhdestvensky Oistrakh	Mdya
ASD2814	Tchaikovsky: Symphony 4	BPO	Karajan	
ASD2815	Tchaikovsky: Symphony 5	BPO	Karajan	
ASD2816	Tchaikovsky: Symphony 6	BPO	Karajan	
ASD2817	Haydn: Symphonies 83/101	BPO	Karajan	
ASD2818	Haydn: Symphonies 92/95	Philh	Klemperer	
ASD2822	Elgar Overtures (Cockaigne/Froissart/etc)	LPO	Boult	
ASD2823	Verdi: Don Carlos (excerpts)	ROHCG	Giulini Caballe Domingo	
ASD2824	Mozart: Song Recital		Fischer-Dieskau Barenboim	
ASD2825	Tchaikovsky: Piano Concerto 2 (complete original version)	ORTF	Martinon Kersenbaum	
ASD2826	Canteloube: Songs of the Auvergne	Lamoureux Orch	De Los Angeles	
ASD2830	Elgar: Serenade for Strings/Arensky Vns	Philh	Barbirolli	
ASD2831	English String Music	ASMF	Marriner	
ASD2834	Mozart: Overtures and Ballet Music	ASMF	Marriner	
ASD2835	Poulenc: Gloria/Organ Concerto	FNRO	Pretre Duruflé	
ASD2836	Bruckner: Mass No 3 in Fmin	Philh	Barenboim	
ASD2837	Wagner: Rare Orchestral Pieces	LSO	Janowski	
ASD2838	Mozart: Piano Concerto 22	ECO	Barenboim	
ASD2844	"Elizabeth Schwarzkopf Songbook" Vol 4		Schwarzkopf Moore	
ASD2845	Stravinsky: The Firebird (complete original 1910 version)	OdeP	Ozawa	
ASD2846	Rimsky-Korsakov: Symphony 3/Piano Concerto Moscow	RSO	Rozhdestvensky	Mdya
ASD2847	Vaughan Williams: Srnd to Music/Lark Ascending	LPO	Boult	
ASD2851	Chopin/Franck: Cello Sonatas	Du Pre	Barenboim	
ASD2852	Bruch: Violin Concertos 1/2	LSO	Menuhin Boult	
ASD2855	Daniel Jones: Symphony 4/7 (In memory of Dylan Thomas)	RPO	Groves	
ASD2856	Schubert: Symphony 9	LPO	Boult	
ASD2857	Shostakovich: Symphony 15	MRSO	Maxim Shostakovich	Mdya
ASD2858	Glazunov: Symphony 2/Rachmaninov: The Crag	MRSO	Rozhdestvensky	Mdya
ASD2863	Dvorak: "New World" Symphony/Smetana: Vltava	BPO	Karajan	
ASD2870	Wieniawski: Two Violin Concertos	LPO	Perlman	
ASD2871	Brahms: Symphony 1	LPO	Boult	
ASD2872	Rachmaninov: Piano Concerto 1/Franck: Symphonic Vns	BPO	Karajan Weissenberg	
ASD2873	Brahms: Piano Quintet in Fmin	Yale Quartet	Previn	
ASD2874	Sibelius: Symphony 7/Tapiola	BNSO	Berglund	
ASD2875	Shostakovich: The Song of the Forests	MPO	Kondrashin	Mdya
ASD2876	Bach,JS: Cantatas	ASMF	Marriner	
ASD2877	Massenet: Manon (excerpts)	Philh	Rudel Gedda	
ASD2878	Arnold: Peterloo Ov/4 Cornish dances	CBSO	Arnold	
ASD2883	Elgar: Violin Concerto	RLPO	Groves Bean	
ASD2884	Mozart: Haffner Serenade	ECO	Zukerman	
ASD2887	Mozart: Piano Concertos 18/24	ECO	Barenboim	
ASD2888	Strauss,R: 4 Last Songs	BRSO	Szell Schwarzkopf	
ASD2889	Rachmaninov: Symphony 2	LSO	Previn	TASEC
ASD2890	Rachmaninov: The Covetous Knight	MRSO	Rozhdestvensky	Mdya

ASD2891	Strauss,J: Die Fledermaus (hlts)	Boskovsky	Rothenberger Fischer-Dieskau	
ASD2892	Schmitt: Psalm 47/La Tragedie de Salome	ORTFO	Martinon	
ASD2893	Shostakovich: Symphony 13 ("Babi Yar")	MPO	Kondrashin	Mdya
ASD2894	Tchaikovsky: Ov 1812/Romeo&Juliet	LSO	Previn	
ASD2900	Glazunov: Symphony 3	MRSO	Khaikin	Mdya
ASD2901	Brahms: Symphony 4	LPO	Boult	
ASD2902	Concert by Elly Ameling			
ASD2903	Music from a Golden Age (Bach,Handel,Rameau,Telemann)	Fischer-Dieskau		
ASD2904	John McCabe: Symphony 2	CBSO	Fremaux	
ASD2905	Concert	Beverly Sills		
ASD2906	Elgar Cello Concerto	Boult	Tortelier	
ASD2907-9	See SLS 851			
ASD2911	Beethoven: Fidelio (excerpts)	BPO	Karajan	
ASD2912	Hindemith: Harmonie der Welt Symphony	LenPO	Mravinsky	Mdya
ASD2913	Moeran: Symphony in Gmin/etc	English Sinfonia	Dilkes	
ASD2914	Vaughan Williams, The Wasps, concerto for 2 pianos	LPO	Boult Vronsky Babin	
ASD2915	Bizet: Carmen Suite/L'Arleienne Suite/Jeux D'Enfants	OdP	Barenboim	
ASD2916	Mozart: Clarinet Concerto/Bassoon Concerto	BPO	Karajan	
ASD2917	Shostakovich: Symphony 8	LSO	Previn	TASEC
ASD2918	Mozart: Symphonies 36/38	BPO	Karajan	
ASD2919-21	Offenbach: Tales of Hoffmann	LSO	Rudel	[SLS858]
ASD2924	Shostakovich: Cello Conc 1/Walton	BNSO	Berglund Tortelier	
ASD2925	Glazounov & Keller: Chopiniana (Les Sylphides)	Bolshoi	Zuraitis	Mdya
ASD2926	Mendelssohn/Bruch Violin Concertos	LSO	Previn Perlman	
ASD2927	Miaskovsky: Symphony 23/Schedrin: Symphony 1	MRSO	Kovalyov	Mdya
ASD2928	Rachmaninov: Songs (Answer,Lilacs,Storm,Vocalise,etc)	Gedda	Weissenberg (piano)	
ASD2929	"Janet Baker Favourites"	Baker	Moore	
ASD2934	Wagner: Valkyries,Forest Murmurs,Tannhauser,Tristan, etc	Philh	Boult	
ASD2935	Prokofiev: Peter and the Wolf/Britten: YPGO	LSO	Previn	
ASD2936	Shostakovich: Violin Conc 1	Philh	Maxim Shostakovich Oistrakh	
ASD2938	Haydn: Trumpet Conc/Telemann: Trumpet Conc	ASMF	Marriner Wilbraham	
ASD2942	Schubert: Symphonies 5/8	Philh	Fischer-Dieskau	
ASD2945	Berlioz: Symphonie Fantastique	ORTF	Martinon	
ASD2946	Saint-Saens Symphonies 1/2	ORTF	Martinon	
ASD2947	Prokofiev: Ballad of the Boy who remained Unknown	Moscow	Rozhdestvensky	Mdya
ASD2951	Mozart: Piano Concertos 17/24	LSO	Boult/Previn	
ASD2952	Grieg: Peer Gynt Suites 1/2/etc	BNSO	Berglund	
ASD2953	Dukas: Symphony in C/etc	ONRF	Martinon	
ASD2954	Tchaikovsky: Rococo Vns/Grieg: Holberg Suite/etc	Northern Sinfonia	Tortelier	
ASD2955	Strauss,R: Sinfonia Domestica	BPO	Karajan	
ASD2956	Mozart: Piano Concertos 12/19	ECO	Barenboim	
ASD2958	Delius: Sea Drift/Song of the High Hills	RLPO	Groves	
ASD2959	Mozart: Mass in Cmin K427	Philh	Leppard	
ASD2960	Beethoven: Symphony 5	LSO	Previn	
ASD2961	Sibelius The Tempest	RLPO	Groves	TASEC
ASD2962	V Williams Toward the Unknown Region	LPO	Boult	
ASD2963	Chopin: Fantasie, Berceuse, Barcarolle, Polonaise, etc	Barenboim		
ASD2964	Bartok: Music for Strings, Percussion, & Celeste Honegger: Symphony 3	LenPO	Mravinsky	Mdya
ASD2970	Bach-Elgar: Fantasia & Fugue in C min	LPO	Boult	TASEC
ASD2971	Bach: Piano Transcriptions		Weissenberg	
ASD2973	Rachmaninov: Vespers	USSR Chorus	Sveshnikov	Mdya
ASD2974	R-Korsakov: Antar Symphony/Glazunov: Scenes de Ballet	MRSO	Rozhdestvensky	Mdya
ASD2985	Various Horn Concertos	ASMF	Marriner Tuckwell	
ASD2988	Mozart: Violin Concertos 3 (K216)/5 (K219)	BPO	David Oistrakh	
ASD2989	Honegger: Pacific 231	CBSO	Fremaux	TASEC

ASD2990	Walton: Symphony 2/Portsmouth Point Ov	LSO	Previn	
ASD2992	Brahms: Piano Concerto 1	LSO	Giulini Weissenberg	
ASD2993	Mozart: Flute Conc K313, Flute & Harp Conc K299	BPO	Karajan Galway	
ASD2994	Villa-Lobos: Bachianas Brasileiras Nos 2,5,6,9	OdP	Capolongo	
ASD2999	Mozart: Piano Concertos 11/16	ECO	Barenboim	
ASD3000	Wagner: Siegfried Idyll, Parsifal	Philh	Boult	
ASD3001	Encores (Paganini, Kreisler, Sarasate, etc)		Perlman	
ASD3002	Holst: Planets	Previn	LSO	TASEC
ASD3003-5	see SLS 885			
ASD3006	Grace Williams: Fantasia on Welsh Nursey Tunes	LSO	Groves	
ASD3007	Bach,JS: Harpsichord Concertos Vol 3	MFO	Malcolm	
ASD3008	Ravel: Bolero/Chabrier Espana/etc	CBSO	Fremaux	
ASD3009	Mendelssohn: "The First Walpurgis Night"	LGO	Masur	
ASD3010	Shostakovich: Symphony 11	MPO	Kondrashin	Mdya
ASD3013	Rachmaninov-Respighi: 5 Etudes Tableaux		Krasnapolsky	TASEC
ASD3014	Bartok: Violin Concerto	LSO	Previn Perlman	
ASD3015	Boccherini: Cello Concerto/Handel/Paganini/Vivaldi	ECO	Tortelier	
ASD3016	Mozart: Symphonies 35/39	BPO	Karajan	
ASD3017	"The Academy in Concert" (Albinoni,Bach,Handel,etc)	ASMF	Marriner	
ASD3018	Tchaikovsky: Manfred	LSO	Previn	TASEC65
ASD3019	Rachmaninov: Prince Rostislav/Scherzo	USSR	Svetlanov	Mdya
ASD3020	Bliss: Music for Strings,Howells: Conc for String Orch	LPO	Boult	
ASD3023-4	See SLS 884			
ASD3028	Telemann/Handel	ASMF	Marriner David Munrow	
ASD3029	Shostakovich: Symphony 6/Prokofiev: Lt Kije	LSO	Previn	
ASD3032	Mozart: Piano Concertos 6/26	ECO	Barenboim	
ASD3033	Mozart: Piano Concertos 8/25	ECO	Barenboim	
ASD3034	Rodrigo: Concerto de Aranjuez	Spanish National Orch De Burgos		
ASD3035	Bernstein: Chichester Psalms/Britten	KCC	Ledger Bowman Ellis	
ASD3036	Dvorak & Tchaikovsky: Serenade for Strings	ECO	Barenboim	
ASD3037	Schumann: Frauenliebe und Leben op 42, Liederkreis op 39	Schwarzkopf Parsons (piano)		
ASD3038	Sibelius: Symphony 5/En Saga	BNSO	Berglund	
ASD3039	Bizet: Symphony in C/Roma	CBSO	Fremaux	
ASD3040-2	see SLS5001			
ASD3043	Beethoven: Piano Concerto 5	BPO	Karajan Weissenberg	
ASD3044	Trumpet Concertos by Hummel,Vivaldi,Telemann,Mozart	BPO	Karajan Andre	
ASD3045	Shostakovich: Symphony 1/Symphony 3 ("May 1st")	MPO	Kondrashin	Mdya
ASD3046	Bartok: Concerto for Orch.	BPO	Karajan	
ASD3047	Rimsky-Korsakov: Scheherazade	OdeP	Rostropovich	
ASD3050	Elgar: Triumphal March/Dream Children/Elegy/Polonia	LPO	Boult	
ASD3051	Tchaikovsky: The Nutcracker (hlts)	LSO	Previn	
ASD3053	Schumann:Piano Concerto, Intro&Allegro Appassionata op 92	LPO	Barenboim Fischer-Dieskau	
ASD3054	Prokofiev: Romeo & Juliet	LSO	Previn	
ASD3058	Saint-Saens: Cello Concerto/etc	CBSO	Fremaux Tortelier	
ASD3060	Prokofiev: Scythian Suite/Cantata "7 They Are 7"	MRSO	Rozhdestvensky	
	Shostakovich: Symphony 2	MPO	Kondrashin	Mdya
ASD3061	Rachmaninov: Trio Elegiaque in Dmin	Kogan	Svetlanov Luzanov	Mdya
ASD3062	Miaskovski: Symphony 22, Svetlanov: Festive Poem op 9	USSR	Svetlanov	Mdya
ASD3063	Nielsen: Symphony 5	BNSO	Berglund	
ASD3064	Chopin: Piano Sonatas 2, 3		Barenboim	
ASD3065	Fauré: Requiem	OdeP	Barenboim	
ASD3066	Strauss: Cello Sonata, Beethoven: Variations	Rostropovich Devetzi		
ASD3067	Tchaikovsky: Piano Concertos 1/3	NPO	Maazel Gilels	
ASD3071	Wagner: Dutchman, Rheingold, Tannhauser, Rienzi	LPO	Boult	
ASD3072	Shostakovich: Piano Quintet, 2 Pieces for String Octet, Stravinsky: 3 Pieces for String Quartet	Borodin Quartet		Mdya

ASD3073	Cherubini: Requiem	Philh	Muti	
ASD3074	Strauss,R: Don Quixote/Rosenkavalier	Dresden	Kempe	
ASD3075	Joplin: "The Easy Winners"	Perlman	Previn	
ASD3076	Bach,J.S: Violin Concertos	ECO	Barenboim Perlman	
ASD3077	Stravinsky: Dumbarton Oaks/Concerto in D/etc	LACO	Marriner	
ASD3078	Kabalevsky: Piano Concerto 3/Violin Concerto/etc	MPO	Kabalevsky	Mdya
ASD3079	Bruckner: Mass 2 in Emin	ECO	Barenboim	
ASD3080	Berlioz: Ovs: Royal Hunt&Storm/Carnival Romain	CBSO	Fremaux	
ASD3081	Shostakovich: Piano Concerto 2, Concerto for Piano and Trumpet	BNSO	Berglund Ortiz	
ASD3082	Strauss,R: 4 Last Songs etc	LSO	Previn Rothenberger	
ASD3083	Gounod: Melodies	Souzay		
ASD3084	Rameau: Ballet Music for Les Fêtes d'Hébé	ECO	Leppard	
ASD3088-9	See SLS5020			
ASD3090	Shostakovich: Symphony 14	MPO	Rostropovich Vishnevskaya	Mdya
ASD3091	"Choral Music of Schumann and Brahms"	KCC	Ledger	
ASD3092	Sibelius: 4 Legends	RPO	Groves	TASEC
ASD3093	Tchaikovsky Capr Italien/Rimsky Capr Esp	LPO	Boult	
ASD3096	John McCabe: The Chagall Windows/etc	Halle	Loughran	
ASD3097	Holst: The Wandering Scholar/Perfect Fool/etc	LSO	Previn	
ASD3101	Mussorgsky: Night on Bare Mt/Boris Godunov Khovanschina/etc	USSR	Svetlanov	Mdya
ASD3102	Russian Choral Music of the 17th & 18th Centuries	USSR Russian Chorus Yurlov		Mdya
ASD3103	Mussorgsky: Songs and Dances of Death, Songs by Tchaikovsky & Rachmaninov	Irina Arkhipova (mezzo) Wustman (piano)		Mdya
ASD3104	Stravinsky: Mavra (Comic Opera)	MRSO	Jarvi	Mdya
ASD3105	Prokofiev: Violin Sonata 1, Bartok: Violin Sonata 1	Oistrakh	Richter	Mdya
ASD3106	Taneiev: Symphony in Cmin Op 12/etc	MRSO	Rozhdestvensky	Mdya
ASD3107	"Showpieces for Symphonic Band" (Prokofiev,Tchaikovsky,etc)	USSR Symphonic Band		Mdya
ASD3108	Khachaturian: Symphony 3/ Concert Rhapsody for Cello & Orch	MPO	Kondrashin etc	Mdya
ASD3115	Prokofiev: Symphony 5	LSO	Previn	
ASD3116	Songs of the Great Patriotic War, 1939-45	Soviet Army Chorus & Band Alexandrov		
ASD3117	Orff: Carmina Burana	LSO	Previn	
ASD3118	Strauss: Don Quixote	BPO	Karajan Rostropovich	
ASD3119	Beethoven: Symphony 7	LSO	Previn	
ASD3120	Dvorak: Violin Concerto/Romance	LPO	Barenboim Perlman	
ASD3124	"Songs I Love" (Schubert, Schumann, Wolf)	Schwarzkopf		
ASD3125	Saint-Saens: Havanaise/Chausson Poeme/etc	Martinon Perlman		
ASD3126	Strauss,R: Ein Heldenleben	BPO	Karajan	
ASD3127	V Williams: Symphony 6/Conc for Oboe & Strings	BNSO	Berglund	
ASD3128	Haydn: Piano Concertos in D and G	Zurich CO De Stoutz Michelangeli		
ASD3129	Schumann: Carnaval/etc	Michelangeli		
ASD3130	Wagner: Tannhauser, Lohengrin, Tristan	BPO	Karajan	
ASD3131	Andre Previn's Music Night	LSO	Previn	TASEC73
ASD3132	Strauss,J: (Blue Danube, Eperor Waltz, etc)	BPO	Karajan	
ASD3133	Grieg&Schumann: Piano Concertos	Monte Carlo Von Matacic Richter		
ASD3134	Canteloube: More Songs of the Auvergne	Paris	De Los Angeles	
ASD3135	Tchaikovsky Suite 3	LPO	Boult	
ASD3136	Haydn: Symphonies 82,84	MFO	Menuhin	
ASD3137	Rachmaninov: Symphony 1	LSO	Previn	TASEC98
ASD3138	Saint-Saens: Symphonies in A and in F	ORTF	Martinon	
ASD3139	Delius North Country Sketches	RLPO	Groves	TASEC
ASD3140	"Music of Victor Herbert"	LSO	Beverley Sills	
ASD3141	Rimsky-Korsakov: Golden Cockerel/Prokofiev: Summer Night	BNSO	Berglund	
ASD3145	Dutilleux: Cello Conc/Lutoslawski: Cello Conc	ODP	Baudo/Rostropovich	

ASD3146	Bruckner: Symphony 2 (Novak ed)	Vienna SO	Giluini	
ASD3147	Ibert: Escales/Ouvertures de Fete/etc	FNRO	Martinon	
ASD3148	Handel: The Choice of Hercules	ASMF	Ledger	
ASD3153	Fauré: Cello Sonatas 1/2/Élégie, Serenade, Papillon	Tortelier Heidsieck		
ASD3154	Britten: 4 Sea Interludes	LSO	Previn	TASEC
ASD3155	Sibelius: Symphony 6/etc	BNSO	Berglund	
ASD3158	Mozart: Symphonies 35/41	LPO	Boult	
ASD3159	Liszt: Piano Concertos 1, 2	Philh	Atzmon Ohlsson	
ASD3160	Wagner: Mastersingers, Flying Dutchman, Parsifal	BPO	Karajan	
ASD3161-3	as SLS5018			
ASD3164	Franck: Psyche	Liège SO Paul Strauss		
ASD3165	Tchaikovsky: Choral Music	USSR	Sveshnikov	Mdya
ASD3166	Purcell: Come ye Sons of Art	EMCL	David Munrow	
ASD3167	Haydn & Beethoven: Scottish Folk Songs	Menuhin Baker		
ASD3169	Dvorak: Symphony 6	RPO	Groves	
ASD3173	Strauss,R: Alpine Symphony	Dresden SO Kempe		
ASD3174-5	as SLS5036			
ASD3176	Ibert: Symphonie Marine/Bacchanale/etc	CBSO	Fremaux	
ASD3182	Handel: 2 Double Concertos, Ov to Agrippina & Arianna	ASMF	Marriner	
ASD3184	Mendelssohn: Symphony 3/Calm Sea&Prosp Voyg	Philh	Muti	
ASD3185	Frank Martin: Polyptique, Ballade, etc	MFO	Menuhin	
ASD3186	Haydn: The Paris Symphonies (Nos 85/87)	MFO	Menuhin	
ASD3188	Respighi: Ancient Dances and Airs	ASMF	Marriner	
ASD3190	Bridge: The Sea/Summer/Cherry Ripe/etc	RLPO	Groves	
ASD3191	Mozart: Oboe Concerto K314/Sinf Conc K297b	BPO	Karajan	
ASD3193	Borodin: Sym 2/R-Korsakov: Skazka/Balakirev	BNSO	Brusilov	
ASD3197	Rachmaninov: Rhapsody on Paganini Theme Dohnanyi: Variations on a Nursery Theme	NPO	Koizumi Ortiz	
ASD3198	Mozart: Violin Conc K271a/"Adelaide" Concerto	MFO	Menuhin	
ASD3199	Sibelius: Violin Concerto	BNSO	Berglund Haendel	
ASD3200	Soviet Army Ensemble: Cavalry Song			
ASD3201	Scriabin (arr Nemtin): Universe	MPO	Kondrashin Lyubimov (piano)	
ASD3202	Schumann: Album for the Young	Weissenberg		
ASD3203	Schubert: Symphony 8/Haydn: Symphony 104	BPO	Karajan	
ASD3208	Mendelssohn: piano Conc 1/S-Saens: Piano Conc 2	RLPO	Groves Adni	
ASD3209	Lalo: Symphonie Espagnol/Cello Conc	CBSO	Fremaux Tortelier	
ASD3212	Berlioz: Ovs Le Corsair/Francs Juges/Carnival Romain	LSO	Previn	
ASD3213	Tchaikovsky: Symphony 1 ('Winter Dreams')	Philh	Muti	
ASD3214	Haydn: The Paris Symphonies (Nos 83/86)	MFO	Menuhin	
ASD3215	Ravel: Boléro, Rapsodie Espagnole, La Valse, etc	OdP	Martinon	
ASD3216	Sibelius: Symphony 1/Scenes Historiques	BNSO	Berglund	
ASD3217	Schumann: Frauenliebe und Leben/Liederkreis	Baker	Barenboim	
ASD3218	Mozart: Piano Concertos1 - 4	ECO	Barenboim	
ASD3219	Stravinsky: Duo Concertant/Suite Italienne/etc		Perlman	
ASD3222	Shostakovich: Satires, 7 Romances on Poems of Alexander Blok	Vishnevskaya Rostropovich Hoelscher (violin) Dertzi (piano)		
ASD3226	Tchaikovsky: Symphony 6	MRSO	Rozhdestvensky	Mdya
ASD3227	Khrennikov:Piano Concertos 1/2	MPO	Kondrashin	Mdya
ASD3228	Liszt:Piano Sonata in Bmin,Venezia&Napoli,Mephisto Waltz 1		Berman (piano)	
ASD3236	Arutyunyan/Kryukov/Vainberg: Trumpet Concs	Rozhdestvensky Dokshitser		Mdya
ASD3237	Miaskovsky: Violin Concerto/Ysaÿe: Ecstasy	MRSO	Dmitriev/Feigin	Mdya
ASD3238	Glazunov: Symphony 4/Poeme Lyrique/etc	MRSO	Rozhdestvensky	Mdya
ASD3254	Chopin: Preludes op 28/1-26		Barenboim	
ASD3255	Haydn: Cello Concertos in D & C	ASMF	Rostropovich	
ASD3256-7	as SLS5064			
ASD3258	Kreisler: Recital Vol 1		Perlman	

Catalog	Work	Orchestra	Conductor/Artists	Notes
ASD3259	Rachmaninov: Isle of the Dead/Symphonic Dances	LSO	Previn	
ASD3260	Wagner: Wesendonk Lieder/Brahms: Alto Rhapsody	LPO	Boult Baker	
ASD3261	Brahms: Violin Concerto	BPO	Karajan Kremer	
ASD3262	Tchaikovsky: Piano Conc 1/Liszt: Piano Conc 1	LSO	Previn Gutuirrez	
ASD3263	Berlioz: Symphonie Fantastique	ORTF	Martinon	
ASD3264	"Music for Double Bass": Rossini, Dittersdorf, Michael Haydn	ASMF	Marriner Slatford	
ASD3265	Bach: Arias from the Cantatas and Oratorios	ASMF	Marriner Janet Baker	
ASD3266	Elgar: Symphony 2	LPO	Boult	TASEC
ASD3270-2	as SLS5066			
ASD3273-6	See SLS5067			
ASD3277	Bizet: Sym in C/Maid of Perth (suite)/Patrie Ov	OdP	Barenboim	
ASD3278-82	See SLS5071			
ASD3283	"Soiree Musicale" Recital	Tortelier	Maud Tortelier	
ASD3284	Rachmaninov: The Bells	LSO	Previn	TASEC
ASD3285	Dvorak: Symphony 9	Philh	Muti	
ASD3286	V Williams: Thomas Tallis Fantasia/Conc Grosso	LPO	Boult	
ASD3287	Sibelius: Spring Song	RLPO	Groves	
ASD3288-91	as SLS5057			
ASD3292	Verdi: Adia (hlts)	Philh	Muti	[from SLS 977]
ASD3293	Vivaldi: 4 Seasons	LPO	Perlman	
ASD3294	Virgil Thomson: Plow that broke the Plains/etc	LACO	Marriner	
ASD3295	Beethoven: Violin Sonatas 'Spring' & No 4 in Amin	Richter	Kaagan	
ASD3299	Poulenc: Gloria/Piano Concerto	CBSO	Fremaux Ortiz Burrow	
ASD3300	Schubert: The Twin Brothers	BRSO	Sawallisch Fischer-Dieskau etc	
ASD3301	Mathias: This Worlde's Joie	Philh	Willcocks	
ASD3302	"Great Tenors of Today"	Bergonzi Corelli Domingo Vickers etc		
ASD3307	6 Cossack Folk Songs	Don Cossacks of Rostov		Mdya
ASD3308	Franck: Symphony in Dmin/Symphonic Variations	BNSO	Berglund	
ASD3309	Shostakovich: Music for the Film "The Gadfly"	USSRSO	Khachaturian	Mdya
ASD3310	Bruch: Vln Conc 2/Scottish Fantasy	Philh	Lopez-Cobos Perlman	
ASD3311	Offenbach: Ballet music	Rosenthal		
ASD3312	Brahms: Double Concerto	Clvlnd	Szell Rostropovich Oistrakh	
ASD3315	Balakirev: Sym 1/Rachmaninov: Caprice Bohémien	USSR	Svetlanov	Mdya
ASD3316	Purcell: Queen Mary Funeral Music/Anthems	ASMF/King's Ch/PJBE Ledger		
ASD3317	Walton: Facade/Wise Virgins Ballet Suite	CBSO	Fremaux	
ASD3318	Music for Trumpet and Organ (Bach, Albinoni, Purcell, etc)	Andre	Mitterhofer	
ASD3319	Strauss: Aus Italien	Dresden State	Kempe	
ASD3320	Mozart: Flute Concerto K313, Oboe Concerto K314, etc	OdeP	Barenboim Debost (flute) Bourgue (oboe)	
ASD3321	Bach,JS: Suite 3 in D/Couperin	SCO	Tortelier	
ASD3322	Schumann: Piano Sonatas op 11, op 22		Berman	
ASD3325	Dvorak: Symphony 7	LPO	Giulini	
ASD3326	Mozart: Symphonies 25/29	Philh	Muti	
ASD3327	Respighi: The Birds/etc	ASMF	Marriner	
ASD3328	Haydn: Symphonies 88/96	LSO	Previn	
ASD3329	Mozart: Oboe Quartet K370, Flute Quartet K285, Piano Quartet K478, etc	Menuhin	Gendron etc	
ASD3330	Elgar: Symphony 1	LPO	Boult	
ASD3331-3	as SLS5079			
ASD3334	Bloch: Schelomo/Hebrew Rhapsody	ONDF	Bernstein Rostropovich	TAS58/132++
ASD3337	Mozart: Piano Concerto K466/Double Concerto	LSO	Previn Lupu	
ASD3338	Andre Previn's Muisc Night II	LSO	Previn	
ASD3339	Balakirev: Piano Conc Op 1/Medtner: Piano Conc 1	MRSO	Dmitriev	Mdya
ASD3340	Sibelius: Symphony 4/The Bard	BNSO	Berglund	
ASD3341	"Rule Britannia!"	RLPO	Groves	
ASD3342	Bliss: Cello Conc/Suite from Miracle in the Gorbals	BNSO	Berglund	

ASD3343	Delius: Violin Concerto/Double Concerto	RPO	Menuhin Tortelier	
ASD3345	Elgar: Coronation Ode	Philh	Ledger	
ASD3346	Kreisler: Recital Vol 2	Perlman		
ASD3347	Khachaturian: Spartacus & Gayaneh Ballets	LSO	Khachaturian	
ASD3348	Walton: Gloria/Te Deum/Crown Imperial	CBSO	Fremaux	
ASD3349-51 as SLS5083				
ASD3352	Tartini/Corelli: Violin Sonatas	Haendel Parsons		
ASD3353	Arnold: Symphony 2/8 English Dances	BNSO	Groves	
ASD3354	Wagner: Tristan & Isolde (hlts)	BPO	Karajan	[from SLS 963]
ASD3355-6 as SLS5086				
ASD3357	"Improvisations"	Menuhin Ravi Shankar Jean-Pierre Rampal		
ASD3358	Nielsen: Hymnus Amoris Op 12/Sleep Op 18	Danish Radio SO/Woldike		
ASD3363	Glazunov: Symphony 5/Taneyev: Symphony 2	MRSO	Fedoseyev	Mdya
ASD3364	Beethoven: Piano Sonatas 1 Op 2/1, 7 Op 10/3	Richter		
ASD3365	Mendelssohn: Symphony 4, Schumann: Symphony 4	Philh	Muti	
ASD3366	Verdi: Overtures Force of Destiny,Luisa Miller,Vespers,etc	Philh	Muti	
ASD3367	Glazunov: Piano Concerto 1, Yardumian: Passacaglia, Recitative & Fugue	BNSO	Berglund Ogdon	
ASD3368	Bartok: Sonata/Bloch: 2 Suites	Menuhin		
ASD3369	Rachmaninov: Symphony 3	LSO	Previn	
ASD3370	Tchaikovsky: Sleeping Beauty	LSO	Previn	
ASD3371	Dvorak: Piano Concerto	Bav SO	Kleiber Richter	
ASD3372	Respighi: Pines of Rome, Fountains of Rome	LSO	Gardelli	
ASD3373	Mozart: "Coronation" Mass	BRSO	Jochum Moser Fischer-Dieskau	
ASD3374	Sibelius: Finlandia/Tapiola/En Saga/Tuonela	BPO	Karajan	
ASD3375	Mozart: Eine Kleine Nachtmusik/etc	ASMF	Marriner	
ASD3376	Beethoven: Symphony 3/Egmont Ov	LSO	Jochum	
ASD3377	Mendelssohn: A Midsummer Night's Dream	LSO	Previn	
ASD3381	Shostakovich: New Babylon (Film Music), Hamlet Suite	MPO	Rozhdestvensky	Mdya
ASD3382	Bruckner: Symphony 9	CSO	Giulini	
ASD3383	Glazunov: Symphony 6/Saxophone Concerto	MRSO	Fedoseyev	Mdya
ASD3384	Paganini: 24 Caprices	Perlman		
ASD3385	Brahms: Violin Concerto	CSO	Giulini Perlman	
ASD3388	Elgar: Pomp & Circumstance Marches	LPO	Boult	
ASD3389	Berlioz: Harold in Italy	FNRO	Bernstein McInnes (viola)	
ASD3390-2 as SLS5098				
ASD3393	'Monteverdi's Contemporaries'	EMCL	Munrow	
ASD3394	Trumpet Concertos by Albinoni, Handel, Telemann	ECO	Mackerras André	
ASD3395	Handel: Music for Royal Fireworks (orig version)	LSO	Mackerras	
ASD3396	Scriabin: Piano Sonatas 1 & 3	Lazar Berman		Mdya
ASD3397	Berlioz: Symphonie Fantastique	ONDF	Bernstein	
ASD3398	'Kamarinskaya'	Soviet Army Song and Dance Ensemble		
ASD3399	Strauss,R: Violin Concerto/Burleske	Dresden Kempe Hoelscher (vln) Frager (pno)		
ASD3403-6 as SLS5096				
ASD3407	Dvorak: New World Symphony/Ma Vlast	BPO	Karajan	
ASD3408	Goldmark: Violin Concerto/Sarasate	LSO	Previn Perlman	
ASD3409	Sibelius: Symphony 5/En Saga	BPO	Karajan	
ASD3410-3 as SLS5102				
ASD3414	Sibelius: Symphony 2	Pittsburgh SO Previn		
ASD3415	Rodrigo: Concierto de Aranjuez/etc	LSO	Previn Romero	
ASD3416	Bliss: A Colour Symphony/Things to Come	RPO	Groves	
ASD3417	Elgar: Enigma Variations, Britten: Purcell Vns	RLPO	Groves	
ASD3418	Vivaldi: Magnificat/Gloria	Philh	Muti	
ASD3419-20 as SLS5104				

ASD3421	Rimsky-Korsakov: Capriccio Espagnol, Mussorgsky,Borodin,Glinka	OdP Rostropovich	
ASD3425	Brahms: Violin Sonatas 1/2	D Oistrakh Richter	
ASD3426	Mozart: Serenade K 361	ECO Barenboim	
ASD3429	Villa-Lobos: Bachianas Brasileiras No 3/etc	Philh Ashkenazy Ortiz	
ASD3430	"Duets for 2 Violins"	Perlman Zukerman	
ASD3431	Ravel: Bolero/Debussy: La Mer/Faun Prelude	BPO Karajan	
ASD3432-4	See SLS5092		
ASD3435	Holst: Hymn of Jesus/Choral Hymns/etc	LSO Groves	
ASD3436	Recital (Mussorgsky,Shostakovich,Tchaikovsky,etc)	Vishnevskaya Rostropovich	
ASD3437-9	as SLS5108		
ASD3440	Shostakovich: Symphony 4	CSO Previn	
ASD3443	Shostakovich: Symphony 5	CSO Previn	
ASD3444	Milhaud: La Creation du Monde/Le Boeuf sur le toit	ONDF Bernstein	
ASD3447	Schedrin:Not Love Alone, & Petrov:Creation of the World	MPO Kondrashin	Mdya
ASD3448	St-Saens: Carnival of the Animals/Septet Op 65	Ensemble Béroff Collard	
ASD3449	Tchaikovsky: Symphony 3	Philh Muti	
ASD3450	"Music for Holy Week"	KCC Ledger	
ASD3451	Haydn: The 7 Last Words	ASMF Marriner	
ASD3452	Dvorak: Cello Concerto/St-Saens: Cello Concerto 1	Philh Giulini Rostropovich	
ASD3453	"Music for Trumpet & Organ"	André Parker-Smith	
ASD3454	"Guillaume de Machaut and his Age"	EMCL Munrow	
ASD3455	Chausson: Poeme de L'Amour et de La Mer/etc	LSO Previn Baker	
ASD3456	Beethoven: Symphony 6	LPO Boult	
ASD3457	Rachmaninov: Piano Concerto 2/3 Preludes	RPO Fedoseyev Alexeev	
ASD3458	Kodaly: Sonata for Cello/Tortelier: Suite in Dmin	Tortelier	
ASD3459	Operatic Arias (Cilea, Mascagni, St-Saens, Bizet)	Philh Stapleton Obraztsova (mezzo)	
ASD3460	Glazunov: Suite: "From the Middle Ages" Characteristic Suite	MRSO Fedoseyev	Mdya
ASD3461-3	as SLS5111		
ASD3464	Rossini: String Sonatas 2-5	Polish CO Maksymiuk	
ASD3465	Mozart: Divertimento in F for 2 Horns & Strings K247, 2 Divertimenti for Strings K137,K138 ("Salzburg Symphonies")	Polish CO Maksymiuk	
ASD3480	D'Indy: Symphony on a French Mt Song, St-Saens: Piano Concerto 5 ("Egyptian")	OdP Baudo Ciccolini	
ASD3481	Shostakovich: Symphony 14	Leningrad CO Gozman Nestorenko (bass) Dolukhanova (mezzo)	
ASD3482	Charpentier: Te Deum/Magnificat	ASMF/King's Ch Ledger	
ASD3483	Britten: Violin Concerto/Walton: Violin Concerto	BNSO Berglund Haendel	
ASD3484	Beethoven: Symphony 5/Fidelio Ov	LSO Jochum	
ASD3485	Sibelius: Symphony 2/Tapiola	BPO Karajan	
ASD3486	Brian Symphonies 8/9	RLPO Groves	TASEC
ASD3487	Arnold: Conc for flute & strings/etc	Philh Dilkes	
ASD3488	Tchaikovsky: Symphony 2/Romeo & Juliet	Philh Muti	
ASD3489	Poulenc: Concerto for Organ, Strings & Timpani Concert Champêtre	LSO Previn Preston	
ASD3490	Rachmaninov: Francesca da Rimini	Bolshoi Ermler Atlantov Nestorenko	Mdya
ASD3491	Tchaikovsky: Swan Lake (hlts)	LSO Previn	[from SLS5070]
ASD3492	Viotti: Violin Concertos 16 & 22	MFO Menuhin	
ASD3493-5	as SLS5119		
ASD3496	Berlioz: Symphonie Fantastique	LSO Previn	
ASD3497	Sibelius: Symphony 2	BnSO Berglund	
ASD3498	Schubert: Rosamunde	Stkpl Dresden Boskovsky	
ASD3499	Wagner: Die Walkure (Wotan's Farewell), Parsifal (Amfortas), Flying Dutchman	BRSO Kubelik Fischer-Dieskau	
ASD3500	Lehar: The Merry Widow (hlts)	New York City Opera Rudel Sills Titus	
ASD3501	Fauré: Requiem.	CBSO Fremaux Burrowes Cook	
ASD3502	Kalinnikov: Symphony 1/Tchaikovsky: Ov in C/etc	USSR Svetlanov	Mdya

ASD3503	Balakirev: Symphony 2/Ciurlionis Sym Poem/etc	MRSO	Rozhdestvensky	Mdya
ASD3504	Glazunov: Symphony 7/Oriental Rhapsody	MRSO	Fedoseyev	Mdya
ASD3505	Glazunov: Piano Concertos 1/2/Arensky	MRSO	Nikolaevsky	Mdya
ASD3506	Tchaikovsky: Concert Fantasy	USSR	Zhukov	
	R-Korsakov: Piano Concerto	MRSO	Rozhdestvensky	Mdya
ASD3513	"Music from the Slavonic Orthodox Liturgy"	Choir of the Alexander Nevsky Cathedral Sofia & Boris Christoff		
ASD3514	Rimsky-Korsakov: May Night Overture/Glazunov: Valse			
	Sibelius: Karelia/etc	BNSO	Berglund	
ASD3515	Tchaikovsky: Symphony 6	LPO	Rostropovich	
ASD3520	Shostakovich: Symphony 12/5 Fragments	MPO	Kondrashin	Mdya
ASD3521	Grieg: Piano Concerto, Schumann: Piano Concerto	LPO	Tennstedt Gutiérrez	
ASD3535	Maria Callas - The Legend: The Unreleased recordings			
	(Verdi: Ballo, Corsaro, Trovatore, Bellini: Sonnambula)		Callas	
ASD3541	Mahler: Symphony 1	LPO	Tennstedt	
ASD3542	Ketelbey: Orch Works (In a Monastery Garden, etc)	Philh	Lanchberry	
ASD3543	Beethoven: Piano Concerto 3/Andante Favori in F	Philh	Muti Richter	
ASD3544	Bach,J.C: Sinfonias Op 6/3, Op 9/2, Op 18/2&4	BNSO	Montgomery Pinnock	
ASD3545	"Sea Fever" (Songs and Shanties)	Robert Lloyd		
ASD3546	Franck: Piano Quintet	Medici Quartet Ortiz		
ASD3547	Prokofiev: Sonata for 2 Vlns op 56,Shostakovich: Vln Sonata op 134,			
	Schnitke: Prelude to the Memory of Dmitri Shostakovich	Kremer & Grindenko (violins) Gavrilov (piano)		
ASD3548	Gounod: Faust Ballet Music/Massenet: Le Cid/Herold: Zampa	Bolshoi	Rozhdestvensky	Mdya
ASD3549	Rimsky-Korsakov: Tale of Tsar Saltan Suite			
	Pan Voevoda Suite/Procession of the Nobles	MRSO	Ivanov	Mdya
ASD3550	"A Russian Folk Festival"	Various		
ASD3551	Brahms: Piano Sonatas 3,5/2 Rhapsodies Op 79	Ohlsson		
ASD3552	Chopin: 4 Ballades,Polonaise 6,Fantaisie-Impromptu	Cristina Ortiz		
ASD3553	Mozart: Oboe Concertos K314, K294b	Prague CO Kersjes De Vries		
ASD3554	Vivaldi: Concertos for Flute and Recorders	Prague CO Hans-Martin Linde		
ASD3555	Vieuxtemps: Violin Concertos 4/5	Paris	Barenboim Perlman	
ASD3556	Prokofiev: Symphonies 1/7	LSO	Previn	
ASD3557	"Continental Collection" (German and Spanish Part Songs)	Kings Singers		
ASD3559	Palestrina: Missa Hodie Christus Natus Est, 6 Motets	KCC	Ledger	
ASD3566	Schubert: Arpeggione Sonata, Schumann: Fantasiestucke,			
	Chopin: Polonaise Brillante Op 3	Shafran	Gotlieb	
ASD3567	Tchaikovsky: Romeo & Juliet Overture			
	Francesca da Rimini Fantasy	LPO	Rostropovich	
ASD3568-9	as SLS5134			
ASD3571	Prokofiev: Piano Concerto 1			
	Ravel: Concerto for the Left Hand	LSO	Rattle Gavrilov	
ASD3583	Beethoven: Symphony 6	LSO	Jochum	
ASD3584	Highlights from the Tchaikovsky ballets	LSO	Previn Haendel	
ASD3587-9	as SLS5140			
ASD3595	Trumpet Concertos by Bach,Haydn,Telemann	Franz Liszt CO Mackerras André		
ASD3596	Mozart: Piano Concertos K467, K488	LPO	Eschenbach	
ASD3597	Handel: Water Music	Prague CO Mackerras		
ASD3598	Elgar: Violin Concerto	LPO	Boult Haendel	
ASD3599	Field: Nocturnes 1-6, 9,10, 12,13,17	Adni		
ASD3600	Ravel: Gaspard de la Nuit/Balakirev: Islamey/etc	Gavrilov		
ASD3601	Glazunov: The Seasons	Philh	Svetlanov	
ASD3604	Stravinsky: Pulcinella Suites 1 & 2	Northern Sinfonia Rattle		
ASD3605	Brahms: 4 Serious Songs/etc	Previn	Baker	
ASD3606	Rachmaninov: Symphony 2 (complete version)	RPO	Temirkanov	
ASD3608	Britten: The Little Sweep	Medici Quartet Ledger		
ASD3609	Oboe Concertos (Vivaldi, Albinoni, Telemann, Hummel, etc)	BNSO	Wangenheim Williams (oboe)	
ASD3612	Brahms: 2 Sonatas for Cello/Piano	Tortelier Pau		
ASD3613-4	as SLS5144			

ASD3620	Schubert: Piano Sonata in G D894	Christian Zacharias	
ASD3621	The Art of Courtly Love	EMCL Munrow	
ASD3622	Schubert: Piano Sonata D960	Lazar Berman	
ASD3625-6	as SLS5148		
ASD3627	Beethoven: Symphony 4/Leonora 3 Ov	LSO Jochum	
ASD3628	Mendelssohn: Conc for Vln,Piano&Strings/Sym 12	BFCO Menuhin Hephzibah Menuhin	
ASD3629	Sibelius: Symphony 3/Pelleas	BNSO Berglund	
ASD3630	Italian Baroque Concertos	BNSO	
ASD3631	Telemann: Water Music, Overtures	Prague CO Bjorlin	
ASD3633	Orch Works (Janacek, Panufnik, Webern, Ives, Bach, etc)	Various Russian Orchestras Rozhdestvensky	
ASD3636-8	as SLS5152		
ASD3639	Mozart: Violin Concertos K211, K219	ECO Spivakov	
ASD3640	Grieg: Peer Gynt	StDr Blomstedt	
ASD3641	Tchaikovsky: Symphony 5	LPO Rostropovich	
ASD3642	Arensky: Symphony 1/Suite 1	MRSO Serov	Mdya
ASD3644	Sibelius: 4 Legends	Phild Ormandy	
ASD3645	Mussorgsky: Pictures at an Exhibition, Stravinsky: Firebird St	Phild Muti	
ASD3646	Beethoven Symphony 7	Phild Muti	
ASD3647	Tchaikovsky: Symphony 4	LPO Rostropovich	
ASD3648	Schumann: Symphony 2/etc	Philh Muti	
ASD3649	Holst: The Planets	LPO Boult	
ASD3650	Britten: Spring Symphony	LSO Previn	
ASD3651	Grainger: "Grainger on the Shore"	English Sinfonietta Dilkes	
ASD3652	Dvorak: Cello Concerto	LSO Previn Tortelier	
ASD3553-4	as SLS5153		
ASD3655	Bartok: Music for Strings,Perc&Celesta Miraculous Mandarin Suite	Phild Ormandy	
ASD3656	"Victoria de Los Angeles in Concert"	De Los Angeles Gerald Moore	
ASD3660	Balakirev: Tamar, Glazunov: Stenka Razin, Rachmaninov	USSR Svetlanov	
ASD3670	Brahms: Symphony 1	LPO Jochum	
ASD3671	Sibelius: Symphonies 3/7	MRSO Rozhdestvensky	Mdya
ASD3672	Sibelius: Symphony 1/Rakastava	MRSO Rozhdestvensky	Mdya
ASD3674	Saint-Saens: Symphony 3	FNRO Martinon	
ASD3675	Beethoven: Violin Sonatas Op 30/3, Op 47 (Kreutzer)	Zukerman Barenboim	
ASD3676	Schubert: String Quintet in C D956	Smetana Quartet	
ASD3687	Bliss: Adam Zero/Checkmate	RLPO Handley	
ASD3688	Delius: La Calinda/5 Little Pieces/etc	BNSO Fenby	
ASD3690	Vivaldi: Violin Concertos	Prague CO Vajnar	
ASD3694	Dvorak: String Qt 12, Smetana: String Qt 1	Medici Qt	
ASD3695	Beethoven: Piano Sonatas Moonlight, Pathetique, Funeral March	Eschenbach	
ASD3696	Schumann: Symphony 3/etc	Philh Muti	
ASD3698	Telemann: "Paris" Quartets 7-9	Linde, Dael, Savall, Curtis	
ASD3699	Sibelius: Symphony 4/Belshazzar's Feast/etc	MRSO Rozhdestvensky	Mdya
ASD3700	Mussorgsky: Song Cycle – Sunless, Shostakovich: Songs	Nesterenko (bass) Krainev/Shenderovich (piano)	
ASD3701-4	as SLS5154		
ASD3705	Stravinsky: Petruchka/Ravel: Daphnis&Chloe St 2	LenSO Temirkanov	Mdya
ASD3706	Shostakovich: Symphonies 6/9	USSR Svetlanov	Mdya
ASD3707	Anton Rubinstein: Piano Concerto 4 op 70, Scriabin: Piano Concerto	MRSO Serov Bunin (pno) Estonia SO Järvi Zhukov (pno)	Mdya
ASD3709	Balakirev: Islamey/Russia/Ovs on 3 Russian Songs Glinka: Ivan Susanin Ov/etc	USSR Svetlanov	Mdya
ASD3710	Rimsky-Korsakov: Golden Cockerel/Tsar Saltan/Mlada Invisible City of Kitezh/May Night Ov	USSR Svetlanov	Mdya
ASD3711	Tchaikovsky: Suite 4 ("Mozartiana")/Arensky: Suite 2	MRSO Maxim Shostakovich	Mdya
ASD3712	Gretchaninov: Symphony 4/Glinka/Hummel	MRSO Zuraitis	Mdya

ASD3713	Shostakovich: Concerto for Piano,Trumpet & Strings, Prokofiev: Piano Concerto 3	MRSO	Shostakovich Krainev	Mdya
ASD3714	Liszt: Tasso, Wevber: Turandot, Berlioz: Benvenuto Cellini, Le Corsaire	MRSO	Rozhdestvensky	Mdya
ASD3715	Prokofiev: Piano Sonata op 83, Schedrin: Anna karenina, etc		Mikhail Pletnyev (piano)	
ASD3716	"Spanish Soul" (Albeniz,Granados,Falla,Turina)		Ortiz (Piano)	
ASD3717	Tchaikovsky: Symphony 5	Philh	Muti	
ASD3723	Mozart: Requiem	Philh	Giulini	
ASD3724	Schumann: Symphony 3/Konzertstuck for Orch & 4 Horns	BPO	Tennstedt	
ASD3725	Parry: Symphony 5/Sym varns	LPO	Boult	
ASD3726	Tchaikovsky: Violin Concerto/Sernade Melancolique	Phild	Ormandy Perlman	
ASD3728	Schumann: Cello Concerto/Bruch: Kol Nidrei	RPO	Tortelier	
ASD3729	Ravel: Piano Trio Amin/St-Saens: Piano Trio Op 18		Tortelier YP Tortelier De la Pau	
ASD3730	Tchaikovsky : Manfred	LPO	Rostropovich	
ASD3732	Bloch: Concerto Grosso/Martin	ASMF	Marriner	
ASD3735-6	as SLS5169			
ASD3737-9	as SLS5175			
ASD3743	Hindemith: Concert Music for Strings&Brass Symphonic Metamorphoses on themes by Weber	Phild	Ormandy	
ASD3744	"Romantic Music for Flute and Orchstra"	Philh	Dilkes Solum (flute)	
ASD3760	Trumpet Concertos by Haydn, Telemann, Albinoni, etc	LPO	Lopez-Cobos André	
ASD3761	Bizet: L'Arlesienne St 2, Chabrier: Espana, Gounod: Faust, Berlioz: Hungarian Dance	BPO	Karajan	
ASD3762	Brahms: Piano Concerto 1	LSO	Tennstedt Ohlsson	
ASD3763	Mendelssohn: Symphony 4 (Italian)/Hebrides Ov/etc	LSO	Previn	
ASD3764	"Choral Evensong for Ascension Day"	KCC	Ledger	
ASD3769-71	as SLS5176			
ASD3774	Horn Concertos by Michael and Joseph Haydn	ECO	Constable Tuckwell (horn)	
ASD3775	Dvorak: Symphony 8/Slavonic Dance in Gmin	BPO	Karajan	
ASD3776	Mozart: Piano Concertos K271, K595	LPO	Eschenbach (cond & piano)	
ASD3777	Delius: Incidental Music to Hassan	BNSO	Handley	
ASD3778	A Festival of Carols from King's	KCC	Ledger	
ASD3779	Rimsky-Korsakov: Scheherazade	LSO	Svetlanov	
ASD3780	Sibelius: Symphonies 5/6	MRSO	Rozhdestvensky	
ASD3781	Schumann: Symphony 1/Mendelssohn: Symphony 5	Philh	Muti	
ASD3783	Mahler: Symphony 4	PTSO	Previn Ameling	
ASD3785	Bravissima! Recital (Dvorak, Mendelssohn, Bartok)	Haendel	Parsons (piano)	
ASD3786	Dvorak: Symphony 9	LPO	Rostropovich	
ASD3797	"British Music for Film & TV"	CBSO/Dods		
ASD3798	"The Schwarzkopf Xmas Album"		Mackerras Schwarzkopf	
ASD3801	"Mad Scenes from Anna Bolena, Hamlet, Il Pirata"	Philh	Rescigno Callas	
ASD3802	Prokofiev: Piano Sonata 8/Romeo&Juliet Suite	Gavrilov		
ASD3804	Debussy: Images, Prelude de l'Apres Midi d'un Faun	LSO	Previn	(Digital)
ASD3807	Stravinsky: Rite of Spring	Phild	Muti	SM69/154++
ASD3810	Encores Vol 2 (Wieniawski,Stravinsky,Debussy,etc)	Perlman		
ASD3811	Verdi: Opera Choruses (Trovatore, Macbeth, Nabucco, etc)		Welsh Nat Op Armstrong	
ASD3814	Schubert: Grand Duo D812, etc		Eschenbach Franz (piano duet)	
ASD3816	Tchaikovsky: Symphony 4	Philh	Muti	
ASD3817	"Callas Portrays Verdi Heroines"	Philh	Rescigno Callas	
ASD3818	Tchaikovsky: Piano Concerto 1	Philh	Muti Gavrilov	
ASD3820	Elgar & V-Williams: Violin Sonatas		Menuhin Hephzibah Menuhin	
ASD3823	Arnold: Symphony 1/Scottish Dances	BNSO	Arnold	
ASD3825	Bruckner: Symphony 1	Dresden	Jochum	
ASD3839	Haydn: Symphonies 94/104	PTSO	Previn	
ASD3842	Avison: 6 Concertos	BNSO	Thomas	
ASD3844	Kern (arr Bennett): Song Transcriptions		Instrumental Ensemble cond Richardson Tuckwell (horn)	

Catalog	Work	Orchestra	Conductor/Artists	Notes
ASD3845	Ravel: Piano Concs Gmaj/Dmaj - Left Hand	ONDF	Maazel Collard	
ASD3854	Beethoven: Symphony 6	Philh	Muti	
ASD3855	Shostakovich: Symphony 5/Festival Ov	USSR	Svetlanov	Mdya
ASD3857	Elgar: Enigma variations	LSO	Previn	
ASD3858	Mozart: Song Recital		Schwarzkopf Gieseking	
ASD3859	Mozart: Sinfonia Concertante K364, Violin Concerto K216	ECO	Spivakov Bashmet (viola)	
ASD3860	Schubert: Symphonies 3, 5	BPO	Karajan	
ASD3861	Prokofiev: Sonata for 2 violins Op 56, Shostakovich: 3 Vln Duets, Moszkowski		Perlman Zukerman	
ASD3862	"Music from the Movies" (Williams, Rozsa, Gershwin, etc)	BNSO	Alwyn	
ASD3864	Delius: The 3 Violin Sonatas		Menuhin Fenby	
ASD3865	"Victorian Collection"		Kings Singers	
ASD3868	Arnold: Concerto for Flute & Strings, Flute Concerto 2, Serenade for Small Orch, Sinfonietta 3	BNSO	Thomas Adeney	
ASD3869	Dvorak: Symphony 7	LPO	Rostropovich	
ASD3871	Prokofiev: Piano Concertos 2 in Gmin, 3 in C	RPO	Temirkanov Alexeev	
ASD3872	Rachmaninov: Piano Concerto 2, Prokofiev: Classical Symphony	USSR	Svetlanov Petrov	Mdya
ASD3875	Bliss: Meditations on a Theme of John Blow/etc	CBSO	Handley	
ASD3878	Bliss: John Blow/Discourse/Edinburgh Ov	CBSO	Handley	
ASD3879	Miaskovsky: Symphony 11/2 Pieces for String Orch	MRSO	Dudarova	Mdya
ASD3880	Shostakovich: The Gamblers	Leningrad PO	Rozhdestvensky	Mdya
ASD3882	Schubert: String Quartet D887		Alban Berg Quartet	
ASD3888	Martinu: Symphony 4/Sinfonietta La Jolla	RLPO	Weller	
ASD3891	Goldmark: Rustic Wedding Symphony	Pittsburgh SO	Previn	
ASD3894	Mendelssohn & Schumann: Piano Trios		Tortelier Chung Previn	
ASD3896	V Williams: On Wenlock Edge, Elgar, Butterworth	CBSO	Handley	
ASD3897	Strauss,R: Also Sprach Zarathustra	Phild	Ormandy	(Digital)
ASD3899	Violin Concertos by Vivaldi, Couperin, CPE Bach	ECO	Zukerman Harrell	
ASD3900	Orff: Carmina Burana	Phild	Muti	
ASD3901	Tchaikovsky: Symphony 6	Philh	Muti	
ASD3902	Chabrier: Espana, Falla: 3 Cornered Hat, Ravel	Phild	Muti	(Digital)
ASD3903	Rossini Overtures (Barber of Seville,Tell,etc)	Philh	Muti	
ASD3904	V Williams: Symphony 4/Lark Ascending	RPO	Berglund	
ASD3905	Brahms: Double Concerto	Ccgbw	Haitink Perlman Rostropovich	
ASD3906	Liszt: Songs		Baker Parsons	
ASD3907	Procession with Carols upon Advent Sunday	KCC	Ledger	(Digital)
ASD3908	"Favourite Opera Duets"		Callas,Ludwig,Pavarotti, etc	
ASD3910	"The Spanish Album" (Sarasate,Falla,Granados)		Perlman	
ASD3911	Shostakovich Symphony 13	LSO	Previn Petkov	
ASD3912	Ravel: Bolero/Daphnis & Chloe/Pavanne	LSO	Previn	
ASD3913	Strauss,R: Don Juan, Till Eulenspiegel, Tod und Verklarung	VPO	Previn	(Digital)
ASD3914	Vivaldi: Cello Concertos, Violin&Cello Concertos	LMP	Tortelier	
ASD3915	Great Sopranos of our time		Various artists	
ASD3916	Oboe Quartets (Mozart, Bach, Stamitz, etc)		Perlman Zukerman Harrell (cello) Still (oboe)	
ASD3933	Sibelius: Violin Concerto	LSO	Previn Perlman	
ASD3943	Concert: Wagner/Grieg/Fauré	ASMF	Marriner	(Digital)
ASD3948	Bach,JS: Orch Suite2, Telemann: Suite in Amin	LACO	Schwarz	(Digital)
ASD3952	Elgar: The Light of Life	RLPO	Groves	
ASD3953	Holst: A Somerset Rhapsody/VW Wasps	BNSI	Del Mar	
ASD3955	Palestrina: Missa Ave Maria	KCC	Ledger	(Digital)
ASD3956	Tchaikovsky: 1812 Ov, Serenade for Strings			(Digital)
ASD3958-9	See SLS5206			
ASD3960	Grieg: Piano Concerto/Franck:Les Djinns	Philh	Ashkenazy Ortiz	
ASD3963	Mendelssohn: Symphony 4, Schumann: Symphony 4	BPO	Tennstedt	(Digital)
ASD3964	Vivaldi: The Four Seasons	Camerata	Menuhin	(Digital)

ASD3965	"A Different Kind of Blues" (8 original jazz compositions)	Perlman Previn Shelley Manne etc	(Digital)	
ASD3973	Brahms: Violin Concerto	North German RSO Tennstedt Hoelscher	(Digital)	
ASD3979	Verdi Choruses (Nabucco, Traviata, Aida, Macbeth, etc)	Muti		
ASD3980	Kreisler: Recital Vol 3	Perlman		
ASD3981	"Songs for Sunday"	Baker Ledger (organ)		
ASD3982	Gershwin: Porgy & Bess Symphonic Picture, Cuban Ov, etc	LSO Previn Ortiz (piano)	(Digital)	
ASD3983	Verdi: Aida (hlts)	VPO Karajan Carreras Freni etc		
ASD3984	Aria Recital (Rossini, Donizetti)	PCO Rescigno Callas		
ASD3985	Wagner: The Ring (orch hlts)	BPO Tennstedt	(Digital)	
ASD3993	Glazunov: Symphony 3	MRSO Fedoseyev		Mdya
ASD3994	Organ Recital (Franck, Liszt)	Parker-Smith	(Digital)	
ASD4005	Rachmaninov: The Bells op 35	USSR Svetlanov		
ASD4006	Moussorgsky: Boris Godunov (hlts)	Bolshoi Simonov Nesterenko (bass)		
ASD4008	Punto: 4 Horn Concertos	ASMF Marriner Tuckwell		
ASD4009	Bruckner: Symphony 3	DrSt Jochum		
ASD4011	Bartok: 44 Duos for 2 Violins	Perlman Zukerman	(Pressed in Germany)	
ASD4012	Schubert: Rosamunde (hlts)	Berlin RIAS Kuhn	(Digital)	
ASD4013	Mozart: Serenade 7 (Haffner), March K249	Berlin RIAS Kuhn	(Digital)	
ASD4014	Mozart: Symphonies 21, 31	Berlin RIAS Kuhn	(Digital)	
ASD4015	"Ballets from Verdi Operas"	Philh Muti		
ASD4022	Portrait of Renata Scotto	Renata Scotto		
ASD4030	Four Trumpet Concertos (Albinoni,Handel,Barsanti,etc)	Wurttemburg CO Faerber André	(Digital)	
ASD4031	"A portrait of Placido Domingo"	Domingo		
ASD4032	Schubert: Trout Quintet	Borodin Quartet Richter	(Digital)	
ASD4036	Tchaikovsky: Piano Trio	Perlman Ashkenazy Harrell		
ASD4039	Brahms: Violin Sonatas Op 120/1, Op 120/2	Menuhin Kentner		
ASD4041	Strauss,J: Waltzes and Polkas	Vienna Strauss Orch Boskovsky	(Digital)	
ASD4046	Shostakovich: Violin Concerto 1/Cello Concerto 1	Philh Oistrakh/BNSO Berglund Tortelier		
ASD4047	Holst: The Planets	Philh Rattle	(Digital)	
ASD4054	Schubert: Songs (Die Forelle,An die Musik,Sylvia,etc)	Baker Parsons		
ASD4055	Bach,JS: Cantatas 11, 34	ECO Ledger		
ASD4056	Mozart: Flute Concertos K313, K314, Andante K315	Hanoverian Orch/Solum		
ASD4058	Dvorak: Symphony 8 op 88, Scherzo Capriccioso	LPO Rostropovitch		
ASD4059	Beethoven: Violin Concerto	Philh Giulini Perlman	(Digital)	
ASD4060	Sibelius: Symphony 2	BPO Karajan	(Digital)	
ASD4061	Elgar: From the Bavarian Highlands/V Williams	BNSO Del Mar		
ASD4066	Janacek: Glagolitic mass	CBSO Rattle	(Digital)	
ASD4067	Poulenc: Orch Works (Les Biches, etc)	Philh Pretre		
ASD4068	Prokofiev: Romeo & Juliet (hlts)	Phild Muti	(Digital)	
ASD4069	Stravinsky: Petrushka	Phild Muti	(Digital)	
ASD4070	Mendelssohn: Songs	Baker Parsons (piano)	(Digital)	
ASD4071	Cherubini: Requiem in Cmin	Philh Muti	(Digital)	
ASD4072	Operatic Ovs and Intermezzi	BPO Karajan	(Digital)	
ASD4073	Britten: Gloriana Symphonic Suite, Prince of Pagodas Prelude & Dances	BNSO Segal	(Digital)	
ASD4075	Schubert: Arpeggione Sonata, Beethoven : Cello Sonata op 69	Tortelier de la Pau (piano)	(Digital)	
ASD4079	Brahms: Liebeslieder op 52a, 16 Waltzes op 39, Vns op 23	Beroff Collard (pianos)		
ASD4080	Bruckner: Symphony 6	DrSt Jochum	(Pressed in Germany)	
ASD4081	Bruckner: Symphony 2	DrSt Jochum	(Pressed in Germany)	
ASD4082	Rachmaninov: Piano Concerto 3	FNRO Bernstein Weissenberg		
ASD4086	Duruflé: Requiem Op 9/Two Motets	KCC Baker Ledger	(Digital)	
ASD4089	V Williams: Toward the Unknown Region, Norfolk Rhapsody 1, Tallis Fantasia, Dives & lazarus	CBSO Del Mar	(Digital)	
ASD4090	French & Italian Opera Arias (Lakme, Huguenots, etc)	Munich Radio Orch Kuhn	(Digital)	
ASD4091	Walton: Symphony 1	Philh Haitink	(Digital)	
ASD4092	"Sing We and Chant it!" (English Madrigals)	The Kings Singers	(Digital)	

ASD4093	Organ Voluntaries	Organ of Kings Cambridge Ledger	(Digital)	
ASD4097	Sibelius: Symphony 1, Karelia Suite	BPO Karajan	(Digital)	
ASD4098	Prokofiev: Violin Concertos 1, 2	BBCSO Rozhdestvensky Perlman	(Digital)	
ASD4099	Ravel: Daphnis and Chloe	LSO Previn	(Digital)	
ASD4100	Borodin: String Quartets 1/2	Borodin Quartet		Mdya
ASD4101	Mozart: Overtures (Figaro,Flute,Giovanni,Idomeneo,Cosi,etc)	ASMF Marriner	(Digital)	
ASD4103	Strauss,R: Four Last Songs, etc	Welsh Nat Op Armstrong Söderström	(Digital)	
ASD4104	Byrd: Mass in 5 Parts/ etc	KCC Ledger		
ASD4136	Beethoven: Symphony 5, Ov Coriolan	Philh Sanderling	(Digital, from SLS5239)	
ASD4157	Haydn: Cello Concertos in D and C	Wurttemburg CO Faerber Tortelier	(Digital)	
ASD4159	Rodrigo: Concierto de Aranjuez, etc	LSO Bátiz Moreno (guitar)	(Digital)	
ASD4160	Albeniz: Iberia Suite: Navarra	LSO Bátiz	(Digital)	
ASD4164	Prokofiev: The Prodigal Son/Overture Op 42	MRSO Rozhdestvensky		Mdya
ASD4166	"Robyn Archer sings Brecht"	London Sinfonietta Muldowney Archer		
ASD4167	Ravel: L'Enfant et les Sortilèges	LSO Previn	(Digital)	
ASD4168	Sibelius: Symphony 5, Night Ride and Sunrise	Philh Rattle	(Digital)	
ASD4169	Tchaikovsky: Manfred Symphony	Philh Muti	(Digital)	
ASD4170	Grieg:Symphonic Dances,Norwegian Romance with Variations	BNSO Berglund	(Digital)	
ASD4171	Castelnuovo-Tedesco: Guitar Concerto 1, Torroba: Homenaie a la Seguidilla	ECO Torroba Romero (guitar)	(Digital)	
ASD4172	Trio Sonatas (CPE Bach, JS Bach, Goldberg)	Perlman Zukerman Sanders (hpsd)	(Digital)	
ASD4173	Tchaikovsky: Violin Concerto/Capriccio Italien	Philh Ozawa Spivakov	(Digital)	
ASD4174	Ravel:Daphnis&Chloe Suite 2,Bolero, Alborada del Gracioso	Phild Muti	(Digital)	
ASD4175	Franck: Symphony in Dmin, Le Chasseur Maudit	Phild Muti	(Digital)	
ASD4177	Bitten: Young Apollo, Four French Songs	CBSO Rattle Gomez	(Digital)	
ASD4178	"Famous Strauss Waltzes"	Vienna Strauss Orch Boskovsky	(Digital)	
ASD4182	Strauss,R: Four Last Songs, Tod und Verklärung	LPO Tennstedt Popp	(Digital)	
ASD4183	Fauré: Melodies	von Stade Collard	(Digital)	
ASD4185	Mozart: Violin Concertos K211, K218	Philh Muti Mutter	(Digital)	
ASD4186	Sibelius: Finlandia, Tapiola, Valse Triste, Swan of Tuonela, etc	Philh Berglund	(Digital)	
ASD4188	Rimsky-Korsakov: Scheherezade	Phild Muti	(Digital)	
ASD4193	Handel & Mozart: Arias	Goldsborough Orch De Los Angeles		
ASD4194	Bizet/Schedrin: The Carmen Ballet	LACO Schwarz	(Digital)	
ASD4198	Rodrigo: Concierto en Modo Galante, Concierto de Estio	LSO Bátiz Cohen (cello) Ara (violin)	(Digital)	
ASD4202	Schumann: Carnaval, Papillons, Toccata	Youri Egorov (piano)	(Digital)	
ASD4206	Korngold: Violin Concerto/Conus: Violin Concerto	Pittsburgh SO Previn Perlman	(digital)	
ASD4207	Bach,JS: Double Violin Concerto, Violin Concerto in Emaj,etc	LSO Menuhin	(Digital)	
ASD4218	Bruckner: Symphony 9	DrSt Jochum	(Pressed in Germany)	
ASD4221	Stanford: Irish Symphony	BNSI Del Mar		
ASD4234	Fauré: Requiem, Messe Basse	ECO Ledger	(Digital)	
ASD4256	Rossini: Stabat Mater	MMF Muti	(Digital)	
ASD4257	Mozart: Concertos for 2 Pianos & Orch K242, K365	LPO Eschenbach Frantz Schmidt	(Digital)	
ASD4258	Liszt: Music for Piano & Orch	Phild Ormandy Katsaris (piano)	(Digital)	
ASD4270	Opera Duets with Placido Domingo	Various Domingo Caballé/Freni/etc		
ASD4271	Stravinsky: Rite of Spring	MRSO Fedoseyev	(Digital)	
ASD4272	Rimsky-Korsakov: Scheherezade	MRSO Fedoseyev	(Digital)	
ASD4279	Operatic Recital (Rossini, Mozart, Donizetti, Verdi, Mascagni)	Munich RSO Wallberg Baltsa (mezzo)	(Digital)	
ASD4280	Beethoven: Violin Concerto	LGO Masur Menuhin	(Digital)	
ASD4281	Mussorgsky:Pictures at an Exhibition,Ravel:Gaspard de le Nuit	Ousset (piano)	(Digital)	
ASD4285	Tallis: The Lamentations of Jeremiah, Mass, 3 Motets	KCC Ledger	(Digital)	
ASD4286	Haydn: Cello Concertos 1, 2	ASMF Marriner Harrell	(Digital)	
ASD4294-5 as SLS5270				
ASD4305	Beethoven: String Quartets op 127, op 135	Alban Berg Quartet	(Digital)	
ASD4306	Arias from French Operas	FNRO Pretre Callas		
ASD4307	St-Saens: Piano Concerto 2, Liszt: Piano Concerto 1	CBSO Rattle Ousset	(Digital)	
ASD4312	Bach,JS: Keyboard Concertos BWV1052, BWV1058	Moscow CO Nikolayevsky Gavrilov		

ASD4313	Stravinsky: Pulcinella, Suites 1 & 2 for Small Orch	ASMF	Marriner	(Digital)
ASD4315	Beethoven: Piano Trios 6 (Archduke), 7		Ashkenazy Perlman Harrell	(Digital)
ASD4321	Prokofiev: Piano Sonata 6, Rachmaninov, Stravinsky		Peter Donohoe (piano)	(Digital)
ASD4333	Chopin: Piano Works (Fantasia in Fmin, Nocturnes, etc)		Yuri Egorov	(Digital)
ASD4334	Franck: Cello Sonata in A, Debussy: Cello Sonata in Gmin		Maisky (cello) Argerich (piano)	(Digital)
ASD4344	Mahler: Symphony 4	LPO	Tennstedt Popp	(Digital)
ASD4387	Holst: At the Boar's Head	RLPO	Atherton	
ASD4388	Britten: Frank Bridge Variations, Matinees Musicales, etc	ECO	Gibson	(Digital)
ASD4389	"Russian Orch Favourites" (Glinka, Rimsky-Korsakov, etc)	MRSO	Fedoseyev	(Digital)
ASD4390	French Piano Music (Debussy, Ravel, Chabrier, Fauré, etc)		Ousset (piano)	(Digital)
ASD4392	Sullivan: Operetta hlts	BNSO	Alwyn Masterson Tear	(Digital)
ASD4397	Britten: Our Hunting Fathers, British Folk Songs	Welsh Nat Op	Armstrong Soderström	(Digital)
ASD4401	Stanford: Songs of the Sea, Songs of the Fleet	BNSO	Del Mar Luxon	
ASD4402	Weill: The Seven Deadly Sins	CBSO	Rattle	(Digital)
ASD4405	Shostakovich: Symphony 10	LSO	Previn	(Digital)
ASD4409	Mahler: Lieder Eines Fahrenden Gesellen, Kindertotenlieder, Ruckert Lieder	Philh	Barbirolli Baker	
ASD4414	Prokofiev:Symphony 1 (Classical),Lt Kije,Love for 3 Oranges	LPO	Bátiz	(Digital)
ASD4415	Schubert: German Mass, Salve Regina, Psalms, etc	BavSO	Sawallisch Fischer-Dieskau	(Digital)

EMI Box sets

EMI always issued a SLS number for every box set they issued. Inside the SLS box you may find discs that have ASD, HQS, CSD, or SAN numbers (and also BOXnnn numbers). For example, ASD2439-40 (V Williams Sea Symphony) is in a box which also says SLS780/2 (the /2 indicating a 2 disc set). Similarly, SAN121-5 Lohengrin/Kempe also says SLS906/5 (the /5 indicating a 5 disc set). What is even more confusing is that by the time you get to the later label issues EMI also frequently dropped the ASD/SAN/etc number off the box, so that what might have started out as a SAN set ends up as a SLS set!

SLS 755	Bizet: Carmen	ORTF	Beecham De Los Angeles
SLS 753	see ASD307-10		
SLS 757	see ASD359-61		
SLS 759	see ASD373-5		
SLS 760	see ASD385-87		
SLS 762	see ASD409-11		
SLS 765	"Tchaikovsky Ballet Music"	Philh	Kurtz Menuhin
SLS 770	Elgar: Dream of Gerontius	HO	Barbirolli Baker/Lewis
SLS 772	Weber: Der Freischutz	BPO	Keilberth Grummer, Prey, Shock
SLS 773	Mozart: Die Entfuhrung aus dem Serail	RPO	Beecham Marshall, Hollweg, Simoneau
SLS 774	Handel: Messiah	ECO	Mackerras Baker
SLS 775	Wagner: Tannhauser	BPO	Konwitschny Grummer, Fischer-Dieskau
SLS 776	see ASD2336-7		
SLS 777	Smetana: The Bartered Bride	Bamberg SO	Kempe Wunderlich
SLS 778	Mahler: Symphony No6	Philh	Barbirolli
SLS 779	see ASD2429-30		
SLS 780	V Williams: Sea Symphony/The Wasps suite	LPO	Boult
SLS 781	see ASD2491-2		
SLS 782	Bach: Die Kunst der Fuge		Rogg
SLS 783	Ravel: Piano Works		Francois
SLS 784	see ASD2511-2		
SLS 785	Mahler: Symphony 5	Philh	Barbirolli
SLS 786	Brahms: Violin Concerto/Double Concerto	Cllvlnd	Szell Rostropovich Oistrakh
SLS 787	Donizetti: Roberto Devereux	RPO	Mackerras
SLS 788	Beethoven: The 9 Symphonies plus Ovs Prometheus	Philh	Klemperer
SLS 789	Beethoven: Piano Trios		Barenboim Zukerman Du Pre
SLS 790	Beethoven: Symphony 9, Overtures Leonora 3, King Stephen	Philh	Klemperer
SLS 791	Shaporin: The Story of the Battle for the Russian Land In memory of the Victims of the Siege of Leningrad	USSRSO LenPO	Svetlanov Yansons Mdya
SLS 792	Strauss,R: Songs		Fischer-Dieskau
SLS 793	Messiaen: Vingt regards sur l'enfant Jesus		Beroff (piano)
SLS 794	Beethoven: The complete Sonatas		Barenboim
SLS 795	Tchaikovsky: Swan Lake	MPO	Rozhdestvensky Mdya
SLS 796	"Glorious John"		Barbirolli
SLS 797	Donizetti: Lucia di Lammermoor	LSO	Schippers Sills Bergonzi
SLS 798	Bach,J.S: The Cello Suites		Tortelier
SLS 799	Sibelius: Complete Symphonies/etc	HO	Barbirolli
SLS 800	Massenet: Manon	Philh	Rudel Sills Gedda
SLS 801	Buxtehude and his contemporaries		Rogg
SLS 802	St-Saens: The 5 Piano Concertos	OdP	Baudo Ciccolini
SLS 803	Debussy: Preludes		Beroff
SLS 804	Brahms: Symphonies 1-4/Tragic Overture/etc	Philh	Klemperer
SLS 805	Mendelssohn: Songs		Fischer-Dieskau Sawallisch (piano)
SLS 806	Mahler: Symphony 2	Philh	Klemperer
SLS 807	Sibelius: Kullervo Symphony	BNSO	Berglund
SLS 808	Bach: Suites 1 - 4	Philh	Klemperer

SLS 809	Mozart: Syms 35, 36, 38, 39, 40, 41 + rehearsal	BPO	Karajan	
SLS 810	Strauss,R: Der Rosankavalier	Philh	Karajan Schwarzkopf	
SLS 811	Bruckner: Symphonies 4/7	BPO	Karajan	
SLS 812	Schubert: Song Recital		Baker Moore	
SLS 813	Prokofiev: Love of Three Oranges	MPO	Dalgat	Mdya
SLS 814	Scriabin: Piano Works		Ogdon	
SLS 815	Orff: Music for Children	Directed by Carl Orff		
SLS 816	Gounod: Faust	OTNO	Cluytens Gedda/De Los Angeles/etc	
SLS 817	Mozart: Concs (Bassoon, Flute, Clarinet, Oboe, etc)	BPO	Karajan	
SLS 818	Bach: Sonatas & Partitas (complete)	Suk		
SLS 819	Mascagni: Cav Rusticana/Leoncavallo: Pagliacci	La Scala Serafin Callas Gobbi		
SLS 820	Couperin: Messe Solenelle etc		Rogg	
SLS 821	Brahms: German Requiem	Philh	Klemperer	
SLS 822	V Williams: The 9 Symphonies	LSO/LPO Boult		
SLS 823	Lehar: The Merry Widow	Philh	Matacic Schwarzkopf	
SLS 824	Handel: Organ Concertos	BFCO	Menuhin Preston	
SLS 825	Puccini: Tosca	De Sabata Callas		
SLS 826	Glazunov: Raymonda complete	Bolshoi	Svetlanov	Mdya
SLS 827	Bach,J.S: St Matthew Passion	Philh	Klemperer	
SLS 828	Mozart: Violin Concertos 1-5/etc	BPO	Oistrakh	
SLS 831	Bach,J.S: The Brandenburg Concertos & The 4 Sts	BFCO	Menuhin	
SLS 832	Paganini: Violin Concs 1/2/Sarasate: Carmen Fantasy RPO	Perlman		
SLS 833	Tchaikovsky: Symphonies 4-6	BPO	Karajan	
SLS 834	Tchaikovsky: Nutcracker Suite	LSO	Previn	TASEC
SLS 835	Scriabin: Symphonies, Piano Concerto, Poeme	USSR	Neuhaus	Mdya
SLS 836	Beethoven: The Complete Cello Sonatas	Tortelier Heidsieck		
SLS 837	Prokofiev: War and Peace	Bolshoi	Vishnevskaya	Mdya
SLS 838	Chopin: Nocturnes (complete)		Weissenberg	
SLS 839	Karajan Conducts the popular classics	BPO	Karajan	
SLS 840	Schubert: SchØne Mòllerin, Winterreise, Schwanengesang	Fischer-Dieskau Moore		
SLS 841	Beethoven: Symphonies 8/9	LSO	Giulini	
SLS 842	London Festival Ballet Gala	London Festival Ballet Orch Kern		
SLS 843	Chopin: Polonaises		Ohlsson	
SLS 844	Prokofiev: Symphonies etc, Shchedrin: Conc for Orchestra	MPO	Kondrashin	Mdya
SLS 845	Handel: Messiah	ASMF	Willcocks Kings College Choir	
SLS 846	Haydn: Symphonies 93-104 + rehearsal	RPO	Beecham	
SLS 847	Rachmaninov: Symphonies, Isle of the Dead, The Bells,etc	USSRSO	Svetlanov	Mdya
SLS 848	Donizetti: Maria Stuarda	LPO	Ceccato Sills	
SLS 850	Penderecki: Cello Concerto etc	RSO	Penderecki	
SLS 851	Mahler: Symphony 9/Symphony 6	BPO	Barbirolli	
SLS 852	Tchaikovsky: The Maid of Orleans	MPO	Rozhdestvensky	Mdya
SLS 853	Rossini: The Barber of Seville	Philh	Galliera Callas	
SLS 855	Rachmaninov: Piano Concertos 1-4 Paganini Rhapsody	Philh	de Burgos	
SLS 856	Operatic Duets		Callas di Stefano	
SLS 857	Beethoven: The String Quartets	Hungarian String Quartet		
SLS 858	Offenbach: Tales of Hoffman	LSO	Rudel	
SLS 859	Tchaikovsky: Swan Lake/Sleeping Beauty/Nutcracker (hlts)	Philh	Kurtz Menuhin	
SLS 860	Prokofiev: On Guard for Peace, Ivan the Terrible	USSRSO	Stasevich	Mdya
SLS 861	Strauss: Orchestral music Vol 1	Dresden State Kempe		
SLS 862	Mendelssohn: Songs Without Words		Adni	
SLS 863	"The Art of Courtly Love"	EMCL	Munro	
SLS 864	Prokofiev: Romeo and Juliet	LSO	Previn	
SLS 865	Tchaikovsky: Piano Concertos 1, 2, 3	NPO	Maazel Gilels	
SLS 866	Bach: Brandenburg Concertos	LPO	Boult Munrow	
SLS 867	Schumann: The 4 Symphonies, Manfred Ov	Dresden	Sawallisch	

SLS 868	"Pianistic Philosophies" (Britten, Dukas, Lloyd, Messiaen, etc)	Ogdon Lucas		
SLS 869	Verdi: Il Trovatore	La Scala Karajan Callas Di Stefano		
SLS 870	"Hoffnung Music Festivals"	Various		
SLS 871	Beethoven: Violin Sonatas 1-10	Zuckerman Barenboim		
SLS 872	Bruckner : Symphony 8	Philh Klemperer		
SLS 873	Beethoven: Symphonies 3/5/7 ect	Philh Klemperer		
SLS 874	Brahms: Piano Concertos 1/2	Philh Barbirolli Barenboim		
SLS 875	Wagner: Siegfried	ENOC Goodall		
SLS 877	Bizet: Les Pecheurs des Perles	Opera Comique Dervaux Gedda, etc		
SLS 878	Donizetti: Anna Bolena	LSO Rudel Sills, Tear, Lloyd, etc		
SLS 879	Shostakovich: String Quartets 1-13	Borodin Quartet		Mdya
SLS 880	Strauss: Orchestral music Vol 2	Dresden State Kempe Tortelier		
SLS 881	Tchaikovsky: The 6 Symphonies/Manfred	USSR Svetlanov		Mdya
SLS 882	Prokofiev: Piano Concertos 1-5	LGO Masur Beroff		
SLS 884	Schoenberg: Gurrelieder	Janos Ferencsik		
SLS 885	Rimsky Korsakov: The Tsar's Bride	Bolshoi Mansurov Vishnevskaya		Mdya
SLS 887	Shchedrin: Ballet - Anna Karenina	Bolshoi Simonov		Mdya
SLS 889	Tchaikovsky: Chamber Works	Borodin String Quartet, Rostropovich		Mdya
SLS 890	"The Art of Richter". Includes Beethoven Sonata op90	Richter	Mdya	
SLS 891	Ballet form the Bolshoi	Bolshoi		Mdya
SLS 892	Beethoven Symphonies and Overtures	Munich Philh Kempe		
SLS 893	Debussy: Complete orchestral music	Orch de Paris Martinon		
SLS 894	Strauss: Orchestral music Vol 3	Dresden State Kempe		
SLS 895	Favourite Cello Concertos	Barbirolli Barenboim Du Pre		
SLS 896	Puccini: La Boheme	RCAVO Beecham De Los Angeles		
SLS 897	Shostakovich: Symphony 7	BNSO Berglund		
SLS 898	Grieg: Lyric Pieces (complete)	Adni		
SLS 900	see SAN101-2			
SLS 901	see SAN103-6			
SLS 902	see SAN108-9			
SLS 903	see SAN110-3			
SLS 904	see SAN114-6			
SLS 905	see SAN117-9			
SLS 906	see SAN121-5			
SLS 907	see SAN131-2			
SLS 908	see SAN126-7			
SLS 909	see SAN133-4			
SLS 910	see SAN128-30			
SLS 912	see SAN137-9			
SLS 913	see SAN140-2			
SDLS 914	see SDAN143-5			
SLS 915	see SAN146-8			
SLS 916	see SAN151-3			
SLS 917	see SAN149-50			
SLS 918	see SAN154-6			
SLS 919	see SAN157-8			
SLS 921	see SAN159-61			
SLS 922	see SAN165-6			
SLS 923	see SAN172-5			
SLS 925	see SAN180-1			
SLS 926	see SAN163-4			
SLS 927	see SAN184-6			
SLS 928	see SAN170-1			
SLS 929	see SAN189-91			
SLS 930	see SAN195-7			

SLS 932	see SAN201-3			
SLS 933	see SAN204-6			
SLS 934	see SAN207-9			
SLS 935	see SAN212-4			
SLS 936	see SAN215-7			
SLS 937	see SAN210-1			
SLS 938	see SAN242-3			
SLS 939	see SAN244-5			
SLS 940	see SAN252-4			
SLS 941	see SAN238-41			
SLS 942	see SAN228-31			
SLS 943	see SAN235-7			
SLS 944	see SAN246-8			
SLS 945	see SAN249-51			
SLS 946	see SAN256-7			
SLS 947	Berlioz: Damnation of Faust	OdeP	Pretre Gedda Baker	(SAN258-9)
SLS 948	Verdi: The Force of Destiny	RPO	Gardelli Bergonzi Raimondi	(SAN260-3)
SLS 949	Bach,JS: St John Passion	Vienna Consortium Musicum Gonnenwein		(SAN264-6)
SLS 950	Verdi: Requiem	Philh	Barbirolli	(SAN267-8)
SLS 951	Tchaikovsky: Eugene Onegin	Bolshoi	Rostropovich Vishnevskaya	(SAN270-2) Mdya
SLS 952	Bizet: Carmen	Paris Opera De Burgos Bumbry Vickers		(SAN273-5)
SLS 953	Bellini: Il Pirata	RTI Rome Gavazzini		(SAN276-8)
SLS 954	Beethoven: Fidelio	BPO	Karajan	(SAN280-2)
SLS 955	Mozart: Marriage of Figaro	Philh	Klemperer	(SAN283-6)
SLS 956	Verdi: Don Carlos	ROHCG	Giulini	(SAN287-90)
SLS 957	Wagner: Die Meistersinger von Nurnberg	Dresden	Karajan	(SAN292-6)
SLS 958	Delius: Mass of Life	LPO	Groves	(SAN300-1)
SLS 959	V Williams: Pilgrim's Progress	LPO	Boult	(SAN302-4)
SLS 960	Verdi: La Traviata	RPO	Caccato	(SAN307-9)
SLS 961	Mozart: Cosi fan Tutte	Philh	Klemperer	(SAN310-3)
SLS 962	Puccini: Manon Lescaut	Philh	Bartoletti	(SAN314-5)
SLS 963	Wagner: Tristan & Isolde	BPO	Karajan	(SAN319-23)
SLS 964	Strauss,J: Die Fledermaus	VSO	Boskovsky	(SAN325-6)
SLS 965	Mozart: Idomeneo	Dresden State Schmidt-Issersdedt		(SAN327-30)
SLS 966	Delius: A Village Romeo & Juliet	RPO	Davies	(SAN316-8)
SLS 967	Verdi: Joan of Arc	LSO	Levine	(SAN331-3)
SLS 968	Wagner:Die Walkure Act 1 & Wotan's Farewell	Philh	Klemperer	(SAN334-5)
SLS 969	Haydn: The Seasons	BPO	Karajan	(SAN336-8)
SLS 970	Rossini: William Tell	RPO	Gardelli	(SAN339-43)
SLS 971	Haydn: The Creation	ASMF	Marriner	(SAN347-8)
SLS 973	Boito: Mefistofele	LSO	Rudel	(SAN344-6)
SLS 974	Delius: Koanga	LSO	Groves	(SAN349-50)
SLS 975	Verdi: Otello	BPO	Karajan Vickers	(SAN351-3)
SLS 976	Elgar: The Apostles	LPO	Boult	(SAN355-7)
SLS 977	Verdi: Aida	Philh	Muti	(SAN358-60)
SLS 978	Mozart: Don Giovanni	ECO	Barenboim	(SAN361-4)
SLS 979	Beethoven: Missa Solemnis	BPO	Karajan	(SAN366-7)
SLS 980	Vaughan Williams: Sir John in Love	Philh	Davies	(SAN371-3)
SLS 981	Rossini: The Siege of Corinth	LSO	Schippers	(SAN368-70)
SLS 982	Berlioz: Requiem	CBSO	Fremaux	(SAN374-5)
SLS 983	Weber: Euryanthe	Dresden	Janowski	(SAN376-9)
SLS 984	Verdi: Un Ballo in Maschera	Philh	Muti	(SAN380-2)
SLS 985	Rossini: Barber of Seville	LSO	Levine	(SAN383-5)
SLS 986	Bellini: I Capuleti e I Montecchi	Philh	Patane	(SAN386-8)
SLS 987	Elgar: Dream of Gerontius	Philh	Boult	(SAN389-90)

SLS 988	Instruments of the Middle Ages	EMCL	David Munrow	(SAN391-2)
SLS 989	Beethoven: Missa Solemnis	Philh	Giulini	(SAN394-5)
SLS 990	Wagner: Rienzi	Staats Dresden Hollreiser		(SAN396-400)
SLS 991	Delius: Fennimore and Gerda	Danish RSO Davies		(SAN405-6)
SLS 992	Verdi: Macbeth	Philh	Muti	(SAN402-4)
SLS 993	Massenet: Thais	Philh	Maazel Sills Milnes Gedda	(SAN407-9)
SLS 995	Mozart: Le Nozze di Figaro	ECO	Barenboim	(SAN420-3)
SLS 996	Brahms: A German Requiem	BPO	Karajan	(SAN413-4)
SLS 997	Walton: Troilus and Cressida	ROHCG Foster Baker		(SAN410-2)
SLS 998	Elgar: Caractacus	RLPO	Groves	(SAN418-9)
SLS 999	Beethoven: Leonore (Original version of Fidelio)	Dresden Blomstedt		(SAN415-7)
SLS1000	Mussorgsky: Boris Godunov	Polish Radio Semkow		(SAN424-7)
SLS5001	Tchaikovsky: Sleeping Beauty (cplt)	LSO	Previn	
SLS5002	Brahms: Lieder	Fischer-Dieskau Moore		
SLS5003	Symphonies: Mozart 40, Schubert 8, New World, Berlioz)	Philh	Klemperer	
SLS5004	Violin Concertos by Beethoven, Brahms, Bruch, Sibelius		Oistrakh	
SLS5005	Tchaikovsky: The Queen of Spades	Bolshoi	Khaikin	Mdya
SLS5006	Beethoven: Fidelio	Philh	Klemperer	
SLS5007	Schubert: Complete Symphonies	BFCO	Menuhin	
SLS5009	Brahms: Four Symphonies	LSO	Boult	
SLS5012	"The Incomparable De Los Angeles"		De Los Angeles	
SLS5013	Berlioz: Nuits d'Ete, Elgar: Sea Pictures, Ravel: Scheherazade	Barbirolli Baker:		
SLS5014	Chopin: The Mazurkas (complete)		Ronald Smith	
SLS5015	Puccini: Madama Butterfly	La Scala Karajan		
SLS5016	Ravel Complete orchestral music	Orch de Paris Martinon		
SLS5017	"Viennese Enchantment" (Strauss Family, etc)	Vienna Strauss Orch Boskovsky		
SLS5018	Verdi: Rigoletto	La Scala Serafin		
SLS5019	Karajan conducts popular classics Vol 2	Philh	Karajan	
SLS5020	Mozart: Sonatas K378, K379, K306	Richter	Kagaan	
SLS5021	Bizet: Carmen	ORTF	Beecham	
SLS5022	Art of the Recorder	EMCL	Munrow	
SLS5023	Mussorgsky: Khovanschina	Bolshoi	Khakin	Mdya
SLS5024	Prokofiev: The Stone Flower	Bolshoi Theatre Orch Rozhdestvensky		Mdya
SLS5025	Shostakovich: Symphonies 1-15	USSRSO Svetlanov		Mdya
SLS5026	Beethoven: Piano Concertos 1-5	Philh	Menges/Cluytens Solomon	
SLS5027	Nielsen: The 6 Symphonies	Danish RSO Blomstedt		
SLS5028	Mozart: Cosi Fan Tutte	Philh	Bohm	
SLS5030	Elgar: Symphonies 1/2, Enigma Vns, Falstaff, Cockaigne, etc		Barbirolli	
SLS5031	Mozart: Complete Piano Concertos	ECO	Barenboim	
SLS5032	Wagner: The Rhinegold	ENOC	Goodall	
SLS5033	Piano Concertos by Tchaikovsky, Grieg, Schumann, etc		Ogdon	
SLS5035	Saint-Saens: The 5 Symphonies	ONRF	Martinon	
SLS5036	Elgar: Starlight Express	LPO	Handley	
SLS5037	Verdi: Falstaff	Philh	Karajan Schwarzkopf	
SLS5039	Bach,JS: Harpsichord Concertos	BFCO	Menuhin Malcolm	
SLS5040	Liszt: Transcendental Studies, Hungn Rpsd 3, Rpsd Espagnole, etc		Berman	Mdya
SLS5042	Beethoven: Cello Sonatas	Du Pre	Barenboim	
SLS5043	Chopin: Piano Concertos 1, 2	Polish SOOhlsson		
SLS5044	Shostakovich: Symphonies 5/10	BNSO	Berglund	
SLS5045	Bach: The Unaccompanied Sonatas and Partitas	Menuhin		
SLS5046	Mozart, Brahms, Weber: Clarinet Quintets, Beethoven: Septet	Melos Ensemble De Peyer		
SLS5047	"The Glory of Kings" (Palestrina, Charpentier, V Williams, etc)	Kings College Choir Willcocks		
SLS5048	Mozart: Symphonies 25, 29, 31, 33, 34, 35, 36, 38, 39, 40, 41	Philh	Klemperer	
SLS5049	"The Art of the Netherlands"	EMCL	Munro	

SLS5050	Shostakovich: Katerina Ismailova	MPO	Provatorov	Mdya
SLS5051	"The Art of Caballé and Domingo" (Puccini,Verdi,Boito)	Various	Caballé Domingo	
SLS5052	Mozart: Die Zauberflote	VPO	Karajan	
SLS5053	Beethoven: The Nine Symphonies	Philh	Karajan	
SLS5055	"Russian Songs" (Tchaikovsky,Mussorgsky,Shostakovich)	Vishnevskaya Rostropovich		
SLS5056	Donizetti: Lucia di Lammermoor	Callas Di Stefano Gobbi		
SLS5057	La Divina - The Art of Maria Callas			
SLS5058	Violin Concertos: Prokofiev 1/Bartok 1/Khachaturian	Oistrakh		Mdya
SLS5059	Puccini: La Boheme	La Scala	Votto	
SLS5061	Khachaturian: Spartacus (complete)	Bolshoi	Zuraitis	Mdya
SLS5062	Gliere: Symphony 3, The Bronze Horeman, Ballet Suite 2	MRSO	Rachlin	Mdya
SLS5063	Wagner: The Valkyrie	ENOC	Goodall	
SLS5064	Moneverdi: Vespers (1610)	Kings College Cambridge Ledger		
SLS5065	Haydn: The 6 "Paris" Symphonies	ECO	Barenboim	
SLS5066	Puccini: Gianni Schicchi, Suor Angelica, Il Tabarro	Rome	Santini	
SLS5067	Strauss,R: The Complete Concertos	Dresden	Kempe	
SLS5068	"Popular Concertos"	Various		
SLS5069	"Hoffnung's Music Festivals"			
SLS5070	Tchaikovsky: Swan Lake (complete)	LSO	Previn	
SLS5071	Wagner: Lohengrin.	VPO	Kempe Thomas Ludwig Frick	
SLS5072	Moussorgsky: Boris Godunov	FNRO	Dobrowen Christoff Zareska	
SLS5073	"HMV Concert Classics Festival"	Various		
SLS5074	Strauss,J: Vienna Blood	Boskovsky Rothenberger Gedda		
SLS5075	'Klemperer Conducts Wagner'	Philh	Klemperer	
SLS5076	Offenbach: La Vie Parisienne	Toulouse Capitol Plasson		
SLS5077	Haydn: String Quartets Op 54	Medici Quartet		
SLS5078	Shostakovich: Song Cycles	Moscow CO Barshai Nestorenko		Mdya
SLS5079	Puccini: The Girl of the Golden West	La Scala Matacic		
SLS5080	"20th Century British Piano Concertos" (Ireland, Britten, Bliss, Rawsthorne, Rubbra, Tippett, etc)			
SLS5082	V Williams: Choral Music	Various		
SLS5083	Mozart: Don Giovanni (complete)	Philh	Giulini	
SLS5084	Elgar: Piano Quintet/String Quartet/Violin Sonata	Allegri Qt Ogdon		
SLS5085	Williamson: Sinfonia Concertante, Violin Concerto, etc	LPO	Boult Menuhin	
SLS5086	Bruckner: Symphony 7, Wagner: Parsifal & Tristan Preludes	BPO	Karajan	
SLS5087	Bach,JS: The Complete Organ Music vol 1			
SLS5088	Shostakovich: The Nose	Moscow Musical Theatre Rozhdestvensky		Mdya
SLS5089	Liszt: Hungarian Rhapsodies 1-15		Cziffra	
SLS5090	Verdi: Simon Boccanegra	RomeOp Santini De Los Angeles Gobbi Christoff		
SLS5091	Delibes: Coppelia (complete)	Paris Opera Mari		
SLS5092	Mendelssohn: St Paul	Dusselforf SO de Burgos Donath		
SLS5093	Brahms: 4 Symphonies/Tragic Ov/Acad Fest Ov	LPO	Jochum	
SLS5094	Piano Concertos: Brahms 1&2, Grieg, Schumann, Tchaikovsky 1		Solomon	
SLS5095	Haydn:Baryton Trios 37, 71, 85, 113, 117, 121	Esterhazy Baryton Trio		
SLS5096	Berwald: The 4 Symphonies, Piano Concerto, Violin Conc, etc	RPO	Bjorlin	
SLS5097	Verdi: La Traviata	Rome Opera Serafin De Los Angeles		
SLS5098	Bach,JS: Xmas Oratorio	ASMF	Ledger	
SLS5099	Tchaikovsky: Symphonies 1-6, Manfred Symphony	LPO	Rostropovich	
SLS5100	Alkan: Etudes Op 39, Trois Petites Fantaisies, Allegro, etc		Ronald Smith	
SLS5101	Edward Heath : "Music, A Joy for Life"	Various		
SLS5102	Rimsky-Korsakov: Snow Maiden	MRSO	Fedoseyev	Mdya
SLS5103	St-Saens: The 3 Violin Concertos	NPO	Dervaux Hoelscher	
SLS5104	The Maria Callas Album			
SLS5105	Massenet: Werther	Paris	Pretre	
SLS5106	'The Great Violin Concertos'	Menuhin		
SLS5107	Mascagni: L'Amico Fritz	ROHCG	Gavazzeni	

SLS5108	Verdi: Aida	La Scala	Serafin	
SLS5109	Shostakovich: "Leningrad" Symphony, Execn of Stepan Razin	MPO	Kondrashin	Mdya
SLS5110	Prokofiev: Ivan the Terrible	Philh	Muti Ambrosian Chor	
SLS5111	Verdi: Il Trovatore	BPO	Karajan	
SLS5112	Beethoven: The Five Piano Concertos	BPO	Karajan Weissenberg	
SLS5113	Bizet: Les Pecheurs de Perles	Paris	Pretre	
SLS5114	Brahms: The 3 Piano Trios	Frankl	Pauk Kirshbaum	
SLS5115	Bellini: Norma	La Scala	Serafin Callas Stignani	
SLS5116	De Falla/Halffter: Atlantida	SNO	De Burgos	
SLS5117	Messiaen: Turangalila Symphony	Previn	LSO	
SLS5118	Wagner: Twilight of the Gods	ENOC	Goodall	
SLS5119	Massenet: Manon	Opera Comique Monteux		
SLS5120	Verdi: La Forza del Destino	La Scala	Serafin	
SLS5122	Lehar: Paganini	Bavarian SO Boskovsky		
SLS5123	Tchaikovsky: Yolanta	Bolshoi	Ermler	Mdya
SLS5124	Mahler: Symphony 5, Adagio from Symphony 10	USSRSO Kondrashin		Mdya
SLS5125	Haydn: The Creation	Philh	de Burgos Donath Tear	
SLS5126	Delibes: Sylvia (complete)	PO	Jean Baptiste Mari	
SLS5127	Schubert: The Complete Symphonies, Rosamunde Music	BPO	Karajan	
SLS5128	Puccini: Madama Butterfly	Rome Opera Santini De Los Angeles		
SLS5129	Sibelius: Symphonies (complete)	BNSO	Berglund	
SLS5130	Rachmaninov: Liturgy of St John Chrysostom	Bulgarian Radio Milkov		
SLS5132	Verdi: Nabucco	Philh	Muti	
SLS5134	Bellini: La Sonnambula	La Scala	Votto	
SLS5135	Puccini: Turandot	Strasbourg Lombard		
SLS5136	The Art of David Munrow	EMCL	Munrow	
SLS5137	Brahms: Serenade 1/Serenade 2/Haydn Variations	LPO	Boult	
SLS5138	Schubert: Piano Duets	Eschenbach Frantz		
SLS5139	Strauss: Salome	VPO	Karajan	
SLS5140	Bellini: I Puritani	La Scala	Serafin	
SLS5143	Khachaturian: Gayaneh (complete ballet)	MRSO	Kakhidze	Mdya
SLS5144	Treasures of the Baroque Era	Nat Iranian TV CO Tchakarov		[ASD3613-4]
SLS5145	Humperdinck: Hansel and Gretel	Philh	Karajan	
SLS5147	Bruckner: Symphony 8	DrSt	Jochum	
SLS5148	Rossini: Il Turco in Italia	La Scala	Gavazzeni	
SLS5150	Rimsky-Korsakov: Sadko, Capriccio Espagnol, etc	USSRSO Svetlanov		Mdya
SLS5151	Smetana: My Country	Dresden SO Berglund		
SLS5152	Mozart: Marriage of Figaro (complete)	Philh	Giulini	
SLS5153	Mozart: Die Entfuhrung aus dem Serail	RPO	Beecham	
SLS5154	Verdi: Don Carlos	BPO	Karajan Carreras Freni	
SLS5155	Bach,JS : Brandenburg Concertos 1-6	Polish CO Maksymiuk		
SLS5157	Shostakovich: Lady Macbeth of Mtsensk	LPO	Rostropovich	
SLS5158	Haydn: The Seasons	RPO	Beecham	[from ALP1606-8]
SLS5160	Strauss: Die Schweigsame Frau	Dresden Janowski		
SLS5162	Vaughan Williams: Hugh the Drover	RPO	Groves	
SLS5163	Handel: Solomon	RPO	Beecham	[from CX1397-8]
SLS5164	Albrechtsberger: Organ Concerto, Bach, Haydn	Prague CO Bedford Parker-Smith (organ)		
SLS5165	Rossini: The Barber of Seville	RPO	Gui De Los Angeles	
SLS5166	Donizetti: Lucia di Lammermoor	Philh	Serafin Callas	
SLS5167	Tchaikovsky: The Enchantress	Moscow	Provatorov	Mdya
SLS5168	Handel: Alexander's Feast	ECO	Ledger	
SLS5169	Mahler: Symphony 5, Adagio from Sym 10	LPO	Tennstedt	
SLS5170	Gounod: Faust	Paris	Pretre	
SLS5171	Beethoven: String Quartets Op 59 , Op 74 ("Harp"), Op 95	Alban Berg Quartet		
SLS5172	Debussy: Pelleas& Melisande	BPO	Karajan	

SLS5173	Mahler: Lieder (Knaben Wunderhorn, Ruckert Lieder, etc)	Discher-Dieskau Barenboim	
SLS5175	Offenbach: Orfee aux Enfers	Toulouse Capitol Plasson	
SLS5176	Ponchielle: La Gioconda	La Scala Votto	
SLS5177	Shostakovich: Symphonies 11/6	BNSO Berglund	
SLS5178	Beethoven:Symphonies 1-9,Ovs Egmont,Coriolan,Fidelio, etc	LSO Jochum	
SLS5180	Beethoven: The Five Piano Concertos	Philh Klemperer Barenboim	
SLS5182	Hindemith: Mathis der Maler	Bavarian RSO Kubelik	
SLS5183	Massenet: Werther	LPO Plasson	
SLS5184	Benatzky: White Horse Inn	Munich RSO Rothenberger	
SLS5185	Verdi: Requiem	Phil Muti	
SLS5186	Bellini: Norma	La Scala Milan Callas	
SLS5187	Leoncavallo: Pagliacci; Mascagni: Cavalleria Rusticana	Phil Muti	
SLS5188	Mahler: Symphony 9	LPO Tennstedt	
SLS5191	Tchaikovsky: Eugene Onegin	Bolshoi Ermler	Mdya
SLS5192	Puccini: La Boheme	Philh Levine	
SLS5193	Verdi: Rigoletto	Philh Rudel	
SLS5194	Bruckner: Symphony 7	Dresden Jochum	
SLS5195	Mahler: Symphony 3	LPO Tennsdedt	(Digital)
SLS5196	Dargomizhsky: The Stone Guest	Bolshoi Ermler	Mdya
SLS5197	Wolf: Lieder	Schwarzkopf Moore	
SLS5198	Beethoven: Missa Solemnis	Philh Karajan Schwarzkopf	(SAN366-7)
SLS5199	Schumann: Symphonies 1-4, Ovs Hermann&Dorothea, etc	Philh Muti	
SLS5200	Handel: Saul	ECO Ledger Allen Tear	
SLS5201	Bellini: I Puritani	Philh Muti	
SLS5202	Lehar : Merry Widow	Munich RSO Wallberg Moser Prey	
SLS5203	Gounod: Mireille	Toulouse Plasson	
SLS5204	Strauss: Intermezzo	Bavarian RSO Sawallisch	
SLS5205	Verdi: Aida	VPO Karajan	
SLS5206	Mahler: Symphony 10	BNSO Rattle	(Digital)
SLS5207	Liszt:Complete Works for Piano & Orch	LGO Masur Beroff	
SLS5209	Berlioz: Requiem	LPO Previn Tear	(Digital)
SLS5211	Verdi: Falstaff	Philh Karajan	
SLS5212	"Yevgeny Mravinsky and the Leningrad Philharmonic at the Vienna Festival" (Brahms: Symphony 2, Schubert: Symphony 8, Shostakovich: Symphony 5, Tchaikovsky: Symphony 5, etc)	Leningrad PO Mravinsky	Mdya
SLS5213	Puccini: Tosca	Philh Levine	(Digital)
SLS5215	Bach,J.S: B Minor Mass	BavSRO Jochum	(Digital)
SLS5216	Verdi: La Traviata	ENO Mackerras	
SLS5217	Beethoven : String Quartets op 18	Alban Berg Quartet	
SLS5218	Mozart : Organ Works (Epistle Church Sonatas, etc)	Lausanne CO Gerecz Rogg	
SLS5219	Fauré: Orchestral Works	Toulouse Orch Plasson Tortelier	
SLS5220	Schubert: Secular Vocal Music vol 1	BavRSO Sawallisch Behrens Fassbaender Schreier	
SLS5221	Violin Concertos (Paganini 1, Mendelssohn, Dvorak, etc)	Various Perlman	
SLS5223	Mozart: Die Zauberflote	Bavarian RO Haitink	(Digital)
SLS5224	Strauss: Arabella	Bavarian SO Sawallisch	(Digital)
SLS5225	Rachmaninov: Symphonies 1-3	Previn LSO	
SLS5226	Wagner: The Flying Dutchman	Berlin Opera Konwitschny	
SLS5230	Lehar: Friederike	Munich RSO Wallberg Donath	
SLS5231	Beethoven: Fidelio	BPO Karajan	(SAN280-2)
SLS5233	The Art of Victoria De Los Angeles (Opera, Song and Zarzuela Recordings, 1949-1969)		
SLS5234	Handel: Keyboard Suites 1-16	Richter Gavrilov	
SLS5235	Liszt: Orchestral Works Vol 1 (Les Preludes, Orpheus, Tasso, Dante Symphony, etc)	LGO Masur	
SLS5236	Liszt: Orch Works Vol 2 (Prometheus, Faust Symphony, Mazeppa, Hamlet, etc)	LGO Masur	
SLS5237	Wagner: Lohengrin	BPO Karajan	

SLS5238	Mahler : Symphony 7	LPO	Tennstedt	(Digital)
SLS5239	Beethoven: Syms 1-9, Ovs Egmont, Coriolan, Prometheus	Philh	Sanderling	(Digital)
SLS5240	Verdi: La Traviata	Philh	Muti	(Digital)
SLS5242	Szymanowski: Orchestral Works (Symphonies, Overtures, etc)	Various Orchestras		
SLS5243	Mahler: Symphony 2	LPO	Tennstedt Mathis Soffel	(Digital)
SLS5244	Beethoven : Symphonies 8, 9	Philh	Sanderling	(Digital)
SLS5245	Tchaikovsky: Sleeping Beauty	USSRSO	Svetlanov	Mdya
SLS5246	Walton: Symphony 1, Belshazzar's Feast, Façade, Crown Imperial, Henry V suite, Portsmouth Point Ov, etc	Philh	Walton	
SLS5247	Glinka: Russlan and Ludmilla	Bolshoi	Simonov	Mdya
SLS5248	Monteverdi: The Coronation of Poppea	Glyndebourne Pritchard		
SLS5249	"The Music of Percy Grainger" (Miscellaneous Works)	Various		
SLS5250	"The Art of Nicolai Gedda"		Gedda	
SLS5252	Bruckner: Symphonies Nos 1-9	DrSt	Jochum	
SLS5254	Schubert: Sacred Works vol 1	Various		(Digital)
SLS5255	Gluck: Orfeo ed Euridice	Philh	Muti	(Digital)
SLS5256	Bach,JS : Brandenburg Concertos 1-6	Linde Consort Linde		(Digital)
SLS5257	Bach,JS: St Matthew Passion	North German Orch Leppard		(Digital)
SLS5265	Mozart: Concert Arias vol 1	DrSt	Blomstedt Moser Schreier	
SLS5266	Britten: Violin Concerto, Young Person's Guide, 4 Sea Interludes, Spring Symphony	BNSO	Berglund Haendel	
SLS5267	Concert (Mozart, Beethoven, Grieg, Handel, etc)	ASMF	Marriner	
SLS5269	Sibelius: Orch Works	BNSO	Berglund	
SLS5270	Tchaikovsky: The Nutcracker	Philh	Lanchbery	(Digital)
SLS5271	Tchaikovsky: Swan Lake	Philh	Lanchbery	(Digital)
SLS5272	Tchaikovsky: Sleeping Beauty	Philh	Lanchbery	(Digital)
SLS5273	Tchaikovsky: Sleeping Beauty, Swan Lake, Nutcracker	Includes all of SLS5270,1,2		(Digital)
SLS5274	Lehar: Land des Lächelns	Munich RSO Boskovsky Donath Jerusalem		(Digital)
SLS5275	"The Art of Janet Baker"			
SLS5276	Offenbach: La Périchole	Toulouse Plasson Berganza Carreras		(Digital)
SLS5277	Donizetti: Maria Stuarda	ENO	Mackerras	(Digital)
SLS5278	Schubert: Sacred Works vol 2	Various		
SLS5279	Bruckner : Symphony 4	BPO	Tennstedt	(Digital)
SLS5289	Schubert: Piano Sonatas D575, D625, D664, D784		Richter	(Digital)
SLS5290	Bruckner: Symphony 8	LPO	Tennstedt	(Digital)

Other EMI labels
(Just a small selection of the best on these other EMI labels)

CSD

The CSD label was used by EMI for what they thought of as "lighter" material. The earliest CSDs are contemporary with the white/gold label. Indeed, the earliest CSD label is identical to the white/gold label except that the 'white' is green.

Cat. No.	Title	Orchestra	Artists
CSD1252	Glazounov: Birthday Offering, Lecocq	RPO	Irving
CSD1253	Prokofiev: Piano Concertos 1, 3	Philh	Susskind Lympany
CSD1256	Prokofiev: Cinderella Suite	RPO	Irving
CSD1261	Debussy: Printemps etc	RPO	Irving
CSD1262	Philharmonic Pops	SOL	Irving
CSD1264	"Fame in a Night"	Orchestra Charles Craig	
CSD1267	"The land of Smiles"	Sadlers Wells Tausky	
CSD1268	"Chu-Chin-Chow"	Michael Collins and Orch	
CSD1271	Schumann: Carnaval/Chopin: Sylphides	RPO	Irving
CSD1278	Schumann: Piano Concerto/Franck: Sym Vns	RPO	Silvestri Lympany
CSD1280	Carnival Time	RPO	Irving
CSD1282	"Famous Marches"	Band of the Royal Marines	
CSD1286	Immortal Pas de Deux	RPO	Irving
CSD1287	Songs for Swingers vol 1	Ella Fitzgerald	
CSD1289	"Waltzes from Vienna"	Michael Collins & Orch	
CSD1292	"Ella Fitzgerald Sings the George Gershwin Song Book" v1	Orch cond by Nelson Riddle	
CSD1293	"Ella Fitzgerald Sings the George Gershwin Song Book" v2	Orch cond by Nelson Riddle	
CSD1299	"Ella Fitzgerald Sings the George Gershwin Song Book" v3	Orch cond by Nelson Riddle	
CSD1300	"Ella Fitzgerald Sings the George Gershwin Song Book" v4	Orch cond by Nelson Riddle	
CSD1301	Chopin: Waltzes	Lympany	
CSD1304	"Ella Fitzgerald Sings the George Gershwin Song Book" v5	Orch cond by Nelson Riddle	
CSD1310	"Steve and Eydie"	Steve Lawrence Edyie Gorme	
CSD1311-2	"Merrie England"	Michael Collins and Orch	
CSD1315	"Hello Love"	Ella Fitzgerald	
CSD1316	Offenbach: Orpheus in the Underworld	Saddlers Wells Theatre	
CSD1319	Concert	Sinf London Irving	
CSD1333	Musical Merry-Go-Round	Sinf London Irving	
CSD1338	An Evening with Paul Robeson	Paul Robeson	
CSD1343-4	Chopin: Nocturnes	Lympany	
CSD1346	Springtime	RPO	Irving
CSD1350	"Songs you Remember"	Owen Brannigan Ernest Lush	
CSD1356	"The Blues Hot and Cold"	Bob Brookmeyer Quartet	
CSD1372	"Gerry Mulligan Meets Johnny Hodges"		
CSD1373	Concerto Movements	RPO	Goossens Moiseiwitsch
CSD1378	Offenbach: La Vie Parisienne	Sadler's Wells	
CSD1388	Rachmaninov: Piano Concerto 2, Preludes 4, 5, 12	RPO	Sargent Lympany
CSD1389	"Ella Fitzgerald Sings the Harold Arlen Song Book"	Orch cond by Billy May	
CSD1398	Bizet: Carmen (hlts)	Saddlers Wells Davis	
CSD1399	Sullivan: Pineapple Poll	RPO	Mackerras
CSD1402	"Italiana"	Orchestra Charles Craig	
CSD1406	Mozart: Overtures Idomeneo, Magic Flute, Cosi, Giovanni, etc	RPO	Davis
CSD1415	"Music of the Service" from the Temple Church in London		
CSD1417	"Instruments of the Orchestra"	Menuhin	
CSD1419	Oboe recital	Goossens	
CSD1436	Rossini Overtures: William Tell, Gazza Ladra, Semiramide, etc	RPO	Davis
CSD1441	"Blitz" All the Music from Lionel bart's 1962 Hit Show		

Catalog	Title	Performer
CSD1444	Music to Shakespeare	Sinf London Irving
CSD1447	"Clap Hands, Here Comes Charlie"	Ella Fitzgerald
CSD1449	Organ Recital (Cesar Franck,Liszt,Reger,Widor)	Germani
CSD1458-9	Gilbert & Sullivan: The Mikado	Sadler's Wells Orch
CSD1465	Adam: Giselle	Philh Irving
CSD1466	Verdi: Rigoletto	Sadlers Wells Lockhart
CSD1473	The Bartered Bride	Sadlers Wells Opera
CSD1474	Organ Recital (Cesar Franck)	Germani
CSD1485	Recital	Lympany
CSD1487-8	Music of Shakespeare's Time	Dolmetsch Consort etc
CSD1495	"Holiday in Britain" (Coates, Jacob, Harty, Arnold, Bantock)	Philh Weldon
CSD1499	"Music for Viola & Cello" (Bruch:Kol Nidrei,Handel,Brahms)	Du Pre Downes (vln)
CSD1500	"Fiesta Flamenca"	Mario Escudero
CSD1501	Beethoven: Piano Sonata 8, Schubert: Moment Musiceaux	Stephen Bishop
CSD1505	Offenbach: La Belle Helene (hlts)	Sadlers Wells
CSD1525	Haydn: Symphonies 89, 90	Vienna Somogyi
CSD1530	Macdowell: Two Piano Concertos	Vienna Chavez List
CSD1531	Villa-Lobos: Cello Concerto	Vienna SO
CSD1532	Bartok: 3 Village Scenes, Music for Strings Perc & Celesta	Budapest Radio Orch Lehel
CSD1533	Offenbach: Gaite Parisienne, Graduation Ball	Philh Mackerras
CSD1555	"The Miniature Elgar"	RPO Collingwood
CSD1558	Strauss,R: Metamorphosen, Le Bourgeois Gentilhomme	Lausanne CO Desarzens
CSD1574	Liszt: Dante Symphony	Budapest Philh Lehel
CSD1576	Humperdinck: Hansel & Gretel	Sadlers Wells
CSD1585	Prokofiev: Romeo & Juliet	Philh Kurtz
CSD1589	Bach,JS: Cantatas 4, 54, 59	LGO Thomas
CSD1591	Chavez: Piano Concerto	Vienna Chavez List
CSD1593	Brahms: Vns&Fugue Op 24, Schumann: Drei Fantasiestucke, Liszt: Sonetto 104 del Petrarca, etc	Lympany
CSD1599	Mozart: Piano Concerto K482, Piano Sonata K570	Vienna RSO Somogyi Barenboim
CSD1601	Bach,JS: Chromatic Fantasy&Fugue, Capriccio Sopro, Handel	Fou Ts'Ong
CSD1608	Mozart: Posthorn Serenade, Serenata Notturna	Lausanne CO Desarzens
CSD1613	Schubert: Piano Sonatas D960, D784	Fou Ts'Ong
CSD1637	Concert of Gershwin, Copland	Utah SO Abravanel
CSD3501	Scarlatti: Sonatas	Fou Ts'Ong
CSD3502	Haydn: String Quartets Op 54 (complete)	Allegri Quartet
CSD3503	Haydn: String Quartets Op 55 (complete)	Allegri Quartet
CSD3507	Holst: Hammersmith Suites 1 & 2, Moorside Suite	Band cond Imogen Holst
CSD3528	Bach,JS: Cantatas 51, 71	LGO Thomas
CSD3539	Holst: St Paul's Suite, Warlock: Capriol Suite, Dvorak	RPO Sargent
CSD3690	Music from the film "Tales of Beatrix Potter"	ROHCG Lanchberry
CSD3695	Rotheenberger sings Lehar	Rotheenberger
CSD3696	Butterworth: A Shropshire Lad, Bridge, Bax	English Sinfonia Dilkes
CSD3705	Warlock: Capriol Suite, Ireland: The Holy Boy, Butterworth	English Sinfonia Dilkes
CSD3713	Sullivan: The Tempest etc	CBSO Dunn
CSD3738	Music for Ferdinand & Isbella	EMCL Munrow
CSD3749	Minkus: Don Quixote	Arranged & conducted Lanchberry
CSD3750	St-Saens: Piano Concertos 2, 4	OdeP Baudo Ciccolini
CSD3751	Dufay: "Music of Guillaume Dufay" (Mass se la face ay pale)	EMCL Munrow
CSD3755	Venetian Festival Music	Kings College Choir Willcocks
CSD3761	Praetorius: Motets	EMCL Munrow
CSD3764	Holst: Choral Music	ECO PJBE Baccholian Singers
CSD3769	Arriaga: Symphony in Dmaj, Schmidt	Philh Bauer
CSD3773	Britten: Canticles 1-3	Tear Bowman Civil
CSD3778	Handel: Messiah Choruses	
CSD3781	Greensleeves to a Ground	EMCL Munrow

CSDA9001 Henry VIII and his Six Wives   EMCL   Munrow

ESD (Greensleeve)

ESD7001	Wiren: Serenade for Strings	BNSO	Montgomery	TASEC
ESD7003	Mendelssohn: Overtures Fingals Cave, Ruy Blas, etc	Philh	Atzmon	
ESD7004	Beethoven: Symphony 6	Munich Philh	Kempe	
ESD7006	"Russian Orch Favourites" (Borodin, R-Korsakov,Mussorgsky)	OdeP	Rozhdestvensky	
ESD7009	"The Lighter Elgar"	Northern Sinfonia	Marriner	
ESD7010	Overtures: Nabucco, Ruy Blas, Zampa, etc	RLPO	Groves	
ESD7011	Tchaikovsky: Marche Slave, Prokofiev: Rome & Juliet	LSO	Previn	
ESD7012	Waldteufel: Waltzes and Polkas	Monte Carlo	Boskovsky	
ESD7013	V Williams: Tallis Fantasia, The Wasps, Elgar	BNSO	Silvestri	
ESD7019	Ravel: Bolero, Chabrier: Espana, Prokofiev: Classical Sym	NPO	de Burgos	
ESD7020	St-Saens:Carnival of the Animals, Poulenc:Babar the Elephant	PCO	Pretre	
ESD7028	Sullivan-Mackerras: Pineapple Poll	RPO	Mackerras	TASEC
ESD7029	Shostakovich: Symphony 5	BNSO	Berglund	
ESD7034	Offenbach: Orpheus, La Belle Helene, Vie Parisienne	CBSO	Fremaux	
ESD7038	St-Saens: Symphony 3	CBSO	Fremaux	
ESD7039	Liszt: Hungarian Rhapsodies 1,4,6, Rakoczy March, etc	Phun	Boskovsky	
ESD7040	Massenet: Le Cid	CBSO	Fremaux	TASEC
ESD7045	Lanner: Waltzes and Galops	Vienna Strauss Orch	Boskovsky	
ESD7049	Shostakovich: Symphony 10	BNSO	Berglund	
ESD7050	Xmas Music from Kings Cambridge	Kings College Cambridge	Willcocks	
ESD7058	Liszt: Hungarian Rhapsodies 2,3,5, Mephisto Waltz 1	LPO	Boskovsky	
ESD7065	Arnold: Concertos for Cyril & Phyllis, Bliss, Jacob	CBSO	Arnold Smith Sellick	
ESD7077	Rossini-Respighi: La Boutique Fantasque	LSO	Gardelli	
ESD7078	Enescu: Roumanian Rhapsody, Falla: 3 Cornered Hat, etc	LSO	Previn	
ESD7092	"English Tone Pictures" (Tintagel, etc)	LSO	Barbirolli	
ESD7094	Sibelius: Symphonies 3, 5	BNSO	Berglund	
ESD7095	Sibelius: Symphonies 1, 7	BNSO	Berglund	
ESD7097	Ibert: Divertissement, Satie, Poulenc, Berlioz	CBSO	Fremaux	TASEC
ESD7099	Delius: Appalachia, Brigg Fair	HO	Barbirolli	
ESD7114	Saint-Saens: Carnival of the Animals/Prokofiev	Philh	Kurtz	TASEC
ESD7133	Bliss: Morning Heroes (Symphony)	RLPO	Groves	
ESD7151	Prokofiev: Romeo & Juliet/Cinderella	Philh	Kurtz	
ESD7159	Sibelius: En Saga/Pelleas/Pohjola's Daughter	BNSO	Berglund	
ESD7160	Sibelius: Spring Song/King Christian II/The Bard/karelia/etc	BNSO	Berglund	
ESD7177	Orff: Carmina Burana	Philh	De Burgos	
ESDW718	Berlioz: Requiem	CBSO	Fremaux	
ESDW720	"Andre Previn Music Festival"	2 disc reissue of ASD3131 and ASD3338 (Music Night vol1 and vol 2)		

HQS

HQS1017	Beethoven: Piano Sonatas Op 101, Op 109		Stephen Bishop
HQS1028	Brahms: Variations on theme by Paganini/, Vns on theme by Haydn		Anievas
HQS1029	Beethoven: Cello Sonatas	Du Pre	Bishop
HQS1058	Chopin: 24 Etudes Op 10 & Op 25		Anievas
HQS1060	Vivaldi: 4 Concertos for 2 Orchestras	Solisti di Milano	Bobesco
HQS1061	Sibelius: String Quartet in Dmin, Barber: Adagio for Strings	Lansdowne Qt	
HQS1070	Sibelius: Karelia Ov, The Bard, etc	SNO	Gibson
HQS1076	Beethoven: Piano Sonatas Pathetique, Appassionata, Moonlight		Barenboim
HQS1088	Beethoven: Piano Sonatas Op 81a ("Les Adieux"), Op 111, Op 49/1		Barenboim
HQS1091	"A Pageant of English Song 1597-1961"	Baker	Moore
HQS1107	Beethoven: Piano Sonatas Op 2/1, Op 31/2, Op 49/2		Barenboim
HQS1108	Bizet: L'Arlesienne & Carmen Suites	RPO	Beecham
HQS1120	Mozart: String Quintets K516, K593	Heutling Quartet	
HQS1125	Chopin: 24 Preludes op 28, etc		Orozco

HQS1126	Delius: Florida Suite, Dance Rhapsody 2, etc	RPO	Beecham
HQS1128	Mozart: String Quintets K174, K614	Heutling Quartet	
HQS1135	Mozart: String Quintets K515, K406	Heutling Quartet	
HQS1136	Berlioz: Le Corsaire, Fauré: Dolly Suite, S-Saens, etc	RPO	Beecham
HQS1152	Beethoven: Piano Sonatas Op 10/1-3		Barenboim
HQS1154	Beethoven: Symphony 2, Ruins of Athens	RPO	Beecham
HQS1155	Beethoven: String Quartets Op 18/1, Op 18/2	Hungarian Quartet	
HQS1159	Beethoven: String Quartets Op 59/1 ("Rasumovsky")	Hungarian Quartet	
HQS1160	Beethoven: String Quartets Op 59/2 ("Rasumovsky"), Op 95	Hungarian Quartet	
HQS1161	Beethoven: String Quartets Op 59/3 ("Rasumovsky"), Op 74 ("Harp")	Hungarian Quartet	
HQS1177	Beethoven: Quartets Op 127/Op 135	Hungarian Quartet	
HQS1178	Beethoven: String Quartet Op 130, Grosse Fuge Op 133	Hungarian Quartet	
HQS1179	Beethoven: String Quartet Op 131	Hungarian Quartet	
HQS1180	Beethoven: String Quartet Op 132	Hungarian Quartet	
HQS1181	Beethoven: Piano Sonatas Op 53, Op 110		Barenboim
HQS1185	Beethoven: Piano Sonatas Op 28, Op 2/3		Barenboim
HQS1188	Mendelssohn: Octet/Sphr: Double Quartet	Melos Ensemble	
HQS1189	Chopin: Military Polonaise, Nocturne in flat, Fantaisie Impromptu		Ogdon
HQS1191	Mozart: String Quartets K387, K421	Heutling Quartet	
HQS1192	Mozart: String Quartets K428, K458	Heutling Quartet	
HQS1193	Mozart: String Quartets K464, K465	Heutling Quartet	
HQS1201	Beethoven: Piano Sonatas Op 31/1, Op 31/3, Op 54		Barenboim
HQS1202	Beethoven: Piano Sonatas Op 22, Op 27/1, Op 90		Barenboim
HQS1203	Beethoven: Piano Sonatas Op 2/2, Op 78, Op 109		Barenboim
HQS1205	Beethoven: Piano Sonatas Op 7, Op 79, Op 101		Barenboim
HQS1206	Beethoven: Piano Sonatas Op 14/1, Op 14/2, Op 26		Barenboim
HQS1207	Beethoven: Piano Sonata Op 106 ("Hammerklavier")		Barenboim
HQS1211	Mozart: String Quartets K499, K575	Heutling Quartet	
HQS1212	Mozart: String Quintets K589, K590	Heutling Quartet	
HQS1229	Beethoven: Piano Variations Vol 1		Ogdon
HQS1230	Beethoven: Piano Variations Vol 2		Ogdon
HQS1236	V-Williams: On Wenlock Edge, etc	Music Group of London	
HQS1237	Palestrina: Missa Papae Marcelli, Missa Brevis	Kings College Cambridge	Willcocks
HQS1244	Handel: Messiah (exts)	ECO	Mackerras
HQS1245	Fauré: Piano Qt 1, Andante, Papillon	Menuhin Menuhin Gendron	
HQS1247	Alkan: Piano Pieces		Ronald Smith
HQS1249	Two Renaissance Dance Bands	EMCL	David Munro
HQS1251	Chopin Recital		Adni
HQS1252	Elgar: Violin Sonata, String Quartet	Music Group of London Quartet	
HQS1254	Bach, J.S: Cantata 147, 3 Motets	ASMF	King's College Choir Willcocks
HQS1258	Duparc: 12 Melodies, Fauré: Poeme d'un Jour Lydia, etc	Souzay	Baldwin
HQS1260	Finzi: Dies Natalis	ECO	Holst Finzi
HQS1262	Debussy: 2 Arabesques, Suite Bergamasque, etc		Adni
HQS1285	Britten: A Ceremony of Carols	Kings College Cambridge Choir	
HQS1289	"Encores"		Tortelier
HQS1290	"Chopin Rarities"		Ronald Smith
HQS1291	Schubert: 3 Sonatinas D384, D385, D408, Duo D574	Suk	Buchbinder
HQS1292	Vaughan Williams: String Quartets	Music Group of London	
HQS1295	"Songs of Many Lands"		Souzay
HQS1302	Boyce: The 8 Symphonies	Festival Orch Menuhin	
HQS1306	Bartok: Contrasts for Violin, Clarinet & Piano, Milhaud, Khachaturian, Prokofiev	Melos	De Peyer Hurwitz
HQS1310	Britten: Winter Words, 7 Sonnets of Michelangelo, etc	Tear	Ledger
HQS1327	V Williams: Violin Sonata, 6 Studies in English Folk Song	Bean (violin)	Parkhouse (piano)
HQS1329	Rachmaninov: Etudes Tableuax Op 33 & Op 39		Ogdon
HQS1330	Ravel: Piano Trio in Amin, Shostakovich: Piano Trio 2	Previn	Kirschbaum

HQS1332	"Earl Wild Plays Liszt"		Earl Wild
HQS1337	"Modern British Piano Music"		Ogdon
HQS1344	Debussy: Petite Suite, Fetes, Bizet: Jeux D'Enfants	Ogdon	Lucas
HQS1355	Schubert: Piano Sonata D960		Adni
HQS1362	Shostakovich: String Quartets 14, 15		Beethoven Quartet
HQS1363	Piano Music of Percy Grainger		Adni
HQS1368	Telemann: Six Sonatas for 2 Flutes Op 2	Galway	Debost
HQS1369	Shostakovich: Viola Sonata		David Oistrakh
HQS1380	Brahms: Hungarian Dances	Beroff	Collard
HQS1381	Tchaikovsky: Piano Trio in Amin	Zhukov	Feigin
HQS1398	Schubert: 'Arpeggione' Sonata/Grieg: Cello Sonata		Tortelier
HQS1412	V-Williams: As I Walked Out (Folk Songs)		Tear
HQS1413	Recital (Schubert, Paganini, Brahms)		Spivakov
HQS1415	Renaissance Suite	EMCL	David Munro
HQS1437	Recital		du Pre

SAN (HMV Angel) Series

The HMV Angel series was first issued in 1963. Most (but not all) SANs came in boxes, and the numbering of these causes a lot of confusion since they have SLS numbers as well as their SAN numbers. EMI always issued a SLS number for every box set they issued. For example, SAN121-5 Lohengrin/Kempe also has SLS906 on the spine of the box. What is even more confusing is that on later SAN issues EMI also drop the SAN number from the box, so that what started out as a SAN set ends up as a SLS set!

All Angel boxes were in the SLS 9xx series. By early 1970 when the later yellow label was standard the boxes were issued with only the SLS number and reference to SAN was dropped although the discs inside the box still carried SAN numbers.

The last set that was issued under a SAN number was SAN256-7 and from SLS 947 onwards all reference to SAN had disappeared from EMI's publicity.

Entries for SLS 947 onwards will be found in the SLS section of this handbook though and are cross-referenced from the following SAN listing.

Of course, none of this applies to single disc SAN issues and these are all listed in the SAN listing.

Label: The SAN label came in three forms. The earliest is gold with a white angel at 12 o'clock. After that the label is again gold but at 12 o'clock there is a postage stamp sized rectangle showing the Nipper dog on a coloured background. The third label is yellow with the same postage stamp "coloured dog". There is one special label, used in SDAN143-5 – the "Callas Carmen". This was a special deluxe issue with a special label in which the "Nipper" at 12 o'clock is in red instead of white.

Number	Work	Orchestra	Performers	SLS
SAN101-2	Lehar: The Merry Widow	Philh	Matacic Schwarzkopf Gedda	(SLS 823 & SLS 900)
SAN103-6	Mozart: Cosi fan tutte	Philh	Bohm	(SLS 901 & SLS5028)
SAN107	Fauré: Requiem	PCO	Cluytens De LosAngeles	
SAN108-9	Mascagni: Cavalleria Rusticana	Rome Opera	Santini De Los Angeles	(SLS 902)
SAN110-3	Mussorgsky: Boris Godunov	PCO	Cluytens	(SLS 903)
SAN114-6	Rossini: Barber of Seville	Glyndebourne	Gui	(SLS 904 & SLS5165)
SAN117-9	St-Saens: Samson et Dalila	ONDF	Pretre Vickers Gorr	(SLS 905)
SAN120	Verdi: 4 Sacred Pieces	Philh	Giulini	
SAN121-5	Wagner: Lohengrin	VPO	Kempe	(SLS 906 & SLS5071)
SAN126-7	Monteverdi: Coronation of Poppea	RPO	Glyndebourne Pritchard	(SLS 908)
SAN128-30	Giordano: Andrea Chenier	Rome Opera	Santini	(SLS 910)
SAN131-2	Puccini: La Boheme	Rome Op	Schippers	(SLS 907)
SAN133-4	Verdi: Requiem	Philh	Giulini Schwarzkopf/Ludwig	(SLS 909)
SAN137-9	Mozart: Magic Flute	Philh	Klemperer	(SLS 912)
SAN140-2	Bizet: Carmen	Paris Op	Pretre Callas Gedda	(SLS 913)
SDAN143-5	Bizet: Carmen Special deluxe commemorative issue	Paris Op	Pretre Callas Gedda	(SDLS 914)
SAN146-8	Handel: Messiah	Philh	Klemperer	(SLS 915)
SAN149-50	Puccini: Tosca	Paris Orch	Pretre Callas Gobbi	(SLS 917)
SAN151-3	Verdi: Il Trovatore	Rome	Schippers	(SLS 916)
SAN154-6	Offenbach: Tales of Hoffmann	PCO	Cluytens De Los Angeles Schwarzkopf	(SLS 918)
SAN157-8	Falla: La Vida Breve ; Tonadillas	Spanish NO	De Burgos Los Angeles	(SLS 919)
SAN159-61	Puccini: Turandot	Rome Opera	Molinari-Pradelli Nilsson	(SLS 921)
SAN162	Orff: Carmina Burana	Philh	De Burgos	
SAN163-4	Brahms: Deutsche Volkslieder		Schwarzkopf Fischer-Dieskau Moore	(SLS 926)
SAN165-6	Beethoven: Missa Solemnis	Philh	Klemperer	(SLS 922)
SAN169	Purcell: Dido and Aeneas	ECO	Barbirolli De Los Angeles	
SAN170-1	Berlioz: L'enfance du Christ	PCO	Cluytens	(SLS 928)

SAN172-5	Mozart: Don Giovanni	Philh Klemperer	(SLS 923)
SAN179	Mahler: Das Lied von der Erde	Philh Klemperer	
SAN180-1	Donizetti: L'Elisir D'Amore	Rome Opera Pradelli Gedda Freni	(SLS 925)
SAN182-3	"Homage to Gerald Moore"	Moore De Los Angeles Schwarzkopf Fiescher-Dieskau	(SLS 926)
SAN184-6	Puccini: Madama Butterfly	Rome Opera Barbirolli Bergonzi	(SLS 927)
SAN189-91	Verdi: Aida	Rome Opera Mehta Nilsson Bumbry	(SLS 929)
SAN192	Walton: The Bear	ECO Lockhart	
SAN193	Mozart: Requiem	Philh De Burgos	
SAN194	Andalusian Songs	De Los Angeles	
SAN195-7	Bach: Mass in Bmin	Philh Klemperer	(SLS 930)
SAN201-3	Mozart: Abduction from the Seraglio	BFCO Menuhin	(SLS 932)
SAN204-6	Verdi: Rigoletto	Rome Op Molinari-Pradelli	(SLS 933)
SAN207-9	Wagner: Flying Dutchman	Philh Klemperer	(SLS 934)
SAN210-1	Wolf: The Italian Song Book	Schwarzkopf Fischer-Dieskau	(SLS 937)
SAN212-4	Mendelssohn: Elijah	Philh De Burgos	(SLS 935)
SAN215-7	Strauss,R: Ariadne Auf Naxos	Dresden SO Kempe Janowitz	(SLS 936)
SAN218	Mahler: Des Knaben Wunderhorn	LSO Szell/Schwarzkopf/Dieskau	
SAN228-31	Bach,JS: St Matthew Passion	ViennaConsortium Musicum Gonnenwein Gedda	(SLS 942)
SAN235-7	Gounod: Romeo and Juliet	Paris Opera Corelli Freni	(SLS 943)
SAN238-41	Beethoven: The 5 Piano Concertos	Philh Klemperer Barenboim	(SLS 941 & SLS5180)
SAN242-3	Mascagni: L'Amico Fritz	ROHCG Gavazzeni Freni Pavarotti	(SLS 938)
SAN244-5	Elgar: The Kingdom	LPO Boult	(SLS 939)
SAN246-8	Flotow: Martha	Bavarian St Opera Heger Gedda	(SLS 944)
SAN249-51	Massenet: Werther	OdeP Pretre De Los Angeles Gedda	(SLS 945)
SAN252-4	Verdi: Otello	Philh Barbirolli Fischer-Dieskau	(SLS 940)
SAN255	"A Tribute to Gerald Moore"	De Los Angeles Du Pre Barenboim Schwarzkopf etc	
SAN256-7	Janacek: Jenufa	Prague National Gregor	(SLS 946)
SAN258-9	see SLS 947		
SAN260-3	see SLS 948		
SAN264-6	see SLS 949		
SAN267-8	see SLS 950		
SAN270-2	see SLS 951		
SAN273-5	see SLS 952		
SAN276-8	see SLS 953		
SAN280-2	see SLS 954		
SAN283-6	see SLS 955		
SAN287-90	see SLS 956		
SAN291	Brahms: Die Schone Magelone	Richter Fischer-Dieskau	
SAN292-6	see SLS 957		
SAN300-1	see SLS 958		
SAN302-4	see SLS 959		
SAN307-9	see SLS 960		
SAN310-3	see SLS 961		
SAN314-5	see SLS 962		
SAN316-8	see SLS 966		
SAN319-23	see SLS 963		
SAN324	Walton: Belshazzar's Feast	LSO Previn Shirley-Quirk	
SAN325-6	see SLS 964		
SAN327-30	see SLS 965		
SAN331-3	see SLS 967		
SAN334-5	see SLS 968		
SAN336-8	see SLS 969		
SAN339-43	see SLS 970		
SAN344-6	see SLS 973		
SAN347-8	see SLS 971		

SAN349-50 see SLS 974
SAN351-3 see SLS 975
SAN354   Holst: Choral Symphony   LPO   Boult
SAN355-7 see SLS 976
SAN358-60 see SLS 977
SAN361-4 see SLS 978
SAN365   Bliss: Morning Heroes (Symphony)   RLPO   Groves
SAN366-7 see SLS 979
SAN368-70 see SLS 981
SAN371-3 see SLS 980
SAN374-5 see SLS 982
SAN376-9 see SLS 983
SAN380-2 see SLS 984
SAN383-5 see SLS 985
SAN386-8 see SLS 986
SAN389-90 see SLS 987
SAN391-2 see SLS 988
SAN393   Hadley: The Hills   LPO   Ledger
SAN394-5 see SLS 989
SAN396-400 see SLS 990
SAN402-4 see SLS 992
SAN405-6 see SLS 991
SAN407-9 see SLS 993
SAN410-2 see SLS 997
SAN413-4 see SLS 996
SAN415-7 see SLS 999
SAN418-9 see SLS 998
SAN420-3 see SLS 995
SAN424-7 see SLS1000

SCX

The great majority of the SCX series is popular and jazz. The following list includes all the classical music entries in the series.

SCX3251	Waldteufel: Les Patineurs, Mon rêve, Grenadiers, etc	Philh Prom Krips H.
SCX3256	Suppe: Overtures	Philh Prom Krips H.
SCX3260	"Palm Court Concert"	Max Jaffa Orchestra
SCX3269	Viennese Dances I	Philh Prom Krips H.
SCX3279	Viennese Dances II	Philh Prom Krips H.
SCX3281	Bernstein: On the Town	Lotis Blair and Orch
SCX3291	Chopin: Les Sylphides, Ponchielli: Dance of the Hours, Meyerbeer: Les Patineurs	Philh Mackerras
SCX3305	Overtures (Offenbach, Thomas, Rossini, etc)	Band of the Scots Guards
SCX3340	"The Immortal Puccini"	Michael Collins & String Orch
SCX3346	J.Strauss: Waltzes	Philh Prom Krips.H.
SCX3362	Waltzes	Philh Prom Krips H.
SCX3387	Weill: Excerpts from the Musicals	Orch cond Sandloff
SCX3416	Grieg: Holberg Suite/2 Elegaic Melodies/etc	Philh Weldon
SCX3427	Slavonic Music (Dvorak,Smetana,Enesco,Bartok)	Philh Mackerras
SCX3446	Orchestral Pieces (Greensleeves,Figaro,Love for 3 Oranges,etc)	Philh Weldon
SCX3467	Bach,JS:Organ Recital at Lyon Cathedral	Commette
SCX3499	Tchaikovsky: 1812 Ov,Dvorak: Carnaval Ov,Mendelssohn,etc	Philh Weldon
SCX3503	"Pop Concert USA" (Bernstein, Copland, Gershwin, etc)	Cleveland Pops Orch Louis Lane
SCX3514	"Magic Vienna" (Waltzes and Polkas)	Clvlnd/Szell
SCX3525	"Romances and Serenades" (V Williams,Delius,Warlock, etc)	Clevelnd Sinfonietta Louis Lane Druian
SCX3539	"Music for a Golden Flute"	Cleveland Sinfonia Lane Sharp (flute)

SCX3541	Beethoven: Piano Concertos 2,4	Clvlnd	Szell Fleisher
SCX3567	Beethoven: Piano Concerto 1	Clvlnd	Szell Fleisher
SCX3568	French Music for the Harp	PCO	Cluytens Annie Challan (harp)
SCX3570	V Williams: Hodie, Xmas Cantata	LSO	Willcocks Baker
SCX3572	Beethoven: Piano Concerto 3	Clvlnd	Szell Fleisher
SCX3575	Beethoven: Emperor Concerto	Clvlnd	Szell Fleisher
SCX6014	Kodaly/Bartok/Britten	Kodaly Girls Choir of Budapest	
SCX6053	Dvorak: Slavonic Dances 1-16 op 46 & op 72	Clvlnd	Szell
SCX6054	Smetana: Ma Vlast (Vltava), Bartered Bride (3 Dances)	Clvlnd	Szell
SCX6132	Lieder (Mahler & Mendelssohn)	Raskin (sop) Schick (pno)	
SCX6159	Harpsichord Recital (Clarke,Handel,Byrd,Purcell,etc)	Kipnis (hpsd)	
SCX6163	Mayer: Quintet for Strings & Sitar, Frankel: String Quartet 5	Lansdowne Quartet Motihar	

SXLP: HMV "Concert Classics" series

The HMV "Concert Classics" series was first published in 1959 as a mid priced series and consists of a mixture of original recordings and reissues of material from a number of sources, most notably including some of the most famous recordings from the HMV and EMI Columbia catalogues. The final issues in the series were released in 1983.

No fewer than six labels were used during its history, the first four being blue with silver lettering, including one with the traditional Melodiya logo. The final two labels, towards the end of the series, were in HMV red.

This listing includes cross references to the original issues. Where no cross reference is given it can be assumed to be the first issue in the UK.

In some cases the original issue shown is a mono such as ALP or 33CX. This indicates that, at the original recording sessions, as well as the original mono recordings, there were also stereo recordings made. This happened because, in those very early days of stereo, HMV and EMI were experimenting with stereo recordings. An eventually issued LP record consists of a selection of "takes" made during the total recording session, and it is perfectly possible that the stereo SXLP consists of a different selection from the original mono release. So where we cross reference to a mono, all that can be said with certainty is that the SXLP originates from the same series of recording sessions as did the original mono.

SXLP20003	Sullivan: Overtures Mikado,Gondoliers,Yeoman,Pirates,etc	Pro Arte	Sargent
SXLP20004	Beethoven: Emporor Concerto	BPO	Kempe Gimpel
SXLP20007	Elgar: Enigma Variations, V Williams: Tallis Fantasia	Philh	Sargent
SXLP20008	"Popular French Overtures" (Suppe,Auber,Offenbach,Herold)	RPO	Gamley
SXLP20010	Brahms: Piano Concerto 1	BPO	Kempe Gimpel
SXLP20019	Mozart: Eine Kleine NachtMusik, Serenata Notturna, etc	Philh	Davis
SXLP20023	Tchaikovsky: 1812 ov, Marche Slave, Romeo&Juliet, Beauty	RPO	Sargent
SXLP20024	Tchaikovsky: Nutcracker, Swan Lake	RPO	Weldon
SXLP20025	Grieg: Piano Concerto, Norwegian Dances, Lyric Suite	RPO	Weldon Bachauer
SXLP20026	Rimsky-Korsakov: Scheherazade	Philh	Kletzki
SXLP20027	Tchaikovsky: Symphony 6	Philh	Kletzki
SXLP20028	Liszt: Piano Concertos 1 & 2	Philh	Silvestri Francois
SXLP20029	Schubert: Symphony 8, Rosamunde	RPO	Sargent
SXLP20030	French Orch Works (Dukas, Chabrier, Debussy, Ravel, etc)	Colonne Concerts Orch	Dervaux
SXLP20031	Beethoven: Ovs (Egmont, Coriolan, Prometheus, Fidelio,etc)	BPO	Vandernoot
SXLP20032	Sullivan: Overtures, German: Dances	Pro Arte	Sargent
SXLP20033	Handel: Water Music, Royal Fireworks	RPO	Weldon
SXLP20034	Overtures Mastersingers, Romain Carnival, Fingal's Cave, etc	RPO	Sargent
SXLP20035	Mozart: Piano Concerto K491, Piano Sonata K576	Philh	Blech Kentner

SXLP20036	Berlioz: Symphonie Fantastique	PCO	Silvestri
SXLP20037	Mendelssohn: Symphony 4, Midsummer Nts Dream	Philh	Wallberg
SXLP20038	Beethoven: Symphony 7	RPO	Davis
SXLP20040	Beethoven: Symphony 3	RPO	Sargent
SXLP20041	"Strauss Waltzes" (Vienna Woods,Emperor,Blue Danube,etc)	RPO	Sargent
SXLP20042	Tchaikovsky: Capriccio Italien, Eugen Onegin (hlts)	RPO	Weldon Shuard
SXLP20043	Beethoven: Violin Concerto	RPO	Pritchard Campoli
SXLP20044	Bizet: L'arlesienne Suites 1&2, Carmen Suite 1	Philh	Wallberg
SXLP20045	Beethoven: Piano Concerto 3	BPO	Cluytens Tacchino
SXLP20046	Operatic Recital (Verdi, Mascagni, Puccini, Giordano)	ROHCG	Downes Shuard
SXLP20047	Berlioz: Damnation de Faust Suite, Bizet: Jeux d'Enfants Suite,La Jolie Fille de Perth Suite	Colonne Orch Dervaux	
SXLP20048	Mozart: Piano Concertos K466, K488	PCO	Vandernoot Heidsieck
SXLP20049	Chopin: Les Sylphides, Rossini: William Tell Ballet Music	ROHCG	Sargent
SXLP20050	Rachmaninov: Piano Concerto 2, Weber	PCO	Cluytens Tacchino
SXLP20051	Mozart: Piano Concertos K456, K503	Bavarian RSO	Engel Prohaska
SXLP20052	Lalo: Symphonie Espagnole, Wieniawski: Violin Concerto 2	Vienna SO	Rudel Olevsky
SXLP20053	Tchaikovsky: Violin Concerto	Philh	Rodzinski Morini
SXLP20058	Grieg: Holberg Suite, Bach, Barber	Philh	Fistoulari
SXLP20059-60	Tchaikovsky: Nutcracker	Philh	Rodzinski [WST203]
SXLP20061	Schubert: Trout Quintet	Barylli Quartet Badura-Skoda	[WST14074]
SXLP20064-5	Smetana: Ma Vlast, Dvorak: Symphonic Variations	Philh	Sargent
SXLP20069	Haydn: Trumpet Conc, Horn Conc 2, Sinf Concertante op 84	Consortium Musicum Fritz Lehan	
SXLP20071	Mendelssohn: Octet Op 20	Janacek and Smetana Quartets	[WST14082]
SXLP20075	Dvorak: Sextet Op 48, Quintet Op 97	European Quartet	
SXLP20078	Massenet: Scenes Pittoresques, Chabrier: Joyeuse Marche, Habanera,Fte Polonaise,Boure Fantasque	PCO	Dervaux
SXLP20080	The Voice of the Violin	Collier (vln) Lush (pno)	
SXLP20081	Beethoven: Triple Concerto Egmont & Coriolan Ovs	Philh BPO	Sargent Oistrakh Knushevitsky Oborin [SBO2753] Vandernoot [SXLP20031]
SXLP20088	Berlioz: Symphonie Fantastique	BPO	Kempe
SXLP20090	Britten: Matinees Musicales, Rossini-Respighi: Rossiniana	Vienna SO	Zeller
SXLP20091	Strauss,J: Die Fledermaus (hlts)	Philh	Ackermann [SAX2336-7]
SXLP20092	Dvorak: Piano Concerto, Slavonic Rhapsody Op 45/2	Vienna SO	Somogyi Firkusny
SXLP20093	Mozart: Symphonies 1-5	Philh	Leinsdorf
SXLP20094	Liszt: Hungarian Rhapsodies 1, 2, 6, 12	Bavarian RSO	Ludwig
SXLP20096	Famous Contralto Arias (Handel,Gluck,Mozart,Purcell)	Vienna Op	Zeller Forrester
SXLP20097	Liszt: Years of Pilgrimage (First Year: Switzerland)		Edith Farnadi
SXLP20098	Liszt: Years of Pilgrimage (Second Year: Italy, Venice, and Naples)		Edith Farnadi
SXLP20099	Prokofiev: Symphony 5, Shostakovich: Festival Ov, Kabalevsky: Colas Breugnon Ov	SNO	Gibson
SXLP20100	Liszt: Years of Pilgrimage (Third Year: Italie)		Edith Farnadi
SXLP20101	Tchaikovsky: Swan Lake	Vienna SO	Lanchberry
SXLP20102	Bach: Cantatas 35, 42	Vienna	Scherchen Stich-Randall
SXLP20103	Schubert: Rosamunde	BavRSO	Heger Rothenberger
SXLP20104	Beethoven: Piano Concerto 5	Philh	Leitner Gelber
SXLP20105	Bach: Organ Works		Vollenweider (organ of Zurich)
SXLP20106	Tchaikovsky: Piano Concerto 1 R-Korsakov:Spanish Caprice,Borodin:Steppes of Central Asia	Philh Philh	Cluytens Mdivani Cluytens [SAX2355]
SXLP20107	Beethoven: Piano Concerto 3, "Les Adieux" Sonata	Philh	Leitner Gelber
SXLP20108	Schumann: Carnaval op 9, Etudes Symphoniques op 13		Bruno Leonardo-Gelber (piano)
SXLP20109	Beethoven: Symphony 1,Overtures Coriolan, Leonora 3	BPO	Cluytens
SXLP20110-1	Bach,JS: Brandenburg Concertos 1-6	Philh CO	Littaur Leppard (hpsd)
SXLP20112	Mozart: Sinfonia Concertante K364, Symphony 29	Netherlands CO	Zinman Brainin Schidlof
SXLP30002	Balakirev: Symphony 1	RPO	Beecham [CX1450]
SXLP30012	Tchaikovsky: Sleeping Beauty Suite	Philh	Weldon [SX1095-6]

Other EMI labels

Catalog	Title	Orchestra	Conductor/Artist	Reference
SXLP30018	Dvorak: Cello Concerto	Philh	Sargent Tortelier	[ALP1306]
SXLP30019	Verdi: Ballet Music (Trovatore, Vespers, Forza, etc)	Philh	Mackerras	
SXLP30022	Delibes: La Source, Messager: Les Deux Pigeons	ROHCG	Mackerras	[CLP1195]
SXLP30027	"Wiener Schnitzel" (Viennese Waltzes)	Philh Prom Orch	Krips	[SX1167]
SXLP30032	Mozart: Symphony 28, 4 Minuets K601, etc	LMP	Blech	[CLP1102]
SXLP30033	D'Indy: Symphony on a French Mt Air, Fauré, St-Saens	LSO	Goossens/Collingwood	[CLP1255]
SXLP30035	Waldteufel: Waltzes	Philh	Henry Krips	[SCX3251]
SXLP30037	Suppe: Overtures (Light Cavalry, Pique Dame, etc)	Philh	Henry Krips	[SCX3256]
SXLP30038	Weber: Ovs Euryanthe, Abu Hassan, Jubel, Freischutz, etc	Philh	Sawallisch	[SAX2343]
SXLP30046	Rossini-Respighi: La Boutique Fantasque, Dukas: Sorcerer	RPO	Goossens	[BSD752]
SXLP30054	Mahler: Symphony 4	Philh	Kletzki Loose	[SAX2345]
SXLP30055	Franck: Symphony in Dmin, Psyche and Eros	Philh	Giulini	[CX1589]
SXLP30056	"Johann Strauss Favourites" (Emperor Waltz, Fledermaus, etc)	Philh	Henry Krips	[SCX3346]
SXLP30057	Lumbye: Copenhagen Tivoli Music	Copenhagen SO	Friisholm	[CSD1536]
SXLP30060	"Viennese Delights" (Vienna Woods, Radetzky March, etc)	VPO	Kempe	[ASD279]
SXLP30061	Sibelius: Symphony 2	Philh	Kletzki	[SAX2280]
SXLP30062	The Soviet Army Ensemble	Red Army Ensemble		[SAX2487]
SXLP30063	Brahms: Violin Concerto	Philh	Kondrashin Kogan	[SAX2307]
SXLP30065	Tchaikovsky: Symphony 5, Borodin: Prince Igor Ov	Philh	Silvestri	[ASD338/ASD261]
SXLP30066	Tchaikovsky: Symphony 4, Glinka: Russlan & Ludmilla Ov	Philh	Silvestri	[ASD338/ASD253]
SXLP30067	Stravinsky: Firebird, Ravel: Mother Goose Suite	Philh	Giulini	[SAX2279]
SXLP30068	Mussorgsky: Pictures, Respighi: Fountains of Rome	RPO	Goossens	[ASD366]
SXLP30070	Borodin: Prince Igor, Moussorgsky, R-K: Russian Easter Ov	Philh	Matacic	[SAX2327]
SXLP30075	Chopin: Piano Music		Moiseiwitsch	[CLP1282]
SXLP30076	R-Korsakov: Coq d'Or, Tale of Tsar Saltan, Dubinushka, etc	Philh	Kurtz	[ASD376, ASD582]
SXLP30077	Popular Overtures (Oberon, Fingals Cave, Orpheus, etc)	VPO	Kempe	[HMV Originals]
SXLP30078	Tchaikovsky: Symphony 6, Rimsky-Korsakov: May Night Ov	Philh	Silvestri	[ASD273/ASD338]
SXLP30080	Beethoven: Triple Concerto	Philh	Sargent Oistrakh Oborin Knushevitsky	[SBO2753]
	Overtures Egmont, Coriolan	BPO	Vandernoot	[SXLP20031]
SXLP30081	Beethoven: Symphonies 5, 8	BPO	Cluytens	[ASD267, new recording]
SXLP30083	"Viennese Nights" (Fledermaus, Emperor Waltz, etc)	VPO	Kempe	[HMV Originals]
SXLP30085	Beethoven: Symphony 9	BPO	Cluytens	[Original]
SXLP30086	Beethoven: Piano Concerto 4	Philh	Ludwig Gilels	[SBO2752]
	Mozart: Violin Concerto 3	Philh	Oistrakh	[SAX2304]
SXLP30087	"Nights at the Ballet" (Carnaval, Giselle, Nutcracker, etc)	various	Irving	[HMV Originals]
SXLP30088-9	Sullivan: HMS Pinafore, Trial by Jury	Glyndebourne	Sargent	[ASD472, ASD419]
SXLP30091	Chopin: Piano Sonata 2, Ballades 1-4		Malcuzynski	[SAX2444, SAX2509]
SXLP30094	"Rossini & Verdi Overtures" (Barber, Ladder, Forza, Vespers)	Philh	Giulini	[SAX2377]
SXLP30098	Beethoven: Symphony 4, Overtures: Ruins of Athens, Prometheus, Fidelio	BPO	Cluytens	
SXLP30099	Opera&Operetta Recital (Lehar, Mozart, Heuberger, etc)	Various	Rothenberger	[DSD1756, DSD1757]
SXLP30100	Brahms: Symphony 3, Tragic Ov	BPO	Kempe	[ASD406]
SXLP30101	Tchaikovsky: The Tempest, Luigini: Ballet Egyptian, Glinka	RPO/Philh	Fistoulari	
SXLP30105	Grieg: Peer Gynt Suites 1,2, Symphonic Dances	Philh	Susskind	[SX1057]
SXLP30107	Borodin: Symphony 1,	Philh	Galliera	[CX1356]
	Balakirev: Overtures	Philh	Matacic	[CX1280]
SXLP30110	Dvorak: New World Symphony, Scherzo Capriccioso	BPO	Kempe	[ASD380/ASD449]
SXLP30111	Offenbach: Gaite Parisienne, Strauss: Graduation Ball	Philh	Mackerras	[CSD1533]
SXLP30112-3	Sullivan: Iolanthe	Glyndebourne	Sargent	[ASD282-4]
SXLP30114	Britten: Purcell Vns, Simple Symphony, Walton: Facade 1,2	BBCSO/RPO	Sargent	[BSD754, ASD443]
SXLP30117	"Sparkling Overtures"	Sadlers Wells/RPO	Tausky	[Various reissues]
SXLP30119	"Russian Concert Favourites" (Glazunov, Prokofiev, Borodin)	Philh	Fistoulari	[HMV Originals]
SXLP30120-1	Sullivan: Yeoman of the Guard	Glyndebourne	Sargent	[ASD364-5]
SXLP30122	Tchaikovsky & Mendelssohn: Violin Concertos	Philh	Silvestri Ferras	[ASD278]
SXLP30123	British Concert Pops	Philh/Pro Arte	Weldon	[HMV originals]
SXLP30124	Mozart: Piano Concertos K467, K482	Philh	Sawallisch Annie Fischer	[CX1630]

Catalog	Work	Orchestra	Conductor/Soloist	Reissue
SXLP30125	"Bohemian Festival" (Bartered Bride, Schwanda, etc)	RPO	Kempe	[ASD449]
SXLP30126	Elgar: Serenade for Strings, Holst, Warlock	BBCSO	Sargent	[CSD3539, BSD754]
SXLP30127	Tchaikovsky:1812 Ov,Capriccio Italien,Eugen Onegin,etc	Philh/RPO	Weldon	[SXLP20042,SCX3499]
SXLP30128	Berlioz: Roman Carnival, Corsair, Beatrice&Benedict, Benvenuto Cellini, King Lear	LSO	Gibson	
SXLP30129	Beethoven: Piano Sonatas Pathetique, Moonlight		Gieseking	[Columbia Originals]
SXLP30130	Chopin: The Waltzes		Malcuzynski	[SAX2332]
SXLP300131-2	Sullivan: Pirates of Penzance	Glyndebourne	Sargent	[ASD381-2]
SXLP30133	Strauss,R: Also Sprach Zarathustra, Till Eulenspiegel	Philh	Maazel	[SAX2467]
SXLP300135	Schubert: Impromptus 1-4, Moments Musicaux		Foldes (pno)	
SXLP30136	Organ Recital (Liszt,Franck,Reger,Widor)		Germani (Selby Abbey)	[CSD1449]
SXLP30137	Sibelius: Violin Concerto, Bruch: Violin Concerto 1	Japan Philh	Ozawa Ushioda	
SXLP30138	Walton: Symphony 1	Philh	Sargent	[ASD2299]
SXLP30139	Walton: Film music for Henry 5th, Hamlet, Richard 3rd	Philh	Walton	[SAX2527]
SXLP30140	Falla: 3 Cornered Hat, Ravel: Daphnis, Alborado	Philh	Giulini	[SAX2341/SAX5265]
SXLP30141	Bach,JS: Harpsichord Works		George Malcolm	
SXLP30143	Rossini:William Tell,Tancredi,Gazza Ladra,Semiramide, etc	Philh	Giulini	[SAX2560]
SXLP30144	"Viva Vivaldi"	Toulouse CO	Auriacombe	
SXLP30146	Debussy: Nocturnes, La Mer	Philh	Giulini	[SAX2463]
SXLP30147	Recital (Schubert, Brahms, Fauré, Debussy, Granados, etc)	De Los Angeles	Moore	[HMV Originals]
SXLP30148	Mozart: Piano Concertos K466, K488	Philh	Boult Fischer	[SAX2335]
SXLP30149	Sibelius: Symphony 5, Karelia Suite	London Sinfonia	Hannikainen	[ST42]
SXLP30150	Mozart: Flute Concertos 1, 2, Andante K315	Philh	Kurtz Shaffer (flute)	[ALP1676]
SXLP30151	Dvorak: Symphony 7, Enescu: Roumanian Rhapsody 1	VPO	Silvestri	[ASD396/ASD417]
SXLP30152	Falla: Nights in the Gardens of Spain, Turina	PCO	De Burgos Soriano (piano)	[ASD545/ASD570]
SXLP30153	Bliss: Checkmate (Suite)	Sinfonia of London	Bliss	[World Records T52]
	Britten: Matines Musicales & Soires Musicales	Philh	Irving	[CLP1172]
SXLP30154	Trumpet Concertos by Hertel,Hummel,L Mozart	Consortium Musicum	Lehan Tarr (trumpet)	
SXLP30155	Prokofiev: Violin Concerto 2	Philh	Galliera Oistrakh	[SAX2304]
	Miaskovsky: Cello Concerto	Philh	Sargent Rostropovich	[ALP1427]
SXLP30156	Handel: Love in Bath	RPO	Beecham	[ASD298]
SXLP30157	Tippett: Concerto for Double String Orch	Moscow CO	Barshai	[ASD512/ASD637]
	Britten: Variationns on a Theme by Frank Bridge	BFO	Menuhin	
SXLP30158	Overtures:Corsair,Midsummer Nts Drm,Thieving Magpie,etc	RPO	Beecham	[HMV&Columbia Originals]
SXLP30159	Saint-Saens: Violin Concerto 3,			[Original]
	Intro & Rondo, Chausson	Philh	Fistoulari Milstein	[SP8528]
SXLP30160	Chopin: Piano Concerto 1	Philh	Kletzki Pollini	[ASD370]
SXLP30161	Handel: Water Music, L Mozart: Toy Symphony, etc	Philh/BPO	Karajan	[Various reissues]
SXLP30162	Sibelius: Scenes Historiques, Pelleas & Melisande, Swan of Tuonela, Rakastave	Halle	Barbirolli	[HMV ASDs]
SXLP30163	Dvorak: Symphony 9, Carnaval Ov	Philh	Giulini	[SAX2405]
SXLP30164	Beethoven: "Spring" and "Kreutzer" Violin Sonatas		Menuhin	[ASD389]
SXLP30165	Mahler: Das Lied von der Erde	Philh	Kletzki Fischer-Dieskau/Dickie	[ASD351-2]
SXLP30166	Operatic aria recital (Carmen, Don Carlo, Macbeth, etc)		Callas	[HMV&EMI Columbia originals]
SXLP30167	Bruckner: Symphony 4	Philh	Klemperer	[SAX2569]
SXLP30168	Beethoven: Violin Concerto	FNRO	Cluytens Oistrakh	[SAX2315]
SXLP30169	Rachmaninov: Piano Concerto 4, Ravel: Concerto in Gmaj	Philh	Gracis Michelangeli	[ASD 255]
SXLP30170	Dvorak: Violin Concerto, Tchaikovsky: Trois Souvenirs	Amsterdam	Kersjes Krebbers	
SXLP30171	Borodin: Polovtsian Dances, Balakirev: Symphony 1	RPO	Beecham	[SXLP30002, original]
SXLP30172	Sullivan: Overtures	Pro Arte	Sargent	[HMV Originals]
SXLP30173	Strauss,J: Emporor Waltz, Die Fledermaus, Polkas, etc	Philh	Krips	[SCX3346]
SXLP30174	"Favourite String Music" (Turina,Rachmaninov,Paganini,etc)	Stokowski & his Orch		[Various reissues]
SXLP30175	Bach,JS: Concerto for 2 Pianos, Mozart: Double Piano Conc	Philh	Galliera Haskil Anda	[CX1403]
SXLP30176	Dvorak: Cello Concerto	RPO	Boult Rostropovich	[ALP1545]
SXLP30177	Bloch: Violin Concerto	Philh	Kletzki Menuhin	[ASD584]
SXLP30178	Mendelssohn: Symphony 4, Schumann: Symphony 4	Philh	Klemperer	[SAX2398]
SXLP30179	Beethoven: Romances 1&2, Mozart, Schubert	ASMF	Marriner Suk	[ASD2725]

Catalog	Work	Orchestra	Conductor/Artist	Reissue
SXLP30180V	Williams: A London Symphony	HO	Barbirolli	[ASD2360]
SXLP30181	St-Saens: Carnival, Bach, Schubert, Brahms, etc	Smith	Sellick (piano)	[CSD originals]
SXLP30182	Schubert & Mahler: Song Recital		Ludwig Moore	[SAX2358,SAX5272,SAX5274]
SXLP30183	Tchaikovsky: Romeo & Juliet, Francesca da Rimini	USSRSO	Svetlanov	Mdya
SXLP30184	Mozart: Piano Concerto K414, Haydn: Piano Concerto Op 21	Moscow CO	Barshai Devetzi (pno)	Mdya
SXLP30185	Brahms: Double Concerto	Philh	Galliera Oistrakh Fournier	[SAX2264]
SXLP30186	Brahms: Violin Concerto	BPO	Kempe Menuhin	[ASD 264]
SXLP30187	Falla: Three Cornered Hat	Philh	De Burgos De Los Angeles	[ASD 608]
SXLP30188	"Springtime in Moscow" (Paganini,Dvorak,etc)	Bolshoi	Reyentovich	Mdya
SXLP30189	Mozart: Piano Sonatas for 4 hands K311, K381, Schubert: Fantasia for 4 hands		Rozhdestvensky Postnikova	Mdya
SXLP30190	Russian Opera Choruses (Glinka, Tchaikovsky, etc)	Bolshoi	Ermler	Mdya
SXLP30193	Goldmark: Violin Concerto, Moussorgsky, Glazounov	Philh	Milstein	[SAX2563]
SXLP30194	Britten: Serenade for Tenor, Horn & Strings, Les Illuminations	Northern Sinfonia	Marriner	[CSD3684]
SXLP30195	Vivaldi: The Four Seasons	Leningrad CO	Shinder Vaiman (vln)	Mdya
SXLP30196	Mendelssohn: A Midsummer Nights Dream	Philh	Klemperer	[SAX2393]
SXLP30197	Sibelius: Pelleas & Melisande, Tapiola, Oceanides	RPO	Beecham	[ASD468, ASD518]
SXLP30198	Ravel: Daphnis&Chloe St 2,Pavane,Alborada,Rhapsodie Esp	Philh	Giulini	[SAX2341,SAX5265]
SXLP30199	Tchaikovsky: Romeo&Juliet, Smetana: Bartered Bride (hlts)	LPO	Boult	[World Records ST665,ST683]
SXLP30200	Tchaikovsky: Sleeping Beauty, Swan Lake Ballet Suites	Philh	Karajan	[SAX2306]
SXLP30203	Rossini: Overtures (Italian in Algiers,Semiramide,Barber,etc)	Philh	Karajan	[SAX2378]
SXLP30204	Schubert: Symphonies 3 & 5	RPO	Beecham	[ASD 345]
SXLP30205	Operatic Arias (Puccini,Giordano,Mascagni,etc)	Philh	Susskind Joan Hammond	[ASD302]
SXLP30206	Gounod: Messe Solenelle, etc	PCO	Hartemann	[ASD589]
SXLP30207	Mozart: Horn Concertos	Philh	Klemperer Civil	[SAX2406]
SXLP30208	Tchaikovsky: Symphony 6	Philh	Giulini	[SAX2368]
SXLP30209	Beethoven: Symphony 3	BBCSO	Barbirolli	[ASD2348]
SXLP30210	Overtures (Mendelssohn,Nicolai,Wagner,Weber)	Philh	Karajan	[SAX2439]
SXLP30213	Mozart: Overtures and Ballet Music	ASMF	Marriner	[ASD2834]
SXLP30214	Brahms: Symphony 4	Philh	Klemperer	[SAX2350]
SXLP30215	Recital (Villa-Lobos, Turina)		Irma Costanzo (guitar)	
SXLP30216	Tchaikovsky: Symphony 5	BPO	Kempe	[ASD 379]
SXLP30217	Brahms: Symphony 1	Philh	Klemperer	[SAX2262]
SXLP30218	Rachmaninov: Piano Concerto 3	MPO	Kondrashin Mogilevsky	Mdya
SXLP30220	Tchaikovsky: Violin Concerto, Chausson: Poeme	MPO	Rozhdestvensky Oistrakh	Mdya
SXLP30223	Beethoven: Piano Concerto 5	Clvlnd	Szell Gilels	[World Records SM156-60]
SXLP30224	Gounod: Faust, Offenbach: Gaite Parisienne, etc	Philh	Karajan	[SAX2274]
SXLP30225	Tchaikovsky: Violin Concerto, etc	Pittsburgh	Steinberg Milstein	[SP8512]
SXLP30226	Weill: Suite the Threepenny Opera, etc	Philh	Klemperer	[SAX2460]
SXLP30233	Moussorgsky: Pictures at an Exhibition		Bachauer (piano)	[DLP1154,1st stereo]
	Moussorgsky: Pictures at an Exhibition	Philh	Maazel	[SAX2484]
SXLP30234	Liszt: "Dante" Symphony	Bolshoi Theatre Orchestra	Khaikin	Mdya
SXLP30235	Prokofiev: Violin Concertos 1, 2	Philh	De Burgos Milstein	[SAX5275]
SXLP30236	Walton: Belshazzar's Feast, Partita for Orch	Philh	Walton Bell	[SAX2319]
SXLP30237	Mozart: Requiem Mass K626	Philh	de Burgos Bumbry	[SAN193]
SXLP30238	Brahms: Symphony 2, Tragic Ov	Philh	Klemperer	[SAX2362]
SXLP30239	Tchaikovsky:Serenade for Strings,Arensky: Tchaikovsky Vns	LSO	Barbirolli	[ASD 646]
SXLP30240	Britten: Young Persons Guide to the Orch, 4 Sea Interludes	Philh	Giulini	[SAX2555]
SXLP30243	"British Concert Pops" (Greensleeves, Elgar, Grainger, etc)	Philh	Weldon	[Various reissues]
SXLP30244	Tchaikovsky: Suite 1	Moscow RSO	Yansons	Mdya
SXLP30245	Mendelssohn: Violin Concerto, Bruch: Violin Concerto	Philh	Barzin Milstein	[SP8518]
SXLP30246	Mozart: Clarinet Concerto, Bassoon Concerto	RPO	Beecham Brymer Brooke	[ASD344]
SXLP30248	Berlioz: The Trojans (hlts)	LSO	Gibson Baker	[ASD2516]
SXLP30249	Beethoven: Romances 1&2, Wieniawski, Chausson, Berlioz	Philh	Pritchard Menuhin	[ASD 618]
SXLP30253	Rimsky-Korsakov: Scheherazade	RPO	Beecham	[ASD251]
SXLP30254	Grieg: Norwegian Dances, Lyric Suite, Peer Gynt hlts	Halle	Barbirolli	[ASD2773, TWO269]

SXLP30255	Brahms: Symphony 3, Acad Fest Ov	Philh Klemperer	[SAX2351]
SXLP30256	Franck: Symphony in Dmin	FNRO Beecham	[ASD 458]
SXLP30257	Haydn: Symphonies 103,104	RPO Beecham	[ASD 341]
SXLP30258	Tchaikovsky: Piano Concerto 3	MRSO Rozhdestvensky Zhukov (pno)	
	Symphony 7	USSRSO Ginzburg	Mdya
SXLP30259	Works for Strings (Tchaikovsky,Liadov,Glazunov,etc)	Bolshoi Violinists Reyentovich	Mdya
SXLP30260	Bizet: Symphony in C, Berlioz: Trojan March, Delibes, etc	FNRO Beecham	[HMV Originals]
SXLP30263	Debussy: Images - Iberia, Ibert: Escales, Ravel: Alborada	FNRO Stokowski	[SP8463]
SXLP30264	Brahms: Violin Concerto	ONRF Klemperer Oistrakh	[SAX2411]
SXLP30265	Haydn: Symphonies 101, 102	RPO Beecham	[ASD340]
SXLP30266	Prokofiev: Sinfonia Concertante op 125	RPO Sargent Rostropovitch (Cello)	[ALP1640]
	Classical Symphony	Philh Kurtz	[ASD263]
SXLP30267	Schubert: Symphony 9	HO Barbirolli	[ASD2251]
SXLP30268	Elgar: Symphony 1	Philh Barbirolli	[ASD540]
SXLP30273	Haydn: Cello Concerto in D, Monn: Cello Concerto in Gmin	LSO Barbirolli Du Pre	[ASD2466]
SXLP30274	Bach,JS: Organ Works	Germani (at Royal Festival Hall)	[CSD1318]
SXLP30275	Purcell: Dido and Aeneas	ECO Barbirolli De Los Angeles	[SAN169]
SXLP30276	Bizet: Carmen Suite 1, L'Arlesienne Suite 1,2	FNRO Beecham	[ASD252]
SXLP30277	Lalo: Sym Espagnole, St-Saens: Intro & Rondo Capr, Havanaise	Philh Goossens Menuhin	[ALP1571]
SXLP30278	Schubert: Symphony 8, Brahms: "Haydn" Variations	Philh Giulini	[SAX2424]
SXLP30279	Falstaff, Froissart, Intro & Allegro	Halle Barbirolli	[ASD originals]
SXLP30280	17th Century Arias (Scarlatti, Monteverdi)	ECO Leppard Baker	[ASD2615]
SXLP30283	Brahms: Piano Concerto 1	NPO Barbirolli Barenboim	[ASD2353]
SXLP30284	Beethoven: Mass op 86	RPO Beecham	[ASD280]
SXLP30285	Haydn: Symphonies 93, 94	RPO Beecham	[ALP1624]
SXLP30286	Beethoven: Symphony 7	RPO Beecham	[ASD 311]
SXLP30287	Elgar: Symphony 2	HO Barbirolli	[ASD610-11]
SXLP30289	Bach: Cantatas 82, 169	BFCO Menuhin Baker	[ASD2302]
SXLP30290	Sibelius: Symphony 7, Tapiola, Oceanides	RPO Beecham	[ASD468, ASD518]
SXLP30293	Strauss,R: Ein Heldenleben	RPO Beecham	[ASD421]
SXLP30294	Bach: Concerto for Violin,Oboe,Strings,Handel,Vivaldi	BFCO Menuhin Goossens	[ASD500]
SXLP30295	Berlioz: Symphonie Fantastique	ONRF Beecham	[ASD 399]
SXLP30297	Schubert: Wanderer Fantasy D760, Piano Sonata D664	Richter	[ASD 561]
SXLP30298	Strauss,R: Till Eulenspiegel, Don Juan, Dance of 7 Veils	Philh Klemperer	[SAX2367]
SXLP30299	"Beecham conducts French Lollipops"	RPO Beecham	[HMV Originals]
SXLP30300	Mozart: Don Giovanni (hlts)	Philh Giulini	[SAX2369-72]
SXLP30303	Mozart: Marriage of Figaro (hlts)	Philh Giulini	[SAX2381-4]
SXLP30304	Bizet: Pearl Fishers (hlts)	Opera Comique Dervaux	[SAX2442-3]
	Gounod: Romeo & Juliet (hlts)	Paris Op Lombard	[SAX2580]
SXLP30305	Verdi: La Traviata (hlts)	Rome Op Serafin	[ASD359-61]
SXLP30306	Puccini: Madam Butterfly (hlts)	Rome Op Santini	[ASD373-5]
SXLP30307	Beethoven: Fidelio (hlts)	Philh Klemperer	[SAX2451-3]
SXLP30308	"Choral Favourites from Kings"	College Kings College Willcocks Ledger	[HMV Originals]
SXLP30310	Beethoven: Symphony 3, Fidelio Ov	Philh Klemperer	[SAX2364,SAX2451-3]
SXLP30313	Beethoven: Symphony 6, Egmont Ov	Philh Giulini	[ASD2535]
SXLP30314	Berlioz: Harold in Italy	Philh Davis Menuhin	[ASD 537]
SXLP30315	Prokofiev: Symphony 5	LSO Previn	[ASD3115]
SXLP30414	Sibelius: Symphony 2	Philh Karajan	[SAX2379]
SXLP30415	Delius: Florida St, Over the Hills&Far Away, etc	RPO Beecham	[ASD329]
SXLP30416	Bach,JS: Overture in the French Style, Italian Concerto	Rosalyn Tureck	[ASD 372]
SXLP30418	Mozart: Piano Concertos K175, K271	ECO Barenboim	[ASD2484]
SXLP30419	Vivaldi: The 4 Seasons	Virtuoisi di Roma Fasano	[ASD367]
SXLP30420	Janacek: Sinfonietta Taras Bulba	RPO Kubelik	[ASD2652,ALP1675]
SXLP30423	Grieg: Peer Gynt	RPO Beecham	[ASD258]
SXLP30427	Prokofiev: Alexander Nevsky	USSRSO Svetlanov	[ASD2521] Mdya
SXLP30428	Strauss,R: Don Quixote, Der Rosenkavalier Waltzes	Dresden Kempe Tortelier Rostal	[SLS880]

Catalogue	Work	Orchestra	Conductor/Artists	Original
SXLP30430	Sibelius: Symphonies 5, 7	Philh	Karajan	[SAX2392, CX1341]
SXLP30433	Tchaikovsky: Symphony 4	BPO	Karajan	[SAX2357]
SXLP30436	Wagner: Overtures (Tannhauser,Rienzi,Lohengrin Act 1)	Philh	Klemperer	[SAX2347]
SXLP30437	Prokofiev: Love of 3 Oranges, Classical Symphony	Philh	Malko	[CLP1060,CLP1044]
SXLP30440	Bantock: Fifine at the Fair, Delius: Songs of Sunset	RPO	Beecham	[ASD2766]
SXLP30444	Handel: Dixit Dominus	ECO	Kings College Willcocks	[ASD2262]
SXLP30445	Mussorgsky: Pictures, Khovanschina, Polovtsian Dances	Philh	Karajan	[Columbia originals]
SXLP30446	Ravel: La Valse,Rapsodie Esp,Tombeau,Alborada	OdeP	Karajan	[ASD2766]
SXLP30447	Liszt: Symphonic Poems Les Preludes, Tasso, Rimsky-Korsakov:May Night Ov	Philh	Silvestri	[ALP1648] [ASD338]
SXLP30448	Bruckner: Symphony 6	Philh	Klemperer	[SAX2582]
SXLP30449	Mozart: Violin Concertos K216, K219	BFCO	Menuhin	[ASD 473]
SXLP30450	Respighi: Pines of Rome, Berlioz: Roman Carnival Ov, Liszt	Philh	Karajan	[SLS5019]
SXLP30454	Mozart: Violin Concertos K218, K271a	BFCO	Menuhin	[ASD533]
SXLP30456	Elgar: Pomp&Circumstance Marches 1-5, Ov Froissart, Elegy	Philh	Barbirolli	[ASD2292]
SXLP30457	Mozart: Cosi fan Tutte (hlts)	Philh	Bohm	[SAN103-6]
SXLP30505	Brahms: Symphony 4	Philh	Karajan	[CX1361]
SXLP30506	"Karajan in Concert" (Wagner,Beethoven,Schubert,etc)	BPO	Karajan	[HMV originals]
SXLP30508	Verdi: 4 Sacred Pieces	Philh	Giulini	[SAN120]
SXLP30509	Tchaikovsky: Symphony 2, Francesca da Rimini	Philh	Giulini	[SAX2416,SAX2483]
SXLP30510	Chopin: 4 Scherzos		Richter	[United Artists UACL10016]
SXLP30513	Brahms: Symphony 2, Schubert: Symphony 8	Philh	Karajan	[CX1355,CX1349]
SXLP30514	Bartok: Piano Concerto 3, Shostakovitch: Piano Concerto 2	NPO	Sargent Ogdon	[ASD2347,ASD2709]
SXLP30515	Beethoven: Piano Concertos 2, 4	Clvlnd	Szell Gilels	[World Records SM156-60]
SXLP30523	Schubert:Piano Quintet 'Trout',Beethoven:Piano Trio 'Ghost'	Amadeus Qt	Gendron Menuhin	[ASD322, ASD2258]
SXLP30525	Wagner: Lohengrin, Mastersingers, Tristan, etc	Philh	Klemperer	[SAX2347]
SXLP30526	Schumann: Symphonies 1, 4	Dresden	Sawallisch	[SLS867]
SXLP30527	Mozart: Symphonies 39, 40	BPO	Karajan	[SLS809]
SXLP30528	Wagner:The Ring (Entry of Gods,Valkyries,Rhine Journey)	Philh	Klemperer	[SAX2464]
SXLP30529	Brahms: Symphony 2, Alto Rhapsody	LPO	Boult Baker	[ASD2746]
SXLP30530	"Beecham Favourites" (Handel,Rossini,Grieg,etc)	RPO	Beecham	[HMV&Columbia originals]
SXLP30533	Bartok: Violin Concertos 1,2	Philh	Dorati Menuhin	[ASD2323, ASD2281]
SXLP30534	Tchaikovsky: Symphony 6	Philh	Karajan	[CX1377]
SXLP30536	Bartok: Music for SPC, Hindemith: Mathis der Maler	BPO	Karajan	[SAX2432]
SXLP30538	Offenbach: Les Contes Hoffmann (hlts)	PCO	Cluytens Schwarzkopf	[SAN154-6]
SXLP30539	Elgar: Symphony 2	USSRSO	Svetlanov	Mdya
SXLP30540	Beethoven: Piano Conc 1, 12 Vns on a Russian Theme	Clvlnd	Szell Gilels	[World Records SM156-60]
SXLP30546	Bruckner: Symphony 9	CSO	Giulini	[ASD3382]
SXLP30547	Moussorgsky: Boris Godunov (hlts)	PCO	Cluytens	[SAN110-3]
SXLP30548	Mahler: Symphony 1	CSO	Giulini	[ASD2722]
SXLP30552	Rachmaninov: Piano Conc 2, Tchaikovsky: Piano Conc 1	Philh	Pritchard/Barbirolli Ogdon	[ASD492,ASD542]
SXLP30553	Schubert: Lieder		Fischer-Dieskau Moore (pno)	[HMV originals]
SXLP30556	Song Recital (Wagner, Schubert, Poulenc)		Jessye Norman Gage (pno)	[EMI Electrola]
SXLP30557	Wagner: Duets (Walkure & Dutchman)	Philh	Ludwig Hotter Nilsson	[SAX2296]
SXLP30558	Schubert: Symphony 9	LPO	Boult	[ASD2856]
SXLP30562	Puccini: Operatic Arias (Butterfly,Tosca,Turandot,etc)	LSO	Mackerras Caballe	[ASD2632]

SXDW (2 disc gatefold SXLPs)

SXDW3019	Sullivan: The Mikado	Glyndebourne Sargent	[ASD256-7]
SXDW3020	Brahms: Piano Concerto 1	RPO Kempe Gelber	[HQS1068]
	Brahms: Piano Concerto 2	Munich Philh Kempe Decker	[original]
SXDW3021	Mahler: Symphony 9	Philh Klemperer	[SAX5281-2]
SXDW3022	Liszt: Faust Symphony, Lalo: Symphony	RPO Beecham	[ASD317-8, ASD388]
SXDW3023	Humperdinck: Hansel and Gretel	Sadlers Wells Bernardi	[CSD1576-7]
SXDW3024	Bruckner: Symphony 8	BPO Karajan	[CX1586-7]
SXDW3025	Tchaikovsky: The Seasons op 37b (pno & orch versions)	USSRSO Svetlanov Cherkassov(pno)	Mdya
SXDW3026	Prokofiev: Cinderella (complete ballet)	MRSO Rozhdestvensky	[ASD2429-30] Mdya
SXDW3027	Sullivan: The Gondoliers	Glyndebourne Sargent	[ASD265-6]
SXDW3028	Tchaikovsky: Nutcracker	Bolshoi Rozhdestvensky	Mdya
SXDW3029	Sullivan: Ruddigore	Glyndebourne Sargent	[ASD563-4]
SXDW3031	Sullivan: Patience	Glyndebourne Sargent	[ASD484-5]
SXDW3032	Beethoven: Overtures (Egmont, Coriolan, King Stephen, Leonora 1-3, Prometheus, Consecration of the House)	Philh Klemperer	[CX and SAX originals]
SXDW3033	Sullivan: Yeomen of the Guard	Glyndebourne Sargent	[ASD364-5]
SXDW3034	Sullivan: HMS Pinafore, Trial by Jury	Glyndebourne Sargent	[ASD415-6, ASD419]
SXDW3041	Sullivan: Pirates of Penzance	Glyndebourne Sargent	[ASD381-2]
SXDW3042	Strauss,J: Vienna Blood (complete)	Philh Ackermann Schwarzkopf	Electronic stereo [CX1186-7]
SXDW3043	Strauss,J: A Night in Venice	Philh Ackermann Schwarzkopf	[CX1224-5]
SXDW3044	Lehar: The Land of Smiles	Philh Ackermann	[CX1114-5]
SXDW3045	Lehar: The Merry Widow	Philh Ackermann	[CX1051-2]
SXDW3046	Strauss,J: The Gypsy Baron	Philh Ackermann Schwarzkopf	[CX1329-30]
SXDW3047	Sullivan: Iolanthe	Glyndebourne Sargent	[ASD323-4]
SXDW3048	"Karajan Favourites"	BPO/Philh Karajan	[EMI Columbia Originals]
SXDW3049	"Favourite Operatic Arias"	Philh Various Schwarzkopf	[EMI Columbia Originals]
SXDW3050	Mozart: Serenades 11,12, 13 for Wind Instruments	Philh Klemperer	[Columbia originals]
SXDW3051	Beethoven: Symphony 9, Ovs Leonora 3, King Stephen	Philh Klemperer	[SAX2276-7, SAX2542, SAX2373]
SXDW3053	Busoni: Piano Concerto, etc	RPO Revenaugh Ogdon	[ASD2336-7, ASD434]
SXDW3054	Bach,JS: Brandenburg Concertos 1-6	BFCO Menuhin	[ASD327-8]
SXDW3055	Verdi: Requiem Mass	Rome Op Serafin	[ASD353-4]

TWO (EMI Promenade Series)

This series was first introduced in January 1966 with the aim of producing demonstration quality stereo sound, although many of the earlier issues had already appeared as mono records.

The majority of releases were of popular material and the following list includes only those items of most interest to the classical collector.

The label: The label is black with white lettering. The letters "*STUDIO* 2 *STEREO*" are about 1cm above the spindle hole, and the familiar "Columbia Magic Notes" logo is at 12 o'clock about 2cms above the spindle hole. This is the same logo as appears on the latest SAX label but black rather than red.

TWO101	"Men O'Brass"	various bands Sargent
TWO139	Tchaikovsky: 1812/Capriccio Italien/etc	BNSO Silvestri
TWO150	"Semprini Plays Favourite Melodies"	Piano and Orch
TWO166	"Nocturne for Four" (Borodin,Mozart,Mendelssohn,Haydn,etc)	Lansdowne Quartet
TWO167	Rimsky-Korsakov: Scheherazade	BNSO Silvestri
TWO176	Grieg: Peer Gynt (extracts), Air from Holberg Suite. etc	Orch Tausky Semprini
TWO180	Viennese Prom Concert (J Strauss, R Strauss, Lehar)	HO Barbirolli

TWO181	"Glorious Melodies" (Liszt,Dvorak,Bizet,Schubert,etc)	Reginald Kilbey and his Strings	
TWO183	Tchaikovsky: Nutcracker/Sleeping Beauty	RPO Boult	
TWO190	Overtures: Ruy Blas/Nabucco/Zampa/etc	RLPO Groves	
TWO199	Borodin: Nocturne/Albinoni: Adagio/etc	RLPO Groves	
TWO200	"Invitation to the Dance"	BNSO Susskind	
TWO208	Organ Recital (Bach,Widor,Elgar,Franck,etc)	Danby at Blenheim Palace)	
TWO221	"Stereo Showcases" (Finlandia, Bare Mt, Danse Macabre, etc)	BNSO Silvestri	
TWO226	"The Best of Eric Coates"	RLPO Groves Brymer (sax)	
TWO232	Gershwin: Rhapsody in Blue, etc	Orch Pourcel Tacchino	
TWO234	Lehar: The Merry Widow (hlts)	Orch Tausky Bronhill	
TWO239	Respighi: Pines & Fountains of Rome , Stravinsky	Philh De Burgos	
TWO243	Novello: Glamorous Night (hlts)	BBC Concert Orch Dods Woodland Sinclair	
TWO246	Lehar: The Count of Luxemburg (hlts)	Orch Tausky Bronhill	
TWO259	Prokofiev: Peter and the Wolf, Britten: Young Person's Guide	OdeP Markevitch	
TWO264	Dukas: Sorcerer, St-Saens: Danse Macabre, Chabrier: Espana	OdeP Jacquillat	
TWO269	Grieg: Peer Gynt	HO Barbirolli	
TWO272	Popular Music of William Walton	RLPO Groves	
TWO275	Favourite Ballet Music (Coppelia, Sylvia, Faust)	Philh Mackerras	
TWO276	"Glorious Melodies" (Dvorak,Franck,Schumann,etc)	Reginald Kilbey and his Strings	
TWO286	Mussorgsky: Pictures at an Exhibition, Ravel: Mother Goose	OdeP Baudo	
TWO288	"Starlight Concert" (Puccini,Chabrier,Gounod,etc)	Studio 2 SO Tausky	
TWO295	Percy Grainger: Country Gardens, Handel in the Strand, etc	Light Music Soc Orch Dunn	
TWO297	"Britain's Choice" (Binge,Farnon,Langford,etc)	Light Music Society Orch Dunn	
TWO299	Johann Strauss Concert	SNO Gibson	
TWO302	Copland: Appalachian Spring, Bernstein: Fancy Free	Concert Arts SO Irving	
TWO304	"Intermezzo" (Mascagni,Leoncavallo,Puccini,Bellini,etc)	Bavarian State Op Patané	
TWO313	Franck: Symphonic Vns, Grieg: Piano Concerto,Liszt	Budapest SO/OdeP Cziffra Jnr Cziffra	
TWO317	Semprini Plays Liszt	New Abbey Light SO Tausky Semprini	
TWO319	Opera and Operetta Arias (Puccini,Bizet,Lehar,etc)	CBSO Fremaux Hughes (tenor)	
TWO320	Grand Operetta Gala (Lehar,Strauss,etc)	Rothenberger Bumbry Streich etc	
TWO321	Coates: London Suite/Cinderella	RLPO Groves	
TWO338	Famous Toccatas (Bach,Reger,Widor,Mathias,etc)	Rawsthorne at Liverpool Cathedral	
TWO348	Strauss Waltzes (Johann&Josef)	Vienna SO Stolz	
TWO350	Massenet: Le Cid, Massenet: Scènes Pittoresques	CBSO Fremaux	TASEC
TWO360	Liszt: Piano Concerto 1,Rachmaninov:Piano Concerto 2	OdeP Cziffra Jnr Cziffra	
TWO361	Eric Coates: The Three Elizabeths Suite, etc	CBSO Kilbey	
TWO368	"The Sound of Vienna" (Radetzky, Champagne Polka, etc)	Strauss Orch of Vienna Boskovsky	
TWO380	Sibelius: Finlandia/Karelia/Tuonela/Valse Triste/etc	BNSO Berglund	
TWO384	"Golden Operetta Favourites"	Rothenberger Bumbry Streich etc	
TWO388	Offenbach Overtures	CBSO Fremaux	
TWO389	"Boskovsky Bon-bons" (Vienna Woods,Light Cavalry,etc)	Strauss Orch of Vienna	
TWO390	Italian Opera Choruses (Verdi,Mascagni,Puccini,etc)	ROHCG Gardelli	
TWO394	Semprini Arrangements (Schubert,Mendelssohn,Mozart)	New Abbey Light SO Tausky Semprini	
TWO395	"Russian Festival Gala" (Borodin, Moussorgsky, R-Korsakov)	OdeP Rozhdestvensky	
TWO398	"250 Years of Film Music" (Bach,Borodin,Mahler,Gershwin)	LSO Keating	
TWO403	Sullivan Overtures	RLPO Groves	
TWO404	Saint-Saens Symphony 3	CBSO Fremaux	TAS40/159 TASEC
TWO409	Ravel: Bolero, Pavane, Alborada, La Valse	Philh Maazel	
TWOX1062	Vivaldi: The Seasons	Koto Vivaldi Japanese Drum Ensemble	

Lyrita

The List: This list is believed to be complete for all stereo Lyritas (see companion "Mono Record Collector's Handbook" for list of mono Lyritas).

Pressings: Despite what has been said in some sources about Lyrita pressings, I have never heard any bad sounding Lyrita, regardless of pressing. The earliest were pressed by Decca and were, in my view, the best. Then came Nimbus pressings. Finally there were a number of different pressing sources including EMI.

The basic rule is that the lower the SRCS number the more likely it is to be a Decca pressing. Conversely, with the higher SRCS numbers it is increasingly unlikely to be a Decca pressing. Beyond around SRCS116 most were never pressed by Decca at all, but were pressed by Nimbus. So it can confidently be said that there is either a Decca or a Nimbus pressing for every Lyrita.

The Decca pressings are easily recognised by the fact that the engraving on the vinyl carries a stamper number in the standard Decca SXL typeface, and is of the form ZLY-nnnn-na, e.g. ZLY-5069-2G. This engraving will be found on the vinyl on both sides of the record.

Nimbus pressings are also readily identified (though more care is needed): Somewhere on the vinyl you will find engraved the word NIMBUS on top of the word ENGLAND, but this engraving is very small.

The pressings after this have 'hand written' scrawl on the vinyl and are easiest identified by the negative fact that they have neither the Decca nor NIMBUS engravings.

Number	Work	Orch	Conductor/Performers	Notes
SRCS 31	Ireland: London Ov/Concertino/Pastorale.	LPO	Boult	
SRCS 32	Ireland: Forgotten Rite/Sym Rhapsody	LPO	Boult	
SRCS 33	Bliss: Mus for Strings/Medn on Theme by J Blow.	CBSO	Rignold	TAS 36/182++ TASEC
SRCS 34	Holst: Lyric Mvmt for Viola&Small Orch./etc.	ECO	Imogen Holst	TASEC
SRCS 35	Bax: Symphony 6	Philh	Del Mar	TAS 35/155+ TASEC
SRCS 36	Ireland: Piano Concin F/etc	LPO	Boult Case Parkin	
SRCS 37	Bax: November Woods/Moeran/Holst	LPO	Boult	TAS 35/155+,39/146+
SRCS 38	Finzi: Before and After Summer-songs		Case Tear Ferguson	
SRCS 39	Elgar: Symphony 1	LPO	Boult	
SRCS 40	Elgar: Symphony 2	LPO	Boult	
SRCS 41	Rubbra: Symphony 7/V Williams: Tallis Fantasia	LPO	Boult	
SRCS 42	Moeran: Cello Sonata in Amin/etc		Coetmore Parkin	
SRCS 43	Moeran: Cello Conc/Rhapsody 2/etc	LPO	Boult Peers Coetmore	
SRCS 44	Holst: Double Concerto/Capriccio/etc	ECO	Imogen Holst	
SRCS 45	Ireland: Tritons/Symphonic Studies/Overlanders.	LPO	Boult	
SRCS 46	Still: Symphonies 3/4	LSO	Goossens/RPO Fredman	TASEC
SRCS 47	Lyrita Lollipops (Delius, Benjamin, Walton, Bliss)	Various		
SRCS 48	Parry: English Suite/Symphonic Variations/etc.	LSO	Boult	
SRCS 49	Walton: Sinf Conc for Orch+Piano/etc	LSO	Walton Katin	
SRCS 50	Holst: Japanese Suite/other composers	LSO	Boult/etc	
SRCS 51	Finzi: A Young Man's Exhortation		Case Jenkins Ferguson	
SRCS 52	"Contemporary Welsh Chamber Music" (Parrott: String Quartet 4, Harries, Wynne		University Ensemble of Cardiff	
SRCS 53	Bax: Symphony 1	LPO	Myer Fredman	

Cat#	Title	Orchestra	Conductor/Performer	TAS
SRCS 54	Bax: Symphony 2	LPO	Myer Fredman	
SRCS 55	Bliss: PRS Birthday Tribute:Serenade/Rout/etc	various		
SRCS 56	Holst: A Somerset Rhapsody/Hammersmith	LPO	Boult	
SRCS 57	Maconchy: Overture Proud Thames/Alwyn/Bush/etc.	LPO	Handley/etc	
SRCS 58	Bax: Symphony 5	LPO	Leppard	
SRCS 59	Ireland: Sextet for Clar,Horn,Qt/etc	Melos Ensemble/etc		
SRCS 60	Baines, W: Silverpoints/Paradise Gdns/etc.	Eric Parkin (piano)		
SRCS 61	Alwyn: Mirages:Song Cycle for Bar&Pno	Luxon Wilson Robles		
SRCS 62	Bax: Garden of Fand/Tintagel/etc	LPO	Boult	TAS 35/155+,39/146+,41/125+
SRCS 63	Alwyn: Symphony 3/Magic Island	LPO	Alwyn	
SRCS 64	Ireland: Violin Sonatas 1/2	Neamen	Parkin	
SRCS 65	Ireland: Songs Vol 1	Luxon	Rowlands (piano)	
SRCS 66	Ireland: Songs Vol 2	Luxon	Rowlands (piano)	
SRCS 67	Brian: Symphonies 6/16	LPO	Fredman	
SRCS 68	Herbert Howells: Quartets Op 21/25/31	Richards Ens Thea King		
SRCS 69	Howells: Merry Eye/Elegy/etc/Butterworth.	Philh/LPO Boult		TAS 11/381++
SRCS 70	Moeran: Symphony in Gmin	Philh	Boult	TAS 11/381
SRCS 71	Adrian Boult conducts Marches	Philh	Boult	
SRCS 72	Searle: Symphonies 1, 2	LPO	Boult/Krips	(Symphony 1 from SXL2232)
SRCS 73	Bridge: Suite for string orch/etc	LPO	Boult	TAS 36/182+
SRCS 74	Berkeley: Div Op 18/Sernd Op 12/etc	LPO	Berkeley Winfield	
SRCS 75	Finzi: Intimations on Immortality.	Guildford PO&Chorus Handley TASEC		
SRCS 76	Alwyn: Symphonies 4/5	LPO	Alwyn	
SRCS 77	Elgar: Enigma/Falstaff/etc	Philh	Andrew Davis	
SRCS 78	Cooke, Arnold: Symphony 3/Jabez&the Devil.	LPO	Braithwaite	TAS 36/179+
SRCS 79	Williamson: Organ Concerto	LPO	Boult	TASEC TAS 36/181+
SRCS 80	Berkeley: Sym 1/Conc for 2 pnos.	LPO	Del Mar Beckett McDonald	
SRCS 81	Scott, Cyril: Piano Concerto 1 in C	LPO	Herrmann Ogdon	
SRCS 82	Scott, Cyril: Piano Concerto 2	LPO	Herrmann Ogdon	
SRCS 83	Bax: Symphony 7	LPO	Leppard	TAS 11/381, 37/171+
SRCS 84	Finzi: A Severn Rhapsody/etc	LPO	Boult	TAS 35/159++
SRCS 85	Alwyn: Symphony 2	LPO	Alwyn	
SRCS 86	Alwyn: Symphony 1	LPO	Alwyn	
SRCS 87	Ireland: Piano Music Vol 1	Eric Parkin		
SRCS 88	Ireland: Piano Music Vol 2	Eric Parkin		
SRCS 89	Ireland: Piano Music Vol 3	Eric Parkin		
SRCS 90	Rawsthorne: Symphony 1/Symphonic Studies.	LSO	Pritchard	TAS 11/382+
SRCS 91	Bridge: Phantasm/Rhaps for Pno&Orch/Moeran.	Philh	Braithwaite	TAS 11/382+, 36/182
SRCS 92	Finzi: Clarinet Conc/etc	Philh	Handley Denman Katin	TAS11/381+ TAS33/133,37/133+
SRCS 93	Finzi: Let Us Garlands Bring/etc	Philh	Handley Case Partri	
SRCS 94	Berkeley: Symphony 2/Piano Conc Op 29	Philh	Braithwaite Wilde	TAS 36/179++
SRCS 95	Overtures (Arnold/Alwyn/etc)	Various		TAS 32/147
SRCS 96	Rubbra: Symphony 2	Philh	Handley	
SRCS 97	Morgan, David: Violin Concerto/Contrasts.	RPO	Handley Gruenberg	TAS 16/509++ 35/159+
SRCS 98	Ireland: Phantasie Trio in A min/Trios 2/3	Neaman Webber Parkin		
SRCS 99	More Lyrita Lollipops	Various		
SRCS100	Hurlstone: Piano Conc/Fantasie varns	LPO	Braithwaite Parkin	
SRCS101	Rawsthorne: Piano Concertos 1/2	LSO	Braithwaite Binns	TASEC
SRCS102	Stanford: Piano Concerto 2	LSO	Braithwaite Binns	
SRCS103	Rootham: Symphony 1/Holbrook	LPO	Handley	TAS 36/179++
SRCS104	Bridge: Oration etc	LPO	Braithwaite	TAS 33/98++
SRCS105	Moeran: Violin Concerto	LSO	Handley Georgeadis	TAS 37/171+
SRCS106	Hadley: Trees so High/1 Morn in Spring	LPO	Boult Allen	
SRCS107	Coates: The Merrymakers Ov/Summer Days St/etc	Philh	Boult	
SRCS108	Alwyn: Lyra Angelica-Harp concerto	LPO	Alwyn Ossian Ellis	TAS 43/155+ 42/150+

SRCS109	Arnold: Eng, Scot & Cornish Dances	LPO	Arnold	TASEC TAS 29/119++ 44/160+
SRCS110	Lambert: Romeo and Juliet	ECO	Del Mar	TAS 33/98++
SRCS111	Britten: Sinfonietta/Tippett/etc	ECO	Del Mar	TAS 38/168+
SRCS112	Finzi: Cello Concerto	RPO	Handley Yo-Yo Ma	TAS 33/133+
SRCS113	Lloyd: Symphony 8	Philh	Downes	TAS 30/114+ 33/131+
SRCS114	Bridge: Ov 'Rebus'/Dance Poem/etc	LPO	Braithwaite	
SRCS115	Arnold: Sinfonietta 1/Bush/Benjamin	LSO	Braithwaite	
SRCS116	Maconchy: Symphony for double string orch.	LSO	Handley	TAS40/159++ TASEC
SRCS117	Hurlstone: Pno Trio in D/Pno Qt in Emn		Tunnell Piano Quartet	
SRCS118	Ireland: Songs.		Mitchinson Hodgson Rowlands	
SRCS119	Rubbra: Symphony 7	LPO	Boult	[as SRCS41]
	Soliloquy for Cello&Orch	LSO	Handley Saram	
SRCS120	Warlock: Old Song for Small Orch/Holst.	LPO/LSO	Boult	TAS 43/155++
SRCS121/2	Alwyn: Miss Julie: Opera in 2 acts	Philh	Tausky Gomez Luxon	TAS 33/98++
SRCS123	Stanford: Irish Rhapsody 4/Bantock	LPO	Braithwaite	TAS 43/155+
SRCS124	Lloyd: Symphony 5	Philh	Downes	TAS 30/114+ TASEC
SRCS125	V Williams: Sons of Light	LPO	Willcocks Bach Choir	TASEC
SRCS126	Leigh: Concertino for Harps&Strings	LPO	Braithwaite Pinnock	TAS 42/143+++ 43/156 TASEC
SRCS127	Rubbra: Symphonies 6/8	Philh	Del Mar	TAS 36/179++
SRCS128	Holst: The Lure/Morning of the Year	LSO	Atherton	TAS 33/132
SRCS129	Lloyd: Symphony 4	Philh	Downes	TAS 35/177++
SRCS130	V Williams: Piano Concerto in C/etc	RPO	Handley Shelley	TAS 35/177+
SRCS131-2	Elgar: Symphonies 1/2	LPO	Boult	[As SRCS39/40]

* * * * *

Readers Digest

There are many Reader's Digest record sets, but only a few are of any real interest. Having said that, some of them are extremely good and should definitely be sought after.

They were made for Readers Digest by RCA in USA and by Decca in England. Given that the vintage of the best of these is early to mid 60s, it should be clear that we are speaking of the highest quality records available.

Listed below is a good selection of the Readers Digest sets, and I have put a * beside those that are, in my opinion, definitely worth getting. ** indicates that the set is outstanding and much sought after.

Record numbers are not very useful where Readers Digest sets are concerned, so I have left them out.

**	Beethoven: The 9 Symphonies	RPO/Leibowitz
*	Eric Robinson's World of Music	
**	Festival of Light Classical Music	
	Joyous Music for Xmas Time	
**	Most Unforgettable Music (This one includes Brahms Symphony 1, Symphonie Fantastique, and is extremely rare)	
*	Music of the World's Great Composers	
**	'Scheherazade' ('Rhapsodic Mood Music')	
*	Treasury of Great Music (includes Reiner Brahms Symphony 4)	
	Treasury of Great Operetta	
	8 Great Piano Concertos	
	8 Great Symphonies	
*	Handel: Messiah	RPO/Sargent
**	Rachmaninov: The Romantic Rachmaninov	Horenstein/Wild

A note about the "Eric Robinson" set: This is a very good box set of various orchestral pieces - rather similar to "Festival of Light Classical Music". Eric Robinson was a well known figure at the time; he conducts 13 of the tracks and his name was used to promote the set. In America the identical set goes under a similar name but using Arthur Fiedler as the promoter. The set includes an unusual version of Tchaikovsky's 1812 which includes a full chorus, as well as cannon, etc, and was produced by the Charles Gerhardt/Kenneth Wilkinson team.

* * * * *

Useful Names and Addresses

Peter Fulop	www.mikrokosmos.com

Gramophone Publications	www.gramophone.co.uk

The Absolute Sound	www.theabsolutesound.com

Stereophile	www.stereophile.com

Bibliography

Mono Record Collector's Handbook. Gives complete listings for English EMI ALP, BLP, 33CX, 33C, COLH, LXT, etc. Available from the same source as this book.

Classic Record Collector (CRC) is a quarterly magazine published by Orpheus Publications (www.classicrecordcollector.com) and is an excellent source for information on these early recordings, though it does tend to refer more to recent CD reissues than to the LP originals.

Penguin Stereo Record Guide, 1975, 1977, 1982, 1986. Authors: Edward Greenfield, Robert Layton, Ivan March

Penguin Guide to Bargain Records, 1966. Authors: Edward Greenfield, Ivan March, Denis Stevens

The Golden Era of RCA Records, 1985, 1989. Author: James A Mitchell.

Full Frequency Stereophonic Sound, 1990. Authors: Robert Moon, Michael Gray

The RCA Bible. Author: John Valin. Published by Music Lover's Press, 3537 Epley Road, Cincinnati, Ohio 45247, USA. Tel: (513) 385-4055

Mercury Classical Record Collection, 1989. Author: Robert J Corsetti, private publication.

RCA Classical Record Collection (LSC series), 1989. Author: Robert J Corsetti, private publication.

Labelography. 1999. Author: Peter Fulop, web: www.mikrokosmos.com

For further copies of this book and of its companion "Mono Record Collector's Handbook" please go to:

www.cranmorepublications.co.uk

www.ingramcontent.com/pod-product-compliance
Lightning Source LLC
Chambersburg PA
CBHW081919170426
43200CB00014B/2765